WRITING EARLY AMERICA

The Revolutionary Age

Francis D. Cogliano and
Patrick Griffin, Editors

Writing Early America

From Empire to Revolution

Trevor Burnard

UNIVERSITY OF VIRGINIA PRESS
CHARLOTTESVILLE AND LONDON

University of Virginia Press
© 2023 by the Rector and Visitors of the University of Virginia
All rights reserved
Printed in the United States of America on acid-free paper

First published 2023

1 3 5 7 9 8 6 4 2

Library of Congress Cataloging-in-Publication Data

Names: Burnard, Trevor G. (Trevor Graeme), author.
Title: Writing early America : from empire to revolution / Trevor Burnard.
Description: Charlottesville : University of Virginia Press, 2023. | Series: The Revolutionary age | Includes bibliographical references and index.
Identifiers: LCCN 2022042542 (print) | LCCN 2022042543 (ebook) | ISBN 9780813949192 (hardcover) | ISBN 9780813949208 (paperback) | ISBN 9780813949215 (ebook)
Subjects: LCSH: United States—History—Colonial period, ca. 1600–1775—Historiography. | United States—History—Revolution, 1775–1783—Historiography. | Indians of North America—History—18th century—Historiography. | Great Britain—History—18th century—Historiography.
Classification: LCC E187.2 .B87 2023 (print) | LCC E187.2 (ebook) | DDC 973.20072—dc23/eng/20230118
LC record available at https://lccn.loc.gov/2022042542
LC ebook record available at https://lccn.loc.gov/2022042543

Cover art: Detail of *The Tea-Tax Tempest, or the Anglo-American Revolution*, engraved by Carl Guttenberg, after John Dixon, 1778. (John Carter Brown Library, Brown University)

CONTENTS

Introduction: Themes and Methods ... 1

Part I. Context and Background

1. The Historiography of Early America ... 21
2. Wealth, Commerce, Environment ... 40

Part II. Current Themes

3. Slavery ... 63
4. Indigenous Peoples ... 83
5. The Imperial Turn ... 104

Part III. Traditional Themes

6. Gender ... 131
7. Eighteenth-Century British History ... 150
8. The American Revolution ... 173

Conclusion ... 195

Appendix A. Early American History in Academic Journals ... 211

Appendix B. Citational Practices in Early American History ... 217

Acknowledgments ... 221

Notes ... 225

Index ... 293

WRITING EARLY AMERICA

INTRODUCTION

Themes and Methods

∽

I

This book examines the writing of early American history in the period between the early eighteenth century and the formation of the United States in the 1780s. Its main conclusions are based on a reading of 393 articles published in journals that concern the history of early America and eighteenth-century Britain written between 2012 and 2021.

I used these recently published articles to assess historical scholarship on what can been termed the "short eighteenth century," from the Treaty of Utrecht in 1713 and the ascent of the Hanoverians to the British throne in 1714 to the end of the American Revolution and the creation of the American Republic in 1783–84. The articles reviewed cover a historical period of imperial competition between Britain, France, and Spain in the Americas; the beginning but not completion of the transition of mainland North America from being largely Indigenous-controlled to polities in the Eastern Seaboard and in the Caribbean becoming dominated by people of European descent; and the development of a mature plantation system dependent on chattel slavery and the accompanying large increase in the numbers of people of African descent, almost all enslaved people living in Atlantic empires that were more African than before or since.

This was a period in which we can discern the economic success and massive social failure of colonization in the Caribbean based on plantation agriculture and its immiseration of the African-descended working population, as well as the development of settler societies, especially in British North America, that enjoyed levels of prosperity and well-being and a cultural confidence that made them very different places than their more embattled and distinctly poorer seventeenth-century counterparts.[1]

My research strategy was a very simple one: to read all recently published articles and thus acquire a greater knowledge of contemporary academic research in eighteenth-century American, Atlantic, Indigenous, African, and British history so as to understand the state of early American historiography in the early 2020s. I make conclusions only about work published in article form from about 2012. This book is thus not a complete survey of early American history writing. The field has grown too large for that kind of comprehensive survey to be possible. Nor is it designed to promulgate a certain vision of what I think early American history should be. It is a summary of hundreds of articles, outlining where I think the writers of journal articles see the field evolving. I am very conscious that it is a partial report. Some of the absences in the journal literature are addressed in other forms, such as articles published in decades previous to the one under study; in monographs; and as chapters in edited volumes.

Readers may disagree with my conclusions about the larger meanings discerned in a consideration of a sizeable body of disparate research articles. That would be a good thing, as this book is meant to provoke discussion. If there is a single lesson that this book wants to convey, however, it is that historiography matters. It matters where we locate ourselves in relation to the work of historical writing both of this generation and of preceding generations. The writing of history is not only about finding new empirical information that enriches our understanding of past events. It is also about arguments and debates and how the present and the past are deeply intertwined through changing historical interpretations and investigations. How we write early American history today tells us much about what themes have grown or disappeared as historians have found some topics more interesting, important, or illustrative than others.

Most books on historiography deal with the craft of history, such as methodological issues and concerns, and treat the writing of history more in abstract than real terms. This book, by contrast, deals explicitly with practice—the findings of hundreds of authors writing in a time-limited period upon a delimited subject. What I want readers to come away with on reading this book is a sense that historians of early America and scholars of eighteenth-century Britain situate their work within longer conversations generated over many decades, in which the work of one generation feeds off, develops, and occasionally contradicts the research done by previous generations.

I believe that if we are to understand any historical field, we will be better placed in our endeavors if we appreciate how what we are writing about or reading fits within longstanding arguments, debates, and conversations. Moreover, to make a meaningful contribution to these conversations, it is a good thing to be literate in what elements lie behind such conversations and how those assumptions and conditions shape how arguments are expressed. Doing early American history now is thus practicing it differently than was done for most of the last century, up to and including the 1990s.[2] My hope is that readers will have a stronger appreciation of the journey that the field of early American history has been on since the 1990s and especially as it is manifested in recently published journal articles. The result will enable readers to catch a historical field of analysis developing at a moment in time and be able to link that moment to historiographical discussions and research findings as well as to the swirl of events in the present that blend with historiographical currents to produce a body of work that relates to the times we ourselves are living in. Thus, I believe that the fact that early American historians focus so heavily on the three themes of Indigenous power, the contours of racial difference, and the manifestations of empire when writing about eighteenth-century American history—and do so often with reference to the American Revolution as the defining event in that century—speaks not just to historical preferences but also to themes that resonate with present-day events and concerns.

II

First, a word about the database on which I based my assessment of early American history writing, which is 393 articles in major specialist and general-interest academic journals published in English since 2012, of which 317 (80.7 percent) appeared in early American history, broadly defined.[3]

My analysis serves one general and one specific aim. The general aim is to contribute to historiographical debate by examining how a field of scholarship develops and changes over time through assessing the influences that help scholars determine what topics they want to work on and prompts journal editors to decide what scholarship they want to publish. It seeks to determine why some themes become dominant while others fade in importance and relevance within a subfield of the discipline of history. I hope to reveal patterns that will be interesting to scholars who do the history of other periods and topics. I would be pleased if my findings from this extensive survey of journal literature about early American and eighteenth-century British history have some applicability to understanding development of historical scholarship in the last decade more generally.[4]

My more specific aim is to chart major trends in the historiography of early America in the decade of the 2010s that might point the way to scholarship that will be done in the 2020s and beyond. I have chosen early American history and the history of the American Revolution because this is my area of expertise, knowledge, and interest, but I expect that some of my conclusions will be able to be replicated in other subfields of historical research.

I have chosen to do research in the journal literature of part of early American history for frankly practical reasons. I have not looked at articles on seventeenth-century American topics nor on the history of the early republic and antebellum America. Early American history is substantial enough as a field to contain a multitude of voices, but it is not so large—as would be the case, say, for modern American history or early modern European history—that a comprehensive study of the great majority of journal literature would be impossible for a single researcher. And the dates I have chosen to bracket this look at journal literature (roughly the last decade, between 2012 and 2021) do not mark any event in the world or in the field of early American history but rather provide a manageable decade-long overview of the latest trends in the field. Occasionally, I refer to articles and books published outside of that period, but I thought it important to place some limits on my data set in order to be able to offer an analysis of a field.

Why choose articles in journals as the means to evaluate recent trends in the writing of early American history? It is a reasonable question, given the centrality of monographs to the profession of history. My choice to look only at journal literature rather than the whole output of scholars in early American history is again a practical one. I could not have provided a comprehensive overview of scholarly trends without making some limitations as to the range of the topic and the medium through which research is communicated. Joyce Chaplin started her 2003 survey of works on early American history by quipping that if she were a gambling woman, she would start a betting pool to estimate how many books would be included in an update of a 1989 bibliography of most books in the field that listed 2,001 titles.[5] She speculated that it might by 2003 have reached 5,001 or even 10,001 books.[6] For my part, I have been editor in chief of the Oxford Online Bibliography in Atlantic History since 2009, during which time nearly three hundred articles on topics in Atlantic history have been published, each article containing in its selected, annotated bibliography between sixty and one hundred titles. Even bearing in mind the duplication of titles in different articles, the sheer abundance of information available to students and scholars in the form of academic outputs is formidable.

Aside from practical considerations, there are three important reasons for choosing to look at only journal literature in evaluating recent trends in early American historiography. It is in journal literature that we can best appreciate the dimensions of a field and how it changes and develops over time. Indeed, journal output is such an extensively peer-reviewed part of the profession and operates such a ferocious process of rejection that one can be confident that almost all articles have been judged, commented upon, edited, and copyedited numerous times. For example, the leading journal in the early American field rejects nearly 90 percent of article submissions.[7] A published article on early American history will have gone through a formidable process of submission, review, resubmission, then perhaps resubmission again before publication. The extent of this peer-review process gives one great confidence that whatever has been published meets very high standards of acceptability to the general audience of academics invested in doing early American history.

Second, although this is not always the case, it is common that some of the principal arguments later advanced in monographs are first tried out in journals. A telling example of a journal article foreshadowing an important later monograph is the famous article by Edmund Morgan in 1972 as his presidential address to the Organization of American Historians that was incorporated into his definitive work on early Virginia, *American Slavery, American Freedom*.[8] Publishing in journals can often be excruciatingly slow, with the time elapsing between first submission and eventual publication being measured in years rather than months. But it is often a quicker form of publishing than monograph publication, which means that it is in article production more than in monographs where we can discern the ebb and flow of scholarship, making writing articles in journals potentially more connected to evolving historiographical trends.

Finally, what makes assessing early American historiography through journal articles viable is its practitioners' close relationship to its specialized journals, especially the long-established *William and Mary Quarterly*

(*WMQ*), one of the most celebrated of all specialist journals of history published in the United States.[9] Until the twenty-first century, *WMQ* had the field largely to itself. It was the place where early American historians sent their most important work, where they published articles they believed would most influence their early Americanist peers. In 2017 a survey of articles in *WMQ* on the American Revolution published since the start of the third series of the journal in 1944 proclaimed that one can discern interpretive patterns in the scholarship of the American Revolution—"from whig, progressive, imperial, neo-whig, neo-progressive and, most recently, neo-imperial alternatives"—by examining only *WMQ* articles.[10] As its authors, Michael McDonnell and David Waldstreicher, state, "The *Quarterly* grew [from 1944] into its undeniable state as gatekeeper and avatar of new work." They qualify this statement in a footnote, noting that *WMQ* is "the gold standard in the field and is still extremely well regarded, even if it has a lot more company now."[11]

McDonnell and Waldstreicher's assessment of the importance of the journal in shaping scholarship is fair. Their comment on *WMQ* having "a lot more company now" is also worth noting. The McNeil Center at the University of Pennsylvania began its own journal in 2002, *Early American Studies* (*EAS*), which has come to resemble *WMQ* in the rigor of its editorial processes and the quality of its published articles. In recent years a third journal, the *Journal of Early American Studies* (*JEAS*), published in the Netherlands and catering as much to a European as to an American audience, has joined the two American journals as a forum for work on early American studies.

That concentration of specialist journals on a particular period of American and Atlantic history makes early American history distinctive.[12] In addition to the specialist journals on early American history, historians have a variety of other venues in which to present work, depending on the nature of the article and on the audience that is intended to reach. If one wants to reach an audience interested in economic history, then it would be a good idea to publish in the *Economic History Review* (*EcHR*); if the intended audience is on cities, then *Urban History* would be a good outlet; articles on women might find a suitable home in *Gender History*; and articles that concentrate on imperialism would be attractive for the editors of the *Journal of Imperial and Commonwealth History* (*JICH*). I have found articles on either early American history or eighteenth-century British history in fifty journals.

III

Topics of interest to early Americanists wax and wane over time. What is the subject of intense attention from one generation becomes an object of indifference in the next. The remainder of this book will examine and evaluate in depth the topics that are of interest to early American historians now, but it also touches on themes that have diminished in importance. Let me preview here that my reading in journals over the last decade reveals that racial African slavery and Indigenous history have become important areas of interest. Articles in these two areas outstrip by a margin the number of articles on all other areas of early American scholarship combined.[13] The American Revolution remains the event most studied; as Michael McDonnell and David Waldstreicher note in their survey of recent writing on the American Revolution, empire has become a major theme both in scholarship on the revolution and in early American history generally. Indeed, these three subjects, broadly conceived—race and slavery; Indigenous history; the American Revolution—attracted 74, 40, and 36 articles, respectively, over the last decade, meaning that they account for at least 150, or 51.2 percent, of articles in my sample devoted to early America. Other wars except for the American Revolution are largely absent.

Although the American Revolution remains well covered, the most noticeable absence from recent early American historiography is debate on its causes.[14] That topic was a hardy perennial for early American historians for many decades, fought over in impassioned terms. Writing in 1964, Keith B. Berwick commented that the *WMQ* between 1944 and 1964 saw an "abiding preoccupation with the causes and consequences of the American Revolution."[15] That interest in the origins of the American Revolution has now plummeted.[16] There has been only one intervention into the debate on the causes of the American Revolution in the last decade, by Staughton Lynd and David Waldstreicher. They argue that the revolution was a struggle for economic autonomy that became a colonial independence movement.[17] This claim met with lukewarm responses from Barbara Clark Smith, Robert G. Parkinson, and especially from Jack Rakove, who dismissed the article as a "provocation." Only Michael McDonnell was sympathetic, thinking it axiomatic that the revolution arose from economic reasons and only criticizing the authors for being too attentive to elites rather than to ordinary people.

There are two possible reasons why debating the causes of the American Revolution has largely ceased to exist. For some historians, such as

Rakove in response to Lynd and Waldstreicher, there is no need to discuss origins because the causes are clear and undebatable. Rakove notes that it is indisputable that the American Revolution was a political and imperial crisis between Britain and the embryonic country of the United States that was brought to a head by "ideological perceptions that inclined political actors in both countries to view each other's escalating actions with increasing suspicion" with the accelerant being specific and historically contingent events in Massachusetts happening from December 1773.[18] In short, the argument over the causes of the American Revolution ceased because one side had won.

Perhaps more interesting than these potentially resolved topics are topics that do not attract much attention because that is not where the direction of scholarship is heading. Looking at these "neglected subjects" tells us a good deal about the priorities and perspectives of writing on early American history as we enter the third decade of the twenty-first century. One such neglected subject is farming folks—the great majority of the White population of colonial British North America. Besides an article on West Indian planter Nathaniel Phillips, which is about his wealth rather than his work as a planter, there is only one article in all 393 surveyed that touches on the lives of White people involved in agriculture: a study of overseers in Virginia and South Carolina by Laura Sandy, which argues that overseers' bad reputation is ill deserved.[19]

Rather, historians are drawn to the middling classes of well-off White women, urban merchants (not merchants' clerks), and amateur scientists. Merchants are especially well-favored within the journal literature. If farmers and the countryside are underemphasized, then merchants and cities are overemphasized. In the towns of early America, small though they were compared to cities in subsequent centuries, and in the merchant class, which was at the apex of the dynamic social and commercial structures of urban life, we can discern most clearly the transformative effects of modernization in the eighteenth-century world. In her introduction to a special issue of *EAS* on port cities in 2017, Jessica Chopin Roney argues that early Americanists study towns and merchants because "port cities were at the front lines of change and being affected by the changes wrought by the global consumer revolution" where they "amplified opportunities for new groups and individuals" in places that were "often disproportionately female." She concludes that "positioned along the saltwater edge, early modern port cities shared much in common with their landlocked urban counterparts, but they diverged in their particular relationship to space, the movement of people, goods, ideas, and pathogens, and their frontline role in forging new circuits of commerce and colonization."[20]

Another neglected subject is migration and population history. There are just six articles in this sample on these topics, five of which are about African migration and African American demography; only one, Timothy Shannon's case study of mid-eighteenth-century servant migration, examines European migration or demographic patterns.[21] These "neglected subjects" indicate how much the field has moved on from the many works in the 1970s influenced by E. P. Thompson's *The Making of the English Working Class* (1963). Indeed, the article in this sample that most reflects the kind of interest in the working class that Thompson elicited is Diana Paton's investigation of the working lives of enslaved women in the last quarter of the eighteenth century.[22]

Other neglected subjects include a lack of interest in the Founding Fathers, even when such people are a relentless focus of attention in popular history and in general culture, as might be seen in the enormous success of the musical *Hamilton*.[23] Only one article in this sample concerns directly the thought of a Founding Father—an examination of the religious thinking of George Washington—while Sophus Reinart and Alan Houston write about Benjamin Franklin as a mid-eighteenth-century writer of popular economic thought and a somewhat vindictive politician. There is also a treatment of Franklin's wife and daughter, Deborah Franklin and Sally Franklin Bache, as political actors in the age of revolution.[24] The only early Americans otherwise who might be household names are the preachers Jonathan Edwards and George Whitefield, each discussed in a single article, and Black writers Phillis Wheatley and James Albert Ukawsaw Gronniosaw.[25]

It shows that one trend of history-from-below from the heyday of the Annales school of history in the 1960s through 1980s has remained, which is a view of history shaped by the collective rather than the individual, with individuals tending toward the unheralded rather than the historically famous. The people written about are people otherwise unknown, such as Hannah Beamon, an elderly and mentally incapable wealthy New England widow; Lene Kühberg, a mixed-race Danish-Ga female slave broker in Osu on the Gold Coast; John Perkins, the first person of Black heritage to attain high rank in the British navy; and James Petiver, an inveterate collector closely associated with the Atlantic slave trade.[26]

In addition, early American historians show little interest in evaluating the work of famous historians who wrote a long time ago about early

American history. Homage toward older historians who had shaped how early American history was written was a decided characteristic of a previous generation's writing on early American history, especially prominent when *WMQ* was the sole specialist journal in the field. From its first issue in 1944, when there was an appreciation of the recently deceased Charles MacLean Andrews, editors of *WMQ* regularly interviewed or assessed the leading figures in the field.[27] Such introspection has stopped in the last decade, although it has been replaced to an extent by forums on important books by major figures.[28] The only homage to a senior person in early American history was a series of appreciations of Mary Maples Dunn in *Early American Studies* in 2019.[29] In addition, the *Journal of the History of Ideas* published in 2016 a series of articles on J. G. A. Pocock's six-volume *Barbarism and Religion*, itself a meditation on the eighteenth-century historian Edward Gibbon.[30]

Yet a decline in deference seems to have been accompanied by a rise in civility. Academic arguments, at least in early American history, are less vicious than before, at least within journal literature.[31] Historians today do not get rewarded for aggressive attacks—smiting an erring colleague to gain a great reputation, as Oxford historian Hugh Trevor-Roper was accused by R. H. Tawney of doing in the celebrated spat between historians of the seventeenth-century English gentry.[32] Martin Ridge notes how his generation of male academics, prominent in the 1960s and 1970s, saw history as a sport, with the reward going to those with "a taste for blood." He references Samuel Eliot Morison's notorious attack on Charles Beard in 1948 as an example of a senior academic being decidedly uncivil.[33]

Historians writing today are less inclined to see the history profession as a place for combat. The tradition of scholarly differences, sometimes strongly expressed in competing sets of articles—as illuminated in debates in the 1970s and 1980s on republicanism and rural capitalism, for example—has largely disappeared.[34] Moreover, very few articles express directly a strong political stance (either conservative or center-left or left-leaning) in ways that were more common in the past, as seen in Jesse Lemisch's attack on the politics of Bernard Bailyn in 1976 or Marcus Rediker's account of a trip to Moscow as the Cold War ended.[35] Only one article in this sample situates itself as directly replying to another article, while another article provoked a critical response directly about its perceived errors. What is noticeable in both cases, however, is that the differences in interpretation are approached with courtesy, in contradiction to the often highly polarized and aggressive confrontations between historians with varying views in a previous generation.³⁶

IV

One consequence of a decline in aggressive historiographical debates is a concentration by historians on outlining new empirical information rather than on engaging in disputes. History is a profession based on a concern for the past, but historians, at least in the field of early American history as written in the last decade, are little interested in exploring its historiographical traditions and in making polemical arguments in favor of certain historical interpretations. Early American historians work within a historical tradition of writing about problems rather than placing them, as sociologists are wont to do, within competing theoretical positions. Certainly, the overarching problems that used to animate earlier generations of scholars, such as the causes of the American Revolution and to what extent the origins of the American nation can be discerned in its colonial past, have become less urgent concerns in the last decade of writing on early America and the American Revolution. What interests early American historians is adding more empirical information to their subject. "Plus ça change," one might say, but the tendency toward empiricism has increased in the twenty-first century as historians have retreated from their interest in social science. In addition, the vast majority of what they read and find important are works written within the discipline of history.³⁷ In other words, early American history is self-referential; it can be glossed as a uni-discipline rather than a multi- or interdisciplinary enterprise.

This conclusion may seem surprising to many readers, given the repeated pronouncements of interdisciplinary intent made within the history profession, not least by early Americanists, but it is a conclusion that comes from what early American historians love best: their references to the works of other scholars (which can be seen in appendix B, my empirical investigation into early American historians' citational practices). Few early American historians work outside the discipline of history; they do not have favorite scholars, either within the discipline or outside it, to whom they often refer; and the majority of articles written by early American historians are discipline-specific.

This statement does not mean that early American historians are unreflexive about what they write or that they embrace archival techniques that are unsympathetic or are indifferent to how archives reproduce knowledge.³⁸ Marie Houllemare, for example, has done indispensable work, tracing through the organization of archives the legal dynamics of the early eighteenth-century French empire.³⁹ There is a growing consciousness, especially by writers on the histories of slavery and the enslaved, that historians need to be aware of the ethics of working on sensitive materials in archives.⁴⁰ This reanimated interest in the politics of the archive is accompanied by an increased concern for the positionality of historians in relation to the topics they study. The boldest of such attempts at reflexive positionality place historians themselves at the center of narratives in ways that highlight the limitations of objectivity and authorial invisibility. Past and present can merge, often deliberately so, especially for scholars of Indigenous history, who follow the scholarly practices of Native American and Indigenous Studies (NAIS).⁴¹ The essential point of these NAIS guidelines is that it is imperative for historians to work with descendant communities and to prioritize those communities' goals. *WMQ* has devoted a forum, including several articles informed by Indigenous Ways of Knowing methodology, to show how scholarly research following these guidelines can be done.⁴²

Yet behind this sensitivity toward context and concern about reception lies a deep introspection in the field and a sharp drawing of boundaries based on the disciplinary orientations and principles of history writing in the empirical manner. Early American history is an insular field. The days of experimentation with the techniques and methodologies of the social sciences or even the biological sciences appear gone. I counted just seventeen articles that make a serious engagement with other disciplines, not including five articles written by literary scholars employing the techniques of their disciplines in their research and several articles by economic historians who employ the tools of their trade and training in economics.⁴³ The engagement with other disciplines is of three kinds. The first uses other disciplines as additives to historical research, meaning that the engagement is incremental. For example, Chris Evans delves into the history and practice of metallurgy in order to write about the hoe as a commodity on plantations.⁴⁴ The second is through having a knowledge of the literature in another field that helps inform a historical analysis. Various scholars have read extensively in the literature on onomastics, linguistics, anthropology, the history of technology, and business studies in composing their work.⁴⁵

Finally, there are six articles by four writers who use theoretical models drawn from the social sciences and sciences to structure the whole of their analyses—in this respect having other disciplines lead the history rather than the other way around. Turk McCleskey, in two articles on that most traditional of topics, debt in Virginia, has teamed up with lawyers, economists, and an engineer in two articles in which they use game theory to explain the nature of debt litigation, using robust quantitative data to justify their conclusions. Robert Michael Morrissey exploits the theory of social networks to understand kinship relations in Illinois country in French Louisiana, while Zachary Dorner does the same for analyzing the career of Silvester Gardiner, a surgeon-druggist and land speculator in Boston in the early 1740s. And Simon Newman, who, like McCleskey, collaborated with a range of social scientists and scientists, has used digital humanities to examine, from many perspectives, runaways in eighteenth-century Jamaica and has used the science of DNA analysis to argue for the strong likelihood that we can connect modern Jamaicans' DNA heritage to the early eighteenth-century Gold Coast.[46]

Engagement with major intellectual thinkers who are not historians is also limited. When early American historians do reference such thinkers (generally they are French, including Pierre Bourdieu, who is the most cited thinker not from history; Michel Foucault; and Bruno Latour), they do so generally in passing and without relying too extensively on their work for their own analyses. Only three essays—an article on early American historiography by Johann Neem; Nathan Perl-Rosenthal's examination of revolutionary epistolary practice; and Ian Chambers's investigation of a Cherokee delegation to midcentury London—rely for their analyses on a theoretical model: in Neem's case, Bourdieu's field theory, and in Rosenthal's and Chambers's cases, Bourdieu's concept of "habitus."[47] Significantly, there is no engagement with any living theorist, or anyone writing in cognate fields in the twenty-first century.

The exception to the rule of early American history as virtually a theory-free subdiscipline is the recent, intense, and growing interest in the Antipodean export of the idea of settler colonialism as an overarching methodology within which to place early American history. The increasing prominence of settler colonialism as a paradigm useful for early Americanists has the chance of transforming the field, similar to how interest in social sciences changed not just the practice but the themes of early American history from the 1960s onwards.

Indigenous legal scholar Maggie Blackhawk makes the challenge of settler colonialism discourse clear when she argues that having a slavery-to-freedom narrative as the central dynamic of United States legal doctrine, as she argues is now standard, diminishes how Indigenes are central to the American experience and to the laws that govern the nation. She argues that the United States of America's "tragic history of colonialism and violent dispossession of Native American lands, resources, culture and children" has much to teach us about reimagining the constitutional history of the United States.[48] Ned Blackhawk in the *American Historical Review* (*AHR*) also emphasizes that "American history begins not with Europeans but with Native Americans, whose lived experiences, historical agency, and ongoing struggles for autonomy form the foundations for all subsequent colonial and national histories."[49] Blackhawk considers the lessons of settler colonialism the "primary operative theoretical formation" that was "central to any engagement with Indigenous history, which in itself [was] central to American history."[50] He cites Boyd Cotheran approvingly: that "settler colonialism is the logic that gives meaning to the history of North America."[51]

In the last couple of decades, scholars have extensively mobilized settler colonialism committed to postcolonial studies. What do they mean by this concept? For some scholars its utility is political. Alicia Cox, for example, sees settler colonialism in entirely adversarial form, as a pernicious form of colonialism intended to dispossess Indigenous people of land, power, and, eventually, identity. She defines settler colonialism as "an ongoing system of power that perpetuates the genocide and repression of Indigenous people and cultures [which] includes interlocking forms of oppression, including racism, White supremacy, heteropatriarchy, and capitalism." She refers to what she calls the "ground-breaking" theory of the late Australian scholar Patrick Wolfe and his expression of the "logic of elimination" to "show that settler colonialism is a system, not an historical event, and that as such it perpetuates the erasure of native peoples as a precondition for settler expropriation of lands and resources, providing the necessary conditions for establishing the present-day ideology of multicultural neoliberalism."[52]

The concept of settler colonialism is derived from nineteenth-century Australian and American history and is read back into early American historiography.[53] It paints the opposition between settlers and Indigenous peoples in stark terms that, according to some scholars, understate the complexity and fluidity of seventeenth- and eighteenth-century America. In a 2019 forum in *WMQ*, the historian of New France, Allan Greer, was dismissive of the concept. Greer notes how the concept of settler colonialism developed from Wolfe's thinking about the case of Australia as a kind of ideal type of modern settler colonialism, "a place where Indigenous resistance was weak, where the complexities of pre-Enlightenment territoriality were absent and where the brutal logic of appropriation could operate on what looked like (but was not) a clean slate."[54]

Nevertheless, the reservations that Greer expresses about settler colonialism are not shared by all early Americanists. Two immediate benefits present themselves for early Americanists in adopting some of the language of settler colonialism. First, as Jennifer Spear concludes in her contribution to the *WMQ* forum in 2019, settler colonialism is useful because it forces us to confront what it means—then and now—to live in stolen lands worked by stolen labor.[55] Second, settler colonialism connects early American scholarship to the scholarship of other places, especially within the colonies established by European empires in the Atlantic archipelago. It also allows early American historians to connect with colleagues who work in imperialism, colonialism, the American West, Indigenous history, and settler relations during the "settler revolution" of the nineteenth century.[56]

Early American scholars acknowledge that settler colonialism may have value as an analytic concept—"an actual historical phenomenon," as Jeffrey Ostler puts it[57]—but contend that the theoretical explications needs to be more nuanced and more attentive to the realities of colonial life and to settler populations that interacted with Africans at least as much as with Indigenous people.[58] Nancy Shoemaker, for example, comments in the *WMQ* forum of 2019 that we need to contextualize settler colonialism in a *longue durée* and especially within a lengthy English history of being invaded and invading others. Settler colonialism was thus, she believes, a forward-looking ideology specific to the English and rooted in their cultural inheritance—a cultural inheritance that shaped attitudes to Indigenes at least as much, and probably more, than the postsettlement interventions usually considered by historians.[59]

It is noticeable that the principal advocates of a settler colonial approach to the study of early America are scholars whose work straddles the colonial–early Republic divide. In the forum of 2019, the most enthusiastic supporters of a settler colonial approach were Michael Witgen and Jeffrey Ostler, who work as much in the nineteenth as in the second half of the eighteenth century.[60] Witgen concludes his generally favorable treatment of settler colonialism in the American interior by arguing, with reference to the early nineteenth century, that "the United States was founded, and continues to be, a nation of settler immigrants locked into a struggle over the meanings of place and belonging with the Native nations of North America."[61] Ostler has been particularly eager to extend settler colonialism backward from the nineteenth century into the late eighteenth century. He preceded his coeditorship of the 2019 forum on settler colonialism with, in 2015, the first settler colonial–influenced foray into early American history. He argued that—contrary to other accounts that read settler statements that they wanted Indigenes dead as mere bluster—Indigenous people were right to think that settlers wanted to practice genocide against them given many examples of settler violence and bad intentions.[62]

Settler colonialism, however, remains a minority interest, with enthusiasm for the concept diminishing the further back in history one goes and the closer one gets to when North America was everywhere populated by and controlled by Indigenous people. It is becoming more popular, with two articles published in 2020 and early 2021 directly referencing settler colonialism. But there are strong countervailing historiographical currents to settler colonialism in an Indigenous American historiography that emphasizes Indigenous agency and the political power of Native peoples rather than the overwhelming power and violence of settlers.[63]

V

It remains to be seen whether settler colonialism will have sufficient analytic purchase and interpretive utility to reshape the field of early American history around a single concept or whether it will be a theoretical perspective confined to Indigenous history and to understanding the shift from colonial to early national history.[64] Settler colonialism is one perspective advanced that to its advocates holds the key to understanding all aspects of early American history. So, too, the topics of race and slavery and the contention that slavery is the fundamental story that shapes the entirety of American history (as advocated in the 1619 Project advanced by the *New York Times*) could be themes around which early American history can be oriented.[65] Another theme around which early American history is increasingly written is empire, in its many forms. The idea that early America was "vast" and encompassed much more than just the histories of the thirteen colonies as they moved toward independence from Britain has also been advanced as a structuring device by scholars associated with *WMQ*, as will be discussed in depth in the first chapter.[66]

Part II of this book deals in turn with each of these possible ways to interpret the story of early America. I have written substantive chapters on slavery and race; on Indigenous history; and on early America and empire as themes in early American history that attract a lot of current attention. This section is preceded by two chapters that will help orientate readers into this field. The first chapter of this book places the last ten years' historiographical developments in a longer context, which, in part, will help to differentiate what is happening now in the writing of early American history from the ways in which early American historians conceived of the field thirty years ago. The second chapter deals with the material realities of early America—wealth, commerce, environment—with an aim to provide the necessary contexts of lived reality in early America that can help readers place slavery, Indigenous history, empire, and (starting the final section of this book), gender within the chronological and spatial boundaries that comprised early America. The first of two final chapters examines a cognate area of historical research—eighteenth-century British history—to highlight what is distinctive and what is not distinctive about early American history as a discrete field. The last substantive chapter then deals with the scholarship around the event that continues to attract most attention in the writing of early American history—the American Revolution. The revolution is depicted in recent works as a contingent event with bad consequences for Indigenes, enslaved people, and in part White women. It is also written about increasingly as an event that was an end to a period of history and an important shaper of larger processes of imperial formation, colonialism, and postcolonialism. The conclusion attempts to sum up what has been written (and tries to avoid being a crystal ball predicting the future direction of the field). Appendix A outlines some of the empirical findings drawn from this analysis of 393 journals. Let's start, therefore, on this historiographical journey by exploring how recent writing on early American history has developed from what generations of previous historians have written on the subject.

PART I
Context and Background

1

The Historiography of Early America

∽

I

When early American historians write about the short eighteenth century (1713–84) they do so after reading contemporary accounts written by settler historians who stress that early America was a success story. Much of the recent writing on early America, as the following chapters will demonstrate at greater length, contests these self-satisfactory accounts by contrasting the successes of settler colonialism with the travails of the Indigenes and enslaved people whose oppression underpinned the success of settlers in establishing societies that they thought were credits to the British empire.[1] The short eighteenth century was a period of empire and intense colonization, but it was also a time of war and revolution, with the Seven Years' War (1756–63) and the American Revolution (1776–83) especially prominent. For the most fortunate members of European Atlantic empires, this was a period in which chests could be puffed up with pride at European settler accomplishments in what Europeans thought of as a New World. Less fortunate people, especially those who got in the way of European settlement, were more inclined to think of the period as a time of continuing disaster and ever greater stress and dismay. For settlers of European descent, however, this was a time, as Jack P. Greene puts it, "of extraordinary growth ... in terms of the volume and value of all colonial trades and in the territorial, demographic, economic, social, political and cultural development of the American colonies."[2]

The eighteenth-century world of early America and the American Revolution in the twenty-first century is historiographically a much-expanded and more imperial world than it used to be. It is hugely more inclusive, with Indigenes no longer playing a passive role and with White male settlers of British descent not being the only Americans or West Indians with any agency. Instead, White women influence matters at all points; German and Scots-Irish settlers in the interior press hard on established governments; and the massive population of enslaved people of African descent puts the lie to any simple declarations that these societies were lands of freedom. If anything, this was an empire driven by slavery and by dreams of continental expansion at the expense of Indigenous inhabitants.

Indigenes are now the principal actors in many of the events that happened in eighteenth-century British America, while enslaved Africans have also been placed front and center of analyses. In addition, women are not subsumed within the general category of men. As well as being a more spatially extensive world, it is a world in which an older idea—that the purpose of studying early America is to understand the roots of the formation of the nation of the United States—has largely vanished. By examining various retrospectives on trends in the written scholarship of early American history, this chapter looks at how scholars from the early 1990s until 2020 have evaluated changes in the writing of early American history in the last half century. It shows that while the field of early American history was transformed through its encounter with and enthusiasm for social sciences as a method of analyzing the past in the 1970s and 1980s, the extent of transformation in the field has slowed in the last quarter century. The most important new orientation today is toward a more expansive and capacious history in which the spatial focus of early America is being steadily extended into the American interior and into Canada, the Caribbean and even into West Africa and Ireland. This move to #VastEarlyAmerica, as a social media hashtag has it, has garnered mostly positive commentary but also has some critics, who lament what they see as an increasing disconnection between the study of the colonial period of American history and investigations into the origins of the American nation.[3]

II

A great deal of what we think of as the traditional story of early America emerged in a period of scholarship between the late 1940s and the early 1990s, with the principal ferment of activity being in the intellectual history and social science dominated years of the 1970s. The study of colonial British America, which was the term mostly used in the twentieth century to describe the study of British America in the seventeenth and eighteenth centuries, was in the doldrums when the Institute of Early American History and Culture (now renamed the Omohundro Institute of Early American History and Culture) was formed in 1947, three years after the leading specialist journal in the field, *WMQ*, was refashioned into its third series. Carl Bridenbaugh, the director, wrote a state-of-the-field report in which he argued that the study of early American history was in crisis by almost all measures. It was a "neglected subject," and it would thus take from the beleaguered historians still interested in a field, which Bridenbaugh denied had "all been written" and "mined out," "a concerted effort to re-establish the field as a prominent [area of] study."[4] That "concerted effort" paid off beyond the dreams of any early Cold War historian of early America. Introducing a series of field-defining essays on early American history in 1984, at the peak period of early American history's infatuation with social science history, Jack P. Greene and J. R. Pole exclaimed that the previous quarter century before 1984 had seen the colonial period "acquire such an integrity" that it had "become one of the most exciting and attractive areas of American historical study."[5]

In 1993 *WMQ* surveyed what had happened in the fifty years following the start of the third series. It commissioned a doyen in the field, Joyce Appleby, to examine the last five decades of scholarship. She painted a very different picture from that advanced by Bridenbaugh. She was full of praise for what early American scholars of her generation had achieved in the previous half century, in moving early American history from the doldrums of neglect in 1948 to the center of attention of not just historians but social scientists of all kinds.[6] Fred Anderson and Andrew Cayton echoed this enthusiasm for the vitality of the field, declaring that there was "never a better time to be an early American historian than now" [1992] due to the advances made in applying what was still then called the "New Social History" to the period, as highlighted in the so-called annus mirabilis of 1970 when four pioneering social history and Annales-inflected studies of New England towns emerged simultaneously.[7] They also commended then-recent works of synthesis by Jack P. Greene and Bernard Bailyn in which socioeconomic approaches were paramount, as well as noting as exemplary a recent "Needs and Approaches" survey of early American economic history by John McCusker and Russell Menard.[8]

All seemed good in the early American vineyard at this time of reflection in 1993.

Appleby welcomed, almost without reservation, the fruits of this radical transformation of early American history affected through a turn to the social sciences, especially anthropology, and a deep involvement since the 1960s by early Americanists in adopting a "European frame of reference," which she argued had a liberating effect on their scholarship. She listed what she found valuable about recent historiographical interventions: New England town studies and the finely grained studies of the seventeenth-century Chesapeake; works on the historical demography of slavery; the long-running debates about capitalism in rural America and if and when America became capitalist; the upsurge of works on Indigenous America; and the beginnings of Atlantic history.

Her article echoed Anderson and Cayton in seeing this as a blissful time to be practicing early American history. Any undergraduate contemplating entering graduate studies reading Appleby's article could not help but think that they were entering a highly exciting and vibrant field. She argued that the historiography of the previous twenty years and the influence of an onslaught of publications in New Social History had put an end to Whiggish historiography and allowed for a liberation from American exceptionalism. She commended current tendencies urging early Americanists to worry less about American origins and origin stories and to lessen their fixation on when and how Americans became democratic. She thought that this trend in scholarship was a good thing, approving how early American historians were "turning away from grand events, exceptional lives and transcendent ideas," the latter comment seemingly aimed at the multifaceted debate over "republicanism" and the American Revolution.[9]

Appleby was especially thankful that the study of early Americans as done through the lenses of New Social History had dispelled, she thought forever, the idea that America was born free, rich, and modern and that as it became more modern, it became more secular. She concluded that in 1993, early American historians were "no longer the custodians of colonial origins and liberal heroes." They had become "able to reconstruct ways of living and thinking quite different from those that triumphed after the Revolution." The only thing she lamented in this general paean of praise to the field was that in historians' embrace of the social sciences they had downplayed the role of individuals and the importance of human agency in shaping events and processes.[10]

That these were good times in the writing of early American history was echoed a couple of years after Appleby's encomium to the field-as-is by Gordon S. Wood in his survey of one hundred years of writing in early American history for the *AHR*. He thought, like Appleby, that the writing of early American history was in very good shape. There was not any sign of real crisis in the field, with an embarrassment of riches in the current historiography as of 1995 that showed that early American history writing was in "a period of greatness" in which scholars were "enjoying the bountiful fruits of the seeds planted by our professional predecessors of a century ago." He was less inclined than Appleby to emphasize changes over continuities in history writing, arguing that "most historians of early America seem to be going about their craft in much the same way" as did historians a century earlier.[11]

Wood acknowledged, however, as did Appleby, that the biggest change in history writing in the generation before the early 1990s was the gradual acceptance in the field of the conceptions and notions of social science. He agreed with Appleby that early American historians believed that "society" should be the major category of analysis, allowing for "a radical transformation of their discipline." (Appleby thought it was more sudden and more inflected by French and British scholarship than did Wood.) Wood's analysis two years following was not empirically different from Appleby's, but he adopted a less celebratory tone, one that has become more pessimistic in his recent ruminations on the direction of the field of early American history, especially on the period around the American Revolution and the making of the American Constitution.[12] He agreed with Appleby that early American historians had become less interested in studying early America for its own sake and as a means of understanding American nationhood and more concerned with seeing early America as an example (of one among many possible societies) of how societies transform from being premodern to modern ones.

For Wood, however, such tendencies were to be lamented more than celebrated as it was a "narrowing of perspective." It implied that in focusing on such small topics ("towns, or counties or even obscure single families"), scholarship retreated into antiquarianism. Unlike Appleby, who argued that 1990s scholarship was better than in the past, Wood believed that one problem with contemporary scholarship as of 1995 was that an earlier cosmopolitan outlook and disdain for local history as antiquarian history had been cast aside in favor of history that looked at "the private spaces and personal lives of ordinary people," leaving to historians working outside of the academy the important task of seeing early America as the "place where we Americans most readily got a bearing on where we have come from and what kind of people we are." It might be noticed the deliberate way by which he used the first-person plural, when he did not need to do so, to emphasize that understanding American history was not for non-Americans but was attached to an American enterprise in civic education. What Wood saw as a relentless emphasis on studying diversity in the colonial period took historians away, he believed, from understanding American identity and the United States as a nation.[13]

In retrospect, Appleby's and Wood's surveys of the field are reflections of a period at an end rather than pointers to how the field of early American history developed in the next generation of scholarship. The moment that Appleby celebrated and Wood lamented—the attachment to society as the principal object of early American history and "its integrative mechanisms, its systems for distributing power, authority and respect, its colonial repertoire"[14]—very quickly disappeared. If there is one thing that has gone from the majority of early American scholarship in the last thirty years, it is the "embrace of the social sciences."[15] Early American historians, despite a continuing rhetoric of a need for interdisciplinary research, have turned inward in the last three decades, focusing on scholarship within the discipline of history rather than taking methods, techniques, and approaches from other disciplines, especially anthropology but also sociology and economics.

III

The then-editor of the *WMQ*, Michael McGiffert, invited present or former fellows at the Institute of Early American History and Culture to write short articles to accompany the larger survey by Appleby. Of the nine articles (one article had two authors), three are on topics that have continuously engaged early American historians since 1993—gender; Africans and slavery; and Indigenous people. The other six articles, each about ten pages long, deal with topics and issues whose importance has declined over time. Fred Anderson and Andrew Cayton, for example, worried about the lack of thematic unity in social histories of the colonial era, reflecting a concern Bernard Bailyn had raised in a presidential address to the American Historical Association in 1981.[16] Saul Cornell wrote on another theme that attracted little attention in the next generation but that was of pressing concern in 1992, which was how to incorporate poststructuralism into works of colonial history. That theme is part of two other articles, too: Michael Meranze on the ethics of history writing and Darren Marcus Staloff on the thought of the "thinking class."[17]

Even those articles that deal with topics that have continued to attract early Americans' historical attention did not accurately predict the scholarly future when read from thirty years' distance. Daniel K. Richter feared that his chosen area of Indian history was in decline. He lamented that perspectives on Indigenous peoples and their relations with European colonizers developed since the 1970s "belong only to a tiny sect within the already small scholarly priesthood of early Americanists." His account was mostly downbeat, arguing that work on Indian history had not been incorporated into the mainstream of early American history and that, worse, this "sect" had "tried to seize title to an Indian past that rightfully belongs only to native communities."[18]

Richter's comments about the irrelevance of Indian history are overly pessimistic since in 1993 so-called Indian history had just had its annus mirabilis like that of New England towns in 1970, with several iconic books just published, including one by Richter himself.[19] In retrospect, this period seems a significant turning point in early American history, when it became impossible not to argue, as Ned Blackhawk declared in 2005, that "colonial Indian historians have now resoundingly demonstrated the centrality of Native peoples to early America in a way that seemed nearly inconceivable a generation ago."[20] For Richter, however, Indigenous history in 1993 seemed "not a period of new departures, but the end of the line," with its major legacy being a means of helping scholars understand catastrophe in early American history more generally and therefore providing readers with a more "inclusive narrative" that "may even help the cultural descendants of European males rise above mere guilt to discover the strands that entwine their heritages with those of other ethnic groups."[21]

Jon Sensbach and Kathleen Brown were more enthusiastic than Richter about recent achievements in writings about early American history in their surveys about African Americans and gender, respectively.[22] Both authors were strongly invested in the movement away from social history to cultural history. That was especially true for Brown, who noted how cultural history reinforced feminist scholarship. She had little time for a previous generation's interest in developing empirical information about how women contributed to colonial life and even less for their concern about if and when the colonial period had been a "golden age" for women that heralded a subsequent decline as patriarchy became stronger and more supported by state power. She dismissed the still-prevailing declension theory about the position of women getting worse over the colonial period; rightly, it seems, as this theme has disappeared in scholarship.[23]

She pointed to two trends that she believed, correctly, would become dominant within women's and gender history in the next three decades. As with other commentators, she argued for a more spatially expansive version of women's history, in what she called "a new cultural history within a reinvigorated comparative framework." Brown emphasized a theme she was to develop in a subsequent book, about how the peopling of the Atlantic world created "gender frontiers." She argued that "by employing the concept of gender frontiers—cultural encounters that extend from Europe, to Africa, across the Atlantic, to the Americas—we can begin to appreciate the centrality of gender to colonial exchanges and contests for power."[24] The one area where her crystal ball failed her was in urging for more work on manhood and masculinity in order "to deconstruct the false opposition of human (male) experience to the particular gendered experience of women."[25] As will be noted below, such explorations of masculinity from a gender history perspective have been limited in recent journal literature, at least for Atlantic America though not for eighteenth-century Britain.

Jon Sensbach was similarly perceptive about where African American history was moving in the future, following what he described as "a prodigious burst of scholarship on African-American history" triggered by the civil rights movement in the 1960s.[26] Sensbach predicted that the future would involve research around three wide-ranging concerns. These were "a broader regional, international, and temporal focus; more intense scrutiny of the ambiguities in the dyadic master-slave relationship and other change over time; and a greater willingness by historians to accept race as a defining category of American history."[27]

The last ambition has been the one most realized. Race is indeed at the center of the early American experience as written about in the twenty-first century. It has been central in particular to how Atlantic history has evolved. The major contribution of Atlantic history has been to bring Africans decisively into the history of the Atlantic world as active agents and to make slavery essential to how the Atlantic world operated and became successful. As Barbara Solow has noted, "What moved in the Atlantic was primarily [African] slaves, the output of slaves, the import of slave societies, and goods and services produced with the earnings on slave profits."[28] Africans are noted not just as the largest body of migrants into the Americas before 1820 but celebrated also for what they did when they got there, economically, culturally, and ideologically.[29]

Sensbach made a prediction that by making race central to the American experience, "we shall have created a forum for historical discussions wherein glib generalizations about democracy and national destiny will perforce stumble hard on the ramification of race slavery."[30] Such a prediction has been realized with an increasing focus now on race as a defining feature of American history in American culture, as can be seen in the popularity of museums throughout the world devoted to either transatlantic slavery or to African American life. It can be seen in the Smithsonian National Museum of African American History and Culture, opened in its permanent home in 2016; in American politics, as seen in 2020 in the high visibility of the Black Lives Matter movement; and in projects such as the 1619 Project of the *New York Times*, for which its journalist author, Nikole Hannah-Jones, received a Pulitzer Prize. That sudden prominence, however, has also led to controversy, notably over the 1619 Project, but also about how Black history ought to be presented: either that this concentration on the centrality of race lacks historical nuance or that it feeds into a US-centric narrative that presumes what Hazel Carby calls a "gated community of knowledge" that "mirrors the theory of exceptionalism and separates the history of African Americans from the histories of the descendants of other survivors of the crossing."[31]

Where Sensbach's recommendations for future research have been least persuasive has been his advice that the study of slavery in early America ought to demonstrate a greater degree of temporal and spatial specificity. Slavery is still often viewed as a timeless institution without a history connected closely to time and place, and few studies since the works of Ira Berlin and Philip D. Morgan in 1998 delineate between patterns of slavery in different times and places, a theme developed at length below.[32]

In the special issue from 1993 three articles by Daniel Vickers, Allan Kulikoff, and Russell Menard point to directions for future scholarship that were generally not followed. Vickers's essay was narrowly focused. It examined the position of early American sailors, asking why maritime subjects were paid so little recent attention by historians and suggesting that scholars need to rescue such men—Jack Tar—from the condescension of posterity. It was a clarion call both for a social history from below and a desire to unite maritime history with landward history.[33] Vickers's insistence that sailors held the key to understanding important things about early American history has only been fitfully addressed in recent scholarship.[34] In this specific case, sailors are not ignored but tend to be seen less through the lens of labor history or as political actors as was common in the heyday of social history but as avatars of a multiracial proletariat in which racial solidarity is examined more often than class politics.[35]

Kulikoff's article is a companion piece to Vickers's, if more broadly conceived and more tendentious in its conclusions.[36] He was interested in farmers, who comprised three-quarters of White Americans during the eighteenth century. Farmers played a crucial role in a debate that was very contentious in the 1970s and 1980s, which was the origins of rural capitalism. The issue at stake was how farmers and merchants in early America were changed as they encountered the encroachment of the market, described usually in abstract terms, along with social questions about the shift in the eighteenth century to wage labor. Did farmers willingly embrace capitalism or did merchants force them to engage with the market against their will? By the 2000s this debate seemed worked out and stale. Scholars with an economic history orientation turned to other topics, such as Atlantic networks of trade and to the murky areas separating legal from illegal trade.[37] It is only recently that scholars have returned to the study of capitalism, and they have done so mainly through extending studies of nineteenth-century slavery back to the colonial period.[38] Farmers have disappeared from the agenda of early American history, despite their numerical predominance in the population of settler society in North America.[39] Emma Hart argues that historians came to a consensus that the main issues in understanding how the early American economy worked did not revolve around what farmers thought about the market or what they did in the economy. She believes that "this consensus released early Americanists and Atlanticists to roam in pastures new. Abandoning the colonial farmer to his fate, they moved to a grander scale of discussions," being interested "less in the producers of commodities than in the commodities and how they were produced, distributed and exchanged."[40]

Russell Menard's article illustrates most clearly the roads not taken in the last thirty years.[41] He argued that what was most needed for forthcoming research was to establish empirically the lineaments of British North American demography. As with every other contributor in this forum, Menard paid relatively little attention to the Caribbean, which, as Atlantic history picked up steam, was becoming an ever-greater object of study among early American historians.[42] He also relegated Indigenous people to essentially an afterthought. Menard described the Indigenous experience as a holocaust of decline, destruction, and death. He did so even though any account of the population history of early America necessarily has to deal with Indigenous population decline as a major factor in early American history. Moreover, a central motif of early American scholarship has stressed the continued presence of Indigenes as a force shaping and constraining the populations and settlement policies of all the other people surrounding them on the North American continent.⁴³

But Menard knew he was fighting against the tide of historiographical change. He understood that his call for a new research agenda on population history was unlikely to succeed as historians were moving away from the rigor and perceived aridity of research into demographic history into the uplands of cultural history. Population history was a subdiscipline that Menard noted was seen by many historians and certainly by students and the general public as too technical, too narrowly focused, and "increasingly irrelevant to central intellectual concerns." Indeed, things were so bad that the field might be considered dead. Menard believed that it should be resuscitated around migration as a subset of population history so as to give it coherence and purpose. His ambition was not realized. Demographic history plays a smaller role in early American history than when Menard was doing his pioneering work in the area in the 1970s.⁴⁴ There is only one strictly demographic article in the articles analyzed here, and that article is oriented toward antebellum rather than colonial history.⁴⁵

The special issue of *WMQ* on the state of early American history is a useful place to start thinking about historical trajectories in journal literature in the last decade, as it marked a division between one period of early American scholarship and more recent scholarship. There has been less change in the writing of early American history between 1993 and 2020 than there was between 1964 and 1993.⁴⁶ Indigenous history and the history of race slavery have cemented their place as the central topics in early American history while, as Michael Meranze asserts in his meditation on the responsibility of the study of the past to the demands of the present, the critical time period continues, as always, to be the American Revolution.⁴⁷ The primacy of the American Revolution as the peak moment of interest for early Americanists can be seen in another publication from 1993. To celebrate its fifty-year anniversary, the *WMQ* sent a volume of the eleven best essays of the approximately 750 published since 1944 to subscribers. Essays on the American Revolution accounted for eight of them; another two focused on the seventeenth century, and only one, by James Henretta on rural capitalism, could be said to be about the eighteenth century prior to the American Revolution.⁴⁸

In a commentary on changes in early American historiography occurring between 1993 and 2010, Christopher Grasso and Peter Mancall note that the most substantial shift in the writing of early American history had been a sustained focus on early modern Atlantic history whereby developments in North America were placed within the context of a wider world.[49] The other area of scholarship to see a substantial increase was the field of imperial history—a subfield related to but not conterminous with Atlantic history. Eric Hinderaker and Rebecca Horn note in their 2010 appreciation of what they call a hemispheric history of the Americas both the increased number of works that place early America in an imperial context and also the persistence of American exceptionalism, although they feel that such exceptionalism is no more apparent in early American history than in other historiographies. They too welcome scholarship on early America that has comparative dimensions and is hemispheric. As with other commentators, they think this comparative work might be done through paying closer attention to imperial competition.[50] Grasso and Mancall make similar statements seeking more comparative work under the ambit of studying empires, as well as commending Atlantic history as a positive historiographical development.[51]

IV

Since the burst of historiographical reflection as part of significant journal anniversaries in 1993 and 1995, there have been four sustained evaluations of the field: by Joyce Chaplin in 2003, Claudio Saunt in 2008, Christopher Grasso and Karin Wulf, also in 2008, and Johann N. Neem in 2020. Three shorter reviews were part of introductions to special Huntington-Omohundro forums published in *WMQ* by Fred Anderson and Drew Cayton, Eric Hinderaker and Rebecca Horn, and Christopher Grasso and Peter Mancall.[52]

Chaplin's account in 2003 was more critical than Appleby had been a decade earlier about the recent direction of early American scholarship. She provided a downbeat analysis of the field, arguing that it promised more than it delivered. She saw early American history as inward looking, paying limited attention to non-Anglophone colonies and neither drawing from or influencing British history except in specific and limited ways.[53] It was slow to take up new methodologies, not very theoretical, and too inclined to publishing accounts that reeked of "regular guy history" that validated a pro-American view of colonial history. For all the talk of a more expansive and less US-centric history that Appleby had promoted, what Chaplin found in her survey of trends, mostly in the decade after Appleby had written her celebratory article, was an increasing gravitational pull in the field toward studying the history of the early republic with little real interest in comparative colonization in favor of a Manifest Destiny view of North America's history, teleologically driven toward the creation of the American Republic. She supported her argument with empirical findings from an analysis of *WMQ* articles. She showed that the percentage of articles on the short eighteenth century declined from 61 percent between 1944–53 to 53 percent between 1973–82 and to a low of 35 percent between 1992–2002.[54]

In short, Chaplin argued that Wood was wrong in seeing early American historians as moving away from telling stories about the national origins of the United States. Instead, she discerned a strong tendency toward a long-standing narrative about American exceptionalism. This exceptionalist tendency was limiting, in her opinion, as it showed a lack of interest in a wider perspective. Chaplin expressed some early doubts about the lasting power of Atlantic history, tartly wondering whether it was a flash in the pan, the 1990s equivalent of the obsession with republicanism in the 1970s. Early American history, she argued, was "situated firmly within a national historiography and geography" that "assesses, at most, the influence that overseas events had on its corner of the world," with little appreciation of wider comparative perspectives. Moreover, Chaplin argued that for all the talk about new subjects and paying attention to the subaltern voice, historians remained obsessed with White settlers with any inquiries into the history of non-European populations being done only within a settler-dominated understanding of the past. Her advice to aspiring authors was to move more firmly toward seeing early America outside exceptionalist lenses. She stressed how early America was enmeshed in imperial webs and global networks, making colonialism and postcolonialism matters requiring more discussion.[55] Similarly, Chris Grasso and Karin Wulf writing in 2008 hoped that this move to studying empire would not entail an abandonment of the cultural turn but would lead to better efforts to connect culture to "analyses of longer strictures, institutionalized processes, and broader patterns of historical change."[56]

Claudio Saunt's survey also was a mainly negative view of the field. He wrote as someone interested in the history of the American West and as an American concerned that many of the residents of the contemporary United States found their historical past underrepresented in the *WMQ*. His empirical research showed how inattentive early American scholars were to studying places outside the thirteen colonies. The practice of early American history, he claimed, was unduly biased toward Atlantic rather than continental histories. Through mapping techniques, he highlighted a persistent eastern bias in both the subject matter that early American historians studied and the places where early Americans were mostly trained (although he ignored historians trained outside America). Yet matters were changing: there was a reduction in the percentage of articles on the thirteen colonies from 90 percent to 50 percent from the 1980s to the 2000s; there were more articles on ethnohistory and cultural history than before; and there was a decline in a few traditional early American topics, such as the military history of the American Revolution and the drafting of the American Constitution.

But, like Chaplin and Wood (though in different ways), Saunt did not see as much change in topics between 1993 and 2008 as Appleby suggested had occurred in the period of historiography between the early 1970s and 1993. The world of early America, he thought, was about the East rather than the West and reflected priorities of the imperial government in the 1760s rather than the interests of contemporary readers living in the expansive, multiethnic world of twenty-first-century America. There were limits, however, to Saunt's idea of expansiveness, such as the mismatch between the amount of attention paid to regions in America and the population of those regions. Like Wood, and indeed like Appleby and Chaplin, Saunt imagined not just the authors but the audience for early American history to be confined to Americans. This national parochialism is endemic within the whole field. In this way, a certain kind of American exceptionalism dominates the field.[57]

V

Such proclamations fit with the aims of the Omohundro Institute and *WMQ* in their mission statement of #VastEarlyAmerica—"three simple words for a complex reality." The institute's director between 2012 and 2021, Karin Wulf, and the current editor of the *WMQ*, Joshua Piker, have each advocated that early Americanists should take a capacious approach to the study of early America. Doing so, they suggest, will uncover a past that is "infinitely complex, dynamic, globally connected and violent." Understanding such a world better highlights, in this reading, the "origins of an ambitious, powerful and democratic nation." "What we need," they suggest (without explaining who the "we" might be in this formulation), "is an early American history that fully grasps the depth, breadth and complexity—the vastness—of early America. This would just be good history, and it is good civics."[58]

Of course, as a mission statement #VastEarlyAmerica needs to be all things to all people. It does, however, skillfully reflect the direction of scholarship in early America—all the surveys noted so far, except that of Wood, urge scholarship to be more "capacious." For Wulf, #VastEarlyAmerica can be "a shorthand for the chronologically, geographically, and methodologically capacious early American scholarship that has characterized the last decade" (since about 2010). It has had its admirers (the majority) and detractors (the minority), the latter of whom Gordon Wood is the most prominent representative. He has extended his arguments of 1995 into a stronger critique of an early America, which he sees as having few clear boundaries and being mushy and indistinct.[59] He thinks the concept as too present-minded, "condemning the past for not being more like the present," and so far from being objective and dispassionate that it veered academic historians to believing "that their history writing should become simply an instrument of moral handwringing."[60]

Johann Neem writing in 2020 comes from a different political perspective than Wood and was trained in the period when cultural history was in the ascendant. But he shares Wood's disquiet over #VastEarlyAmerica as a governing paradigm in his survey of recent historiographical trends in early American history, even though he is careful to distinguish himself from Wood's concern about excessive political correctness as distorting scholarship. Neem concludes his essay with a concern that Wood shares—that early American history provides no useful guide to democratic politics, even though democracies depend on citizens having a sense of themselves as a people, a sense that can only emerge from historical writings.[61]

Employing the concept of bounded space as outlined by French sociologist Pierre Bourdieu,[62] Neem argues that the problem with the concept of #VastEarlyAmerica is "an epistemological gap between two distinct, coherent, and incompatible fields of historiography." Wood believes, Neem argues, in polity—how his work explains political situations. However, the proponents of #VastEarlyAmerica are interested in exchange—movement across porous boundaries, rather than political and cultural solidities.[63] Neem sees a historiography based on exchange as problematic since it involves an unthinking acceptance of the language and practice of neoliberalism and economic globalization. He argues that accounts of early America that adopt a methodology of exchange rather than polities are in the ascendant and that they draw their vocabulary and categories of analysis from discourses around globalization, made by theorists such as Saskia Sassen. What Neem draws from the presentist account of globalization by these theorists is that contemporary globalization has led to a declining intelligibility in respect to the question of national sovereignties.[64]

Like other commentators, Neem notes the increasing emphasis on imperialism as an early American history topic.[65] He finds this enthusiasm for the workings of the eighteenth-century British empire wanting. He argues that early Americanists increasingly see empire as a creative force, a highly flexible institution that sustained and protected a fluid and mobile world full of diversity and intergroup exchange across territorial boundaries. It was, in this account, a world with fragmented, competitive layers of sovereignty and free exchange. Sovereignty in this world did not depend on place or borders, Indeed, early American historians, he argues, celebrate a borderless world, citing me in particular in commending studies of early America that welcome pluralism, fragmentation, hybridity, and mobility.[66] Also citing Jeffers Lennox on Nova Scotia and Lisa Ford on Georgia (both colonies founded in the second quarter of the eighteenth century), Neem comments, without approval, how "in some recent interpretations, freedom was secured not through citizenship in a democratic nation" but was gained "outside it, in the empires and borderlands where porous boundaries and weak or distant sovereign authority enabled exchange and sustained pluralism." He cites Lisa Ford to this point: "Sovereignty and jurisdiction have always been intertwined but they have not always been territorial in nature."[67]

Neem suggests that it is not accidental that early American historians have become enamored of imperialism today given that he thinks the current global order resembles the eighteenth-century British Empire. Thus, it can be, as Krishnan Kumar argues, a prism through which we can examine the contemporary world.[68] Empire is increasingly seen not just as important but as a positive force for bringing cultures together: "As scholars turn their attention away from empire as a category to analyzing empire as a set of practices they have discovered complexity, plurality, contradiction, and even fragility at the heart of imperial projects."[69] He sees a new narrative emerging in works such as Kathleen Duval's exploration of imperial entanglements in the lands near the Gulf of Mexico where the end of empire was a tragic event in which "a world of cosmopolitan diversity and free exchange was overturned in 1776 by a modern democratic nation-state determined to achieve territorial control and cultural uniformity."[70]

This valorization of empire—and belief that empires, for all their faults, managed diversity better than was done in a nation-state, so that the creation of the United States was "independence lost," in Duval's phrase, rather than paradise gained—is a consequence of the historical shift Neem sees from polity to exchange. It is not a move he welcomes, as he makes clear in a penetrating and critical analysis of the career to date of the double Pulitzer Prize–winning historian Alan Taylor. He argues that whereas Taylor's works in the 1990s on the revolution and early republic in the American northeast were careful examinations of political contestations between elites and ordinary people, the latter emboldened by the American Revolution's egalitarian ideals, over time Taylor has dropped his concerns with "polity" in favor of a new story of exchange in which he argues that a diverse society needs a more pluralist narrative that is based on multicultural "encounters." Such a story would allow "us" (by which Taylor seems to mean Americans) to move beyond a national story and embrace today's globally interconnected world in which national boundaries are porous and in which national identity is fragile. In this new story of a diverse and porous imperial order, Taylor's critical perspective on empire falls away to be replaced by what Neem criticizes as a narrower and less sophisticated version, derived from histories of exchange, in which the story he tells is not of political contestation between classes of White people but of White people pursuing a vision of White liberty and non-White exclusion.[71]

By the time Taylor was writing his synthesis of the American Revolution in 2016, class politics had disappeared from his work and a narrower interpretation had emerged. Taylor, Neem argues, now writes about freedom within the rubric of diversity. His vision of freedom, in this account, is one of exchange and diversity, sustained through empire and threatened by American independence, primarily because Taylor sees race as uniting White Americans, rather than a shared commitment to ideas of liberty and republicanism as central to the American story.[72] At bottom, therefore, the American Revolution for Taylor was a crisis over whiteness with, as Neem interprets him, "the ideals of the Revolution and democratic class politics that animated Taylor's early work float[ing] like ephemera over a deeper racial story." Neem's conclusion is harsh: Taylor's "focus on pluralism and exchange leads him to conflate democratic rule with whiteness, which stands in contrast to the multicultural imperial world. In short, the language and plot offered in Taylor's more recent work echo the vocabulary and aspirations of contemporary neoliberal globalization."[73]

VI

It is worth paying close attention to Appleby writing in 1993 and Neem in 2020 because they enunciate, as Neem makes clear, two different versions of what early American history ought to be about. Explicating these differences highlights what is at stake in the recent historiography of early America. Neem is in a minority of early Americanists in being dubious about some of the assumptions behind #VastEarlyAmerica. It is not a minority opinion I myself share, as might be expected given my longstanding advocacy of the virtues of an Atlantic history approach to early America and given how Neem cites me as an especially egregious proponent of histories that are all about exchange.[74] But his reservations about "vastness" as a catchall definition of the ambition of early American history in the twenty-first century are worth considering because the term elides examination of the political in favor of a bland attachment to multicultural pluralism. It is a strong accusation that early Americanists' antagonism to the teleological pull of the nation-state really means that people taking this position are too accepting of global capitalism and are cheerleaders for its neoliberal excesses.[75]

As Bob Dylan sang, it appears you always have to serve somebody. Neem's view of the differences between historians of the polity and historians of exchange is a stark one. He argues that historians of exchange fail to recognize that freedom is possible only in a republic. Instead, Neem argues, they serve what he thinks is the wrong God. He suggests that the noble dream of tracing how freedom emerged in the creation of a sovereign self-governing people through the establishment of a visionary if flawed American republic is being replaced. Neem suggests that historians have increasingly abandoned trying to understand how people pursued various forms of freedom-seeking in favor of analyzing how people had an increased ability to exchange goods freely and to maintain cultural pluralism. His charges are rooted very much in the politics of the present rather than in the dynamics of the past. I am not sure that early American historians would recognize in their attempts to understand how people, ideas, and things moved around the Atlantic and indeed the world that they are substituting narratives of quests to gain freedom for the banal search for the acquisition of material objects in a developing world of goods. The use of the word "neoliberalism," with all its contemporary connotations, to describe histories whose purpose Neem disagrees with is deliberately provocative.[76]

There is a constancy of purpose between what Appleby wrote in 1993 and how #VastEarlyAmerica was conceptualized by Wulf in 2016. The language used in Karin Wulf's advocacy of #VastEarlyAmerica—dynamic, complex, globally connected, expansive—is redolent, as I have noted about the project of doing British Atlantic history in general, of the language of neoliberalism, when that was not a dirty word, in the time of Bill Clinton and Tony Blair and Third Way politics.[77] Neem's critique of the field is very much designed to draw attention to, and to move away from, the ways in which the Blair-Clinton "Davos man" approach to the inevitability of globalization under a benevolent Anglo-American leadership has shaped a generation of scholarship on early America in ways Neem feels unfortunate.

Yet the high hopes of that period, both in politics and in history, as in Appleby's enthusiasm for a glorious future of early American scholarship to match a distinguished recent past, is worth not just remembering but reflecting upon. The ethics behind #VastEarlyAmerica are worth pursuing for their own sake because they increase the quantum of good scholarship on ever more diverse themes and places. As Steve Sarson argues, "What the idea of vastness also encompasses, especially with its advocates' stated attention to depth as well as breadth, is something more than mere inclusion." The push towards a more "capacious" view of early America means "something more like recognizing or validating, perhaps even embracing and celebrating, the vast diversity of early American life, and with that the vast diversity of early American scholarship."[78]

2

Wealth, Commerce, Environment

I

In the middle of the eighteenth century, Benjamin Franklin was convinced of North American greatness, claiming that the rapid demographic advance of the White settler population in the northern colonies and the abundant availability of land (mostly taken from Indigenes without proper compensation) made North America a decided addition to the national strength of Great Britain. The colonies of British North America, Franklin thought, were much more valuable that the rich sugar colonies of the British West Indies which were, according to Bostonian James Otis, "a compound mixture of *English, Indian* and *Negro*" and which were ruled over by tyrants who liked nothing better than "to whip and scourge the poor Negroes according to their own brutal will and pleasure."[1]

Franklin crowed in *Observations on the Increase of Mankind* (1755) that rapid population increase among the White population in North America meant that it "will in another century be more than the People of England" and that "the greatest Number of *Englishmen* will be on this Side of the Water." "What an Accession of Power in the *British Empire* by Sea as well as Land!" he exclaimed, and "What Increase of Trade and Navigation! What Numbers of Ships and Seamen!"[2] Of course, much of what Franklin bragged about was wishful thinking. Indigenous American power was far from nugatory in this period, whatever Franklin thought, and however much he urged Britain to embark on an aggressive policy of western expansion into the Ohio valley, noting, for example, in 1766, that "a well-conducted western colony would be of great national advantage with respect to the trade, and particularly useful to the old colonies as a security to their frontiers."[3] Indigenous people controlled much of the interior of the continent and all of the western lands to the Pacific, knowing precisely where their domains began and where others ended. The reality of Indigenous power was palpable. As Pekka Hämäläinen notes, "From one bridgehead to another and across the continent's edge, European pretensions to empire crashed against indigenous territoriality."[4]

Some European writers were not as blindingly patriotic and enthusiastic as was Franklin about the future glory of settlement in the Americas. William Robertson in Scotland and the Abbé Raynal in France considered the European conquest of the Americas a moral monstrosity, costing the lives of millions of Indigenous Americans and implicating Europeans in the crime of the Atlantic slave trade in return for relatively modest improvement in science, a quickening of transatlantic commerce, and some useful if not essential commodities such as sugar, tobacco, and potatoes. The educated view then, and to some extent now, was that early America was not an epic but a tragedy, a catastrophe, a horror story.[5]

There was another view, one that accorded with Franklin's positive assessments of a grand American future, that was vigorously put forth by intellectuals like Thomas Jefferson, part of an American set of thinkers who were unimpressed with French intellectual condescension to North America. In an ongoing argument with George-Louis Leclerc, Comte de Buffon, about whether things degenerated or improved when they were placed in the Western Hemisphere, Jefferson praised not just American animals but hailed the achievements of White settlers in colonizing continental America.[6] One achievement of European settlement, he contended, following Franklin, was the development by the middle of the eighteenth century of viable, flourishing, and influential settler colonies, full of happy, contented, and prosperous Whites. America had the first settler colonies where people of European descent enjoyed materially better living standards and greater degrees of racially exclusive egalitarianism than Europe in what James Belich describes for the period between 1783 and 1939 as "settler revolutions," encompassing not just the United States of America but Canada, Australia, New Zealand, and, to an extent, South Africa.[7]

These settler colonies were dynamic worlds. As Saul Dubow writes about nineteenth-century South Africa, "The static mechanical and spatial metaphors" that characterized imperial and colonial history in the mid-twentieth century have been discarded in recent historiography "along with the uni-directional outward diffusion of forces, ideas and people from the metropole [which] contrasts markedly with the resonating language of the postcolonial metaphorical repertoire: hybridity, fluidity, ambiguity and decenteredness."[8] But alongside settler achievements were the gross injustices of European colonization, marked by Indigenous dispossession and African American and Afro-Caribbean destitution.[9] In evaluating the world of early America before and during the American Revolution and the War for American Independence, scholars writing in the last decade in academic journals oscillate between these two poles whereby their subject can be judged—the view of Franklin or those of Robertson and Raynal. Such a duality of opinion is interspersed with less dominant but still vital preoccupations such as wealth and standards of living, environmental change, religious diversity and the centrality of established Protestantism, and gender frontiers, all of which have shaped the evolving world of early American historiography. This chapter focuses on the material realities of early America—wealth, trade, and adaptations of the environment—and their effects on individuals from many backgrounds.

II

Franklin's glowing endorsement of the achievements of the settler populations of the northern colonies in the mid-eighteenth century was founded on demography and material reality. So too were Robertson's and Raynal's doubts about the moral purpose of the Americas and about how to evaluate European interactions with non-Europeans. Franklin observed that British North America was rich and populous. Raynal and Robertson focused on the demographic disaster that had befallen Indigenous populations. Modern historians add to these concerns an appreciation of the horror and brutality of eighteenth-century slavery and the terrors of the slave trade.[10] Thus, any assessment of what early America was like in the eighteenth century needs to be founded on an understanding of the material reality that early Americans experienced.

Delineating such material reality, so important in the social history heyday of the 1970s, has not been a notable feature of recent early American scholarship and is less prominent in journal literature in this field than it is for the study of eighteenth-century Britain. Nevertheless, enough work has been done in this area to establish the basic foundations of the underlying economic structures governing life for early Americans. It was not a period of especially dramatic changes, as happened in the middle of the seventeenth century when the transition to plantation agriculture occurred or in the transition to industrialization in the nineteenth century. There were no notable economic step changes in colonies experiencing moderate but steady economic growth, notably in towns and on the plantations, evident everywhere in settler-dominated areas, including the West Indies, with a partial exception in more sparsely settled New France.

Whites enjoyed very high standards of living in remarkably egalitarian societies where the gap between rich and poor was at historically low levels, especially compared to the industrializing nineteenth century. Crucially, however, not everyone was included in such egalitarian paradises. Blacks, Indigenous Americans, and most French Catholics did not enjoy high standards of living, as measured by Gross Domestic Product and by access to consumer goods and life-sustaining foods. Peter Lindert and Jeffrey Williamson outline the empirical evidence to support this economic interpretation, increasing by 20 percent previous estimates of colonial American wealth. They emphasize less wealth than living standards. Americans were no richer than the average Briton and much less wealthy than White West Indians, but they lived better than the first group because the cost of the necessities that were needed to live in a modicum of comfort was relatively low in British North America. Lindert and Williamson suggest that the cost of obtaining a reasonable basket of commodities necessary for comfortable living was 54 to 68 percent less in North America than in Britain.[11]

It meant that colonial White Americans had enviable lifestyles. Certainly, as Robert Allen, Tommy Murphy and Eric Schneider show, they lived better than settlers in Latin America. Including slavery does not alter that picture much. What was important in British North America was the excess demand for White labor and the inadequate supply of such labor. This imbalance encouraged wages to be as high as those in London, while the costs of living were nowhere near commensurate with those pertaining in the empire's capital.[12] This finding accords with Lindert and Williamson's findings. They argue that even if enslaved people are included in calculations, the thirteen colonies in 1774 were *still* the most egalitarian places on the planet. But we do have to consider just how poor were enslaved people. Enslaved people were at the bottom of the income distribution rankings and in 1774 had an average total income worth only £13.37 per capita, under one-tenth of the average wealth of White settlers in the American South. Including them in estimates of annual income reduced average American income from £76.9 to £69.1.[13]

Lindert and Williamson find it empirically difficult to include the enslaved and especially Indigenous people in their analyses due to a paucity of evidence. It provides an opening for fresh research into the wealth, income, and living standards of the enslaved in North America. J. David Hacker's reconstruction of enslaved demography in British North America shows that, unlike the West Indies, the enslaved population in British North America, despite its poverty and dreadful mistreatment, experienced rapid natural population growth, especially from the 1740s. If judged by such things as anthropometric data, the standards of living of the enslaved appear higher than almost any population on earth in the late eighteenth century, save for the White American population.[14] But enslaved people suffered in other ways. High levels of natural demographic growth, for example, fueled a massive internal slave trade and the breakup of enslaved families, as White Virginians sold "excess" slave populations south to places like Alabama.[15]

More work needs to be done on wealth and income levels among Indigenous Americans. There has not been any significant research into this area since a pioneering study by Peter Mancall and Thomas Weiss in 1999, where they suggested that including them in eighteenth-century conjectures of economic growth reduced it appreciably. They argue that output per capita for Indigenes was equal to about 56 percent of that made by non-Indigenes.[16] We still await research that incorporates an updated analysis of the wealth of Indigenous America into the work that Lindert and Williamson have done for people living in the thirteen colonies.

Nevertheless, Lindert and Williamson's findings on non-Indigenous American wealth and living standards are largely supported by the only intensive study of economic growth of an American region, Joshua Rosenbloom and Thomas Weiss's analysis of the economy of the Middle Colonies. They show that the region's economy was strong enough to achieve respectable growth (for premodern periods) of about 0.6 percent per annum. Output per worker, including both Whites and Blacks, increased by 0.25 percent per annum, despite limited increases in productivity that were offset by rising population levels that reduced the growth of Gross Domestic Product per capita.[17]

This comfortable picture looks different if groups other than White Americans are analyzed. Laura Panza, Jeffrey Williamson, and I have made an analysis of Jamaican incomes and standards of living for 1774 that demonstrates that the living standards of enslaved Jamaicans were incredibly low at the same time as the incomes of the people who enslaved them were unfeasibly high. If Pennsylvania was the most equal place on earth, Jamaica was the least equal of any place so far analyzed for evidence on standards of living. Enslaved people in Jamaica scraped by at the best of times barely above subsistence. In less good times they faced starvation. One such bad time was during the American Revolution when the cost of living soared to unheard of heights and enslaved people suffered from hunger as a consequence.[18]

Wealth varied by region. The West Indies was easily the richest; next was the plantation South; followed by the Middle Colonies, New England, and, last, New France.[19] New France's poverty is striking, especially when the wealthiest colony in the eighteenth-century Americas was undoubtedly French Saint-Domingue, even though there is no data that is sufficiently explored to ascertain incomes there.[20] The differences in wealth between colonies in British America were less pronounced than inequalities between French colonies. Vincent Geloso notes that the residents of French North America had real wages less than three-quarters of wages of people in New England. This poverty was compounded by the high burden of seigneurial taxes, peculiar to French America, which reduced per capita income from between 5 to 10 percent. Geloso argues that seigneurial taxes were highly detrimental to the Quebec economy, reducing by over one-half the potential returns that could be made in the colony from a potential migrant. Unsurprisingly, migration from France to Quebec in the eighteenth century was minimal to nonexistent. Low migration rates slowed down population growth, although such growth was still strong as families had even larger numbers of children than in New England. This limited population growth deprived the colony of its most efficient methods of sustaining increases in per capita income.[21]

III

That Lindert and Williamson tracked the start of rapid economic growth back to the 1650s and 1660s is hardly coincidental. It happened at the same time as chattel slavery developed in Barbados and Virginia. The wealth of British America and to a large extent that of Britain as well was dependent on plantation slavery, as an increasingly large numbers of writers assert.[22] The importance of slavery and the slave trade in early America is made manifest by the multitude of articles about various kinds of enslavement in the short eighteenth century as covered in the next chapter. Accounts of plantation wealth typically focus on Jamaica, the richest plantation colony. Research on this colony is done in the shadow of Eric Williams.[23] Williams used Jamaica as a case study of a West Indian society based around slavery whose great wealth began to dissipate after facing the twin existential shocks of the American Revolution and the challenge, as planters saw it, of abolitionism. He noted how abolitionism became a major protest movement at the same time as increased industrialization meant that Britain was less dependent on slave-produced wealth than had been the situation a generation earlier.

Ahmed Reid comprehensively denies Williams's contention that the West Indies economy was in decline as abolitionism took hold. Using an abundance of quantitative data, he suggests that the plantation system in Jamaica was productive and profitable until the abolition of the British slave trade in 1807. He contends that "Jamaica's productive capacity could be compared to emerging industrial economies at the time." He sees Jamaica's plantation system as "dynamic and efficient," using rising slave prices as a proxy for increased productivity and, in an article cowritten with David Ryden, in constantly buoyant land prices.[24] Reid's conclusions about the relentless increase in slave productivity and total factor productivity in Jamaica are in line with previous estimates made by David Eltis, Frank Lewis, and David Richardson in 2006. They also can be combined with evidence from Peter Mancall, Joshua Rosenbloom, and Thomas Weiss about similar increases in slave productivity in the South Carolina rice industry. We should note, however, that the latter three authors insist on a considerable downturn in slave productivity during the American Revolution, which undermined advances in productivity made in South Carolina between 1722 and 1775.[25]

Plantations were hugely profitable and produced wealth for their owners and for the many people in Britain and the colonies involved in the slave plantation economy.[26] That wealth came from the hard work by enslaved people who were workers before they were anything else.[27] The centrality of work to the enslaved experience is emphasized in recent articles on the Caribbean, in which human factors are combined with environmental agency. These interactions created a hugely profitable but malign ecosystem in which humans, animals, and the land all suffered so that Europeans could satisfy their craving for sweetness in the form of sugarcane. Neil Oatsvall and Vaughn Scribner, for example, equate work and energy to evaluate enslaved work practices on West Indian plantations. They comment that "the preponderance of work on early modern sugar plantations took place at the nexus of human labor and environmental processes. When we understand work as a form of energy transfer, and place it at the center of sugar production, then the Atlantic world emerges as a series of interconnected energy flows rather than merely a collection of shared human experiences." Their analysis "suggests that Caribbean sugar plantations should be defined by abstracted energy transfers as much as by human slavery. Humans worked and so did sugarcane."[28]

The plantation was envisaged by planters to be a pastoral paradise. They thought of the plantation as a White-controlled place of peace and harmony, where hierarchical deference kept people knowing their place, producing a satisfying sense of order and social coherence. Scholars discern their ideology about ideal plantation space through examining how the plantation was depicted visually and in literature. John Crowley examines how sugar plantations in the Caribbean were depicted by European artists in ways that validated European dominance. The visual representation of sugar plantations changed, he argues, over time, doing so alongside the rhythms of metropolitan disdain for West Indian plantation culture as abolitionism developed into a major social reform movement from the 1750s onward. Until the 1770s painters privileged machinery over people, and the work of enslaved people was largely taken for granted—virtually no Blacks were ever included in pictures. The plantation was depicted through its technology, a technology repeatedly described as progressive and modern. Slavery and the Atlantic slave trade were rationalized as necessary for British economic culture and thus unremarkable as an institution valorized for its modernity. From the 1770s, however, British artists broadened their perspective to include picturesque landscapes and genre scenes of everyday life. The violence of slavery was airbrushed out. Nevertheless, despite the saccharine nature of these landscapes of harmonious and orderly plantations, this change betokened a response by artists and planters to the beginnings of antislavery. It provided a proslavery perspective on the plantation in which the *absence* of visual representations about how sugar was a killing machine contested abolitionist accusations of planter cruelty.[29]

Plantations were also depicted in literature, such as James Grainger's Georgian epic *The Sugar Cane* (1764), a poetical evocation of West Indian plantations that served as something akin to a management manual for planters. Britt Rusert calls Grainger's outline of the experimental plantation "an enclosed site from which empirical knowledge is produced, extracted, and transplanted from tropical lands and bodies." Grainger, in Rusert's view, tried to see the plantation as a counter to a dangerous Caribbean environment and as a place of Enlightenment improvement and serenity. Nevertheless, Grainger could not prevent his Georgic poem of praise toward the plantation complex from showing a high degree of anxiety, even among White beneficiaries of enslaved labor, about the plantation project, how it could be maintained, and how it might last into the future. Grainger viewed the plantation, Rusert argues, "as a productive, pleasing and healthful environment, produced and managed by the colonial plantation class," but the evidence told against him. Tristan Schweger examines Grainger as a defender of property rights who tried to advance a view of the planter as a beneficent patriarch, with his authority predicated upon "a Whiggish concept of labour bestowing ownership and political agency," as if the plantation was like an English aristocratic state.[30] In fact, the plantation was a site of contestation and chaos, ruled over by planters who symbolized to hostile commentators the worst of eighteenth-century avarice. As Sarah Yeh comments, West Indian "planters, who ruthlessly and repeatedly imported fresh slaves to replace those who had not survived the brutal conditions of Caribbean plantation agriculture, were a disturbingly extreme version of the new 'improving' landlords in rural Britain who callously hired and fired tenants and laborers according to their needs without any sense of moral obligation or responsibility to those beneath them."[31]

Studies of how West Indian plantations operated show them to be uncertain and threatening places, where wealth was accumulated by people willing to take great risks through the exploitation of their workers. They were sites of creation but also of destruction, notably of the environment. Artists may have depicted the Caribbean as Edenic, but it was, in reality, a place of environmental danger. The transformation of the landscape meant that the ecological balance of the Caribbean was broken, making plantations prey to all sorts of climate-caused problems. One challenge was insect infestation, as Matthew Mulcahy and Stuart Schwartz outline in a study of ant invasions that severely disrupted plantation productivity in Barbados, so that planters thought that "nature seems to have waged war on us." They note that "the human decision to cultivate certain plants in extensive monocultural units in particular soil types [was] responsible for new ecological balances and new landscapes in which specific insect pests could flourish."[32] Climate change, Katherine Johnston contends, was even more existential, threatening the very viability of the Caribbean plantation. It was induced by planters' continuing eagerness to cut down forests to maximize land available for cropping. Deforestation caused drought, which in turn made planters work enslaved people harder. Tragically, the harsh conditions of plantation work resulting from environmental changes caused in part by climate change confirmed for Whites that only Blacks had the physiological capacities to labor in harsh tropical heat on drought-parched lands.[33]

Sugar cane work was a brutal business, as shown in three articles by Justin Roberts, Nicholas Radburn, and Diana Paton.[34] Radburn and Roberts provide sobering data on a little-studied part of the enslaved labor force, the 10 percent of the enslaved population employed in "jobbing" gangs. These gangs were enslaved people owned by relatively poor White Jamaicans who hired out their enslaved laborers at high prices to planters so that the slaves in jobbing gangs would do the hard and debilitating work, such as holing, that wrecked their health instead of destroying the health of these planters' own enslaved laborers. Jobbers made huge profits but at the expense of their workers, more women than men. Jobbing was "universally regarded by the negroes as the worst kind of service."[35] That service showed just how devastating it was to work producing sugar on a Jamaican estate.

Given this endless brutality, the best hope for an enslaved person was to survive. That survival was hard, however, in a society where Whites and Blacks were engaged in an everlasting battle, with Whites' fascination with quick profits compromising at every turn any attempt by the enslaved to act collectively rather than individually. The slave community was seldom a source of support to newly arrived Africans, who invariably suffered social ostracism and physical difficulties when placed on plantations. It was, Roberts shows, a Hobbesian dog-eat-dog world. Those enslaved people who enjoyed advantages on the slave plantations (invariably Creole men working in privileged positions such as being drivers or tradesmen) treated the less fortunate (women and the recently arrived from Africa) with contempt, either treating them with indifference or, as was more likely, bullying vulnerable enslaved people. The result was highly fraught populations fighting each other rather than collaborating.[36] The slave communities Roberts describes were full of interpersonal violence and sexual exploitation, with the "better sort" of enslaved people humiliating and mistreating "poorer sorts." Planters took advantage of these divisions, all founded on the bedrock of a grueling work routine that left most enslaved people, and especially those employed in jobbing gangs, destitute, exhausted, and with greatly diminished health prospects. It was a world of chaos and dysfunction.[37]

And it was worse for women than for men, as Paton argues in her interpretation of the predicaments faced by enslaved women as workers and mothers. The slave plantations of Jamaica saw the first example of a modern tendency: the selection of categories of women who could be used to care for other women's children. This was an innovation within slavery and in society in general. Planters were aware from abolitionist discourse from the 1760s onwards that the poor health and bad material conditions endured by enslaved women made it impossible to believe planters' claims that they were humane and benevolent men with a real interest in advancing better conditions for pregnant women or women with infant children. Thus, they adopted new strategies to try and improve West Indian enslaved reproduction rates. These new strategies arose from two contradictory impulses: pressure from below by enslaved women that their children be given some minimal care instead of being ignored and mistreated; and managers' drive to increase the efficiency of women's work by transferring maternal duties from prime female field hands to women unable, due to age, to work in the fields. Paton argues that "the large scale and hierarchically managed organization of childcare on Caribbean plantations should be understood as an important aspect in what [Sidney] Mintz terms the Caribbean's 'precocious modernity.'"[38]

IV

The beneficiaries of the wealth produced by the enslaved were wealthy planters and merchants in the Americas; merchants and manufacturers in Britain; and merchants and rulers in West Africa. Karl Koth and John Serieux chronicle the career of wealthy Jamaica planter Nathaniel Phillips (1733–1813), suggesting that for those men willing to take great risks and leverage themselves to the hilt with debt, profits could be massive. Phillips made profits that in his best year exceeded 21 percent. Even during the American Revolution, contrary to what the Eric Williams's thesis presupposes, he made annual profits of 14.8 percent, including a 2.2 percent increase in the value of his land per annum. He came to Jamaica in 1759 with good connections but no money and by 1780 was worth £110,000 in money, excluding the tens of thousands of pounds he owned in the form of enslaved people. Such wealth made it possible for him to plough £20,000 into buying a large Welsh estate, Slebech Hall, in Pembrokeshire, South Wales.[39]

Wealth cascaded into Britain, as has been revealed extensively in the British digital project *The Legacies of British Slave Ownership* and in articles by Sheryllynne Haggerty and Susanne Seymour on the Dukes of Portland and their involvement in slavery.[40] It was not just owners of West Indian estates resident in Britain or slave traders or merchants trading to Africa who made serious money from slavery. Significant sums could be made from humble forms of manufacture. Chris Evans writes about the manufacture, sale, and agricultural use in sugar cultivation of the hoe, a ubiquitous agricultural implement heavily used in sugar cultivation in the West Indies. It made, Evans notes, ironmongers such as the Crowley firm of Newcastle and London very rich.[41]

Nuala Zahedieh has investigated the copper industry from when it grew from nothing in the seventeenth century to a major industry in the eighteenth century as a result of demand from plantations for copper. She shows how an individual coppersmith like the Scotsman William Forbes made such a large fortune in Atlantic trade, with annual growth of 12 percent per annum between 1750 and 1775, that he could purchase one of the most expensive landed estates in his native country. Unlike Reid, Koth, and Serieux, she supports Williams's argument that the American Revolution was economically devastating, noting that the copper trade virtually collapsed after 1776. She estimates that before this collapse, copper supported the employment of 13,000 enslaved people in the Caribbean and 4,500 Whites in Britain. She describes a circle in which employment in England created the purchasing power to consume more sugar and rum, the production of which required more copper equipment and created more employment in England and fostered industrial development in South Wales.[42]

Zahedieh supports Williams's argument that special interests accumulated much of the profits from plantation agriculture, emphasizing the way rent-seeking distorted regulation in the Atlantic trade in the early eighteenth century. Klas Rönnbäck has provided empirical data to back up this argument. He shows that the people who mostly benefited from Britain's quickly growing sugar market were not sugar planters, who operated in highly competitive markets where they could not manipulate prices, but a small group of highly placed and extremely rich sugar refiners. Their market position and access to government contacts made the price of refined sugar considerably higher in Britain than it presumably would have been in a free market.[43]

Zahedieh's and Rönnbäck's arguments fit into a larger discussion about the utility of the eighteenth-century concept of mercantilism in understanding the Atlantic economy. They frame their analyses within a mercantilist framework, thus supporting Jonathan Barth's 2016 argument in *WMQ* that scholars should not get obsessed with how various people in eighteenth-century Britain defined mercantilism in different (and usually self-serving) ways and should focus instead on how it was the major organizing principle in Atlantic commerce, the ideological basis for seeing the value of the empire to the metropolitan economy, as well as a coherent economic system whose dimensions continue to be worth studying.[44]

Whether Barth's strong argument in favor of mercantilism is correct is hotly contested. A substantial body of opinion, especially within British historiography, sees mercantilism as an outmoded and analytically useless concept by which to understand the Atlantic economy. Steven Pincus and Julian Hoppit have been especially critical of mercantilism as an ideology and practice. Pincus, in an article in *WMQ* in 2012 accompanied by several replies and his response, argues for mercantilism to be discarded as an unhelpful concept. Mercantilists, he asserts, "did not agree on fundamental economic principles," meaning "there was no mercantilist consensus." To argue otherwise is thus to promulgate a "historical myth."[45] Barth, by contrast, bases his support of mercantilism on ideas about money in the early eighteenth century, thus focusing on the links between mercantilism and bullionism as the conceptual foundations behind economic theory. Money, he argues, "was the locus of mercantilist consensus." His focus on money has been taken up by other scholars, as features of the money supply are once again becoming topics of interest to early Americanists.[46]

V

I started this chapter with Benjamin Franklin as the champion of settler America, crowing about the future glories of the British empire in North America. Franklin was unprepared to recognize the extent to which White wealth depended on Black labor, but others were more prepared to admit the mutual relationship. The political economist William Wood, for example, wrote in 1718 that the "*Labour of Negroes* is the principal foundation of our *Riches* from the *Plantations*."[47] Slavery undergirded this empire, as did land appropriated from Indigenous Americans, but it was undeniable that for settlers of European descent there was much about Franklin's analysis with which they could agree.

Franklin is worth coming back to as he represents a particular position in favor of a highly dynamic and successful settler world, dominated by commerce, capitalism, and "improvement." As Sophus Reinart proclaims in his study of the global impact of *The Way to Wealth* (1758), Franklin's most popular book (1,100 editions in twenty-six languages by 1850), this tome represents "an exceptional historiographical case, globally spanning the emergence of political economy and the codification of a quintessentially capitalist ethos."[48] Franklin's world in this text, Reinart argues, was one defined by "improvement," and although Franklin constantly elided slavery as providing the material means whereby "improvement" could be achieved, he praised "the pursuit of useful knowledge, the establishment of more rational institutions, the enhancement of agricultural outputs, the expansion of infrastructure and industry, and, more generally, the development of a virtuous and commercial, if parsimonious, society."[49]

It was a distinctly urban vision.[50] The chief architects of such a vision were merchants. It was merchants who fashioned how a distinctly American market culture emerged, as Emma Hart dissects in an anatomization of vibrant livestock and real estate markets in Charleston and Philadelphia. These markets were relatively unregulated by European standards and operated less by rules and rituals, as in northern England and lowlands Scotland, than through bargaining between sellers and buyers. Ellen Hartigan-O'Connor stresses one particular feature of this market culture: the auction or vendue sale, which taught Americans how to judge goods and assess value.[51] The urban environment was a vibrant space full of commercial innovation, including the "bills in the bottom" system described by Nicholas Radburn; bills of lading, which Hannah Farber looks at with reference to how these bills worked in material culture; and marine insurance, also outlined by Farber. She sees the latter as especially important, central to integrating transatlantic commercial networks and demonstrating the conceptual framework of a transnational *lex mercatoria*. Farber shows that the merchant and financier class had an outsized influence through their involvement in the robust transatlantic system of marine insurance in matters of political economy, in an area that regulated commercial behavior, and also provided a conduit for mercantile control of public policy.[52]

The Atlantic merchant was important because he or she connected the people of British America and Africa to the world of goods. As David Hancock explains in regard to merchants, "Out of necessity they were international thinkers and actors who viewed the world as a connected series of markets that they could integrate and improve." Max Edelson expands: "Planters and merchants, locked in competition in their small corner of the Atlantic world, behaved as if they acted on an expansive international stage."[53] Nancy Christie outlines this process for Quebec. Small shopkeepers, including several women merchants, used goods they sold to incorporate French Canadian inhabitants into British trading and consumption networks. French Canadian peasants and artisans were so keen to acquire ready-made British clothing and other goods that this became part of a broader assimilative process in which merchants as the agent and goods as the objects were essential to making the British conquest a means of modernizing Canada. She concludes that "despite a relatively small population, post-Conquest Quebec experienced the same kind of renaissance in material culture as the other colonies of British North America."[54]

Emma Hart and Cathy Matson stress how merchant networks were spatially grounded in towns. They show this connection to locality in a study of three merchants in three different British Atlantic ports—Newcastle, Philadelphia, and Charleston. Matson notes in another article a detailed case study of a Philadelphia merchant sailing the *Lydia* to Kingston in 1764.[55] Christine Walker has provided another case study of a woman merchant in local trade in Kingston, while Robert Gamble describes how itinerant merchants, including female hucksters, linked consumers in the countryside to merchant networks in the city, thus expanding rural abilities to acquire fashionable and necessary goods.[56]

Hart and Matson note that being "a successful trader was thus not only a matter of building transatlantic networks and crafting a reputation across oceans, but a question of embedding oneself in the local relationships, customs, and institutions of a port city." "Integrating and improving across great spans of time and space," they argue, "the British Atlantic merchants formed coherent networks that shared a language of credit, trust, and profitable exchange." They insist that "these entanglements in turn led to merchant importations not only of goods but of new architectural forms, technologies, and institutional improvements that they introduced to other city dwellers."[57]

Benjamin Franklin was a materialist and an optimist, mostly secular in how he thought, even if everything he wrote was tinged with a Protestant religious sensibility. Recent writings on early American history tend to confirm his materialism and his optimism. In material terms, White Americans lived very well. They troubled themselves little about how their enviable standard of living was often founded on Black labor in the plantation machine and from the fruits of produce grown on appropriated Indigenous land. Looking just at their world, Franklin's Panglossian approach seems justified. Other peoples in the America, as shown in the examination of Black people and their lives in the next chapter, faced Hobbesian lives of horror.

VI

Of all the material changes that occurred in early America, two are especially important. One change was the replacement of one population—Indigenous Americans—as the dominant population of early America by the twin populations of African and European migrants and their Creole descendants. The other is the transformation of the landscape that occurred mainly as a result of the growth of the latter two populations and the ways in which settlers used and altered the landscape to create new forms of economic activity, notably in plantation areas.[58] The second change is globally at least as important as the first. It signaled how the Americas entered the Anthropocene midway through the eighteenth century, the Anthropocene being a term popularized in 2000 by the atmospheric chemist Paul Crutzen to describe a world fundamentally altered by human activity. John McNeill notes that "the last 250 years amount to the most tempestuous period in the relationship between humankind and the natural world since the eruption of Mount Toba some 73,000 years ago," an event that led to a prolonged volcanic winter that nearly pushed the human species to extinction.[59] The Anthropocene is marked by what Joyce Chaplin calls the "other revolution," or the Industrial Revolution, and is characterized by the "Great Divergence," a term invented by the historian of China Kenneth Pomeranz to describe the process by which the economies of the West, including the neo-Europes of North America, became more powerful and important than the traditional economic powerhouses of India and especially China in the East.[60]

One sign of the limited interest in environmental and global economic history in the journal literature of early American history is that neither *WMQ* nor *EAS* has published an article on the Great Divergence.[61] There is a similar lack of interest by early Americanists in the Industrial Revolution.[62] Chaplin notes the relative indifference of early American historians to industrialization and especially to the concept of the "preindustrial" by comparing the number of references to the American Revolution in *WMQ* (2,476) to the Industrial Revolution (146), while the term "preindustrial" is noted 85 times.[63] What might be possible if the Great Divergence became a subject of inquiry in early American history can be seen in Paul Warde's *Past & Present* (*P&P*) article of 2018, where he explores the role of potash, the precursor of the modern chemical industry, in breaking the limits on E. A. Wrigley's concept of an "organic economy" in premodern Europe. North America is incidental to this analysis, but Warde shows how North America's great forests, as well as forests in Scandinavia and eastern Europe, provided the "ghost acres" needed in Pomeranz's theory to provide the raw materials needed for early industrialization.[64]

Early American historians have not published as much in journal literature on environmental history as the influence of two major environmental historians with an interest in early America, William Cronon and Alfred W. Crosby, might suggest.[65] The number of articles in *WMQ* on environmental history is low—none at all in this field were published between 1973 and 1993. There are more environmental history articles in my sample than that, but not more than ten in total, depending on how the field is defined.[66] Three of these articles—two by Joyce Chaplin and one by James Rice—are surveys. Chaplin and Rice differ in how they evaluate the field. Chaplin is less positive about the topic than Rice. She believes that an increase in interest in environmental history in the 1990s coincided with a decline in social history and that the field started from a low base, given the limited prominence in the United States, compared to Canada and Britain, of the field of historical geography. Thus, she concludes that early American environmental history is at the edge of early American historians' interest. She concludes that "just when early Americanists were most prepared to think in terms of a lost preindustrial world, and perhaps primed to think of its implications for the natural world, they lost interest."[67]

Chaplin deplores this indifference to physical nature. She wants scholars to pay more attention to the Industrial Revolution and the move to the Anthropocene than to the American Revolution because "the development of fossil fuel economies has had far greater effect on the globe than did the creation of the United States."[68] She argues that more could be done on climate history and the Little Ice Age, asserting that if environmental history is on the margins of early American history, then climate change is on the margins of environmental history, especially in studies of the eighteenth century.[69] Scholars could also do more, she continues, on energy regimes and how they connect to plantation agriculture, slavery, and industrialization. Historians are beginning to do this, as is seen in how Neil Oatsvall and Vaughn Scribner look at energy reserves and energy deficiencies as a way of understanding labor patterns on plantations. In addition, Jean-François Mohout makes a direct comparison between historical slave ownership and contemporary usage of fossil fuels.[70] Natale Zappia outlines how grasslands were transformed during the age of revolution in the American West, which saw inedible grasslands changed into a seemingly inexhaustible bank of storable and transferable energy that made these regions "food frontiers" that fostered the "near complete globalization of food systems."[71] Chaplin makes a similar point about how contemporary debate on fossil fuels makes imperative the need to write environmental histories. She asks: "Isn't it important to examine whether or to what extent enlightenment, stable justice among humans, and intellectual and physical security actually depended upon fossil-fuel technology?"[72]

James Rice takes a different and more positive approach to evaluating recent work in environmental history. He notes that the number of articles in environmental history are steadily increasing both in number (eight in *WMQ* between 2002 and 2016) and in influence (these articles won eighteen prizes and honorable mentions).[73] One advantage of such work is its close association with science. Rice argues that early American environmental histories are heavily weighted toward interdisciplinary approaches, including archaeology, natural sciences, and a strongly anthropological take on the functioning of political and social structures and their relationship to the environment.[74]

Examples of such engagement with climatological research include articles by Adam Hodge and Robert Michael Morrissey on how climate changes caused bison scarcity and changes in hunting patterns on the northern Great Plains and the Illinois valley for Indigenous groups like the Kaskaskias, a subgroup of the Illinois Nation. Another example is Thomas Wickman's exploration of the effects of severe cold on Wabanaki power in the early eighteenth century. Each writer shows how it was climate more than conflict with settlers that caused these groups of Indigenous people the most concern.[75]

The several articles by Robert Michael Morrissey on social networks of the Kaskaskia people in Illinois country and the complex ecology of bison hunting in the tallgrass prairie borderlands deserve special attention as examples of how close attention to ecology and climate change can enrich early American history.[76] Morrissey writes about what Stephen Aron calls the "American Confluence."[77] This is the area bounded by the Mississippi, Missouri, and Ohio Rivers, into which the Kaskaskia people, the largest group within the Illinois Nation from the upper Illinois valley, moved in the late seventeenth and early eighteenth centuries. They did so, he explains, less as a reaction to French colonization, as customarily argued, but as a reaction to environmental change brought on by drought. This movement happened in a crucial area of North America. The Illinois country was a major ecological transition zone, a biome-scale ecotone dividing grasslands in the West from conifer forests in the East. Morrissey's research shows the benefits of connecting ethnohistory, ecology, and climate history so as to evaluate the respective impact of environment and social and political conditions on one Indigenous nation.

Morrissey shows that old ideas about the prairies as an almost timeless and pristine landscape that was not altered until colonization put pressure on the people and lands who lived in this area are incorrect. The tallgrass prairies were not especially ancient, contrary to older interpretations, and indeed were one of the newest biotic communities on the continent, formed through the dynamic influence of forest and fire. It was an area, moreover, full of bison, which had appeared in great numbers in the region after 1,000 CE and which the Illinois hunted extensively. That worked well when bison numbers were high but proved disastrous when drought struck. The Illinois people compounded their problems by destroying forests, and soon a portion of them decided to head southward. They were trying, Morrissey argues, to preserve their ecotine lifestyle in the face of drought-induced environmental change. He notes that changes to this bison-hunting economy had significant social changes, such as increasing Kaskaskia involvement in Indigenous slave trading; shaping distinctive kinship systems in which women left their families to reside with others, often with French traders; greatly increasing the size of Kaskaskia villages; and involving people in a seemingly endless cycle of violence and exploitation.[78] Morrissey contends that climate change, the bison economy, and pressure of European colonization "*combined* to produce devastation for the Illinois in ways that were unique and particularly intense."[79] Many of these changes occurred in the 1680s and 1690s, but they had lasting effects into the eighteenth century. The usual cycle of decline for Indigenes involved diseases, trade (especially alcohol and guns), and warfare.[80] In the Illinois country these factors intersected with an ongoing cycle of violence and conflict that the bison economy had created, including the Illinois's penchant for slave raiding.

Morrissey's environmentally oriented exploration of the changing world of the Kaskaskias in the Illinois valley insists that early America was rapidly transforming, even if scholars don't fit these transformations into the historiography of industrialization or the Great Divergence. His account should be placed within a scholarship on wealth, commerce, and environment in early America that oscillates between seeing the period as one of catastrophe, especially for Indigenous peoples and the enslaved, and one of increasing wealth and an increasing cornucopia of goods under the direction of urban merchants, as key figures in early American wealth and commerce. The overall tone is one of nuance and moderation, with good things balanced by bad. It suggests that early American historians remain divided about whether to take the Panglossian view of Franklin or the Hobbesian perspective of Raynal and Robertson.

PART II

Current Themes

3

Slavery

I

If, as Charles McLean Andrews argued in 1914, commerce and colonies were "unthinkable without the other," the recent expression of automatic linkages is between slavery, imperialism, and capitalism. Thomas Truxes, in his 2021 survey of British American overseas trade, concludes that "without the slave trade and chattel slavery, the overseas trade of British America could not have existed in the form—and on the scale—that it did."[1] As the most significant component of early American wealth and as an institution that was distinctively racialized and increasingly based around skin color, ensnaring both Indigenous Americans and especially Africans trafficked to the Americas and their descendants, slavery may once have been hidden in plain sight but is in the early 2020s insistently everywhere. The 1619 Project of the *New York Times*, for example, declared that it "aims to reframe the country's history by placing the consequences of slavery and the contributions of Black Americans at the very center of the United States' national narrative."[2]

Early American historians may not yet go as far as the *New York Times* in reorienting early America around slavery or even around slavery and Indigenous dispossession, but slavery, the plantation system, and race in all its manifestations are crucial to the story of early America as written in the last decade. Slavery influenced everything, from commerce to culture. Africans were the most numerous migrants to British America—3.5 million carried in the Atlantic slave trade between 1619 and 1807. The buying and selling of enslaved men, women, and children was big business. And no region in early America can now be studied without considering the impact that slavery had on social and cultural patterns in an imperial system dependent on slavery in manifold ways. Most important, the enslaved African is one of the key figures defining early American history and how these millions of men and women suffered yet survived under slavery has become an urgent subject of study.

II

Studies of slavery in the last decade have concentrated on two very different places: Massachusetts and Jamaica. Jamaica is an obvious place to study early American slavery. It was an economically prosperous but socially monstrous society. It produced great wealth for a fortunate few. Its small White population, including White women, as Christine Walker has demonstrated, lived very well, but their particular and peculiar culture was one of unattractive debauchery, oriented around the relentless pursuit of profit, heavy drinking, frantic sociability, and sexual exploitation. Meanwhile, the enslaved majority lived lives of misery and deprivation.[3]

Why, however, should there be such interest in slavery in Massachusetts, a place with a small and economically insignificant enslaved population? This interest reflects a growing feeling that slavery was important everywhere in early America and that as Sven Beckert, citing Barbara Solow, argues, slavery and its by-products constituted the foundation of the very Atlantic economy that was at the center of British economic power.[4] If slavery was important everywhere, does the customary division between societies with slaves (like Massachusetts, where slavery was not constitutive of all social and economic relations) and slave societies (like Jamaica, where slavery was fundamental to all social, economic, and political relations) any longer make sense?

Russell R. Menard thinks not. In a study of slavery in St. Mary's, Maryland (and the only article in this sample to look at the previously traditional topic of Chesapeake slavery), Menard argues that the dichotomy customarily used to distinguish between places with differing proportions of enslaved people in the population should be replaced by the idea of a spectrum of slave societies. He shows that slavery was as important in the 1720s, when the enslaved population was just 12 percent of the total population, as it was in 1774, when 40 percent of the population was enslaved and when most households owned slaves. His preferred description of changes over time is that slaveholding changed from being elite to being "popular." The implication is that studying slavery in places like Massachusetts, where the proportion of the enslaved in the population was small, is just as important as studying slavery in places like Jamaica, where the population was overwhelmingly enslaved.[5]

A relative torrent of scholarship on Massachusetts—seven articles by three authors—supports Menard's contentions.[6] Slavery in the colony was both similar to slavery elsewhere and also distinctive. It changed over time, especially as the bound labor force was transformed in the early eighteenth century from Indigenous to African and again in the 1760s as Boston filled up with poor White people who fled a collapsed rural economy into the city, displacing Black tradesmen in the process.

III

Jared Hardesty, Wendy Warren, and Gloria McCahon Whiting have created a powerful picture of slavery as a dynamic presence in Boston and the Massachusetts countryside, although Blacks, both enslaved and free, were forced out of the city in the 1760s by a sudden influx of poor Whites who displaced them in the workforce.[7] Hardesty cites the politician John Adams (1735–1826), who claimed that the end of slavery in Boston was due to the "multiplication of laboring White people" and who believed that they should not have to compete with the enslaved for work. Adams declared that "common people would not suffer the labor, by which alone they could obtain a substance, to be done by slaves."[8]

Hardesty and Whiting differ considerably in how they treat slavery in Massachusetts. Hardesty's view is the harsher one. He stresses the extent to which Boston merchants were tied into an Atlantic world with its nodal center in Jamaica and how these merchants used their Atlantic-derived wealth to buy estates in Boston's hinterland, which they filled with enslaved people. Enslaved people were forced through their small numbers to accommodate themselves to European norms, such as adopting Christianity, as did the most famous enslaved person in the colony, the poet Phyllis Wheatley. Yet adopting Christianity, Hardesty declares, did not mean assimilation. Black Christians, including Wheatley, appropriated Christian ideas mainly as a way of decoding the Euro-American world and then fashioned a Christianity of their own that was in its way a form of resistance.

Whiting focuses not on religion but on family. She shows how far Black marriages deviated from the western European household system. Enslaved men found it hard to assume customary patriarchal responsibilities such as providing material support for their families. And they found it difficult to become household heads and assert male privilege when they lived in households separate to those of their wives and children. The result was that New England slavery was remarkably matrifocal by the standards of New World enslavement. Because slave-owners possessed few enslaved people, most enslaved couples did not cohabit. Children belonged to the masters of mothers, not fathers. White New Englanders owned enslaved people for profit and cared little about Black family structures. Wendy Warren shows that infants mentioned in runaway advertisements sometimes had no (or negative) financial value to their masters because they were not laborers. Early in the eighteenth century African labor replaced Indigenous labor as the main source of non-White bound labor in New England, to the satisfaction of White farmers and merchants, as Indigenous people, located within large family networks, were harder to bring under control compared to Africans, who did not have the networks of support that would have allowed them to challenge their masters and mistresses. Whiting notes that New England's early dependence on indentured European labor was replaced by an "near-complete reliance" on African slavery with little reliance on Indigenous people as a source of bound labor.[9]

Where Hardesty and Whiting most differ is in how slavery ended in New England. Both agree that the American Revolution was crucial in moving Blacks from slavery to forms of freedom, and both agree that the move away from slavery preceded rather than followed 1780 legislation that gradually removed slavery as an institution. On other matters, they disagree. Hardesty stresses how bad the American Revolution was for Blacks, even if some of them gained opportunities as soldiers through which a proportion claimed rights for freedom. He finds it unlikely that they became mostly free of their own volition, but rather became free out of contingency, as they were forced out of labor markets and were either sold to other less-hard-pressed colonial places or encouraged to join the British or Continental army. He argues that many enslaved men, women, and children gained their freedom less as a result of abolitionist pressure but because enslavers saw the way the wind was shifting and decided to sell their enslaved property to slaveholders in other colonies where slavery was legal and profitable. Manumission, therefore, was more self-serving than later narratives supposed.

Whiting, on the other hand, has a more positive view of the ending of the institution of slavery during the early years of the American Revolution. She provides empirical evidence from inventories about how Blacks vanished from sight in this period. What freedom they got, she argues, came from actions Black people took themselves to ease themselves out of conditions that were similar to slavery. The American Revolution dealt slavery a major blow, but it did not itself cause manumission. She argues that slavery was abolished by "public opinion" more than by any constitutional activity or by the courts, as previous interpretations have suggested. The emancipatory process, she argues, was more bottom-up than top-down, implemented by ordinary people, both Blacks and Whites.

IV

When scholars look at how enslaved people experienced slavery, they concentrate on the difficulties that are involved in extracting individual lives from intractable and compromised sources. Stephanie Smallwood, for example, stresses how the archive of slavery is a representation of power that in itself is unaccountable to the enslaved, stating that the "silences we encounter in the slavery archive reflect the necessary failure of the attempt to represent subalterns in that idiom."[10] Kelly Wisecup similarly argues that the archive of slavery is necessarily incomplete because it "functions not just as a repository for records and memorials of the past but as spaces of knowledge production that aim to define what can be known about slavery as well as what kinds of terror and violence are permissible on certain Black bodies." "As a result," she concludes, "working in the archive is always compromised by its propensity to reproduce itself and its ways of seeing." She goes so far as to see the archive of slavery as so compromised as needing to be discarded: "Merely expanding the archive or recovering additional texts does not escape the archive and its epistemes." Thus, historians "need to destabilize the project of the colonial archive itself" by creating projects (she references the visual representation of Tacky's Revolt by Vincent Brown as an example of desired practice) that "undercut or compromise their original purposes."[11]

What scholars find alarming and indeed distressing about the archive of slavery is its founding origins, as Saidiya Hartman puts it, in "a violence that determines, regulates and organizes the kinds of statements that can be made about slavery" and in how women in particular enter the archives "in little more than fragments" with "snippets of their lives, loves and losses, emerg[ing] from records imputed with the possibility of yielding profits."[12] This may be the reason why writing about individual enslaved lives is uncommon in the journal literature. The individuals readers learn about, moreover, are those extraordinary individuals who managed to achieve prominence, meaning that they avoided the customary silences of the archives. One example was Captain John Perkins, whose career Douglas Hamilton has chronicled. Perkins was the most senior Black officer in the British Navy, finishing his career just below flag rank. Hamilton notes that such a career was only possible in the armed services, where the demand for manpower was such that it allowed a few enslaved men a route to freedom not possible in civilian life. Perkins's "unique career speaks to the capacity of the maritime service to subvert race and slavery in the Caribbean."[13] The same capacity for subversion was true to a more limited extent in the army, where Black soldiers, at least in the Caribbean, were common from the 1740s onwards, as Maria Alessandra Bollettino has shown. The motives behind employing Black men in battle were mostly malign—they were seen as cannon fodder, with their deployment meant to protect British regulars from the ravages of West Indian diseases. For a few Blacks who served as soldiers, however, the result was some limited social advancement. Moreover, as Bollettino notes, the valor of some Black soldiers in battles such as the Battle of Havana in 1762 encouraged Britons to see such soldiers "as their adept and skilled protectors rather than as their inveterate enemies."[14]

Scholars who stress the silence of the archives and the violence inherent in its construction and in how it represents Black people—Marisa Fuentes relates her shock of doing research on Black women in the Barbados archive when all she read about were women who were "battered, beaten, executed and overtly sexualized"—raise important points about "how the archive and history have erased Black bodies." It is a question of particular concern for scholars who are the descendants of some of the people serving as "objects" of archival disdain, who find that immersion in such archives forces them to see their "own ancestors in these accounts ... to hold and inhabit deep wells of pain and horror."[15]

The archive, however, is not everywhere as compromised as suggested in recent writings on its politics and structured violence. A concern with the voices of the enslaved, moreover, is not as new as is sometimes proclaimed and is addressed thoroughly in literature on slavery in French America, literature that is seldom addressed in Anglophone studies.[16] Cécile Vidal, Emily Clark, Dominique Rogers, and Sophie White have shown in their in-depth investigations of testimony from the enslaved in court documents from New Orleans just how much evidence can be obtained from digging in colonial archives and in reading those cases against the grain.[17] Nevertheless, the evidence in the archives is not easy to access and often reveals a violence that manifests itself in the very way events are recorded. Sasha Turner argues that this is the case for documenting the deaths of enslaved Jamaican children, whose only mention is usually a dry note of a financial "loss" in an account book. Turner suggests that it is the duty of the historian to acknowledge these traumatic events less through repeating the dry notes contained in colonial bookkeeping than through imaginative speculation and sympathetic identification with the women who suffered such losses. Her work on the maternal grief of these women is an attempt not to recover and recuperate but to affirm loss: "Maternal loss, archival loss, and historical loss."[18]

The most conspicuous act of archival retrieval in this sample are two articles on a single enslaved man, Frank, who lived a peripatetic life in the Leeward Islands, Jamaica, and England in the 1720s and early 1730s. Keith Mason focuses on Frank's work roles on the Stapleton plantations of Nevis in the 1720s. His analysis is predicated on an evaluation of plantation management on these estates, which he describes as one where the absentee owners and their White agents in Nevis operated a management style that Mason calls paternalistic humanitarianism. Stapleton chose to run his plantations like an extended transatlantic patriarchal household that functioned through a tiered hierarchical structure of command that incorporated trusted kin, clients, and servants acting as attorneys, managers, and overseers while the absentee himself stood at the apex, dispensing commands, justice, and rewards.

This management strategy depended on effective White managers and capable Black subordinates serving as drivers. But this did not work in this case: the White employees fought with each other in ways that meant that William Stapleton lost confidence in their ability to act in his interests. This loss of confidence in White management gave an opportunity for "key" or "privileged" enslaved men like Frank to make an impact. Frank replaced an elderly driver, Andrew, in 1722 and quickly impressed with his skill, intelligence, and leadership qualities. By 1725 he had become an overseer. He had considerable responsibilities and garnered significant rewards, such as having his own house and livestock and having his marriage and family ties acknowledged and, to a degree, accommodated. It all fell apart, however, when Frank was implicated in an islandwide slave conspiracy. Usually, this would have led to torture and execution, which is certainly what the White residents of Nevis wanted. But Frank had so impressed his master that he was able to survive this episode, though he had to be transferred to Oxfordshire in England for his own safety.[19]

James Dator, however, disputes Mason's version of Frank's life. The differences between Dator's and Mason's accounts show how different readings of the limited archival traces of an enslaved person can lead to strikingly divergent interpretations. Dator is not interested in the particularities of slave management practices and criticizes Mason for what he thinks is a too-uncritical acceptance of how Frank is depicted in White-created records, in which Frank is seen through the prism of Stapleton's patriarchal sentiments. He tries to avoid seeing Frank within a master-slave dialectic and instead sees him as having a surprisingly "cosmopolitan sensibility." Frank took advantage, in this telling, of living in a period of profound social transformation that was marked by greater antagonism between Whites and Blacks within a dynamic Atlantic economy that exhibited increased regional connectivity. Frank, in Dator's eyes, was a traveler more than a worker: he navigated between mountains, plantations, and the sea in a life marked by mobility and by a diversity of experience as a field slave, rebel, and traveler.

He warns against reading Frank's life solely through White-created plantation records, comparing him to a well-known enslaved person, the Afro-Brazilian healer Domingo Alvares. The sources, however, handicap scholars in learning about Frank. His life between 1722 and 1730 is documented, but he then disappears from the record after having moved back to Jamaica from Oxfordshire in 1730.[20] Of course, Frank's very presence in the archival record points him out as an unusual person, but two features of his life connect him to the experiences of other enslaved people. He was a rebel, who used violence and had violence used against him, and he was a runaway, who tried to gain his liberty through flight. If a previous period of scholarship emphasized culture as a feature of enslaved life, the violence of slavery is a dominant theme today, in ways that links this scholarship to that on Indigenous people and on the American Revolution. Much of this has been outlined in the previous chapter, in discussions on the brutal character of slavery in Jamaica.[21]

Another way in which scholars highlight the violence of slavery is through an examination of runaway ads, an abundant and much-used source on early American slavery. There are six articles on runaways in this sample, three by Simon Newman. One question that Newman poses is whether "runaway" is an appropriate term for historians to use about enslaved people escaping from their owners, given that "runaway" has connotations with criminality. That enslaved people were conducting a criminal act when fleeing without permission is, of course, how masters and mistresses saw it and how they framed advertisements seeking the return of people they considered their property. Newman's work on runaways spans escaped enslaved people in England, Scotland, Africa, Barbados, Jamaica, and Virginia in the middle of the eighteenth century and includes a digital history of runaways in late eighteenth- and early nineteenth-century Jamaica that employs a variety of media to show how enslaved people escaping their masters could be "hidden in plain sight." He places runaways squarely within the realm of labor history. He shows that in most cases the act of running away has to be understood within a complex pattern of unequal labor relations, more akin to protest or strikes than to what slaveholders tried to depict as criminal actions.[22]

Scholars pay particular attention to the language and format of these advertisements, as can be seen in articles by Simon Middleton, Jordan Taylor, and Stefanie Hunt-Kennedy. Middleton concentrates on the increasing tendency of runaway advertisements to offer financial rewards to those who returned escaped enslaved people to their masters. He details how such offers of monetary rewards confirmed slaveholders' property rights so that enslaved people were increasingly seen as convertible into cash, like other forms of property. Taylor shows the complicity of the community in the whole business of slavery, especially newspapers. Publishing advertisements about runaway slaves was a reliable and valuable source of income for newspapers, augmented by editors playing an important role in returning runaways, through services associated with these advertisements, such as dealing with enquiries about how enslaved people were to be returned and how claimants were to receive rewards. Newspapers became brokers and supporters of the institution, even when their editorial pages opposed aspects of slavery.[23]

Hunt-Kennedy focuses on the language of runaway advertisements in Barbados and Jamaica to show how frequently they refer to bodily disfigurement, thus providing a graphic example of slavery's violence. Indeed, what she stresses in the mundane nature of such violence is its quotidian repetition within thousands of runaway advertisements. That violence, if anything, increased over time. Her survey of ninety-seven years of runaway advertisements shows that deformities, disfigurements, amputations, and marks of punishment all increased, although evidence of branding declined. She attributes the latter not to any sudden outbreak of humanitarianism but to enslavers becoming conscious of how these descriptions of branded slaves were being used by abolitionists for polemical purposes. She notes the differences between how Black disability was rendered—usually as a matter of indifference—and how White disability was described. White disability was treated as a consequence of doing service in the military or other institutions and as incurred in the preservation of enslavement. Significantly, Whites were offered compensation for their bodily disfigurement while Blacks received none. Black disability was discounted, she suggests, because such disability was fundamental to how slavery operated.[24]

V

The violence of slavery and the slave trade was distasteful. It fueled a growing abolitionist movement. But the wealth produced from enslaved labor was considerable. It encouraged a corresponding proslavery campaign. Recent work has concentrated more on proslavery than on abolitionism. What work there is on abolitionism locates the abolitionist impulse firmly within the religious framework of Evangelical opposition to slavery outlined a generation ago by Roger Anstey. It shows that Evangelicalism spread well before abolitionism did. Yong Hwi Yoon describes how antislavery sentiment spread in North America largely due to the twin influences of the Great Awakening and the American Revolution on Evangelicals' sensibility. It took some time, however, for Evangelicals to make the connection between sin and slavery, which then fueled the growth of the movement in the 1780s. Philippa Koch shows how until the mid-eighteenth-century, Protestants in Britain and North America (abolitionism never had a hold in the proslavery Caribbean or the plantation South) tended to think about the morality of slavery, when they thought about it at all, within providentialist thought. It usually meant that churchmen of all persuasions defended slavery as economically and morally necessary even if these churchmen deplored aspects of slavery, such as its violence. This was a view greatly informed by missionary activities to convert the enslaved. Koch notes, for example, how the Evangelical preacher George Whitefield tended to accept slavery, seeing it as a providentially ordained means to provide economic stability to his mission to convert Africans.[25]

John Coffey, in a 2012 article on the origins of abolitionism, outlines what happened next. He, like Koch, emphasizes the importance of providentialism as the ideology that shaped abolitionist thought. The early rise of abolitionism was not provoked by humanitarianism or the growing recognition that Africans were as human as Europeans and as deserving of the rights to freedom that were the birthright of Europeans. In Coffey's view, accounts that neglect providentialism thus "drain abolitionism of some of its sound and fury." He argues that most of the existing literature on the rise of abolitionism relegates unnecessarily its religious foundations. He notes that in reading abolitionist texts the historian encounters the "insistent testimony of human fear of divine wrath." Nicholas Guyatt calls this testimony "judicial providentialism," The Evangelical Christians who dominated the abolitionist campaign lived in what Boyd Hilton calls "the age of atonement" and were moved,

Coffey argues, by an "overwhelming conviction that Providence regulates the affairs of men and in so doing chastises errant nations." Coffey's argument, in short, "puts the fear of God back into abolitionism," showing that providentialist abolitionism contained a strong transcendental and nationalist element. Early abolitionists believed that slavery was such a sin that if Britain did nothing to stop it, it would incur the disfavor of God and render naught Britain's global triumphs from 1763 onwards. One virtue of Coffey's approach is that he connects abolitionism to wider British nationalist and imperial currents. "Abolitionism," he concludes, "was about national shame and honour; it was about national guilt and divine favour," and about "restoring Britain's ruptured relationship with Heaven."[26]

A belief in providentialism, however, cuts both ways. One could be a providentialist proslavery advocate as easily as being an abolitionist. Ryan Hanley shows how a belief in providentialism, in this case derived from deep immersion in Calvinism through the Dutch Reformed Church, encouraged the ex-slave James Gronniosaw to take a proslavery stance in his *Narrative*, a pioneering Black Atlantic text. His theological training led him to present enslavement as socially and spiritually beneficial for the enslaved. It might seem surprising that someone who had experienced slavery could be so dismissive of its horrors, but his stance derived from his close involvement with the epicenter of Calvinist Evangelicalism in 1720s New England and his close friendship with George Whitefield.[27]

Other supporters of proslavery came to their views through less surprising mechanisms. The proslavery movement had some prolific and influential advocates. The most notable was Jamaican historian Edward Long. Long's historical investigations into English villeinage proved to his satisfaction that African enslavement could be justified through reference to an English history in which slavery was acceptable. Devin Leigh shows that Long thought enslaving Africans, whom he depicted when writing about the Coromantees of the Gold Coast as being barbarous, was perfectly legitimate and indeed desirable for people he thought were barbarous. Long based his justification of transatlantic enslavement through fusing his ideas about White supremacist racial hierarchy in the colonies with a sophisticated understanding of English notions of class subordination.[28] Further theoretical support for proslavery was given through the idea of "just war"—the notion prevailing in European doctrines that it was the prerogative of the winner of such wars to decide whether captives should be killed or enslaved. Jeffrey Ostler explores this topic at length, noting that abolitionists such as Anthony Benezet approached this question head-on, denying that Africans transported in the Middle Passage had been enslaved as a result of being on the losing side in "just wars." The attention Benezet and other abolitionists gave to this issue, Ostler believes, "represented the first attempt to secure protections for African slaves in international spaces." On the other hand, international commerce was as likely to enhance as to impede proslavery beliefs, as Nicole Dressler explains in an article on ideas about convict transportation. She argues that such ideas "evoked new discussions on punishment, reform and morality" that were used by thinkers and writers like the Jamaican historian Edward Long, who cited the convict trade of Britain to justify African nations' mechanisms for commodifying and then enslaving individuals these states deemed criminals. Long, for example, argued that African states had the same right to sell their offenders into the Middle Passage as the English state had rights to send convicts to labor unpaid in the colonies.[29]

What is noticeable about the journal literature on abolitionism and proslavery thought is that it is slanted strongly to early modern ideological predispositions. What is absent is an attempt to connect these intellectual ideas to economic motivations, a subject central to the heated past debates around the origins and nature of abolitionism.[30] There is a disconnect, as a result, between the burgeoning literature on the multiple links between slavery and capitalism and the more limited literature on abolitionism. The many articles and books that have restored historical attention to the role of slavery in shaping European modernity have little to say about the impulses behind antislavery. Why did Britain and then other European nations abolish an institution that was so economically profitable? The question that has animated the debate started by Eric Williams in 1944 and has consumed so much academic attention in the last fifty years is entirely absent from this literature.[31]

For example, abolitionism is not mentioned once in a recent special issue devoted to Europe and slavery in *Slavery & Abolition* (*S&A*). The religious motivations that galvanized abolitionists, Black and White, to oppose slavery are absent. Moreover, there is never any hint in the publications concerning slavery's importance to the development of capitalism that thousands of ordinary Britons and Americans, Black and White, male and especially female, signed petitions against slavery based on their belief that slavery was a sin and a national disgrace. Such a disconnect between studies of slavery's importance in fostering capitalist development in Europe and explanations of why, even so, the push to abolish the slave trade and slavery succeeded are an opportunity for historians to restart this debate and reconnect materialist explanations with religious investigations in discussing slavery's rise and fall.³²

It would be useful to make these connections if only to reestablish the importance of religion as a field of inquiry within early American history as a whole. Religion is not ignored, but it is sidelined. There is only one article in the sample on a standard early American topic for this period, the Great Awakening of the 1720s through 1750s, and that article, on Jonathan Edwards and his connections to Scotland, is not directly on this event.³³

Catherine Brekus notes, in a general survey of religion in early America, that religious practice and religious belief—what religion is and how it was real to the people who practiced it—is neglected in favor of accounts that stress what religion did.³⁴ Relatively few articles in this sample deal with religious experience, and even then religion is approached indirectly rather than directly, as in Janet Moore Lindman's examination of how the idea of "spiritual friendship" nourished relations between pious, middle-class Protestant women.³⁵

One partial exception to early America as mostly secular is the treatment of non-Christian religions, such as obeah, and how they related to Christianity. Katherine Gerbner's concept of "Christian slavery" illuminates the attitudes of Protestantism to race, and her study of obeah within the Moravian mission to Jamaica between 1754 and 1760 shows that obeah was not just an Afro-Caribbean practice, as often thought, but was the frame through which Afro-Caribbeans interpreted European religion and medical practices. The cultural interplay between different groups of early Americans as manifested in religion is also a subject that is getting some attention in regard to medicine and natural history, as seen in an article by Kristen Block on European and African understandings of yaws and leprosy and Christopher Parsons's investigation of how ginseng became a medical treatment as a result of combinations between Indigenous people and French Jesuits in the 1720s.³⁶

VI

Renewed attention to slavery has meant fresh studies of the Atlantic slave trade. In the past, historians of the slave trade concerned themselves about the size and composition of the slave trade and the extent of its profitability and contribution to European and especially British economic growth. The first question has largely played itself out, as assiduous work in the Trans-Atlantic Slave Trade Database has documented the volume of the slave trade and charted where enslaved people came from in Africa before they arrived in the Americas, though Africanists contest some of the definitions used to describe African regional origins.[37] The debate on the profits of the slave trade in Britain have been settled so that those profits are being calculated as around 6–10 percent per year, with similar results seen for France, though historians disagree strongly about the relevant figures for the Netherlands, and data on Portugal is still limited. Less work has been done on the profitability of the slave plantations, but a consensus has emerged that annual profits were around 8–12 percent.[38]

Currently, scholars are examining the workings of the British Atlantic slave trade as a commercial enterprise. The commercial importance of the slave trade in the urban economies of southern and West Indian towns has taken a long time to percolate into scholarship. In part this slow realization that the slave trade was big business is due to the influence of a seminal article by Jacob Price in 1974 that posited, based mainly on the historiography of the eighteenth-century Chesapeake, that urban development in the American South was hindered by the absence of an entrepreneurial decision-making merchant class located at the center of an important trade, such as grain in Baltimore and Philadelphia or the provision trade with the Caribbean for New York and Boston. Urban entrepreneurs, Price thought, could transform a mere "shipping point" into a spearhead of industrial development through their ability to link people from the city and its hinterlands. That class of people and that urban infrastructure that made cities "electric transformers," to use the apt phrase of Fernand Braudel, was missing, Price thought, in plantation societies where the plantation was autonomous from urban life and where towns were marginal in turn to plantation enterprise.[39]

That interpretation of plantations as disconnected from urban life and from merchants in particular no longer bears scrutiny. Price's analysis ignored the most important and easily the largest form of commerce in early America, the trade in captives from Africa. Recent work on the slave trade has dispelled notions of Charleston and Kingston as being "mere shipping points." The slave trade was big business and "Guinea factors" handling thousands of captives arriving from Africa sold into enslavement on plantations were the greatest merchants in the British empire. Nicholas Radburn's study of John Tailyour in Kingston in the 1780s shows how much money could be made in this trade—Tailyour made enough from selling 17,295 captive Africans, which amounted to

11 percent of total enslaved cargoes from 54 ships between 1785 and 1796, to retire young and buy a large estate in his native Scotland. Radburn also shows how the slave trade was a business that provided the kind of vertical and horizontal linkages that allowed towns to develop and diversify. In particular, massive amounts of credit drove the slave trading business, situating it at the center of a large number of financial innovations. Credit terms varied considerably and were highly erratic, especially in the last quarter of the eighteenth century under the "bills in the bottom" mechanism of granting credit. This was a highly effective and impersonal system of formalizing institutionalized arrangements, which moved away from kinship toward less personal systems reminiscent of modern finance. Radburn argues that the bills in the bottom system solved the problem of debt in the trade, lowering traders' entry costs and enabling Britons to ship more African captives to the Americas, thus outpacing their foreign rivals.[40]

Nevertheless, it was a fragile business, Radburn shows, deliberately so, given the emphasis on impersonal ties. One had to be alert and skilled to take advantage of consistently shifting prices for the enslaved and terms of credit.[41] Those credit terms were consistently higher in the more productive colonies, such as Grenada and most of all in Jamaica, rather than in older and more settled colonies like Barbados and Virginia. Surges were accompanied by collapses. The slave trade, for example, came close to disaster during the War for American Independence, when credit contracted dramatically, prices for the enslaved declined, and merchant houses left the business. Even the biggest Jamaican houses, like Hibbert and Jackson, nearly folded. Three-quarters of slave merchants in Liverpool in 1776 had left the business by 1784. Like most early modern financial mechanisms, Radburn concludes, factorage in in the bills in the bottom system relied on uncertain trust networks that easily broke down during periods of economic uncertainty.[42]

These complex transactions made slavery and the slave trade a crucial part of urban life in the plantation world, as Gregory O'Malley shows in his article on the multiple linkages made by the slave trade in colonial Charleston. This bustling South Carolina capital accounted for nearly one-half of all Africans who arrived in British North America. In short, it was the gateway for North American slavery. O'Malley shows that the transatlantic slave trade brought hundreds of country people into town, not just to purchase enslaved men, women, and children, but to buy consumer goods and to do business of all kinds. He concludes that the slave trade, as the lifeblood of the plantation system, touched everyone in the region, providing multiple economic and social linkages that connected the whole colony. Of course, as he notes, the people most affected by Charleston's slave trade were the unfortunate Africans enmeshed in its machinery. The arrival of Africans into Kingston's or Charleston's harbor marked the momentous step within the trajectory through which African captives were transformed into enslaved people and thus into property. It was the essential moment that allowed planters to purchase human bodies and put those bodies into backbreaking work on plantations.[43]

The next step is to evaluate this process by which captive Africans were transformed into enslaved people and thus into forms of commodities as it occurred on the liminal spaces of the urban waterfront. Sean Kelley has provided two penetrating articles on the commercial side of this process, outlining the precise ways in which Africans were bought and sold. He describes how merchants managed the so-called "scramble" for enslaved Africans by avoiding auctions in favor of orderly sales of captives arranged in sets of categories in a merchant's yard, rather than aboard ship. Sales were preceded by negotiations in which customers agreed with merchants about price and other important matters. He notes how this way of selling captives gave huge advantages to the merchant factors, who could manage a sale effectively for their own benefit and was a further massive indignity for traumatized captives. The "scramble," he concludes, was a brutal feature of a brutal system.[44]

VII

Paying attention to the mechanics of the slave trade means paying greater attention to West Africa as a trading node, similar to how Jamaica was a trading node for the North American provisioning trade.[45] Sean Kelley has shown that British Americans from Barbados and North America were heavily involved in trade with West Africa. New World merchants proved able to turn the agricultural products produced by enslaved people on plantations, especially rum, into marketable trade goods sent to West Africa in order to buy more captives for the plantation system—a vicious circle, in short. His work illustrates strongly that the transatlantic slave trade was global, as Giorgio Riello's "diamond-shaped" model of how Africans bought Indian textiles makes clear. Riello stresses the importance of African demand and the discerning taste of African consumers. They wanted the same goods as North Americans, such as textiles, metalware, alcohol, tobacco, guns, and luxuries.[46]

West Africa was thus a vital cog in a dynamic world trading order. It was a world where African merchants exercised great agency, as Europeans often found out to their cost. Ty Reese outlines how things could go wrong in his account of the limited success of the Company of Merchants Trading to Africa, founded in 1750, in negotiating the palaver system, as the Fante with whom they dealt controlled the company-distributed goods.[47] Anne Ruderman's analysis of inter-European trade shows that trade with Africa was highly profitable for merchants, but it was complicated, uncertain, and difficult as a trading environment: disaster was as easy to achieve as triumph. Nevertheless, if Africans had agency, Europeans had influence. "In the thin trading markets of the African Atlantic," Ruderman notes, "Europeans focused on low quality and damaged goods as rivals charged higher prices than they would have done at home and forced trading partners to get the merchandise they wanted."[48]

European interference in West African commercial networks, Joseph Inikori argues, provided specific benefits to some individuals and some nations, like the kingdom of Dahomey, but in the main was devastating for West African economies. It diverted investment in manufactures that might have led to precocious industrialization and instead led to an unhealthy concentration on the Atlantic slave trade. The slave trade, he argues, slowed or reversed West African population growth in key areas such as the Gold Coast, which had been experiencing slow but steady growth from 1450 to 1650. The next two hundred years saw a shrinking of urban areas and a breaking down of the linkages between towns and the countryside, retarding the growth of capitalism in the region as a whole, thus halting African capitalism at the same time as European involvement in African trade spurred development and economic growth in Europe and the Americas.[49] European colonial ambitions in West Africa were similarly sporadic and unsuccessful, mainly because imperial officials were not sure what were their aims in taking over African territory instead of just concentrating on commercial relations. Matthew Dziennik explains how a brief and failed attempt by Britain to make Senegambia an imperial bridgehead in West Africa shows that trade was not the only consideration shaping British policy toward Africa after the end of the Seven Years' War. He argues that "a colony that became subsumed by the slave trade not only furthered the importance of legitimate commerce to British colonialism but provided abolitionists with a space in which to sketch out the moral culpability of Britons for the miseries of human trafficking."[50]

What is clear is that some Africans prospered considerably from involvement in European trade, including from the Atlantic slave trade. Women were conspicuous among these beneficiaries of the trade. Bronwen Everill and Pernille Ipsen focus on women merchants in West Africa. Everill concentrates on women's roles in domestic slavery in the slave-trading towns of St. Louis and Goree, showing how much support there was for slavery of all kinds among well-placed African women. She argues that slavery was important in developing a commercial culture and economy in Senegambia and important in developing an African version of Jan de Vries's British industrious economy.[51] Ipsen constructs a case study of a mixed-race Danish-Ga woman in Osu in the Gold Coast, Lene Kühberg, who was, she argues, an authentic Euro-African slave trade broker—an intermediary very skilled in negotiating what could be often a dangerous social and economic climate. Kühberg prospered, but only through exploiting her position within European as much as Osu social hierarchies. Randy Sparks builds on such individual case studies in a study of Gold Coast merchant families and their involvement in a distinctive economic practice of pawnship. That practice involved lending family members as "pawns" to secure trust within commercial deals. It often went wrong, especially when African merchants were involved with European traders who were prone to kidnapping "pawns," thus precipitating crises within the delicate European-African web of connected relationships.[52]

VIII

The study of slavery in early America has evolved considerably over the last decade. The focus has moved spatially, to the Caribbean and Jamaica in particular, away from the Chesapeake, which was the center of research in the period of social history in the 1970s and 1980s. A significant subsidiary stream of work is concerned with slavery in northeast America, New England, and New France. The body of work on slavery in Massachusetts proves conclusively that slavery could be very important even when not demographically dominant. Most important, slavery is depicted as vital to the history of everything in early America and never marginal or epiphenomenal. The old idea derived from studies of antebellum America that slavery was a "peculiar" and backward-looking institution has been discarded. Instead, scholars follow the findings of the influential Caribbean anthropologist Sidney Mintz, who saw the plantation as a landmark experiment in modernity, merging field and factory, and the Trinidadian writer and activist C. L. R. James, who described the enslaved population of Saint Domingue in the mid-eighteenth century as people who "from the start lived a life that was an essence a modern life."[53] In short, scholars studying slavery no longer see an early America that was to be left behind in the nineteenth century but are starting to treat slavery in the early American period as highly modern and as pointing the way toward a racial capitalism that threads its way through American history from the early seventeenth century to the present.[54]

What remains often missing, however, despite the best efforts of scholars working hard in archives among intractable sources, are the voices of the enslaved themselves and their active engagement of shaping the times in which they lived and played such important roles. Enslaved people are seldom active agents in their own lives. In most articles examining varying aspects of slavery, they often remain passive recipients buffeted by larger forces that they have little control over, from the Atlantic slave trade as it began in European-African commercial relations on the coasts of West Africa through to their employment and mistreatment on Massachusetts farms and even more so on highly destructive Jamaican sugar plantations.[55] As writers have noted, the inability to recreate the active agency of the enslaved in shaping the contours of slavery derives in part from the assumptions buried in the creation of archival sources about slavery in which the enslaved were peripheral to an interest in plantation profitability. Indeed, we often know about enslaved people only when they are in great trouble, hauled before courts in French Louisiana to defend themselves against criminal accusations that would lead to their execution.[56] But scholars face another problem in addition to the inadequacy of the sources to recapture the lives of enslaved people, which is that understanding slavery as modern means concentrating on the structures that entrapped enslaved people, especially the plantation machine that proved such an important innovation in early American economic life. The relentlessness of this machine and its brutal logic in treating enslaved people as interchangeable units of labor reducible to numbers in ledgers makes it very hard to restore enslaved people's humanity.

It can be done, however, as we have seen in the two articles on Frank, an enslaved man from the Leewards in the 1720s, examined above. Scholars have also examined in depth the only enslaved person in early America who has left enough material behind for scholars and readers to discern a distinctive voice. Phillis Wheatley was an enslaved woman in Boston, born in West Africa, who authored the first book of poetry in America written by an African. She has always been a subject of fascination for literary scholars but increasingly has been of interest also to historians, with Mark Peterson analyzing her thought as a representative of a certain Boston sensibility. In the journal literature, the most conspicuous study has been by David Waldstreicher. He shows how Wheatley had her own idea of what modernity meant for an enslaved person suffering under the tyranny of "our Modern Egyptians." Wheatley, in often oblique ways, pointed out the contradictions of modernity and slavery, making clear that would-be moderns were less friends of liberty than slaveholders depriving Africans their chance of salvation. Her work thus fed into the providentialist modes of thinking that John Coffey sees as underpinning the embryonic abolitionist movement, with which Wheatley was associated. Pinning Wheatley down to a single position is very difficult but, as Waldstreicher argues, paying attention to her and to her accusations of patriot hypocrisy—as slaveholders yelping, as Samuel Johnson quipped, for liberty—provides a different take on what modernity meant for an enslaved American. Wheatley, Waldstreicher insists, was an actor in history, someone more than a poet of Christian doctrine. By writing neoclassical poetry she brought, by stealth or simile, her female African perspective on the politics of slavery, inserting herself into a moment, Waldstreicher contends, when Blacks became participants (even if less powerful than other key figures in the early American lexicon who led settler societies and orchestrated colonial commerce) in the problems of empire. Thus slavery, capitalism, and imperialism came together and can be traced in the writings of Wheatley.[57]

Paying greater attention to the lived experiences of the enslaved and how enslaved people navigated a modern system of slavery that underpinned many capitalist developments in the eighteenth-century Atlantic world is one future direction for studies of early American slavery. Slavery was not an unchanging entity that remained the same into the nineteenth century as it did before the American Revolution. Work on slavery in Massachusetts and Jamaica points the way for what needs to come next, which are studies of slavery in early America that recognize just how varied was early American slavery, especially in the eighteenth century, when the slave trade flourished and when opposition to the institution of slavery was minimal.

4

Indigenous Peoples

∽

I

The history of early America is increasingly the history of Indigenous America. That history has a curious dualism, in which historians stress both how powerful and adaptable Indigenous peoples were, while envisioning them as notably vulnerable to a relentless push from European settlers intent on removing them from their land. One strand of scholarship stresses that Indigenous people made their own history in eighteenth-century America. Pekka Hämäläinen, for example, shows us in a stimulating article on the politics of grass just how capable Indigenous Americans were in altering their ways of life to take advantage of new things, such as horses and guns, and in doing so changing the landscapes they lived in.[1] Yet there is a strong countercurrent to this approach, given especial prominence in the afterwash in 1992 of the five-hundredth anniversary of the start of the Columbian exchange, where historians argued that European arrival caused the death of paradisiacal worlds, leading to an American genocide.[2] In this formulation from the 1990s, the Columbian exchange devastated the Caribbean and started processes by which Indigenous peoples, who formed a dense population by pre-Columbian standards, were quickly eliminated as a people from the region. That proposition, however, current scholarship has shown, applied only to parts of the Greater Antilles, and not to the Lesser Antilles and the Greater Caribbean region that extended into North America and South America. As Melanie Newton argues, the "narrative of aboriginal disappearance" is one of the "foundational imperial myths" of the Caribbean, which has persisted into twentieth-century anticolonial texts.[3] It is a myth also with some purchase for the history of Indigenous nations in the North American mainland, with an underlying theme that once-powerful Indigenous populations declined and disappeared as settlers extended their control over the continent. If that story has any truth to it, however, it pertains only to the history of Indigenous America in the latter half of the nineteenth century. It is not true for the eighteenth century. Indigenous people had many reasons to curse the arrival of Columbus and the thousands of Europeans who came to America in his wake, disrupting beyond recognition the world they had inhabited up until the early sixteenth century. But Indigenous people neither disappeared, as a previous generation of scholarship thought, even in the Greater Antilles, nor did they lose their influence. Recent writing has concentrated on these themes—Indigenous presence and Indigenous power and persistence in early America—as this chapter on Indigenes in early American historiography will show.

The principal actors in this chapter are Indigenous Americans. One of the biggest changes in early American history writing is that Indigenes are now front and center of historical attention. They no longer wait offstage or are included in analyses as an afterthought. Indeed, Indigenous people are so important to current discourses and research that early American history is coming close to being written around Indigenes more than around any other group. Their prominence in the field as historical actors, not just objects of a relentless westward expansion of European settlement, has transformed how scholars think of the colonial period of American history, a period in which it was Indigenes more than European settlers and their descendants who set the historical agenda. The sudden prominence of Indigenes as historical actors in shaping early American history reflects how the continuing reality of Indigenous power in large parts of North America strongly shaped early American history. This recognition that Indigenous Americans were dominant players in early American history has encouraged historians of Indigenous people in early America to question what used to be axiomatic in early American historiography—that early American history was a settler story. "By what right," asks Michael Witgen, "have Anglo-Americans come to see themselves, their imagined community, as the legitimate occupants of North American territory? How are settler societies to justify, or not, the seemingly inherent violence of the colonial experience?"[4]

II

The study of Indigenous American history has exploded within early American history writing to such an extent that Daniel Richter's fears expressed in 1993 of Indian history being in decline and irrelevant are today pessimistic and misplaced.⁵ The centrality of Indigenous peoples to early American history has become as axiomatic today as it was axiomatic in the past to place settlers as the people with agency and influence.⁶ Yet there is a defensive tone still that is evident in much of the scholarship on Indigenous Americans in early America, as if historians are seeking validation that what they are doing is considered by other historians to be worthwhile. Jean O'Brien, for example, notes how American museums continue to subscribe to historical discourses that "insisted that non-Indians held sway over modernity . . . and in the process created a narrative of Indian extinction that has stubbornly remained in the consciousness and unconsciousness of Americans."⁷ Juliana Barr states in a reply to James Merrell's quip that he "wants to see an Indian behind every bush" that "the problem is that in early American history that is actually the only place many folks still locate them—behind bushes, roaming the woods, consigned to the wilderness."⁸ Scholars regularly stress that we cannot understand early America without taking into account Indigenous power and insist that this fact about early American history is not sufficiently appreciated.⁹

We can see this defensiveness in James Merrell's reconsideration in 2012 of an article he had published in 1989 on how historians of colonial America get Indian history wrong. After outlining how "even avatars of traditional approaches to traditional subjects" like Gordon Wood and Joseph Ellis now pay attention to Indigenes and admit that Europeans "invaded" America and cheated Indigenes of their land, Merrell cites leading scholars of Native history, including himself, lamenting how Indigenous peoples are still ignored in the story of early America. He then proceeds to list at length the many ways in which historians use "loaded vocabularies" about Indians and their histories that renders them as outsiders. He concludes that this tendency "keeps American history tethered to the very European structures of thought faced by indigenous peoples centuries ago."¹⁰ Merrell argues the point at length, listing obvious words used about Native peoples that are problematic, such as "precolonial," "discoveries," "backcountry," and some more contentious ones like "settlers." The vocabulary chosen, he argues, had real consequences as these words "were and are told in the imperial project of relieving Indians of their sovereignty and their land."¹¹

Historians of Indigenous America working in the United States have started to advocate for work done in Indigenous languages and for greater sensitivity toward issues of translation. Alyssa Mt. Pleasant, Caroline Wigginton, and Kelly Wisecup, for example, argue that Indigenous

Ways of Knowing center spoken, image-based, material-object, and Indigenous-language texts, and they call for an increase in bringing Indigenous histories and texts into scholarly studies and into the classroom.[12] Yet they, like Merrell, do not mention any work written in European languages other than English, and neither do Pekka Hämäläinen and Samuel Truett in their survey of the state of Indigenous history.[13] Thus, the prizewinning work of Gilles Havard on Indian history in the *pays d'en haut*, including three major studies and a cowritten history of French America with Cécile Vidal, has attracted relatively little attention. When it has been referenced, this referencing is generally in articles dealing with French America rather than with British America.[14]

The problem, Merrell finds, is that scholars "continue to write Indians out of history" because it is hard to escape doing this through following established discourses. He notes that "however imaginative and illuminating the work by scholars of Native history, however successfully it has helped usher Indians back to the early American theater, that theater still resonate with words drafted ages ago by people with an agenda, words that have been (and still can be) weapons."[15] Andrew Cayton, replying to Merrell, argues that Merrell does not go far enough because American history is still framed around "a conflicted tale of men and women seeking acceptance within a language and culture shaped by late eighteenth-century slaveholders and imperialists" that "marginalizes the perspectives of people who were anything but marginal in the eighteenth century." Cayton urges scholars to be bolder, arguing that if we continue to use the narratives and vocabularies of a nineteenth-century genre of nationalist history "we're going to be seriously frustrated by our collective inability to find language that adequately captures what we mean to say."[16]

The dominant narratives that are so hard to escape reflect a centuries-long debate justifying imperial possession in claims to sovereignty and dominion through conquest, discovery, occupation, and use by a supposedly more advanced civilization.[17] These discourses justified the subjugation and incorporation of Indigenous peoples, either to vindicate the appropriation of their land and resources or to defend European pretensions to regions they did not in fact control.[18] Changing such powerful discourse is very difficult.[19] It takes considerable imagination to move from this position to seeing powerful Indigenes controlling most of continental America as late as 1776.[20] That so many early American historians have impressed on readers that this is a principal dynamic of early American history is a major achievement. But many historians of Indigenous America think we still have a distance to go before we recognize just how dominant Indigenes were in shaping early American history before 1800. It is the power of the older discourses on "disappearing" Indigenes and the difficulty of escaping these discourses that shapes the many complaints that vital parts of Indigenous history have been ignored, forgotten, or misrepresented.[21] A significant part of the renaissance in Indigenous history has thus been recuperative—demonstrating how, where, and in what ways Indigenous power persisted, despite concerted assaults on Native culture, language, and memory.[22] Juliana Barr, for example, contests the term "prehistory," noting that it implies there was no Indigenous history before European arrival and stressing that in much of North America Indigenous power was such that as late as 1800 the majority of continental land remained under Native control. In much of North America what colonization there was arose between differing Native American empires, like the Comanches and the Lakotas.[23] Mt. Pleasant and her coauthors reaffirm Barr's argument. They note that the field as a whole continues to overlook the American West and that spatial and temporal boundaries arise out of terms set through settler colonialism.[24]

Barr expands on this theme in an article on geographies of power in the American interior, focusing especially on present-day Texas. She notes the continuing power in this region of Apaches and Comanches, fighting each other for control of huge swathes of land, with the Comanches eventually proving triumphant. She insists that it was these two groups, not Europeans, who defined the politics and the boundaries of the region.[25] That it was disputes between different Indigenous people that shaped early America as much as European colonization is a prevalent theme in many articles. Barr argues that it is instructive to compare how Indigenous Americans fit into US history and how Indigenes play a quite different role within Latin American historiography. Spaniards subjugated Indigenes and took control of much of South and Central America and the Caribbean, but they did not doubt that Indigenous Americans were powerful. Indeed, Barr notes, Spanish colonization rested on "the might and complexity of the Indian polities, economies and civilizations they conquered."[26]

III

One attempt at recovery of important aspects of Indigenous history is Matthew Bahar's insistence that we stop thinking of Indigenes as bound by land and recognize instead that some Indigenous peoples, like the

Wabanakis of northeast America, were highly accomplished sailors. Indeed, their maritime power was such that it shaped and limited colonization until disaster struck the Wabanakis with the Seven Years' War.[27] Another example of recovery is Evan Nooe's investigation of the Creek practice of blood revenge, a custom that backfired badly, he suggests, in the nineteenth century, facilitating war and eventually dispossession.[28]

Chad Anderson's act of recuperation is particularly revealing. He explores references to Indians in the details in John Mitchell's famous map, *A Map of the British and French Dominions in North America* (1755), to demonstrate the density of the Native American presence in America, even in books that were intended to advance British settlement and that might be expected to diminish or deny Indigenous geographies. North America, the Mitchell map shows, was no *terra nullius* in need of European settlers to unleash its potential.[29] Anderson contests Barr's and Edward Countryman's claim that Indigenous settlements were highly profiled in French and Spanish maps but not in British ones, suggesting an early erasure or elimination in the British American mind of the reality of Indigenes in the North American landscape. In fact, Anderson notes, Mitchell included more than two hundred Indigenous settlements on his map, one produced as the interior was exploding into violence at the start of the Seven Years' War, where British weakness in a land of "contested, unclear or even unknown borders" was evident.[30] Moreover, Mitchell's knowledge of what he mapped came from Indigenes themselves, who were the people who mostly contributed to any silences about Indigenous geographies by what they chose to reveal or not reveal about the way they occupied land.[31]

The efflorescence of scholarship on Indigenous peoples in early America has shown the extent to which Mitchell captured the reality of the nature of colonial power in the first three quarters of the eighteenth century. Indigenous people were everywhere and were a major influence on narratives of colonization. They therefore need their own histories, locating them in specific periods of time and showing that Indigenes had as much historical agency as other groups in early American history. Historians of Indigenous America are extremely conscious of temporality.[32] Thus, Georgia Canley insists on how the widespread Indigenous American custom of gift-giving faced significant challenges during the Seven Years' War, contributing to the breakdown of Indian-European relations that led to Pontiac's War in 1763.[33] Carla Cevasco describes how Indian understandings of how to live with scarcity and dearth—their hunger knowledges—not only enabled them to cope with hunger better than Europeans relatively unused to dealing with famine in general but proved important at specific moments of tension when resources ran low.[34]

Bradley Dixon focuses on a dispute in North Carolina in 1730 to examine how the Chowan people used tributary relationship to give themselves a role within North Carolinian politics and policy making while retaining considerable autonomy. In an analysis influenced by the ideas of Richard White's "Middle Ground," he shows that negotiated interactions as much as conflict and the pressures of colonialism shaped how the Chowans placed themselves in a diverse North Carolina environment.[35] Elizabeth Ellis, for her part, examines a major event in Indian history from the year before Dixon's analysis, the Natchez War in French Louisiana in 1729. She situates this war in its place and time very specifically, describing it within a complex ecology of Indigenous politics. She draws especial attention to the Natchez custom, common in many Indigenous American wartime practices, of accepting refugees into their social structure and incorporating them as long as they followed expected and not always well-explained Natchez rules of conduct. French colonists were accepted into the Natchez nation on this basis, too; not knowing, or caring to find out, what rules they were expected to follow, they were thrown out. In revenge, they turned to the Natchez's mortal enemies, the Choctaws, who were delighted to have an excuse to attack their foes. Ellis argues that the war was therefore born out of a relatively common and discrete incident of violence that was grounded in a longstanding pattern of Indigenous politics.[36]

Gregory Smithers is also explicit about temporal specificity in his wide-ranging analysis of how Cherokees thought of things such as friendship, gift-giving, and blood revenge. In the early eighteenth century the Cherokees used their understandings of such matters to establish a modus vivendi with the British. That broke down in the 1750s as the British listened less often and acted more frequently in violent ways, thus abandoning, as the Cherokees saw it, any fidelity to the Cherokees' most valued attribute—consensus. Smithers concludes that Europeans ultimately failed to live up to what the Cherokees understood to be the ideals of friendship, notably during the American Revolution.[37] Andrew Johnson concentrates on an earlier war, the Yamasee War that raged in South Carolina in 1715, arguing that slave trading was at the heart of the conflict, with the colonial government taking control of the Indigenous slave trade, which it used as an important site of state building between 1715 and 1735.[38]

Increasingly, the way stories about moments of change in Indigenous American life are told embraces methodologies informed by Indigenous Ways of Knowing, which portray Indigenes as powerful actors in their own narratives, with information derived in part from descendant communities. Two examples of research that use such methods are by Alejandra Dubcovsky and Christian Ayne Crouch. The former demonstrates how Indigenous Ways of Knowing can show Native Americans as being active in their own histories even if, like the Apalachees of Florida, they were victims of both English aggression and Creek power in sustained campaigns of eradication and enslavement. Thus, the Apalachees are usually seen as objects, not subjects, of southeastern slavery. Dubcovsky disputes this interpretation of victimhood. She uses a single source from a Spanish colonial archive to privilege Indigenous voices and consulted with a range of contemporary Apalachee leaders to show that slave trading had not erased them from colonial America. They survived the slavery holocaust of early eighteenth-century Florida, thereby reshaping a history that is usually fashioned around Apalachee suffering and loss.[39]

Crouch also relies upon NAIS methodologies to "tease out Indigenous presences in documents that appear to be exclusively European in manufacture and meaning." She counterposes sources from European archives, such as maps and documents, with visual and physical objects that lessen "the privileges often implicitly offered to written documents that have been at the heart of early American studies."[40] Her close study of French maps, or plans, of Kanestake, occupied by the Haudenosaunees in southwestern Quebec, shows how even though these documents expressed colonial ambition, projected French fantasies of control, and ignored Indigenous naming practices, their creation probably relied on dialogic exchange with or appropriations of Indigenous knowledge, with Natives participating in the transcription and drafting process.

Jeffers Lennox's deployment of the model of "spaces of power" is a similar interrogation of how maps were made and how spaces influenced British-French-Indigenous relationships in northeastern North America; his work shows that geographies in eighteenth-century Nova Scotia were fluid, seasonal, fleeting, not always imperial, and never static. He notes that "spaces were not established" and that "permanent spheres of interaction and interchange" were "constructed, maintained and allowed to expire as necessary." As he notes, these spaces had a dark side to them, as they moved from being places where people intermingled to becoming places of military confrontation during the Seven Years' War.[41]

IV

How, then, are scholars to escape the straitjacket of seeing Indigenous peoples only through settler eyes and through a powerful discourse justifying European colonization? One answer to how we should rethink the approach to early American history that takes Indigenous power into account is provided by Michael Witgen in his reply to James Merrell's 2012 article. He argues that if we are to take Indigenous people seriously, "we should stop trying to write colonial histories that include Indians and start writing early American histories that embrace a continental perspective."[42] His proposal points to a fact increasingly made about early American history: until the mid-nineteenth century, Indigenous, not European, social formations controlled much of what later became the United States of America and the nation of Canada.

As Witgen states, "The continent was not an unsettled wilderness. It was instead a social world populated by powerful, independent indigenous social formations." He argues that in places like the Great Lakes and the northern Great Plains (he could have added Southwest North America, California, possibly parts of the Lesser Antilles and the Amazon, and Hawaii) "a distinctly Native New World emerged alongside the settler colonies of the Atlantic New World." His clarion call that "we need to explore the history of this Native New World on its own terms, not as an appendage of colonial America but as part of a continental process of historical development" has been taken up by many historians. What is fundamental here is that Indigenous power in this period was real, and European visions of dominance were often fantasies, even though these fantasies had a real punch when realized in the nineteenth century.[43]

The years of 2011 and 2012 were a period of stocktaking in how Indigenous history was envisioned, similar to the years of productivity between 1989 and 1992. In addition to Merrell's meditation, there were two powerful critiques of the future of writing about Indigenous people that appeared in these years: a suggestive article by James Sidbury and Jorge Canizares-Esguerra advocating for ethnogenesis as an organizing concept; and a reconsideration of the utility of borderlands as a way of grasping the nature of Indigenous-European relations by Pekka Hämäläinen and Samuel Truett.[44] Scholars of Indigenous American history have thus an abundance of interpretative models in which to shape their work—Middle Grounds, ethnogenesis, borderlands, and settler colonialism. All these schemas generate empirical data and theoretical discussion, but none have met with overwhelming approval, and criticisms of their deficiencies ring as strong as recognition of their advantages.

Certainly, Sidbury and Canizares-Esguerra's advocacy of ethnogenesis as a means to adapt the theoretical principles of creolization (as developed in the history of the Caribbean) to the differing peoples of North America has not been taken up by other historians, notably not by historians of Indigenous America. They believe that what is key about the movement and settlement in the Americas is the extent of sexual, social, and economic mixing between groups that scholars often keep methodologically apart. This mixing between Europeans, Indians, and Africans led to what Robin Blackburn calls a "disembedding" of individuals and institutions in what was very much a New World.[45] In this New World, according to Sidbury and Canizares-Esguerra, everyone's response to "disembedding" was to seek to re-embed themselves into communities, thus "creating new identities rooted in the transformations that forged the early modern Atlantic world." The result of creative responses to interethnic relationships, they suggest, was the development of new identities, sometime pan-Indian, pan-African, or pan-European, identities that they believe were always connected to fluidity and adaptability, thus echoing the themes so evident in #VastEarlyAmerica about histories of exchange. Identity, in short, was created in the Atlantic crucible of constant expansion and continual exchanges between people coming together across ethnic barriers.[46]

In the commentaries that followed, the Caribbeanist Laurent Dubois endorsed their argument in favor of creolization, an endorsement that is unsurprising given the prominence of creolization in discourses on Caribbean culture. James Sweet, a historian of race relations in Brazil, cautiously agreed but argued that ethnogenesis was more shaped by violence and by stratagems of power than Sidbury and Canizares-Esguerra presented. The Atlantic, Sweet suggests, was "an unrelenting exclusionary space as much as a progressive and inclusionary one." Historians of Indigenous America, however, commented on ethnogenesis from positions ranging from indifference to outright hostility. Claudio Saunt dismissed the concept because ethnogenesis ignores, he claims, how Indigenous Americans, unlike Africans, were organized into sovereign nations. Creolization or ethnogenesis, he believes, erases that difference. He notes that "for many Indians the challenge of the Atlantic world was less to create new identities than to hold onto the identities they had." Pekka

Hämäläinen was equally unimpressed. He argues that ethnogenesis flattens Indigenous experiences into uniformity through an insistence that what united people was how they had to adapt to new conditions.[47]

Hämäläinen and Samuel Truett are reluctant to have fluidity, adaptability, and all the baggage associated with "transformational" encounters define the field of Indigenous history. They do so by examining whether the fashionable concept of borderlands, popular in the 1990s and 2000s, is still useful. They highlight an influential 1999 article by Jeremy Adelman and Stephen Aron in popularizing the concept and note that borderlands history has become part of the mainstream of historical thinking, complementing and even supplementing Middle Ground perspectives.[48] They think, however, that the concept now offers little that is useful as an interpretive framework, mainly because the concept of borderlands is contaminated with frontier connotations and does not sufficiently acknowledge the very real power of Native empires and nations outside borderlands regions. Moreover, they are dubious about the #VastEarlyAmerica project of writing early American history as being about entanglements and shifting accommodations in a timeless sort of way rather than writing temporally and spatially bounded accounts of expansion and contraction.

Their main objections to the concept of borderlands are threefold. First, they see it less as departing from but more as depending on older versions of historical analysis. These versions prioritize European contacts with Indigenes over a view that Indigenous people themselves were creating the conditions for borderlands history and often choosing not to be part of any contact with Europeans, even if such contact started off on terms of their own making. They argue that the concept of borderlands lives in the shadows, "offering a chiaroscuro rendering of America that heightens the impact of the historical portrait but leaves the basic composition intact."

In short, they suggest that borderlands reflect a *fin-de-siècle* sensibility from the 1990s of a multidirectional, multivocal America. Behind borderlands, they argue, lies the frontier thesis of Frederick Jackson Turner, which, they suggest, falls into the epic rather than the romance genre. What the Turner thesis lacks in sensitivity to voices outside those of settlers, they suggest, it makes up for in having a sense of direction—the frontier closing—and a clear sense of winners (settlers) and losers (Indigenes). For Hämäläinen and Truett, borderlands history is delusional, accepting the direction of history posited by Turner but trying to elide it through a Middle Grounds emphasis on egalitarian cultural mixing.

Second, they dislike the concept of borderlands because they see it as a narrow version of the European-American encounter that elides the antagonisms, cultural demarcations, and power imbalances implicit in such encounters. The concept of borderlands, they argue, does not recognize the reality of empire—both Indigenous and European—in shaping activities in the peripheries. In particular, a borderlands approach does not acknowledge the many ways that Indigenous peoples formed themselves into empires and often, as with the Comanches and Lakotas whom Hämäläinen has written about, aggressively targeted dominion over other Indigenous peoples, being uninterested in engaging in anything more than trivial ways with Europeans. Finally, they fault the borderlands approach for its totalizing tendencies. It is easy, if one considers all connections between Europeans and Indigenous Americans to be primarily negotiations rather than contestations of power, to see everything as happening within a borderlands framework. Hämäläinen and Truett would like more precision in how borderlands are defined.[49]

Their mission statement for a replacement of a borderlands approach calls for closer attention to power as enunciated through imperial contestations (rather than concentrating on entanglements, one of their bête noirs). They declare: "We must link borderlands to European and Indigenous power, envision new cores, and embrace more nuanced definitions of power. We need to adopt an approach that shows how imperial and national interpenetrated smaller (regional, local) scales without necessarily dominating them, an approach [that] would destabilize distinctions between core and periphery and would challenge the convention of using the territorialized spaces of empires and nations as points of departure. If previous historians envisioned borderlands as peripheries to European realms, new scholarship is as likely to find them taking shape around indigenous cores."[50] Hämäläinen and Truett posit moving away from histories of exchange to histories of polities, with more concern for issues of power and territoriality in imperial centers (Indigenous as well as European) and less emphasis on exchange and encounter on the peripheries.

These criticisms of possible interpretative models suggest that scholars are at something of a crossroads in how we do Indigenous history. We know what we don't like; we are not sure what to put in place of older models. In particular, the work of Frederick Jackson Turner casts a continuing long shadow, and it is difficult to escape the Turnerian baggage that is fundamental, Hämäläinen and Truett suggest, to the concept of borderlands and to Indigenous history generally.[51] The concept of borderlands is therefore just a more open-ended vision of its harsher sister-term of "frontier," and has been so since Herbert Bolton first defined it over a century ago, in 1921.[52] "Borderlands" as a term thus still resonates with the idea of closure posited by Turner but pushes that closure into an abstract future. Turner knew when the frontier closed and dated it precisely, while for historians writing on borderlands, the eventual end of borders and their closure on European terms is assumed but never dated—borderlands just wither away and ebb out of sight, if not memory.

Settler colonialism has its own Turnerian echoes, and indeed, these are stronger than they are for either ethnogenesis or borderlands. Settler colonialism at its crudest is a form of Turnerian perspective that just takes a different moral viewpoint on whether the ending of the frontier was a good and necessary result of modernization. As Jessica Choppin Roney notes, we don't use frontier theory much now to explain westward expansion, mainly due to the overtones, often explicit, of Eurocentric racism in celebrating the end of the frontier period of American history in the late nineteenth century (a notion that once Indigenous Americans had gone, an overseas American empire could develop). She comments that "the frontier theory has never entirely gone away, perhaps because it too [like settler colonial theory] offers a multifaceted understanding of space and time."[53] The problem is teleology. Both the frontier theory of Turner and the settler colonial theory of Patrick Wolfe are framed within a modernization schema in which dispossession, whether desirable or regrettable, is universal, irreversible, and relentlessly unilinear. Narratives of modernity and progress continue to bind us, however much we try to resist their gravitational pull.[54]

This means that early American historians continue to grapple with the elusive nature of eighteenth-century Indigenous America. It is hard to balance European fantasies of domination with the reality of Indigenous power and even harder to stress how Indigenous people had not vanished nor were in any danger of disappearing in the eighteenth century against our knowledge of what happened to Indian power in the nineteenth century. The question to answer is how the settler empire of the United States in the period of the early republic took over Indigenous empires that were so strong that they had previously successfully resisted settler attacks, notably during the sixty years of war in the Ohio valley between 1754 and 1815. Michael A. Blaakman outlines the paradox. He notes that the US empire was a weak one in a world that it could not command, and one place it could not command was the North American frontier. Yet the solvency and survival of republican governments and the expansion of political and economic opportunity for White male citizens was, he argues, predicated on Indian removal. He notes that "with this equation sitting unresolved at the heart of the new nation's political economy, the United States attempted to trump Native power by couching in the future tense what it could not accomplish in the present."[55]

In short, the United States of America, and even more so settlers in the British Empire before it, wanted to take Indigenous land and expand but lacked the means and often the will to do so. Historians, Blaakman argues, no longer see the American state as paltry and ineffective, though they have not come to see it as powerful in ways that British historians see the British fiscal-military state.[56] If this is the case, then historians still have a problem to solve: How do we describe and understand "a national state that was unable to rule much of the territory it claimed but also succeeded in colonizing regions of the North American interior that European empires had long tried to dominate?" How, then, do we account for eighteenth-century Indigenous American power and also provide the framework for its later decline without reductionist reversion to demographic determinism, in which Indigenous people lost because their populations were in demographic free fall?

This conundrum might be thought a problem that is for nineteenth-century American historians to solve, but it is important for eighteenth-century historians to address, given how often the nineteenth century is read back into earlier periods.[57] Eran Zelnik, approaching the question from the perspective of the aftermath of the War of 1812, thinks that it can be solved by seeing the American state as quite powerful, settler populations and migration westward as considerable and relentless, and Indigenous populations relatively sparse and fragmented. Following settler colonial theory, he argues that in the nineteenth-century United States of America, "we find one of the most fortuitous circumstances for a settler collective to cohere." Such a circumstance made it easy for the settler to contemplate and implement policies to eliminate the Native. It is not an argument that early American historians are likely to accept, mainly because they don't see the American state to be as powerful as Zelnik does, nor do they envision Native settlement in the West to be all that weak and divided.[58]

Addressing this problem, Jessica Choppin Roney suggests three solutions. She argues that we should look at how space, time, and sovereignty are mutually constitutive. She notes that all historical constructs need to be rooted in close studies of particular locales in specific periods;

that scholars need to acknowledge the importance of memory and how Indigenous systems of knowledge provide different ways of constituting the past; and that we need to see the United States as made, remade, and remade again in response to colonialism. Roney concludes in a manner that adherents of #VastEarlyAmerica would approve: that studies ought to embrace chaos, instability, and multipolarity. Early America and the nations that arose out of it contained multitudes, she suggests, and contradictions aplenty. In her view, early Americanists can open analytic possibilities when we consider those multitudes "occupying both space and distinctive temporal phases . . . and still more if we can jettison the idea that those temporal phases necessarily conform to stages along a single arc such as progress or decline, and instead imagine how they may be nonlinear, moving in many different, even contradictory, directions at once."[59]

V

One theme very present in the history of Indigenous peoples in early America is the importance of war and violence in defining their experience and how they interacted with Europeans. In this way, Indigenous history intersects with themes dominant in early American history as a whole, such as envisioning early America as a violent place where war was often present and where it was usually transformative. The experiences of Indigenous people in the two imperial wars in the second half of the eighteenth century—the Seven Years' War and the American Revolution—have been highlighted in five articles over the past decade, which together show how powerful Indigenous peoples were in maintaining their authority and note the challenges that were increasingly troubling to these influential nations.

Paul Kelton and Michael McDonnell stress that we continue to underplay just how important Indigenous peoples were in the Seven Years' War. Kelton covers the whole war and argues that the Cherokees were much more important in the conduct of the war than historians have generally recognized. It was the Cherokees, he argues, who transformed the conflict from one involving the French and British to one that was between the British, French, and Indigenes. They were influential in shaping the conflict, especially through their diplomatic success in allying with the Haudenosaunees, or the Six Nations of the Iroquois Confederacy, on the side of the British, greatly enhancing that empire's war capacities. They were very strong as a military force but also were powerful diplomats who provided the diplomatic breakthrough by which the war in the Ohio valley came to an end in 1758.

Other nations found their position in the war more problematic than did the Cherokees. Michael McDonnell shows how the French-British conflict forced the Anishinaabe Odawas to abandon their careful and remarkably successful strategy of playing off one empire against the other. Before the Seven Years' War, the Anishinaabes, through diplomacy and a great deal of violence, had made themselves indispensable to the French. Their indispensability ended, however, during the Seven Years' War in the face of a tougher opponent. The British were determined not just to live with Indigenous people in the *pays d'en haut* but to conquer them and force them to obey British law and follow British customs.

Not surprisingly, the Anishinaabes did not like what was happening to them and rose up against White authority in Pontiac's War in 1763. It was a great triumph for Indigenes and a disaster for Europeans, who not only could not collect money from Native land and dwellings but had to recognize Indigenous claims to land and sovereignty over that land. British actions could lead to Native counterreactions. In this case, British miscalculations (the most important of which was thinking that Detroit and the Hurons who lived there held the key to controlling a vast "western confederacy" when in reality it was the Anishinaabes at Michilimackinac who were in charge) resulted in the Anishinaabes having the balance of power in the region. Their achievements during Pontiac's War in 1763 gave them long-term stability, including after the American Revolution, in the central and northern Great Lakes region.[60]

White settlers resented Indigenous power, a resentment that was increasingly expressed in racially divisive ways. There is a growing, though far from universal, consensus that developing American nationalism after the Seven Years' War was based on an increasingly strident awareness of racial differences, seen especially in longstanding conflicts between Indigenous peoples and Europeans in the Ohio valley and western Pennsylvania.[61] A key area where ideologies of whiteness took hold was in the backcountry areas so celebrated by Benjamin Franklin as the heartlands of settler fecundity. Racial thinking, especially regarding Indigenous Americas, became foundational to the logic of settler activities in western Pennsylvania and the Ohio valley.[62] Accordingly, the Paxton riots of 1763, which resulted out of settler violence toward Indigenes, have become a focal point in early American history, seen as pivotal to the American experience and attracting more scholarship than traditionally more famous events like the 1765 Stamp Act crisis.[63]

The Paxton Boys' rebellion was a relatively small-scale incident, by the standards of frontier violence generally, when settlers in western Pennsylvania massacred twenty Conestoga Indians. They then marched on Philadelphia to protest the government's wartime policies. The event has moved from being thought of as a minor skirmish to being considered a major event in early American history, now seen as a military challenge to Quaker government in Pennsylvania and, more importantly, described as a prelude to more intense extrajudicial and racially motivated violence. Historians pay great attention to the extensive pamphlet literature around the rebellion and how this literature raises important questions about political representation, authority on the frontier, and, most importantly, the growth of ideologies of whiteness and expressions of hatred towards Indian "savages." The aggressive politics of the Paxton Boys convinced colonial politicians in Philadelphia that White people needed to have governments uphold the prerogatives of whiteness against any challenge from nonwhites.[64] The lesson was learned. When ninety-seven Moravian Indians were massacred in western Pennsylvania in March 1782, the Pennsylvania legislature was notably more indulgent to Whites in the state's interior than it had been two decades earlier.[65]

Jeffrey Ostler develops this theme of an ideological commitment to White supremacy in a study of expressions of genocide directed against Indigenous people during these pivotal decades. Usually, the many expressions of sheer hatred towards Indigenes found in pamphlet literature in this period have been largely ignored as bluster. Nevertheless, Ostler shows, such talk of wishing Indigenous people to face genocide and to vanish from the landscape was taken very seriously by Indigenes themselves—rightly so, Ostler thinks, given the later experience of dispossession and removal that occurred when Whites had the ability to act on their prejudices. He argues, following Indigenous Ways of Knowing methods, that if we listen to Indigenous voices, then they thought the threat of genocide to be real, not just idle talk. "Genocide talk" peaked in the early 1790s but was present during the American Revolution. The discourse of genocide suggested to Indigenes the consistently bad intentions of colonists toward them and encouraged many Native peoples to support the British. Ostler concludes that "to realize that their very existence was at stake provides a deeper appreciation for what exactly Indians survived."[66]

Hatred was not the only emotion that existed in Indigenous-European relations, but it was an important emotion and one that historians argue contributed to partisan politics during the American Revolution. Hatred of Indians helped make colonists hostile toward George III in the 1760s because he and his government were thought to be too favorably inclined to Indigenous interests as opposed to the concerns and desires of settlers. Samuel Fisher argues that Scotch-Irish Americans drew on long traditions of Protestant suspicion of Stuart tyranny and overfondness of "barbarous" Gaels to transfer their hostility from Gaels toward Indians. He references the Paxton Boys' rebellion and the Royal Proclamation of 1763, which limited unrestrained westward expansion, as key moments in turning many Americans against Britain. Likewise, the growing power of Indigenous Americans that Michael McDonnell chronicles in the *pays d'en haut* was a factor promoting settler fears that Indigenous people would stop them from doing what they wanted in westward settlement.[67]

These fears were manifested in contradictory ways. Settlers craved the security of imperial dependency against internal foes, such as enslaved people in Jamaica and Indigenous people in Pennsylvania and South Carolina, but they resented what they saw as an alarming trend toward inclusivity in which White Protestant settlers' special claims to British identity were downgraded so that a Bengali or a Cherokee or a Catholic was thought by the imperial government to be their equal. In Scotland fear of Gaels led to greater support for the Union after 1745. In British North America, by contrast, Americans' determination to maintain exclusionary understandings of Britishness ironically led them toward independence.[68]

The hostility of settlers to Indigenes helped move Native peoples in the opposite direction, toward Britain, as Gregory Dowd explains in a wide-ranging article on Indigenous peoples in the American Revolution. He notes that current scholarship sees Indigenes as distrusting settler intentions so much that they tended to side with the British. The empire offered coexistence and prospective statehood in this interpretation, but the American Revolution only unleashed on Indigenous people settlers who were land-seeking and racist backcountry men, backed by a government receptive to settler demands.[69] Dowd does not doubt the latter point but is unsure that the British Empire was all that solicitous of Indigenous peoples' interests. He accepts many of the assumptions of settler colonialism but denies that the British Empire offered any bulwark for Indigenous people against settler desires.[70] Thus, he follows Johann Neem in seeing as misplaced much of the recent literature on imperialism as a beneficial force in eighteenth-century British America.[71] Dowd notes that the nineteenth-century British Empire in places like South Africa, New Zealand, and Australia showed that it was as unfriendly to

Indigenes as was the US republic with its White supremacist responsiveness to settler desires. The United States may have been the first and most aggressive settler polity. It was not exceptional, however. As Dowd comments, "Outside the Republic, the empire bore down on natives in ways that American Indians would recognize."[72]

Dowd's observation about making comparisons before agreeing to America being an exceptional example of settler hostility toward Indigenous people points to a larger theme neglected in accounts that look at the American Revolution only through American eyes. What Dowd demonstrates is that one should be careful in arguing that Americans were so determined on developing forms of racial segregation that most settlers were made patriots due to outrage at perceived British indulgences toward Indigenous people. Eran Zelnik, summarizing this strand of scholarship, argues that "to a considerable degree, settlers joined the insurgency when the British enemy became associated with race treason." Zelnik notes how the American Revolution saw its most violent warfare in the interior and in the slave society of South Carolina.[73] Zelnik assumes that race-making mainly occurred in North America. He suggests that the hardening of racial boundaries resulted both from new ways of thinking about race and from the practical ways in which White supremacy was implemented as a political imperative by White colonists and then Americans in the early republic. These harder forms of race thinking, he suggests, put North America at odds with a British Empire in which abolitionism was developing and where Britons were beginning to have ideas about the place of nonwhites in the empire that diverged from those held by colonists. Southern slaveholders were dismayed over Lord Mansfield's decision in 1772 in *Somerset* to confine the legality of slavery to the colonies alone instead of the British Empire as a whole and horrified over the clumsy and back-firing decree by the last colonial governor of Virginia, John Murray, Earl of Dunmore, in 1775, to set free enslaved people (and indentured servants) willing to take up arms against colonists. These events are usually thought of as key moments in the hardening of White opinion in North America against a British Empire deemed too soft toward enslaved and Indigenous people.[74]

Divergences in thinking about race between Britain and North America, however, are greatly overstated. The ideological currents in British thinking about race were moving in similar directions to those in the colonies, influenced by an extreme sense of racial caste-consciousness and the need to maintain an absolute commitment to whiteness emanating from the Caribbean in the thought of proslavers such as the Jamaican historian Edward Long, as Matilde Cazzola and Lorenzo Ravano have shown.[75] Brooke Newman, Andrew Wells, and James Delbourgo each demonstrate that the hardening of racial thought was not an American phenomenon but was an intellectual current that was also present in British thought around midcentury. Britain's commitment to slavery and to White supremacy in the West Indies was close to absolute before and during the American Revolution, with abolitionism only becoming a significant issue in British politics very suddenly in the second half of the 1780s.[76]

VI

What this positive view of imperialism elides, with the British as the more reliable friend of Indigenous peoples than reprehensible settlers, is the viciousness of the British Empire to enslaved persons and to Indigenous people in the eighteenth century before the American Revolution. One thing that is very often forgotten in US-centric accounts of imperial policy after the Seven Years' War is that it was less westward but southern expansion that had fueled British, French, and Spanish imperial visions in the two decades before the Seven Years' War. The big money in imperial expansion was directed to investment in southern Caribbean islands such as Grenada, which moved from being a marginal colony in terms of population and wealth under the French to a powerhouse of slave-labor plantation output in the 1760s and 1770s. It was also in the southern Caribbean that some of the most intractable imperial problems in the latter half of the eighteenth century—the expansion of a dynamic Atlantic and interimperial slave trade, inter-European imperial competition, the question of subjecthood—were most debated. Moreover, it was a significant venue for Indigenous-European clashes, notably in the Carib-European War of 1769–73 and in the continuing issue of how to deal with the refusal of the Kalinga Indigenous population to abandon their land so that Europeans could advance their plantation enterprises.[77]

Whatever benefits British imperialism brought to the Indigenes of the Americas and the enslaved were more than matched by its negative impacts. Moreover, such a binary view of imperialism and revolution focused around patriots and loyalists acts against one of the principal themes in the recent writing about Indigenes, which is that Indigenous power and ability to influence environmental change was considerable. Even if colonization was a sustained assault on Indigenous people in the Americas, it was not a one-way process. Recent journal literature makes it emphatically clear that Indigenous people were not passive recipients of whatever colonists threw at them. Scholars might not rewrite early American history so that it is Indigenous people, not Europeans, who are the main players in the drama or claim that the best perspective on early America is an Indigenous one, but the historiographical trends of the last decade, indeed the last thirty years, make clear that we have fundamentally rethought the place of Indigenes in early America. That rethinking—seeing early America as Indigenous country—is still proceeding, but the movement forward is unmistakable. Indigenous people are now front and center of the writing of early American history. That centrality within the historiography is likely to become more evident in future writings on the period.

5

The Imperial Turn

I

One theme that has dramatically increased in prominence within the writing on early American history is imperialism, mostly but not exclusively British imperialism. This chapter focuses more on British imperialism than on Spanish, French or Dutch imperialism because that is where the great majority of articles on imperialism in early America are focused in the journals sampled in this book, but a renewed interest in European imperialism in the Americas in general can also be detected, with several important articles emerging in the last decade in particular on that traditional topic of French-British rivalry and also on the Bourbon imperial reforms in the period following the Seven Years' War.[1] A renewed interest in imperialism arises out of the thirty-year quest to see early America as part of many wider worlds, most of which were part of some kind of imperial configuration. Historians have realized that what united most people's experiences in the Americas was that they lived as colonial subjects within imperial polities. At its most basic level, renewed attention to imperialism allows historians to discuss the relationship between power and authority in the formation of colonial societies and draws attention to the continuing importance of metropolitan influence in the articulation of colonial identities.

Why is imperialism useful as a form of analysis? First, it brings the issue of power firmly back into the equation.[2] Second, it draws attention to a principal tension in early modern political discourse—that between republicanism and monarchism. Over the eighteenth century the latter became more authoritarian than before and more based on a vertical articulation of power, in which colonial subordination was pronounced, as the linkages between monarchy and aristocracy turned from adversarial to mutually supportive.[3] Paul Kramer, in an article on the twentieth-century United States of America seen through imperialist lenses, concisely summarizes the advantages of an imperial approach. The three major virtues he sees in an imperial perspective are the way that power resides in and operates through long-distance connections; the mutual and uneven transformation of societies through these connections; and comparisons between large-scale systems of power and their histories. "It is this particular set of questions," Kramer argues, "about power, connection and comparison—that makes imperial history an indispensable tool in the kit of any historian of the US."[4]

In practice, however, imperial history is not just a way to study "power, connection, and comparison," which are tools in all historiographical kits. It is, more significantly, a way to connect early America to world or global history in a historiography that sees a restored global history as cosmopolitan and meeting the needs of a globalizing world. "The imperial," Kramer adds, "has long been a useful concept in work that attempts to situate the US in global history."[5] He argues that an imperial approach is preferable to its related cousin, transnational history, as it is less the tool of neoliberalist capitalism and more able to recognize that world history is not just about flows, exchanges, and connections but "is wrought in hierarchy and power" and in "violence and coercion."[6]

The "imperial turn" was one that early Americanists were always likely to be receptive toward, not just because, as Karen Kupperman argues, early America was international from the beginning, but also because empires were so much part of the early American landscape. A world map of 1750 would see empires rather than nation-states as the dominant configuration, as they had been for millennia. Nation-states on this map would be, as Jane Burbank and Frederick Cooper note, "a blip on the historical horizon, a state form that emerged recently from under imperial skies and whose hold on the world's political imagination may well prove partial or transitory."[7] Studies of imperialism thus have been a means whereby historians can study processes of globalization. Indeed, at times the term "imperial" has become a synecdoche for "world" in recent historiography, most notably in eighteenth-century British history, in a period when imperialism, globalization, and modernity merged.

Patrick O'Brien's prolegomena for global history in the first essay in the *Journal of Global History* (*JGH*) in 2006 makes this point explicitly, arguing that there was a profound conjuncture in the imperial meridian (he prefers this to the term "age of revolutions") between 1783 and 1825 that made the writing of world history possible, as Europe's geopolitical power became globally hegemonic.[8] In Britain, global and world history are intertwined, as can be seen in important research and teaching programs at Oxford, Cambridge, Exeter, and Warwick, where "global and imperial" are not thought of as separate concepts. This equation of global with imperial in Britain is perhaps not surprising. Danielle Kinsey thinks that it is easy for historians of Britain and its empire, and thus presumably for early American historians, to see how empires were integral to modern transformations in the last three hundred years, more so than revolutions, because modernity has "unfolded slowly over centuries, inhered multiple centers of innovation and occurred unevenly and differently around the world." How this happened can be seen to best effect, she argues, in the case of the British Empire because "the Empire created modern Britain as we know it and modernity transformed the Empire. Industrialization and the development of political economy happened . . . under imperial skies."[9] That British historians are receptive to imperial approaches is unsurprising given the centrality of the British Empire to British history over the last four hundred years. What is more interesting is that this "imperial turn" has reasserted itself, both in respect to writing about the British Empire and increasingly in studying empires in comparative fashion.[10] This chapter explores how imperial perspectives on early America fell out of favor and how they became increasingly popular as historiographical frameworks in the 2000s and 2010s. I suggest that this approach augurs much that is valuable in aligning early American history to the histories of other places in the early modern period and to an American history that, as Kramer notes, an imperial lens illuminates.[11]

II

Early American history in its modern form was oriented from the start around the concept of imperialism, beginning with the writings of Charles M. Andrews in the first third of the twentieth century. One of the luminaries of early American history writing in the next generation was Andrews's student Lawrence Henry Gipson, who penned the multivolume work *The British Empire before the American Revolution* (1936–70) about the rise and fall of empire in North America in the eighteenth century.[12] Andrews and Gipson between them formed the so-called imperial school in early American history.

Imperialism remained historiographically important from the early twentieth century into the Cold War, but significant voices, such as Edmund Morgan, started to argue during that Cold War period that there were better ways to understand early America than through imperialism. From the late 1940s through to the late 1980s, early American historians trended away from the study of empires in early America toward considering how colonial America became a nation. The question of nationalism—and the nature of nationalism—became a primary topic in the history of the American Revolution. The pivotal piece in this move toward nationalism was Morgan's 1948 article on colonial ideology around the time of the Stamp Act.[13] Morgan saw ideas as central to the development of the American nation between the 1760s and the 1780s. One of the key effects of this emphasis on nationalism as a theme was to separate out the revolutionary era from the rest of the colonial era. Another effect was to date the revolutionary era precisely.[14] Morgan's approach separated colonial history, with its old-fashioned emphasis on imperialism, to an exciting Cold War study of revolution and nationalism that was portrayed as a transition to the modern. One indication of this trend was a surge from the 1960s onward in books that focused on the beginnings of America as a nation based on republicanism, the focus heralded in the very title of such books.[15]

Such a demarcation between colonial and revolutionary history has largely disappeared. Early American historians have begun to copy their British peers in extending the period they study into a long eighteenth century, occasionally slipping back into the seventeenth and forward into the early nineteenth century. As Jeremy Adelman argues, increasingly historians do not write, as Morgan did, of a temporally bounded American Revolution but of an age of revolution connected to a global history of the era. The age of revolution is much wider in conception than the previous definition of an American revolutionary period, covering several revolutions without presuming that they were driven by a single teleological purpose.[16]

The interpretive model that has fed into this new emphasis on an age of revolution into which the Seven Years' War and the American Revolution need to be fitted is C. A. Bayly's *Birth of the Modern World* (2004). He identifies a "world crisis," starting around 1700, which intensified as problems multiplied in the landed empires of Asia around 1720. This world crisis provided an opportunity for expanding sea-based European empires to move into Asia while developing their empires in the Americas.[17] It also drew these empires into global conflicts, in which Britain had particular advantages due to its administrative achievements in developing a fiscal-military state that allowed it to fight expensive wars without risking state bankruptcy. John Darwin develops this theme to show that the coming together of commercialization, warfare, social crisis, and "the growth of complexity with these societies" made the age of revolutions global as much as Atlantic, given how the force of revolutionary events "ricocheted around the world."[18]

Jeremy Adelman, Janet Polasky, and Wim Klooster build on this idea of world crisis to stress the imperial nature of these Atlantic disturbances, rather than seeing them as principally democratic revolutions. They see Atlantic revolutions, especially the American one, as settler revolts when political crisis led to demands for increased freedoms for previously excluded social groups. For Adelman, what is imperative is denying the teleological assumptions behind tracing a move from deficient empires to more effective nation-states. He insists that European empires were not "backward and brittle systems cracking under the pressure of global competition and confrontations."[19] Lauren Benton, an important figure in the study of how law and empire developed in the early modern world, argues that states functioned as legally pluralistic organisms that worked usually within multiethnic and constitutionally diverse empires. She suggests that a multitude of political arrangements existed in eighteenth-century states (most of which were empires in Europe, Asia, and the Americas) that did not rely on any single creed or practice but depended on syncretic or mixed forms of governmental organizations.[20]

III

Much of the interpretative energy about the age of revolutions is concentrated after the formation of the United States and is driven by scholars trying to explain the connections between the American, French, Haitian, and Spanish revolutions.[21] Klooster, for example, draws on themes in his analysis of slave-revolt rumors in the Atlantic world in the age of revolutions that are directly related to topics with which early American historians are familiar. He notes that one of the hallmarks of the Atlantic world in the age of revolutions was that it was interconnected and imperially entangled, though he laments how seldom scholars examine these imperial entanglements comparatively.[22] Issues of representation, he argues, would benefit from a comparative approach.[23] So, too, though he does not dwell on this theme, would issues surrounding slavery.

Klooster makes an instructive examination of how rumors of slave revolt shaped the age of revolution in various hemispheric regimes. He argues that a common rumor provoked several slave insurgencies in the age of revolution—that benevolent European monarchs had mandated emancipation but that this act was thwarted in the colonies by self-interested slaveholders and colonial officials. Increased slave insurgencies, however, were not as they are often described, he believes. They were not a result of the politicization of the enslaved as a result of "rights" talk and universalist rhetoric about human rights expressed in the age of revolutions but instead arose out of the immutable principles held by the enslaved on their rights to freedom, which drew on African and Creole notions of kingship that well predated the age of revolutions and which were rooted in the eighteenth-century age of empires more than in the age of revolution. "Like free people," he argues, "slaves inhabited a world held together by a web of rights." What revolutionary events did, he suggests, was not to change the thinking of the enslaved but to provide the impetus whereby the enslaved were able to act upon beliefs they had always held, including the assumption that their enslavement was immoral and illegal. This occurred in a context in which revolutions gave them opportunities, previously denied, to convince European sympathizers that the enslaved deserved to be free.[24] Klooster cites Robin Blackburn on this point: "Emancipation in the Americas was not achieved through slow concessions and customary rights but it was marked by revolutionary ruptures including both interventions from 'outside' the slave system and the action or reaction of the slaves themselves."[25]

The article in the sample that most engages with the global dimensions of the age of revolution, applying a theoretical model of culture in order to arrive at conclusions similar to those of Klooster, is by Nathan Perl-Rosenthal.[26] He distinguishes two approaches that early American historians have taken to the reality that the American Revolution was part of a broader age of revolutions: connective and contextualist approaches.[27] The first, he notes, stresses how the era's revolutions influenced one another. Eliga Gould's 2007 article introducing the idea of entanglement as a way of understanding how empires functioned in this period is a classic example of the connective approach.[28] The contextual approach, which Perl-Rosenthal favors, by contrast, casts the era's revolutions against each other, taking the causal links as given and seeking to establish the distinctiveness and significance of each revolution.[29] Drawing on the French scholarship of Pierre Bourdieu and Michel de Certeau, he attempts such a contextualist approach in comparing epistolary culture in North America in the 1770s with that of Saint Domingue in the 1790s to outline a Bourdieuian "habitus" of letter writing that began in prerevolutionary times, shaped revolutions, and continued well after the revolutions had finished.[30] Although he asserts that Atlantic cultures did not remain unchanged in the face of revolution, the trend of his analysis is toward cultural continuity. This theme connects his work to that done by other scholars influenced by the linguistic turn.[31]

Perl-Rosenthal employs de Certeau to emphasize the role of "tactics" that people use to accept or reject dominant ways of thinking and acting in society, but he stresses that such use of tactics to modify the existing social order was not an unlimited process of invention. "In the revolutionary period," he argues, "people could redefine cultural practices only if they already knew how to use them according to the rules of their society."[32] He stresses continuity over revolutionary change, arguing that we should not expect a single revolution to explain as much as it is usually expected to do. Only through looking at the age of revolutions as a whole, he suggests, can we "see each revolution's significance in more measured terms and . . . hear in them together the deep music of a new world coming into being through the instruments of the old."[33]

Perl-Rosenthal's paean to mystic chords of memory as determining cultural practice points to a conclusion that several scholars have noted about the use of the age of revolution instead of the birth of nations to center the American Revolution as an event and as a process. The term has essentially nonrevolutionary implications that fit with ideas in British history of the long eighteenth century and with current reemphases in European history about the continuing power of the *ancien régime* to survive revolutionary change. The age of revolution in this reading fits well with an imperial perspective. If we see empires as important, effective, and largely beneficent, as is the contemporary take on empires in the writing on early American history, then we can depict revolutions as evolutionary rather than transformative in their cultural, social, and political impact.

Michael McDonnell notes that while historians agree with Bayly's conception of a "world crisis" leading to an age of revolution and the making of modernity—accepting with Bayly that it is clear that something particularly profound happened between 1750 and 1848—they reject theories that see the changes in this age of revolution as especially dramatic.[34] The ubiquity in scholarship now of the phrase "age of revolution" is that the highly influential thesis of Eric Hobsbawm on revolution ushering in the modern age no longer holds the influence that it once did. Hobsbawm's modern world emerged out of a distinct revolutionary epoch in which the Industrial and French Revolutions were the "twin craters" of an eruption from which "world revolution" spread outwards. Hobsbawm's thesis of 1962, long influential and easily incorporated within a view of the American Revolution put forward by Edmund Morgan and the Cold War generation of historians, is too Eurocentric for the current generation of scholars.[35] The age of revolution concept encourages a return to a different scholarship, that of R. R. Palmer, who put forward a view of the interrelated upheavals of the age of revolutions as showing the democratic and egalitarian spirit of the time. Jeremy Adelman argues that it is not coincidental that Palmer's work was revived in the post–Cold War era as scholars searched for a postnationalist, postsocialist turn in history. He suggests that Palmer's insistence that historians should avoid exceptionalist narratives about the rise of the West and his stress on transnational interconnections suited a period in the 2000s when notions of liberal democracy being part of a dominant global tidal process held sway.[36] Historians accept discourses of globalization less readily now than twenty years ago, but Palmer's formulations remain powerful for historians of early American history who are allergic to explanations of historical causation that tend toward exceptionalist narratives.

IV

The (re)turn to imperialism is a surprising development given how irredeemably old-fashioned imperial history was just a generation ago.[37] Patrick Griffin has described how the imperial vision of Lawrence Henry Gipson moved from central within early American historical practice to being irrelevant between the 1930s and the late 1960s. Gipson's interest in empire, his wide synthetic approach, his penchant for arresting narrative, his incessant Anglophilia and indifference to history from below, and his deliberately pedestrian prose (chosen out of distaste for the fervid romanticism of a previous generation of writers) came to be out of step with academic fashion in the period of decolonization and anti-Vietnam protests of the 1960s and 1970s. The generation of social historians taking charge in this period "pooh-poohed the celebratory tone of Gipson's work" on the rare occasion that they even read it. As Griffin notes, "In an age when empire was breathing its last and its oppressive nature had become apparent, celebrations of empire did not resonate." Furthermore, Gipson's "promise of the grand Anglophone alliance of liberty-loving Britons and Americans seemed pathetically quaint."[38]

Gipson does not seem so quaint and out of fashion now as he did a half century ago. But empire was decidedly out of fashion when Gipson died, aged ninety, in 1971. It was outmoded in British as much as in early American history. J. G. A. Pocock, in a famous article from 1975 calling for a wider conception of what constituted the boundaries of British history, lamented how empire had disappeared as something English people recognized they had been involved in (and he meant English, rather than British, having the Oxford historian and television don A. J. P. Taylor firmly in his sightlines). "Within very recent memory," he argued, "the English have been increasingly willing to declare that neither empire nor commonwealth ever meant much in their consciousness that they were Europeans all the time." He described the historiography of the early 1970s as groaning with books on English history "in which Welsh, Scots, Irish and, in the reign of George III, Americans, appear only as peripheral people when, and only when, their doings assume the power to disturb the tenor of English politics." He titled his argument a "plea" and felt that when he called for a more expansive British history that took empire and commonwealth seriously, he was just "a voice crying in the wilderness."[39]

Pocock's former colleague in New Zealand, D. K. Fieldhouse, then at Cambridge, was even more despondent about the future of imperial history at this time. He expressed despair over the fragmented state of the field, imploring: "Can the fragments of the old history be put together again into new patterns which are intellectually respectable?" He feared that imperial history might be "condemned to share the midden of discredited academic subjects with, say, astrology or phrenology."[40] He thought that the options for a reinvigorated imperial history might be to explore the motives behind European expansion; the process of the mechanics of empire building; the organization and bureaucratic impulses of empire; or the costs and benefits of empire. All of these aims were worthy, but they hardly set the world on fire. And they were themes that were from the top-down rather than looking at how people might have experienced empire. Fieldhouse was not alone in his lack of interest in ordinary people and imperialism. Bill Schwarz, for example, notes that the left-leaning *Historical Workshop Journal (HWJ)* was similarly unconcerned about such themes, virtually ignoring until the 1990s any engagement with the activities of the subaltern school of scholars of India, such as Ranajit Guha, who was writing works of enduring importance at the same time as Fieldhouse was lamenting how out of date imperial history seemed to be.[41]

Fieldhouse's fear of the imminent death of imperial history was misplaced. The field revived in the 1990s as social history declined in importance, and it became triumphant in the 2000s as the "imperial turn" replaced the "linguistic turn" as the hot new thing in historical studies.

That turn to a "new imperial history" has not yet ended. We can start to see the change developing in an article by Fieldhouse's successor at Cambridge, A. G. Hopkins, in *P&P* in 1999. Hopkins was not completely convinced that imperial history was the coming trend, claiming at the start of his polemic in favor of imperial history replacing nation-state history that historians of empire, like himself, had a diminished stature. But he thought that imperial history had a future and that it was all the more important as discourses of globalization were taking hold. He proclaimed that "what is needed is a fundamental reappraisal of world history to bring out the extent to which, in recent centuries, it has been shaped by the interaction of several types of empire at various stages of development and decay."[42]

The imperial turn took some time to eventuate, however. The new field of Atlantic history was initially hostile to accusations that it was merely a warmed-over imperial history. Bernard Bailyn, for example, insisted that the genealogy of Atlantic history lay in contemporary international politics in the interwar period and in the creation of the postwar NATO world rather than in imperialism. He noted that neither Charles M. Andrews nor Clarence Haring, the major imperial historians in the early twentieth century, took an Atlantic approach. Alison Games thought along similar lines. She argued that the Atlantic cannot be imperial because an imperial perspective draws attention to a single place or set of places rather to the process whereby places and people were transformed through integrative, transnational Atlantic interactions.[43]

Other historians, especially European-born historians, were less concerned than Bailyn or Games to distinguish Atlantic history from imperial history and were increasingly prepared to think of Indigenous American history in imperial turns. What was common about people in the Atlantic world, in this view, was that they were subjects of kings, emperors, or chieftains, not citizens, and that they lived in empires, not republics. Three European scholars wrote crucial books in the mid-2000s that insisted on the Atlantic world of settlers and Indigenous Americans as being best defined by empire: J. H. Elliott, P. J. Marshall, and Pekka Hämäläinen.[44] In addition, scholars of Iberian America joined with Elliott in trying to see seventeenth- and eighteenth-century imperialism in comparative terms, with Jorges Cañizares-Esguerra making an intriguing argument that the conquistadors and New England Puritans who first extended European power to Spanish and British America were united under broadly imperial themes. That thought has been extended in much recent scholarship, such as a provocative book by a team of authors headed by Pedro Cardim that attempted to explain Iberian hegemony in the early modern Atlantic world, drawing from older work by Elliott on how monarchy and empire fitted together.[45]

Imperial history has an especial resonance in Britain, even if its popularity rises and falls in dizzying succession.[46] But empire is always there, as the Brexit debate of 2016–20 illustrated. As Robert Saunders notes in an analysis of imperial thinking as a factor in Britain's relationship with Europe in the last fifty years, all sides of the European debate in Britain that culminated in Brexit in 2020 debated the issue through the common cultural inheritance of an imperial legacy.[47] What united traditional imperial historians and "new" imperial historians was a belief that imperialism was so wide-ranging as to encompass the whole of eighteenth-century British and British American history. That belief was about culture as much as power. As Eric Hinderaker wrote in 1996, "Empire is a cultural artifact as well as a geopolitical entity; it belongs to a geography of the mind as well as a geography of power."[48] And as Kathleen Wilson argued, "The eighteenth-century British empire presents us with interconnected and interdependent sites of historical importance, territorial and imaginative, that can disrupt oppositions between metropole and colony and allow us to rethink the genealogies and historiographies of national belonging and exclusion."[49]

Studies of empire have abounded recently because they meet significant parts of the twenty-first century zeitgeist, at least that zeitgeist that existed before the rise of populist nationalism in China, America, and much of Europe after 2015.[50] It is not surprising that studies of empire, both celebratory and derogatory, reappeared when international affairs had an imperialist tinge and when the United States was being reenvisioned as an imperial power.[51] Historical imperialism is an interesting topic in an age of transnational globalization when the borders separating countries and economies seem porous. Imperial history also answers questions about the past that bear on the present—notably the cultural history questions of identity and difference—in ways that histories of nation-states were less able to do.[52] Krisnan Kumar explains that "empires, for all their faults, show us another way, a way of managing diversity and differences that are now the inescapable fate of practically all so-called nation-states." "That by itself," he argues, "seems sufficient grounds for continuing to study them, and to reflect on what they might be able to teach us." The study of empires engages current beliefs in multiculturalism, diasporas, migrations, and multinationalism and can be a prism through which the "pressing problems of the contemporary world and even the birth pangs of a new world order" can be addressed.[53]

V

For many early American historians, the imperial turn of the 2000s reestablished links between the colonial and the national period of American history. It encouraged scholars to think through the links between colonialism and postcoloniality and the continuities in the national experiences of countries that emerged from the British Atlantic. Jack Greene wrote an important essay along these lines in 2008, in which he argued for the possibilities of a new imperial history that recognized that the United States from its founding was a postcolonial state formation. That recognition, he thought, "could reshape all of American history" and might turn on its head nationalist histories, "many of which continue to operate within the traditional view that colonial histories are subordinate to national histories and are useful principally for the light that they shed on emergent national institutions and cultures." For Greene, the important point about the American Revolution was that it was a settler revolt that left settlers in full control, with the situation of the colonized unchanged.[54]

Andrew Shankman develops this theme in an article on state formation over the long term. Shankman insists on continuities between colonial and national governance systems, notably the idea, advanced by Greene, that the British Empire and the American nation-state relied on governance being negotiated between elites and the imperial state. He argues that governance in the interior depended much more than at the center on the willing cooperation of those who were to be governed, as coercive authority had distinct geographical limits. The state intervened in the interior less to advance its own interests but to adjudicate local disputes under circumstances that were of the choosing of people in distant places. He concludes that "once there was a reasonably unified and sizeable locality enjoying hegemony over its vicinity, neither the British imperial state nor the republican nation-state could govern within the locality without its voluntary willingness to be governed." He posits as the best example of leading from behind the policies adopted by William Pitt the elder during the Seven Years' War. Pitt, he argues, "understood the organically federal nature of the empire he led and the absolute necessity of approaching the colonists differently in the internal realm than he would need to in the external." By knowing the limits to his authority,

Pitt exercised power especially effectively. He was able to "convince loyal and proud British subjects living in colonial America that they wanted to be governed," as long as they were governed in accordance with colonial cooperation.[55]

Greene and Shankman's views are becoming orthodoxy for scholars of the early republic. Gautham Rao, for example, in a historiographical study of the state in the history writing of the early republic, insists on calling the United States "an imperial state."[56] Rao's idea of the "imperial state" replicates the findings of colonial historians such as Max Edelson, who describes the imperial state as being a shared vision of statecraft and political economy that "cohered around a new ethos of systematic governance" that developed over the eighteenth century and came to fruition in the 1780s.[57] It was an imperial state that relied as much on what was happening in the peripheries, as the study of the relationship between Native Americans and the early federal government shows, as in the metropolitan center. That colonies and nation were linked together is axiomatic in new studies of the beginnings of the American nation. Annette Gordon-Reed and Peter Onuf, for their part, conclude that "the once-conventional Whiggish narrative of the march of liberty and the progressive maturation of democratic institutions culminating in US independence is giving way to a much more complicated and contingent history that cannot be contained within the contested boundaries of a fragile alliance of rebellions [and] self-declared republics."[58]

The work of Rao and others, notably Max Edling and Peter Onuf, points to a notable lacuna in the writing of early American history for the period before 1787 and especially before 1776, which is the role of the state.[59] Journal literature on the state in this sample is surprisingly limited, especially given its prominence in the historiographies of eighteenth-century British history and the early US republic. The standard question of whether the early American state was weak or strong is often addressed but usually obliquely. Thus, Andrew Shankman argues that the state in early modern America was strong, as can be seen in how it enforced the Navigation Acts in the 1720s, but that its power was constrained by the necessity of consulting colonists and developing effective enforcement mechanisms. He examines the White Pines Act in New Hampshire in 1711 as an example of initial failure and eventual success. That success resulted from the ability of a skilled governor, Benning Wentworth, who figured out how to get the owners of New Hampshire forests to welcome regulation that provided the British navy with timber. Wentworth, in short, was good at navigating negotiated authority.[60]

By contrast, John Craig Hammond argues that the state in the colonial and federal periods (the latter being more his focus) had limited control over what slaveholders did. Ironically, the constant support of these governments for maintaining and expanding the institution of slavery showed less a strong state than a weak one. "Ultimately," he concludes "neither a revolutionary promise of an empire for liberty, nor a weak, over-extended nation-state could overcome the post-colonial realities of white settlers clamoring for more slaves, geopolitical conflicts that encouraged European powers to bid for those white settlers' loyalties, and growing trans-Atlantic demand for slave-produced commodities, which dictated that the expansion of European-American sovereignty into the continental interior would be accompanied by African-American slavery."[61]

In general, however, articles (as opposed to books) on the nature of the imperial state are relatively limited.[62] One exception is Robert Aggorworth, who examines the colonial post office, the only continentwide British institution based in North America before the Seven Years' War.[63] Thomas Agostini looks at how colonial states funded provincial soldiers as part of the British Army during the Seven Years' War. He shows that this process was affected by the high wages that ordinary White men received, meaning that colonists had to be given similar wages when joining (much higher than those awarded to British regulars), making the provision of soldiers an expensive proposition. It meant that the colonies that provided such soldiers (mostly in New England) spent considerable sums on providing military support to the British Army. Although they were reimbursed by the British treasury, they were left paying 58.4 percent of the £1.5 million that Britain spent on colonial troops, showing that places like Massachusetts had reason to be resentful in the 1760s of an imperial state that downplayed the colony's financial and manpower contribution to British victory in 1763.[64]

As well, Aaron Graham, a historian of eighteenth-century Britain who has moved into doing research on Jamaica, has contributed to early American history the insights from British historians of the fiscal-military state. He has written five articles on the state in Jamaica: two on legislators and legislation, one on towns as a focus of imperial expenditure, one with me on taxation policies in Jamaica from the 1730s to the 1780s, and a more wide-ranging study of corruption and contracting during the Seven Years' War. In this last article, he downplays ideas that such corruption was either distinctive or contributed much to American disenchantment with imperial rule. He argues that the experience of legislative expansion after the Seven Years' War, similar to what had happened in Britain a generation earlier, often had the secondary consequence of schooling local elites in the advantages and the processes of legislation. One of his principal findings is that attitudes to taxation varied considerably throughout British America with White colonists in Jamaica happy to pay much more than in the plantation colonies and Middle Colonies of North America, as long as they controlled the allocation and distribution of taxes so that it was spent on security and on preventing enslaved rebellion.[65]

The state, however, is beginning to attract historical attention, as can be seen in an article by Jessica Choppin Roney on the failed attempt to create a trans-Appalachian state in 1784 to be called Franklin after the near-octogenarian founding father, Benjamin Franklin. Roney shows that the failure to create this state illustrates "how a small settler revolt on the periphery of a powerful empire developed into and intersected with messy and violent contests for control of the land and resources deep into the North American interior and in the Caribbean." Emphasizing continuity over change in the transit to nationhood, Roney stresses how new governmental structures were fashioned more from below than from above, with governments forced always to respond to settler actions and criticisms. Settlers in this region were now having to deal with "a closer but deeply unstable metropole" rather than with the more distant but safer and more predictable British imperial center. That increased instability was even more significant for the Cherokee and Watangan nations. They had to make choices: the Watangans chose to cast their lot with the new state of North Carolina, while the Cherokees opted for pan-Indian alliances under the umbrella of British support. Neither was satisfactory, as these choices reduced their local autonomy. Roney suggests that relationships between settlers and the state were symbiotic, with the two sides operating in tandem. "Settler-driven expansion," she contends, "did not precede the state; it required the state, as settler communities well knew." Roney's analysis shows the possibilities that can arise from detailed attention to the state and how power worked in theory and in practice as part of state formation. Her work connects world and ground in ways that feed into longstanding early American concerns with regionalism while connecting to the larger discourses of imperialism and nation-building in Britain and in the United States.[66]

VI

The imperial turn has strongly affected the historiography of the American Revolution. Michael McDonnell and David Waldstreicher were commissioned to write a survey of articles in *WMQ* on the subject of the American Revolution published in that journal since its World War II refounding. They see a decided move to neoimperial approaches since the fiftieth-year anniversary of *WMQ* in 1993, with early American historians taking their cues from new Atlantic and continental perspectives, stretching and blurring temporal and spatial boundaries. These studies of the last thirty years see the American Revolution in less parochial and less exceptional ways than in the period of Morgan's revolutionary epoch; more attention is paid than previously on explaining, perhaps justifying, why Britain took the actions that it did. The emerging scholarship in the field, they show, has the entanglements of empire very much in view. This neoimperial tendency in revolutionary scholarship is a principal reason why historians shy away from looking at the causes of the revolution. As McDonnell and Waldstreicher state, "A generation's worth of literature suggests that long- and short-term developments to the east, west and south of the Thirteen colonies created an imperial crisis in which the political and economic stakes were high for all concerned." The result is a decentering of the republican, liberal, and democratic aspects of the emerging nation in favor of imperial and transnational continuities. It is less that the American Revolution shapes the writing of early America than the other way around: Atlantic and global history now informs how scholars see the American Revolution beginning, developing, and concluding.[67]

This new imperial approach to the American Revolution makes it hard to see how it could ever have occurred. The British Empire was effective; the White people within it were happy and prosperous, if often resentful that the benefits of the empire they professed to love were extended to other people, such as Indigenes. And the causes of the American Revolution were mysterious, while the extent of revolutionary change is less extensive than previously thought. All of these arguments, through the imperial prism, suggest continuity rather than change. One article on imperialism and early America that has significant implications for how we view the causes of the American Revolution in this way is Katherine Carté Engel's comprehensive treatment of how Protestants in the eighteenth-century British Empire became connected in vibrant transatlantic networks around a shared commitment to the ideology of imperialism.⁶⁸ In short, it is the ideology of imperialism that drove ideologies of Protestantism rather than ideologies of republicanism, as was stressed in the literature of the 1970s and 1980s.

Carté wants to move away from previous debates about whether Protestantism united or divided Americans in the thirteen colonies over conflicts with Britain and declines to express an opinion over whether religion became more or less important over time. Her argument is that Protestantism was important, was institutionally powerful in the colonies as well as in Britain, and that empire was an important glue in that strength. Empire, she argues, united Protestants (which was a diverse and tolerant body, including Huguenots, Dissenters, and Anglicans, though not Quakers or Moravians) rather than Protestants uniting the empire. The Protestant churches were connected in multiple ways, both within British America and with Britain, and were a vital means whereby imperialism was strengthened in America. "By communicating across the empire," she argues, "British Protestantism developed a collective perspective that prevented its institutions from being turned against the empire." That collective support for imperialism meant that the churches were helpless when imperial conflict developed in the 1760s and 1770s. Protestantism thus played little part in the coming of the revolution, though it was an essential way in which colonists were knitted together in supporting imperial goals for most of the eighteenth century. The effect of the American Revolution, however, was massive, "a fracture within its heart," taking away at a stroke a highly successful and unified Protestant community that had been "a safety valve for controversy, preventing historic religious dimensions from growing into casus belli."⁶⁹

Carté does not mention Catholics in her article, but where Catholics sat within the Atlantic world is a matter of great interest as a way of defining the limits of expansions of ideas of which people might be incorporated as subjects into the empire.⁷⁰ Jessica Harland-Jacobs contends, contrary to a literature suggesting that British America was defined by anti-Catholicism, that the clearest trend after 1763 was toward accommodation and assimilation, sometimes an accommodation forced on reluctant Protestants by British statesmen with a wide view of imperial politics. Aaron Wallis outlines in a case study of Grenada how this accommodation operated. Wallis sees more political conflict over Catholic incorporation than does Harland-Jacobs, but both authors see Catholics as being included rather than excluded from colonial life after the Seven Years' War ended in 1763. For Harland-Jacobs, this relatively unproblematic assimilation shows how empires are "expansive polities that must engage in complex negotiations of diversity management." Wallis sees a harder edge to this story, arguing that the forced assimilation of French Catholics to British laws and customs came about from an insistence by the British that the conquered had to submit to what the conquerors wanted them to do. Nevertheless, both writers see Catholic incorporation into imperial structures as fashioned more by the cultural appeal of Anglicization rather than from coercive authority.[71]

How Catholics were incorporated or excluded from social and political life in late seventeenth-century and early eighteenth-century England has also been addressed by Carys Brown in ways that are suggestive for other places in the Atlantic world. Brown suggests that even for militant Catholics in an England in which anti-Catholicism was virulent—and Brown's case study of the Rookwoods of Suffolk is of an uncompromising Catholic gentry family, with two family members having been executed for treason over three generations—communities were prepared to tolerate Catholics. This tolerance included allowing a member of the Rookwood family to return from exile, something thought desirable when such Catholics were substantial contributors to the local community and its economy.[72]

Nancy Christie does not deal with religion per se in her temporally expansive study of how French Catholics in Quebec aligned themselves with British laws and institutions, but her work fits within a literature that sees Catholic assimilation to British ways as happening all over the British Empire in the second half of the eighteenth century. She argues that the key to such assimilation to Anglicization after the Conquest was French Catholic men's appreciation of British patriarchal values. They identified as much with being male as with being French, seeing themselves as similar to English-speaking men in wanting to be masters of their own homes.[73] Michael Breidenback reinforces such arguments that downplay anti-Catholicism as a force in prerevolutionary British America. He describes how the Catholic doctrine of conciliarism, which denied papal infallibility, was compatible with republicanism and allowed moderate Catholics, such as Charles Carroll from a very wealthy Maryland Catholic family, to support American independence out of his commitment to toleration and religious liberty and his fierce opposition to the idea of an established church.[74]

VII

Given how much attention is paid to slavery in general in early American history writing, historians have also looked at slavery as an imperial issue, paying especial attention to the most important legal case connecting imperialism to slavery, the *Somerset* case of 1772, in which a British judge, Lord Mansfield, ruled in favor of an enslaved man protesting against being forced by his owner to be sent to plantation America. This case has attracted a large amount of attention, including an article by David Waldstreicher as part of a biography of Phillis Wheatley. Waldstreicher memorably describes Wheatley as "Jefferson's Kryptonite." He sees *Somerset* as very important in propelling revolutionary outrage against a perceived lack of British support for slavery.[75]

Matthew Mason, by contrast, sees *Somerset* as being virtually ignored in North America and argues it was unimportant as a cause of revolution. North Americans in 1772 should have been concerned about this case as it showed British willingness to consider slavery un-British and illustrated there were limits to British support of planters. But they were not, Mason argues. Planters in Virginia and South Carolina, he suggests, had "greater concerns," such as protesting British actions in New England and even more so the financial crisis of 1772. He argues that "protesting against *Somerset* would have been politically awkward as it would have cast [planters] as friends of slavery, not liberty."[76] In addition, Mason argues that the founding era was not a "missed opportunity" to abolish slavery.[77] In his view, emancipating the enslaved in the areas where slavery was strong in the thirteen colonies was impossible given rapid demographic increase and how much effort would have been needed from a powerful state to either compensate slaveowners for their freed property or relocate free people to some distant asylum to keep them away from hostile Whites.[78]

Mason takes a "weak" state approach, arguing that it was inconceivable in the 1780s for an American government to be so activist and powerful as to free a rapidly growing population of enslaved people. He concludes that "treating the Founders as omnipotent gives them, ironically enough, too much credit for what they did accomplish, in relation to slavery or any other political issue."[79] Mason's argument, that there was no "missed opportunity," accords with the general tendency in early American history writing on imperialism to note that empires were better at managing diversity rather than in implementing coercive authority, at least against the White settlers they depended upon for their support.

VIII

What is remarkable about writings on empire in early American history is the positive views about how empires functioned. Paul Gilje, for example, is enthusiastic about how successful the British were in increasing commerce with the Americas in the long eighteenth century. Unlike the many historians who see the British empire as inherently expansionist, he argues that an emphasis on internal expansion as part of government policy only occurred after 1812 and was not inevitable. The empire prior to the War of 1812 was, in his view, based around commerce, not conquest. For Gilje, the British Empire in America was a commercial success story. He concludes, in ways that run counter to many of the arguments presented in literature covered in this book, that "despite episodic violence and Anglo-American aspirations for land, most of the time indigenous people and whites managed to live in relative peace, engaging in trade and finance."[80] Jonathan Eacott is more restrained that Gilje about the success of British imperialism in fostering trade, but he too sees Britain as very successful in developing colonial trade as an intrinsic part of its eighteenth-century foreign relations. He notes that "in developing their early modern empire, Britons used leverage to advance their trade advantages, using the assets of a strong foreign power to increase their capabilities and wealth, prizing open one market with assets from another."[81] Jacob Soll reinforces this point when he emphasizes the interplay between mercantilism and laissez-faire economics in Britain's and France's empires. He argues that the remarkable economic expansion of both empires was "based far more on private/state partnerships and close collaboration than on either any victory of one state over the other or the triumph of intervention or economic laissez-faire."[82]

The view of empire dominant in the current literature is dramatically different from older views of a hugely inefficient imperial state. Jack Greene summarizes this view of the imperial state. He quips that no one before 1763 attributed the stunning success of growth in British America to imperial bureaucracy. The Board of Trade did its best, especially under the skilled leadership of its long-time official Martin Bladen, who largely ran the board between 1717 and 1741 and was responsible for appointing some of the best governors ever to serve in the British Atlantic empire. Yet neither the Board of Trade nor outstanding governors like Benning Wentworth in New Hampshire, Edward Trelawney and Sir Henry Moore in Jamaica, Sir William Gooch in Virginia, William Shirley in Massachusetts, or William Bull and James Glen in South

Carolina had the ability to deal with the vast number of imperial issues flowing from the Americas to Britain. As C. A. Bayly observes of a later period, "British colonial affairs were largely ... mediated through groups of complaisant mercantile elites and creoles."[83] Contrary to Jacob Soll, Greene argues that the colonies developed despite, rather than because of, Britain's imperial bureaucracy, citing the agricultural writer Arthur Young, who observed in 1772 that what imperial officials did or thought hardly mattered "because the colonies did the business for them; their increase caused the national trade to increase, and all went on silently, but prosperously."[84]

Greene's view is not how recent writers have seen this topic. The imperial turn in early American history has transformed scholarly assessments of the imperial state. It is no longer seen as the paradigmatic weak state. Instead, writers, especially those scholars writing about the British fiscal-military state, stress how strong and active it was, especially in providing funds and troops to keep the colonies safe and investing in the infrastructure needs of British American settler societies.[85] Indeed, before 1763, when it came adrift in North America (though not in other parts of the globe), the British Empire made few mistakes. The major achievement of the rulers of the imperial state was to recognize imperial difference and to resist calls from the Board of Trade to try and create an integrated and centralized imperial system. As Patrick Griffin argues, "The empire resembled a rabbit warren of differing arrangements passed under different monarchs for different reasons to address different problems."[86] Both in Britain and in France, where the imperial state was also quite effective in managing the combative and sometimes creative tension between imperial dictates and local autonomy, rulers understood that a strong state could not compel one part of the empire to act like another part of the empire.[87] The imperial state, nevertheless, was a powerful beast, even if it did not always choose to exercise the power that it had, balancing central government's desire for rationalization, standardization, and centralization with a recognition that each imperial place had its own history and its own distinctiveness that needed to be acknowledged.[88]

The British Empire, in short, worked (as did the French Empire, at least before 1756). It oversaw remarkable growth; it prevented major colonial disputes, at least before 1776; and it came down hard on its internal opponents, such as Scottish Jacobites in 1745 and Jamaican enslaved rebels in 1760. It had a hard fist that it chose to exercise against Highlanders, Indigenes, and Africans while treating White elites softly. Poor Whites also experienced the harshness of the state, either as criminals in the ferocious justice system of London or as soldiers in the all-conquering British Army. Peter Way provides an illuminating and sobering account of the tyranny fundamental to the running of the British Army in which it, in the pursuit of obtaining a cowed and obedient labor force of soldiers willing to kill for country, insisted on "waging a war of terror against its own men, maiming and killing many to coerce all to do their duty."[89] Way notes the similarities between soldiers—"another form of coerced labor in the capitalist project"—and enslaved people. Like enslaved people, soldiers resisted their harsh treatment and like enslaved people suffered the full brunt of state violence against them for their noncompliance. Deserters, for example, were punished ferociously, being whipped to the point of death (the average whipping was a mind-boggling 742 lashes, and many men received more than 1,000) or else being executed (one in four soldiers tried under military rule were sentenced to capital punishment). Way concludes that "the army settled on exemplary punishment to provoke terror in its men with the intention of promoting order."[90]

An efficient imperial state was founded on sound bureaucratic principles. Asheesh Siddique argues, in an examination of "Instructions" and "Queries" from the Board of Trade, that it was documents that held the empire together, not the imperial constitution. "Through the technology of paper," he writes in two articles that draw on a current interest in how archives are created and transmitted to posterity, "the constitutional edifice of empire was enacted and sustained across vast oceanic distance."[91] Siddique here reinforces the important work of Marie Houllemare, who carefully explicates how paperwork and bureaucracy in the French Empire, especially in law making, increasingly bound the colonial peripheries to the metropolitan center.[92] Law was as important as paper, as Edward Cavanaugh explains in a study of law officers and their advice to government on colonial constitutions. Tellingly, Cavanaugh depicts an imperial state, in which the attorney-general and solicitor-general were significant players, that responded better to colonial differences in the second quarter of the eighteenth century than it did after 1760 and did so through using the royal prerogative rather than the authority of parliament as justification for its actions.[93]

David Chan Smith offers a case study in support of these views of the imperial state in an examination of a British parliamentary enquiry in 1749 into the Hudson's Bay Company (HBC) as it operated in the northern reaches of what it is today Canada. Led by Arthur Dobbs, a member of the British parliament with a dislike of chartered companies, parliament charged the HBC with failing to maintain a positive relationship with Indigenous people and not forming a barrier against French commercial interests. It was a replay of sorts of the concerted campaign against the Royal African Company that led to its demise and replacement by private traders in 1698. Smith shows that things had changed by 1749. The HBC was able to successfully defend itself against such charges and showed that it had been misrepresented in a politically motivated campaign. It was supported by significant imperial players in London and within the company, including the London mercantile elite that had so opposed earlier state monopolies. The testimony of HBC officials revealed, in ways that Jacob Soll notes were true for the empire as a whole, a private-public corporation functioning effectively in a competitive environment. Their testimonies showed that the company sustained Indigenous goodwill, held off French challenges, and imported substantial numbers of beaver skins into Britain. Its officials persuaded parliament that it was a socially beneficent corporation, embedded within larger social networks that exercised responsibly its duties to a range of communities in Britain and in Canada.[94] It was not closed down; indeed, the HBC continues into the present.

The imperial reforms after the end of the Seven Years' War were meant to transform a negligent imperial system. Historians currently don't consider this system as being very bad before the war. But contemporaries thought it was not working properly when they argued for a tighter and more authoritarian imperial system in discussions that occurred in Britain, France, and Spain in the 1760s.[95] Contemporary ambitions for an improved imperial system were seldom achieved. Matthew Dziennik provides a case study, examined in the previous chapter in the context of slavery in West Africa, of an imperial reform in this period—the establishment of Britain's first West African colony, in Senegambia in 1763—that failed in ways that the HBC did not. Senegambia's failure is important because it outlines how the imperial reforms that were instituted after the Seven Years' War did not just fail in North America but did so in other imperial settings. The big change in British thinking after the Seven Years' War was that they were no longer content with giving state support to private commercial concerns and letting those commercial companies run things largely under their own control, on the model of the East India Company in the early eighteenth century.[96] They wanted political control also, through creating loyal and stable colonies based on direct imperial rule. The problem in Senegambia was that the British state was less powerful than African elites who wanted trade and economic expansion without any political management. By 1784 Britain's plans in West Africa were in ruins. The failure of Senegambia, however, was instructive as a pointer to British imperial policy in Africa in the nineteenth century. Britain felt that interference in West Africa was desirable, in order to protect the slave trade at a time when that trade was supported in Britain, and to advance abolition in the early nineteenth century, when the slave trade was no longer an institution that Britons wanted to uphold.[97]

The implications of the imperial turn still have a good deal of mileage in them, even if it is foolish to predict a future, especially as the forces of globalization in the 2020s are taking a battering from a renewed nationalism. One of the consequences of a #VastEarlyAmerica approach, however, will surely be the consideration of multiple imperialisms in early America. This chapter has mainly concentrated on one empire—the British—and how early American history can be increasingly folded within British history. But there is evidence that historians of other empires are doing similar projects, mostly in book rather than article form, in which comparative imperialism is a key theme.[98] As Allan Greer writes, in his survey of the field from a Canadian perspective, "If our aim is to emancipate colonial history from the anachronistic habits of thought established by national historiography, it is important to more than simply expand our spatial range. It is also a matter of examining familiar subjects from unfamiliar vantage points."[99] That means looking at many imperial perspectives, bearing in mind that the colonial formations we study grew, took shape, and in some cases died before the start of nation-states in the Americas.

PART III
Traditional Themes

6

Gender

∽

I

The movement of Europeans and Africans across the Atlantic brought into sharp relief the multiple ways that gender relations operated across these vast spaces and within Indigenous societies.[1] But gender was also crucial to imperialism and needs to be treated within that context as well as being a principal manifestation of how difference was managed in early modern empires. Gender is central to the "new" imperial history, as Kathleen Wilson has stressed. She insists that "the history of the intimate and the 'private' lay at the heart of the public projects of trade, colonization, and the 'arts of discovery.'" In garrisons, forts, factories, plantation societies, and urban centers the utilization of enslaved, Indigenous, subaltern, and "respectable" women's bodies, the regulation of sexuality and lineage, and the demarcation of the roles and privileges of masculinity and femininity constituted in no small part the substance of imperial power and dominion.[2]

Various gender systems—European, African, Indigenous—operated in early America, shaping imperialism, as Wilson notes, in numerous ways. The return of imperialism as a major organizing principle in the field has changed gender studies considerably. It has, to an extent, reinvigorated research in gender history, a field in which, Terri Snyder argued in a survey of early American women's history in 2012, "an explicit focus on women as subjects has waned over the last decade or so."[3] The major change has been one that reflects the drift in historical writing in general, from the concentration on the local to a fascination with the global. In the heyday of town and community studies, scholars assumed that early American lives, especially those of White women, were defined by "persistent localism" and by the relative isolation in which they lived, not much connected to wider social, economic, or cultural patterns; their existences were dominated by face-to-face interactions and by personal relationships.⁴ These assumptions have largely disappeared, as historians strive to see how women fit into larger global patterns.

In the traditional telling of the making of empires, men feature heavily, as discoverers, traders, imperial officials, intermediaries, and as expansionist settlers. It points to one of the most important, if underrecognized facts about early America: it was a heavily male environment, especially in the beginnings of colonization. Women were not great fans of moving to America. They seldom did so willingly, meaning that seventeenth-century colonies were heavily skewed toward a male population. Even after natural population growth took away that bias toward men in British North America (though not in the West Indies), the settler colonies established by Britain and France in the New World were highly masculine places, where masculine values such as competition, aggression, bravery, carousing, and a strong devotion to achieving the main chance and making money at all costs were even more prevalent than they had been in Britain.⁵

If empire is about managing difference, then gender is an important category to consider. Along with race, gender and the notion of "gender frontiers" are where managing differences between people was most consequential. The metaphor that a well-governed state was like that of a family in good order had great purchase in both early America and eighteenth-century Britain. The household, however, was as often a place of conflict as of harmony. And it raises questions that reflect older treatments of gender as much as investigations done recently within the context of imperial gender frontiers. For example, Enlightenment figures increasingly in the eighteenth century saw identity in the form of "fraternity," so that identity became coded increasingly male.⁶

II

The study of gender in early America remains a surprisingly specialist area, compared to its prominence in other periods of American history and within eighteenth-century British history. Terri Snyder notes that most early American historians do not write on gender and most US women's historians do not write about early America.⁷ It is still the case that historians do not think about gender issues even in cases where a gender perspective seems natural and illuminating. The literature in the New History of Capitalism movement, for example, has been criticized for not addressing gender except tangentially. Amy Dru Stanley bluntly declares that "the emergent grand narrative of the New History of Capitalism is blind to feminism, gender and sex difference," while Ellen Hartigan-O'Connor suggests that women exist as minor characters in the history of capitalism and that the consideration of women in the economy as principal actors has gotten worse with the advent of the New History of Capitalism movement, especially as "financialization has replaced industrialization as the engine of nineteenth-century transformations."[8]

These absences testify to the importance of intersectionality—in not compartmentalizing gender as a separate category so that one need not address gender when writing on class and capitalism. Gender, Greta La Fleur reminds scholars in a 2014 article, is a capacious concept. She urges historians to do more to recognize the instability of gender as a way of analyzing early American behavior and suggests that they might connect their studies to those of the present as, she contends, gender in eighteenth-century British North America and England was similar to how we understand gender today—flexible, contingent, and non-self-identical. Early America had periodic bouts of "gender trouble," but these, La Fleur argues, "were as variegated, and as regionally, racially and economically specific as they are in our own time."[9]

Some traditional themes in women's history, such as whether the colonial period was a "golden age" for women as their relative scarcity increased their economic power, have long disappeared.[10] After all, the notion of a "golden age" is very race specific. Black women's experience in British and French America was never "golden." In the journal literature I examined, one of the only hints of this once-vibrant theme in women's history, as well as a concomitant desire to chronicle female contributions to a history from which they had been largely excluded, is in articles by Christine Walker on White women in Jamaica. She sees White women as active commercial agents in Jamaica's mercantile sector and as firmly committed to slavery as an institution. They shared little sense of sisterhood with Black or free colored women (a theme confirmed in Erin Trahey's account of free women of color).[11] Walker argues that Jamaican White women forged a distinctive sexual culture in which their scarcity in the population and their inherited wealth when they became rich widows meant they enjoyed remarkable sexual and economic freedom. Walker wants to restore these women historiographically to the prominence they had in real life, "question[ing] the double erasure of both women and the slaves they owned from the conjoined histories of empire and slavery." These White women were vital players in imperial projects, meaning that reconfiguring women's roles within families "aided in the flourishing of Jamaica's profoundly exploitative and lucrative form of colonialism."[12]

The move from recovering the lived experience of women in early America to examining how they were represented and how they represented themselves has been highly productive, not least in questioning how archival materials relating to women have been created and how they should be carefully interpreted. Some things, however, have been lost in the process.[13] Little has been done recently in establishing female standards of living and material well-being. The standard of living debate for women was once a vibrant subfield in the economic history of early America, notably for the colonial Chesapeake, but while this debate has continued to be important in British and early modern African history, it has faded away within the history of early America.[14] We have no recent publications that examine the standard of living of any group of women or children in early America that might test whether Benjamin Franklin was right to be so confident that American population growth and female fertility were underpinned by women's high standard of living.

This lively area of debate in English economic history should be one of interest to scholars of early American women's history, given the importance of the empirical findings about women's and children's contributions to the relatively strong English standards of living in the eighteenth century, the development in England of a "high-wage" economy, and the move from the "industrious revolution" described by Jan de Vries to an industrial revolution. It is a debate that has been advanced in several significant articles by Sara Horrell, Jane Humphries, and Jacob Weisdorf.[15] These three authors have established that the contributions of women and children were vital to getting ordinary families in eighteenth-century England over the "respectability" threshold, so that families had disposable incomes over what was needed for bare subsistence. When the urban working class and agricultural laborers achieved "respectable" household standards of living, England could escape Malthusian stagnation and was able to move into an era of setback-free growth, culminating in the first Industrial Revolution. Traditional accounts of English standards of living have been highly masculine in nature, based around the earnings of male workers employed full time (250 days a year) in lucrative occupations such as within the London building trades. Horrell, Humphries, and Weisdorf argue that using a fully employed man in a highly paid occupation skews the analysis, because more people worked in other, less well-paid occupations; few men were able to work as many days as

250 per annum; and household income was only maintained through earnings from female work and the contributions of children's labor.

The picture they paint of standards of living once females' and children's labor is included is less rosy than when just considering male employees. The female labor market was segmented, with single women able to work full time but married women confined to casual labor and to less desirable and worse paid jobs. Women, especially married women, tended to do less work over time—the peak women's involvement in York in the workforce was in 1450, followed by a steady decline before picking up a little in the early eighteenth century. If we include women and children in accounts of standards of living in England, we see a considerable reduction in the days that are worked per household and thus a less sustained upward trend in the data. Horrell, Humphries, and Weisdorf note that "men's pay over the year alone [was] clearly insufficient to sustain their families until the early decades of the nineteenth century."[16]

Women's work mattered: "It was the blood, sweat and tears of our family workers in their quest for respectability that turned scientific acumen and inventiveness into the widening flow of goods and services that presaged and then marked the Industrial Revolution." They note that "women and children were mainstays in providing labour for the woolen and small metal goods industries and they made up the additional labour on which the industrious revolution relied" and which led to England becoming a high wage economy en route to industrialization.[17] Most of the benefits of female labor and their crucial role in increased consumption, however, did not accrue to women. These benefits went to men; women remained confined to low paid, intermittent work in overstocked labor markets. By the late eighteenth century, married women and their children in industrial settings were more dependent on men than before.

Early American historians have not yet picked up on this argument, which makes for a lacuna in women's history, but historians of other places, such as West Africa, have drawn on the methodologies of the standard of living debate to work out standards of living in their areas. Despite massive archival absences and gaps in data collection, Klas Rönnbäck has made convincing calculations of wages and living standards among West African laborers, notably canoemen and their families, working for the British Royal African Company in the first half of the eighteenth century. He shows that canoemen's standards of living were on a par to those enjoyed in other parts of the world such as much of Asia and southern and eastern Europe, if not eighteenth-century Britain or North America.[18] It proves an obvious point, though one denied by eighteenth-century proslavers who pretended that African lives improved once they crossed the Atlantic Ocean, which was that Africans enslaved in the New World suffered worse living standards than they had enjoyed in West Africa. That decline in living standards was especially pronounced for female field hands in places like Jamaica, where inequality between Whites and Blacks was extraordinarily high and where enslaved women unfortunate enough to work in the dreadful environment of sugar plantations did not get enough food to sustain themselves while they worked in such harsh conditions that their reproductive capacities were irrevocably harmed and their life expectancies dramatically reduced.[19]

It was different in West Africa, where the more privileged female traders living in coastal towns like Saint Louis and Gorée, in present-day Senegal, were, Bronwen Everill shows, significant economic actors as "producers, consumers, active participants in the marketplace, inheritors of property and managers of the household."[20] Everill takes de Vries's concept of an industrious revolution and applies it to Saint Louis and Gorée to argue that women could participate in this industrious revolution because the commercial demands of port cities allowed them to mobilize household and enslaved labor in ways that allowed them to purchase luxury goods. Women dominated these towns, being twice as numerous as men, and they were extremely avid consumers of European goods, partly due to intermarriage with European traders. They used their household power, including control over enslaved people, to acquire consumer goods such as French shirts, Moroccan shoes, and lots of jewelry. Women did so in societies where such displays of wealth were equated closely to power. In the process they intensified household production. Slavery was central to this industrious revolution, as described by Everill: "Domestic slavery allowed women to accumulate capital, earn interest and rent and invest, all while staying largely within the domestic sphere of the household."[21]

III

Terri Snyder commends gender studies of early America for showing how we look at difference and for enabling historians to examine different patterns of subordination: those that existed between Blacks and Whites, between settlers and Indigenes, and between classes of men. Attention to women also makes us conscious of how women's status was separate to that of men. Snyder highlights the importance of marriage choices and marriage experiences as an example of how attention to gender relations informs larger patterns. Three articles in this sample deal specifically with marriage as an early American institution.[22] In addition, Sara Damiano examines how wives managed husbands' estates when menfolk were temporarily absent, notably on war service during the American Revolution. She shows that such delegation demonstrated how much trust men placed in their female relatives and wives as people able to conduct business on their behalf, outlining how we can't think of economic activities in early America without taking into consideration what Carole Shammas describes as a varied pattern of household government that changed depending on race, class, and location, with some places being propitious to marriage (the European-settled areas of North America) and some, like the borderlands of continental America and the Caribbean, being "marriage-challenged zones."[23]

Implicit in Damiano's work is a negation of the idea of separate spheres for White settlers: women dominant in the home and the private realm; men superior in the public sphere and in work. That White women exercised active agency outside the home is central to recent scholarship. Vivian Bruce Conger, for example, illustrates how Deborah Read Franklin and Sally Franklin Bache, Benjamin Franklin's wife and daughter, involved themselves in imperial and revolutionary politics, exploiting common ideas of female virtue to have their voices heard, though in different ways, since Sally was open to female active agency in ways her mother was not prepared to countenance.[24] White women's roles as businesspeople is addressed by Susan Brandt in her study of White women as medical entrepreneurs in the American Revolution and by Inge Dornan in her work on White women as slaveholders in the South Carolina plantation economy.[25] Historians stress how White women were imperially minded and supportive of imperial projects—there is no article on female rebels or female rebellion. They occasionally strained against the strictures of patriarchy, including, as Sharon Block notes, having to cope with their appearance and physical beauty being continually scrutinized. But there is little appetite in the literature for seeing early America as being a gendered battleground, at least for White women.[26]

British scholars writing on gender are more inclined to be concerned with conflict and transgression. They work within a well-established literature on politeness, which draws from the work of Paul Langford from the late 1980s and which has been central to how historians have conceived of gender relations in the last thirty years. Politeness served as a safety valve in a dynamic and changing eighteenth-century Georgian society that helped to cement stability into that world. It helped to accommodate the restless forces of middling aspirations and imbued common expectations and values across a very broad propertied order.[27] Jonah Miller, for example, examines "stop and search" processes in London, whereby authorities could investigate presumed female criminals by examining invasively their bodies, especially those of poor women, whose personal bodily integrity could be violated easily as they were deemed dangerous, unruly, and in need of constant monitoring.[28]

Garthine Walker also looks at gender outside the prism of politeness. She examines discourses around rape in the early eighteenth century, as represented in popular crime reports. She notes both the low rates of conviction for rape and how it was understood that rape had to be accompanied by extreme violence for a rape conviction to succeed. Her point is that such accounts of rape show the way that this crime was heavily shaped by misogyny and patriarchal double standards.[29] Lisa Wynne-Smith looks at the limitations of politeness in another respect. Through the use of interdisciplinary evidence from medicine and psychology, she examines how trauma operated in the records of the highly dysfunctional gentry Newdigate family of Warwickshire, creating what she calls a pain narrative to understand terrible family disputes.[30] Soile Ylivuori examines female honor and the various meanings associated with female chastity for eighteenth-century English gentlewomen. She shows that the reality and the public understanding of female chastity were not as far removed from notions of male sexual honor as usually understood. What constituted chastity was a highly negotiable concept. It was dependent less on any evidence of physical chasteness and was more dependent on external signs that demonstrated that women exhibited the requisite signs of female purity, even if not physically chaste. She argues that a public loss of a chaste reputation did not necessarily lead to social disgrace and could be compensated through other performative means.[31]

A double standard thus existed but was not absolute. Kate Gibson expands on this fluidity within understandings of sexual behavior in an examination of how aristocratic women, such as Lady Dacre and the Countess of Pembroke, were prepared to act as mothers to the illegitimate offspring of their husbands. She argues that at least in the higher ranks of society, and reflected in literature of the period, women doing "mothering work" by looking after their husband's illegitimate offspring could present themselves as appropriate without meeting any (or much) social disapproval. A great deal of emphasis was placed on familial reputation in eighteenth-century Britain, where women were often defined by their ability to be loving mothers of large families as good stepmothers, even to illegitimate children, in ways that avoided snickering about cuckolding. This double standard was negotiated in ways that worked to some kinds of female advantage and in doing so advanced claims to feminine virtue, increasing elite women's social capital as powerful matriarchs.[32] Another article on elite women, Hannah Greig and Amanda Vickery's outline of how politicians spent their day, shows—in an analysis that follows Peter Mandler's claims that work on elite gender politics was "Namier in petticoats"—the crucial ways in which female powerbrokers operated levees and courts that lessened the impact of homosocial places like parliament.[33]

Elite women are often the focus of scholarship on gender in eighteenth-century England, but Karen Harvey has written several important articles that look outside the narrow confines of middling to aristocratic women. She interrogates the very idea of gender in letters written by middling people between 1726 and 1827, in which women discussed their sense of the relationship between body, mind, and self—embodiment, in short. She finds that gender, or the sense of the body as determined by its sexual and gendered nature, was relatively unimportant in how people experienced their bodies.[34] Instead, letter writers' relationships, religion, or life stages determined how they thought of their bodies. She thus contradicts Dror Wahrman's influential thesis that individual identity, including gender, was based around notions of a physical, naturalized body, with gender increasingly fixed in ideas of biology.[35] It was difficult for eighteenth-century people to view their bodies in biological ways when they did not know how bodies worked. "The experience of embodiment," Harvey argues "was likely to have been affected as much by age as by historical change, reflecting the fact that embodiment is a lived process . . . profoundly affected by the physical state of our corporeal bodies."[36]

Harvey's interest in embodiment and how it relates to gender and sexuality is exemplified in two articles on the notorious case of Mary Toft, a poor woman from Godalming, Surrey, reputed to have given birth to rabbits rather than humans in a *cause célèbre* from 1726. Harvey draws on an impressive mastery of other disciplines, notably forensic psychology, to write an extended detective story about what happened in this remarkable, ridiculous, and tragic case. She casts doubt on the accepted story of Toft as a con woman who played on local superstitions and instead argues that she was a victim of a concerted plot from female kin and other women to try and manipulate the public for financial gain. She places Toft within the context of trauma and abuse and contends that she was a victim of other women exercising their unlawful authority over Mary Toft's body. Thus, Harvey transforms this well-known tale from being about eighteenth-century ideas of the body, about monstrous births, and about fluid ideas of human identity into a story that is rooted in the social and economic context of poor people in a Surrey village. It is thus not a story of knowledge and ideas about medicine but an exploration of the politics of family, neighborhood, town, country, and metropolis. She shows the Toft family as disreputable and marginalized members of the town's laboring poor, thus writing a rare history of ordinary people in eighteenth-century Britain. Mary Toft's deceptions and her victimization were part of a moral panic, Harvey argues, about the dangerous actions of the rural poor, so that her "generation of rabbits exploited the reproductive power of laboring women just as law enforcers were increasingly seeking to bring that power under their control." Mary and the poor people in her family and community were "regarded as real threats in a social world in which ordinary people (and the poor and women in particular) were seen as a tangible and organized threat to the social order."[37]

IV

The concerns of historians of gender in early America are related in many ways to the themes that interest historians of gender and gender relations in eighteenth-century Britain, but they are also distinctive, with a focus on the gender and familial interrelationships between people of different conditions, and especially different races, and on explicating how the history of gender is influenced by colonialism and European settlement. Gender historians of early America over the past decade have focused on how early America was a place of "gender frontiers."[38] Kathleen Wilson connects gender to the performative nature of state power, paying particular attention to three places in the eighteenth-century British Empire. She argues that the workings of the imperial state can only be understood through an appreciation of household governance, including the centrality of White male privilege, marital strategies, and mixed-race concubinage. In her view, "Problems of governance, discipline and population permeated early modern forms of colonial rule," with the family as "the model for and instrument of authority with an irreducible political importance."[39]

To illustrate her thesis, Wilson examines the performative nature of empire in mid-eighteenth-century Jamaica. Colonial governance, she suggests, "lay in the realm of state-making and racial making, as the imposition of racialized and gendered categories of family, household, and national belonging became critical aspects of administration." Jamaica posed a particular problem to a system of governance concerned with family, as its White subjects faced demographic disaster and its terrorized Black population was hugely numerically dominant and thus dangerous for White people. White rule, Wilson argues, was uneasily maintained and was done so "through theatrical performances of privilege and terror."[40] White Jamaicans' Achilles heel was their vulgar manners and their unconventional family policies and penchant for sexual racial mixing, leading to widespread concubinage and mixed-race families.[41] Metropolitan observers attacked White Jamaicans' family life as "an ostentatious transgression of English standards of civility and rule." Irregular families inspired imperial critiques: "The fate of nation, colony and empire was tied to individual sexual choice; the well-governed colony and the self-governing individual went hand in hand."[42]

Wilson cites William Blackstone to insist that the model for social order was familial so that "individuals of the state, like members of a well-governed family, are bound to conform their general behaviors to the rule of propriety, good neighborhood and good manners." The problem with gender and family in Jamaica, however, was that its population, Black and White, did not conform to this patriarchal vision of domestic harmony. No matter how rich White Jamaicans were, their chaotic family and gender lives were worrying because, Wilson states, "it was the regulation of individual and collective behavior that polity depended upon." If White women in Jamaica did not do their duty and reproduce while White men continued their infatuation with "rioting in the goatish embraces of black women," as historian Edward Long put it, then their failure to create families that were recognizably British while living in a society that was grossly disordered meant that they could not contribute to a viable body politic, no matter how much wealth Jamaica produced.[43] Wilson concludes that "the consolidation and extension of British authority . . . required gendered technologies of power that sought to intervene directly in the domestic organization and the sexual practices of its subjects."[44]

V

Jamaica, perhaps surprisingly, is the eighteenth-century British American colony that has attracted the most attention from historians of women, historians of gender and sexuality, and historians interested in the intersection of race and gender. As Christine Walker and Kathleen Wilson have argued, Jamaica had a very distinctive gender and sexual culture, a gender frontier that was an outlier among British American colonies. It was one that was remarkable modern in its indifference to religion, its sexual openness, and (by European standards) its fluidity and deviance.[45] Its modernity was unsettling to many outsider observers, who portrayed Jamaica, as Dallin Lewis notes, as a place of female impropriety, domestic chaos, and sexual and financial rapacity.[46] Walker argues that the reality was very different, suggesting a much more positive view of Jamaica's distinctive sexual culture, at least as seen from the perspective of White women. The wealth and demographic instability of early eighteenth-century Jamaica made Jamaica a "seedbed for innovation," not least in gender arrangements. Jamaica's relaxed attitude to marriage and its extreme commitment to Atlantic slavery gave White women in the island multiple chances to maximize their income through exploiting enslaved labor. They were able to do as sole femmes, living outside conventional wedlock boundaries while remaining sexually active.[47]

Jamaica also pioneered the development of a new class of people, free people of color, most of whom were women and many of whom received their freedom through being either the partners or the children of elite White men. Daniel Livesay focuses on the most privileged section within the class of free people of color, mixed-race descendants of wealthy White men educated in Britain, who stood to inherit large sums of money from their fathers. If they did so, then they occupied a curious position in Jamaica's developing caste system. This was a system in which color was the measure of all things, with wealth going only to people who could assure their White racial purity. Jamaican legislators were torn between familial feelings for people who were their kin and anxieties about how helping free people of color would destroy rigid understandings of racial division Livesay examines the tensions in familial relationships of free people of color, though he looks at free people of color only in relation to their White inheritance, not in regard to the families of the enslaved to whom they were related. He shows how wealthy free women of color formed a point of tension, in being both rich and non-White, in a Jamaica in which these conditions were not meant to exist. They helped reframe, Livesay argues, racial politics in the island. He concludes that "the small opening given to elites of color to become White was, if anything, an experiment to stabilize and augment a failed settler society."[48] Their relative success in breaking down racial hierarchies in Jamaica depended on mobilizing kinship links with wealthy White men. Those kinship links declined over time, as a greater number of free people of color did not have White parents but came from mixed-race backgrounds, a fact that encouraged White Jamaicans to see them as a population group that mediated between Whites and Blacks.[49]

Erin Trahey extends Livesay's analysis of inheritance practices made by relatively wealthy free women of color. She argues that these women worked within, rather than outside, racial systems in Jamaica and did so in ways that subtly undermined some of these seemingly rigid racial rules about how different racial groups should not mix. Over several generations, she notes, free women of color who owned property and who had a commitment in furthering the life chances of other free women of color, only some of whom were their kin, whittled away at the limits of White hegemony. They adopted both African and well as European conceptions of property and family, chipping away at the edifice of White privilege in the island by creating an alternative political community. They did so without ever explicitly attacking the fundamental colonial institutions and beliefs that upheld White supremacy, in part because they were complicit in such systems. Their actions did much to disturb what White Jamaicans thought were established realities.[50]

For most Black women, however, especially the vast majority of such women who toiled in slavery, Jamaica was hell on earth. Heather Vermeulen shows aspects of this hell in a detailed examination of the sexual practices of the well-known Jamaican overseer and slaveholder Thomas Thistlewood, who left explicit diaries outlining his sexual assaults on Black women. Thistlewood controlled Black women, Vermeulen asserts, through systematic rapes, in what the author describes as a "libidinal Linnaean project in which rape, slavery, natural history and surveillance goes together." Thistlewood's violence toward Black women, in this reading, illustrates the dark side of the Enlightenment and shows how central sexual violence was for effective plantation management and domination of enslaved women in the eighteenth century.[51]

The nature of female enslavement in Jamaica was notably brutal but also conspicuously modern, as Diana Paton has stressed in her account of enslaved childcare practices in late eighteenth-century Jamaica. Paton's article both fits within the history of slavery in the Atlantic world and contributes to a gender history in which that gendered Atlantic history of slavery is prominent. In England, childcare before the Industrial Revolution was undertaken alongside other activities.[52] It was never, however, the kind of structured and institutionalized childcare that became routine on Jamaican plantations, in which sugar work was extremely intensive, preventing working women from caring for their infant and toddler children. In Jamaica, the politics of reproduction merged imperceptibly with the realities of harsh work regimes and foreshadowed, in child care, how European and North American White women would work in nineteenth-century factories.[53] Paton argues that looking at the organization of childcare labor on Jamaican plantations and exploring how women workers were separated from their children while working "could help us develop a broader framework for understanding the history of caring labour and its relationship to changing regimes of social reproduction over time."[54] It presaged nineteenth-century shifts in female work patterns whereby childcare became institutionalized, reinforcing the idea that Caribbean "factories in the field," where the work of childcare was separated from the work of production for profit, was precociously modern.

VI

The Indigenous frontier was one that Europeans found alternately fascinating, dangerous, and mystifying, especially where gender and sexuality were concerned. Two articles in particular deal with this (to Europeans) strange gender frontier. To these important articles on Native American women can also be added Susan Sleeper-Smith's extensively researched examinations of female networks and how women exercised power and female involvement in commerce in the Ohio valley and Illinois country.[55]

Felicity Donohue reinterprets some notorious examples of adulterous Indigenous women in the American southeast being seemingly punished by vicious gang rapes in the period between the Seven Years' War and the American Revolution. She argues that White observers who detailed such acts of barbaric behavior to an audience predisposed to see Indigenous people through the lenses of savagery failed to understand the cultural contexts within which such gang rapes occurred. Donohue does admit such events were likely to have happened, though her account gets somewhat close to explaining them away. She provides, however, a close anthropological reading of female Indigenous sexuality, showing that Indigenes such as the Choctaws did not subscribe to European notions that married men owned the bodies of their wives and that sexual incontinence within marriage would disgrace them.

She notes how powerful Indigenous women could be in matriarchal societies and shows that marriage was conceived of in communitarian rather than individual ways. What horrified White observers about harsh punishments for female adultery was misplaced. These punishments, which Donohue thinks outside the normal ways in which adultery was dealt with, were the result of intense pressure on Indigenous societies greatly affected by and splintering under the stresses of war. Punishments, she argues, were intended as deterrents to women seeking sexual connections with outsiders while being also intended to reclaim and internalize anxieties and fears provoked by external conflict. These punishments, horrific though they were, should be seen, she argues, as arising from declining community cohesion more than reflecting male sexual privilege.[56]

Indigenous power was more pronounced in southeast North America earlier in the century. The reality of Indigenous power in the early eighteenth century is made clear in Sophie White's comparison of descriptions of the first Mardi Gras in New Orleans, late in 1729, with the scare of the Natchez War that started on 28 November 1729. In the Natchez War, 237 French people died, sometimes after considerable torture. White connects this trauma for the French in Louisiana with an account in a French pamphlet on the torture and ritualized execution of an Indigenous Natchez woman captured by the Tunicas, a French ally. She concentrates on an account by Marc-Antoine Caillot in which Caillot interweaves his description of a Mardi Gras marked by outrageous costumes, much cross dressing, and an emphasis on clothing and on the general theme of metamorphosis. To the casual reader, the placement of a description of a carnival transplanted to the Americas in between accounts of violence, torture, and death seems incongruous. White demonstrates that the placement of this discussion of the Mardi Gras within a complex text is not accidental.

What disturbed Caillot about the execution by slow fire of the Natchez woman—who endured her ordeal with amazing bravery and who denounced her torturers, in the way approved of in Indigenous societies, with violent abuse, declaring (as turned out to be the case) that her death would be quickly avenged—was the involvement of French men and especially French women in the torture of the woman. To Caillot, the French participation in torture "was a signal that these colonists had violently rejected the social and moral standards of France." It was important for Caillot to stress that any colonial "transformations" of French people into Indigenes was temporary, not permanent, and that Frenchness remained important and stable in the infant colony. White argues that Caillot's "foray into a colonial-pastoral masquerade offered a means for traumatized colonists in New Orleans to safely play with role reversals and metamorphoses that they hoped were temporary and therefore reversible."[57]

White argues that by inserting a masquerade into an otherwise dismal tale of torture and death, and by emphasizing in this carnival tale the many changes of outfits that were part of the Mardi Gras, Caillot "underscored the importance of dress for reclaiming Frenchness and reasserting the colonial order" of Louisiana. If the French were able to keep their cultural practices in lands in which they were outnumbered and surrounded by people willing and able to do them harm. White suggests, the French could stop themselves in being permanently transformed. The Mardi Gras showed that colonial transformations—even into acting as Indigenous people (or, indeed, as Africans, who played a role in the masquerade in which they did not shift into other costumes than those dictated by their enslavement)—were always temporary: French identity could be preserved in colonial places. Gender was a crucial component of such assertions of identity.[58]

VII

One aspect that is underdone in this sample of articles in early American gender studies is masculinity. The relative paucity of such articles suggests that early American historians have not moved toward making masculinity a topic that might inform women's history and questions of the gendered nature of power, as Toby Ditz urged should be the next step in scholarship in an important survey of men's studies from 2004.[59] Snyder's survey of women's history from 2012 does not mention masculinity, for example. There is only one article in the sample—Elizabeth Mancke and Colin Grittner's examination of the well-known diaries of Simeon Perkins of late eighteenth-century Nova Scotia, which describe competing models of manhood within worlds of commerce—that focuses specifically on masculinity in early America, although it is a theme more frequently addressed in eighteenth-century British historiography.[60]

One reason to do more on masculinity is that, as Linda Colley argues, the dominance of discourses around politeness as a model by which masculinity was transformed in eighteenth-century Britain has not led to a reconciliation, or even much consideration, of how the polite and refined gentleman that represented hegemonic masculinity in later eighteenth-century Britain could become a much less polite and genteel man overseas, keen on sexual excess, racial antagonisms, and debauchery of all kinds.[61] Another reason to look more closely at masculinity in imperial settings is that it would allow scholars to respond to Carole Pateman's arresting thesis from 1988 that the celebration of "fraternity" in late eighteenth-century political discourse merely meant that the authority of fathers was replaced by the authority of men. That replacement enhanced the realm of politics open to men while keeping women even more subordinated than before. In Pateman's view, the push to liberty in the age of revolution was "fundamentally, not accidentally, masculinist."[62]

In general, historians still know too little about what women did, thought, how they behaved in relation to men, how they interacted with each other, and need to know more about the particular experiences of women of varying races and classes. The study of enslaved women, especially, could attract more historical attention, similar to what Diana Paton has done in respect to enslaved women's role in childcare.[63] The history of children and empire is another ripe topic for exploration. Troy Bickham has shown how much mileage might be gained from studying children and imperialism in an intriguing exploration of how children learned about empire in formal schooling and outside of it, through such things as playing board games with an imperial theme. By the 1780s Britain was awash with publications for children that engaged with empire and the people and places connected to it. Bickham suggests that the plenitude of imperial material suggests that parents who sought opportunities for their children thought such opportunities might be imperial and thus came to concentrate on empire through reading, conversation, and visits to dedicated spaces of display. This new emphasis on empire was a postrevolutionary development, more connected to the sudden growth of abolitionism and controversy over India than to the loss of America. It was part of the creation of an abolitionist generation in which the United States was seen as outside the imperial family.[64]

If we follow Wilson's recommendation that imperialism is inextricable from gendered technologies of power and expand on Brown's conception of early America as a series of gender frontiers, three significant facts about gender in early America emerge. First, women did not want to go there, with well under one in five female migrants coming to British America doing so as free women and the great majority of all migrants being male, many single men. Second, the dominant cultural impulse in

Britain and the Anglicized parts of British North America in the eighteenth century was polite sociability within a culture of marriage and that sociability within marriage shaped the lives of middling White women markedly. Finally, the great majority of people in early America were dependents of men, including all children, the overwhelming majority of women, and a substantial proportion of men, including almost all Black men. Carole Shammas points out that more adults in British North America were household dependents in the eighteenth century than in eighteenth-century Britain or in nineteenth-century America, legally subordinated to their masters, fathers, and husbands.[65]

If the British West Indies is included in such formulations, the rates of household dependency would be increased. Given how important men were in the lives of women and children, what sort of manliness men envisioned themselves fashioning and how able they were to establish hegemonic models of manhood are important to study. So too are deviations from such models of manliness, including homosexuality, and how we might look at sexuality and intimate histories, both of which have been described in monographs rather than in recent articles.[66] Indeed, sexuality is a rather neglected topic in the journal literature, though less so in monographs. Heather Kopelson's article on the policing of abominable sex in early Bermuda treats transgressive sexuality in early America, although as her focus is on the seventeenth century, it is an article that does not strictly fall within the parameters of this study.[67] It is a topic that has ceased to be quite as important in the literature in the 2010s as it was in the 2000s. John D'Emilio's quip in respect to the historiography of same-sex relationships—that early America can seem like an "unfortunate inconvenience" to historians trying to evaluate the good bits that occur from the early nineteenth century onwards—still seems to have some validity.[68]

The increasingly masculine character of eighteenth-century British and American culture can be canvassed in two visual depictions of sociability in which men dominate in ways that had not been the case so much in the past and which point to the masculine nature of ideas such as fraternity. William Hogarth's *A Midnight Modern Conversation* (1733) takes male sociability as a modern invention. Karen Harvey notes that this printing of gentlemanly conviviality and intellectual discussion lubricated by lashings of rum punch (itself an imperial product) nodded to seventeenth-century genre paintings of tavern scenes but unlike its predecessors excluded women and children.[69] Hogarth's painting might be compared to John Greenwood's *Sea Captains Carousing in Surinam*

(c. 1755–69), another painting set in a tavern, but one in which debauchery features more prominently and where the issue of race is present, in the form of a diminutive, barely clothed Black boy waiter and a half-naked female barmaid. It shows a man vomiting, a man dancing madly, other men in states of severe inebriation, and hints of sexual debauchery.[70] Greenwood's painting shows that politeness was not the only model of manhood available in the imperial world of British men. How gender went global remains a project not yet fully realized.[71]

7

Eighteenth-Century British History

I

Historians of early America and historians of eighteenth-century Britain ought to be thought of as being like casual friends, separated by distance, whose lives are lived usually in different orbits.¹ On rare occasions, however, an early American historian pauses to take stock of what is happening in eighteenth-century British history and how it might be useful for colonial American scholarship. This chapter is one of these periodic attempts at stock taking. What recent trends in the writing of eighteenth-century British history show, however, is a general lack of concern from eighteenth-century British historians about what was happening across the Atlantic. These trends also display a lack of engagement with one of the principal ambitions of early American history, which is to write a more capacious history that includes a variety of perspectives, from Atlantic to continental to African and, in this case, to European and to British history. British historians, by contrast, produce scholarship that tends to the insular rather than to the capacious, running in well-worn grooves of interpretation that have changed little in the last thirty years.²

II

This type of investigation has been done before. Edmund Morgan published a highly influential think piece in 1957 in which he alerted early American historians to the work of Sir Lewis Namier on the culture of the ruling elite of Georgian Britain. He suggested this scholarship should lead colonial American historians away from tired and outdated imperial approaches and limited and teleological socioeconomic explanations of historical change toward studies of the local institutions of the colonies. The aim, he argued, was to do detailed research in colonial archives so that we "know how the individual's picture of society was formed." That meant understanding "the local institutions which produced the American Revolution, the institutions from which were distilled the ideas that enabled men of that age to stand as the architects of modern liberty."[3]

But Morgan was no simple Namierite. He was an intellectual historian who took ideas very seriously, unlike Namier.[4] He advocated Namierite methods of social history in colonial American history but tied such methods to a celebration of the commitment of the revolutionary founders to idealistic ideas about protecting liberty and property from tyranny. Morgan commended historians for asking how American revolutionaries developed a remarkable "breadth of vision and attachment to principle" that contrasted favorably with "parochial English politics" and an "empire dissolving for lack of vision."[5] The result of Morgan's intervention, Michael McDonnell and David Waldstreicher note, was twofold. It led to a forty-year ascendancy of neo-Whig perspectives on the American Revolution, although that interpretation was always contested, with neo-Progressive approaches never entirely disregarded. Where Morgan was overwhelmingly successful, McDonnell and Waldstreicher assert, was in establishing a new chronology, lasting between 1763 and 1789, that was a distinct "revolutionary age," with the Seven Years' War and the 1790s "screened out."[6]

Forty years later T. H. Breen ventured onto the same terrain.[7] His summary of Georgian history, published in 1997, came at a particularly protean period in writing on this era. The mid to late 1980s and early 1990s was a time, Breen noted, in which "Georgian Britain had suddenly become a hot topic." He cited Paul Langford's assertion that scholars working then had discovered a "transformation, social, cultural, religious and economic, which occurred between the 1720s and the 1780s [that] was nothing, if not spectacular" and approved of Kathleen Wilson's comment that "recent studies of popular politics, class relations, crime, and the law have done nothing less than revolutionize the ways in which we view and interpret the expression and exercise of power in eighteenth-century English society."[8] Breen concentrated on the paradigm-busting works of Linda Colley and John Brewer that rethought national identity and the nature of the British state, respectively. He gave a sideways glance to the work on material culture and economic history of Jan de Vries and nodded to Paul Langford's emphasis on politeness as a central animating impulse of the period, while noting works by Colin Kidd and Roy Porter in his analysis.[9] Breen explicitly opposed what he considered old-fashioned and uninformed views of eighteenth-century England as a "traditional, conventional, and conservative" society.[10] Instead, he argued that "dynamism, growth and modernity suddenly seem apposite terms to describe this not-so-traditional England of the eighteenth century."[11] He thus largely disagreed with the controversial and insightful theses of J. C. D. Clark, put forward in two books of 1985 and 1986, that England was an "ancien régime" in what Clark insisted was a long eighteenth century dominated by a pervasive oligarchy in which religion was the central animating impulse in society and politics and Jacobitism the quintessential existential threat to the survival of the Hanoverian regime.[12]

What impressed Breen about eighteenth-century England (and to an extent Scotland and Ireland—he ignored Wales) was the growth of an articulate and powerful middle class who created and benefited from a vibrant consumer economy and who participated in a political system that was more than just a pursuit of place and power. It involved genuine ideological differences, some of which became translated in America into classical republicanism. For Breen, the implications of this British scholarship were that early American historians ought to concentrate on four themes: the impact of a market economy on social and economic patterns; the ramifications of a fiscal-military state and Britain's expanded capacity to fight and win expensive wars; the development of a strong and distinctive national identity among the British that was powerfully exclusionary and that tended to reduce the "other" (a category in which Americans were placed, much to their anger and horror) to second-rate status; and the reaction by Americans to being relegated to second-rate status, which was to develop a political discourse based on republicanism, inspired by Evangelical Protestantism and demonstrated in print by "an angry, shrill, often nervous insistence on natural rights."[13]

III

Morgan and Breen alerted early Americanists to important books that they believed had transformed eighteenth-century British scholarship. Yet no such transformative books have appeared recently that have had the impact of Namier on Morgan or of Colley and Brewer on Breen. Eighteenth-century British historians have lowered their ambitions from the grand aims that were common in the 1980s and 1990s. They concentrate on narrow topics and on case studies. They seldom write panoramic surveys that have arresting new interpretative frameworks.[14] There are exceptions, as always, with a few important books in economic and imperial history recently published that take a *longue durée* and global approach, in which the eighteenth century is central but not dominant.¹⁵ What is notable, however, is that the interpretative schema of the period established in the work surveyed by Breen remains the model for current scholarship.¹⁶

Indeed, scholarship on eighteenth-century British history (from a summary of seventy-one articles between 2012 and 2020) proceeds in customary grooves with an updated Whig interpretation of history having a surprising amount of purchase. The eighteenth century is depicted as a welcome relief from the horrors of the seventeenth century, with a post–Glorious Revolution settlement in place that was glorious insofar as it confirmed a Restoration settlement generally supported by a largely content population. This population welcomed domestic harmony and the fighting of overseas wars that Britain usually won.¹⁷ It was a settlement in which an oligarchical elite under a limited monarchy agreed to pay a reasonable (though not exorbitant) amount of taxes. These taxes funded a strong fiscal-military state and a flourishing economy at home and an empire based on the extraction of tropical or semitropical commodities from America, the Caribbean, and South Asia, using, in America, enslaved people drawn from Africa.

A steady but continuous increase in national Gross Domestic Product spread reasonably far down the social ladder, and the government prioritized the interests of property and a middling class keen on consumption over the poor and especially over non-British imperial subjects. These conditions kept politics stable and society largely happy, at least in England and Wales. They also produced an economy that gradually changed in evolutionary and nonthreatening ways through an industrious, not industrial, revolution away from agriculture toward industry and services. The system did not succumb to Malthusian pressures from a growing population due to the long-term effects of an agricultural revolution largely based around people's willingness to work harder to get more money to purchase more goods rather than on remarkable technological improvement. The dominant theme is continuity rather than change in a "long eighteenth century" undisturbed by revolutionary agitation or serious class conflict.¹⁸

It is a view of Georgian Britain as seen in the artworks of Thomas Gainsborough and Sir Joseph Reynolds, with a nod to the work of William Hogarth, in which themes of British national identity are more stressed than hints of an always precarious social order. Britons, especially the wealthy and well-born, had good reason to feel very pleased with themselves in this prosperous, stable, and self-satisfied realm presided over by a much-loved (if socially derided) George II and his adept chief ministers, Robert Walpole and Henry Pelham. It was a realm that was united by intense Francophobia and ardent Protestantism. Indeed, the most fundamental weakness of this privileged realm was its "chauvinistic self-regard" and its inability to see people other than the metropolitan English as worthy of attention.[19] It was this chauvinistic exclusivity that led to the Hanoverian regime under its naïve new monarch from 1760, George III, coming adrift in the thirteen colonies and, in the long term, in Ireland.[20]

It is important to note, however, that this view of eighteenth-century Britain as oligarchic, politically and socially stable, and comfortable is to an extent an artifact of periodization. If we look at British history using the preferred historiographical convention of the long eighteenth century, then the period after the limits of my study (the contentious 1790s) and even more so the period prior (of party factions, intense political and to an extent social conflict that characterized the reigns of the later Stuarts from the Glorious Revolution in 1688 to the Hanoverian succession in 1714) show a conflicted Britain with a historiography more inclined toward disagreement than in the placid Georgian era.[21] If we extend our analysis back to 1688 in English and British history, we see a Britain in which revolutionary fervor had significant impacts. The current consensus on the Glorious Revolution, for example, is that it was more revolutionary than previously thought, ushering a chaotic cacophony of voices from a variety of political positions in which the contentious 1690s was a time of economic distress combined with political partisanship that created conditions of disorder and encouraged many of the multiple pamphleteers of the period to attack each other with a venom that recalled the anarchy of the 1640s.[22]

IV

This updated Whig interpretation of eighteenth-century Britain finds its strongest support in scholarly work on the English economy and the long-term origins of the Industrial Revolution. Important new research has been done providing data to make long-term reevaluations of the English economy. These findings are underpinned by the work of a previous generation of demographic and economic historians about the essential social and economic structures of premodern England.[23] It provides massive empirical evidence about economic growth and the nature of work from late medieval to modern times.[24] Neither the data nor the findings are uncontested, but we now have a persuasive answer to a key question in English history: How did England move from being a European backwater before 1600 to being the economic dynamo of the world by the mid-nineteenth century? This involved a massive movement of labor out of agriculture into increasingly productive industries and into services, a movement that fortuitously did not lead to a Malthusian crisis of too few resources for too great a population.[25] By recalculating social tables of English occupations made in 1688, 1759, and 1798 and by extensively examining wage rates and measures of agricultural and industrial output, these researchers have shown that explanations of economic growth can be focused on the seventeenth century. Indeed, 1650 marks the year from which we can date a persistent rise in English per capita GDP. It is also around this time when structural changes that ensured such economic growth took off and when fiscal capacity took off in comparative terms.[26]

The explanations for persistent economic growth in England after 1650 are mostly endogenous, with economic change associated with a lengthy process of industrialization rather than a sudden-bang Industrial Revolution in the second half of the eighteenth century. The principal endogenous causes were located within England itself, notably a commercialization of agriculture from after 1600 and the development around 1700 of a high-wage culture in which the economy grew principally through an increase in working hours. A desire for more consumer goods rather than advances in knowledge and technology explains England's steady if unremarkable rising economic growth between 1650 and the 1780s. This explanation means that there is little need for Kenneth Pomeranz's Great Divergence thesis, in which western European economic growth in the eighteenth century is in part explained by Britain's use of colonial land to grow tropical crops that provided the caloric needs of a growing population, allowing Britain to devote less land to the growing of its own food than would have been the case without overseas colonization.[27]

The English settlement of North America and the Caribbean fits poorly into this explanatory model of enduring English prosperity in an economy nicely balanced between agriculture, industry, and services, in which not just men but also women and children contributed considerable amounts of labor. The absence of interest in colonization and slavery and its contribution to British economic growth is surprising given a long history of this issue arising from the pioneering work of Eric Williams on the links between capitalism and slavery and Joseph Inikori's more recent reassertion of the importance of Africa, the slave trade, and slavery to the Industrial Revolution.²⁸ The recent surge of interest in slavery and capitalism from scholars of nineteenth-century American history, which touches on early America and eighteenth-century Britain and which has become a self-proclaimed historiographical "movement" called the New History of Capitalism, has not yet appeared to an appreciable degree in recent journal literature on eighteenth-century Britain.²⁹ Only one article in the sample, by Mark Harvey, a sociologist rather than a historian, addresses the extent to which the development of industrial capitalism intersected with the development of plantation slavery. His interest is primarily on the late eighteenth and nineteenth centuries and is concerned as much with how British industrialism affected the growth and structural development of plantations as with how plantations had an effect on the British economy, arguing that there was "a trajectory of capitalist development marked by the expansion of market exchanges, but also certainly of violence, dislocation and coercion in the exploitation of labour" and that "British industrial capitalism was constituted ... by diverse and dynamically growing combinatory configurations and reconfigurations of historically novel regimes of exploitation."³⁰

Nevertheless, Klas Rönnbäck makes an important empirical contribution to the debate through looking at value-chains connecting Britain to Africa and the Americas. He shows that while the Atlantic slave trade was always of relatively minor economic importance, the percentage of the economy derived from Atlantic plantation economies appreciated considerably over time, from 3.5 percent of British GDP between 1700 and 1710 to 11 percent between 1800 and 1810, although that figure reduces to just over 6 percent if we exclude, as we probably should, the 4.7 percent of GDP derived from the colonial and American goods trade. Importantly, the dramatic rise in the importance of the plantation economies to Britain came after the American Revolution, when cotton became a major commodity in British trade and manufacturing. The contribution of trade with the plantation complex peaked at around 7 percent of GDP on the eve of the American Revolution and fell to under 5 percent during the War for Independence.³¹

Thus, the general view about the importance of slavery to British economic growth is that it was significant and substantial but not as transformative as, for example, endogenous changes in agriculture and consumer culture. The strongest voices suggesting that slavery was important in shaping economic growth, thus adopting a modern update of parts of the Williams's thesis on capitalism and slavery, are from Nuala Zahedieh and Pat Hudson. Zahedieh points to the close connections between the development of the copper industry and plantation agriculture, and Hudson notes that economic activity related to slavery was in areas strongly impacted by Atlantic trade and in areas outside the main centers of Enlightenment and bourgeois values. Slavery helped turn these places from being poor regions in the 1760s to among the wealthiest parts of England by the 1790s. She emphasizes how the business of slavery improved technology and even had a large impact on administrative improvements in the tertiary sector, notably in credit arrangements and on financial institutions.[32]

The reach of slavery-related advances in the economy was limited, however. Chris Evans provides a case study of slavery and its impact in Wales in which he shows that while there were multiple connections to slavery in such industries as copper and especially iron, a commodity that led to significant transformations of economic and political life in West Africa, the "flow of slave-generated wealth into Wales was on a very modest scale and there is nothing to suggest it made a decisive contribution to Welsh industrialization."[33] Jon Stobart's empirical analysis of overseas "exotic" goods in the inventories of rural shops over the eighteenth century suggests that while the penetration of the exotic world of goods from Asia and the Americas throughout England was deep and important, the availability of overseas goods was variable both by region (areas close to London had more overseas items of consumption than shops in Cheshire or Cornwall) and by individual store. Although rural consumers were increasingly exposed to tropical goods such as sugar and tobacco, both becoming consumer staples by the early eighteenth century, Stobart denies that the increasing presence of such goods in rural shops spurred on greater ranges of available items than before, showing that local produce was as important as tropical goods in providing rural folk with a taste of luxury alongside the necessities they bought.[34]

V

What attracts more scholarly attention than economic links between Britain and British America is how the ever-evolving and ever-more-effective fiscal-military state worked and what its impact was on the rest of society and on Britain's geopolitical position. It was an essential precondition for warfare—a constant in much of the eighteenth century—allowing Britain to move aggressively into the world and to win almost every war it fought, save the American Revolution. The basic contours of the historiography of the fiscal-military state were laid down by John

Brewer, Patrick O'Brien, and Philip Hunt a generation ago. What has happened since has been more stress on the flexibility and efficiency inherent in the fiscal-military state and how it started to spread to other parts of the British Empire (principally Ireland and recently Jamaica).[35] Thus, Anne L. Murphy investigates the Bank of England and its role in managing the natural debt as being about "performance and display," in which it convinced the public through its administrative processes that the growing debt was "an intimate compact between state and citizens."[36]

Scholars see the fiscal-military state arising out of politically inspired transformations of state economic policy emerging from what the English ruling elite thought was the catastrophe of the mid-seventeenth Civil Wars. Patrick O'Brien argues that it was not the Glorious Revolution but the English Civil War that fostered the growth of a fiscal-military state and ongoing prosperity. The Civil War was a moment of extreme trauma for the English ruling elite. It made them willing to pay larger taxes than any ruling elite elsewhere in Europe (and in British North America) to keep themselves safe. It helped that most of the aristocracy and gentry were protected from the major burden of taxation. Taxes were seldom extensively levied on landed property but were derived from customs and excise taxes set up in the English republic of the early 1650s. O'Brien argues that there was "an exceptional political consensus, not merely in favour of restoring but of sustaining an increasingly well-funded system of monarchical with aristocratic rule."[37]

England put in place an embryonic but effective system of administration, much enhanced over the eighteenth century, in order to keep the ruling elite safe. As O'Brien concludes, "The fiscal state succeeded in preserving external security, allowing sufficient political stability, safeguarded property rights, and provided subsidies and protection for overseas trade."[38] Just as important as what was done was who remained in charge. As Martin Daunton has argued, one reason the elite agreed to changes in taxation that increased their fiscal obligations was that in the late seventeenth century the position of the aristocracy in Britain was secure; they were who determined the terms of compliance and cooperation by retaining and enhancing their control over all forms of taxation.[39]

The fiscal-military state needed more than the support for state taxation by the wealthiest people in England. It depended on England and then Britain recovering from the economic catastrophe of the mid-century civil wars and having sufficient money to wage war without bankrupting itself. O'Brien argues that from the mid-seventeenth onwards, England had more financial resources than other European empires. England, between 1642 and 1815, had the fastest growing and most economically secure European economy.[40] The growth in the economy meant a concomitant rise in tax receipts. Stephen Broadberry et al., in a somewhat acrimonious argument with Gregory Clark, who contests their figures and wants to lower estimates in annual growth, contend that economic growth was especially pronounced as the fiscal-military state took shape. They conclude that "a growing body of evidence has shown that England ... was escaping Malthusian constraints and slowly raising national income per head well before the onset of the industrial revolution." They argue that annual growth rates in the eighteenth century averaged 0.7, which was well over twice the annual growth rates in the late sixteenth and early seventeenth century.[41]

The significant changes in England's economy in the late seventeenth century associated with the culmination of the first stages of an "agricultural revolution" eased after 1700 and then restarted in the years of rapid industrial growth after 1800. Robert Allen's investigation of social tables made in 1688 and 1759 suggests a period of remarkable social stasis in the first half of the eighteenth century, with the most significant change being a decline in rates of English poverty to an all-time low in 1759, when 13.7 percent of the English population lived below the poverty line.[42] England had a strongly commercialized society with a diverse and productive agricultural sector and a well-developed protoindustry in an increasingly monetized economy.[43] If White Protestants in British America were included in this analysis, then the poverty levels would be even lower.[44] Of course, if the unit of analysis was moved away from White Protestants of English descent and was extended to include all people in the British Empire, such as Irish Catholics, Indigenous Americans, African American enslaved people, and (from 1759) Bengalis, then the wealth and prosperity of Britain decline dramatically and equality even more. Economic prosperity and equality were the province of White Englishmen (and some Lowland Scots), White Americans, and White West Indians.[45]

The development of a strong market economy in England from the late seventeenth century onward has several important implications for early Americanists. Julian Hoppit argues that it was shaped by a "revolution in government activity," as seen in a dramatic increase in parliamentary economic legislation designed to aid England's commercial future. Hoppit insists that these developments suggest a growing efficiency in the workings of the British state.[46] John Beckett argues that we can see the start of parliamentary legislation to promote private economic ambitions as a leading result of the Glorious Revolution, paving the way for conditions that favored Britain becoming the first industrial nation.[47] The transition to a commercial society unleashed concerns, echoed across the Atlantic, that this new focus on finance was destructive and dangerous to social harmony.[48] Aaron Graham explains how contractors funding the massive outlays that government required to meet the demands of fighting a global war in the 1750s mixed patriotism with a self-interest that appeared to observers unfamiliar with high finance as being akin to corruption. In fact, Graham asserts, what contractors were doing was a natural outcome of an increasingly complex financial system. The gap between the cognoscenti in finance who understood how the fiscal-military state worked and the importance of mercantilism in governing this financial system separated the cognoscenti from a populace who associated money culture with vice and foreign influences.[49]

The increasing role of finance in shaping British society and politics made many English people nervous, especially if they did not understand the operation of nebulous concepts such as the "public debt." Some people, like the Scottish financier and historian Adam Anderson (1692–1754), were very comfortable with the increasing role of finance in politics, seeing men of finance as essential for British geopolitical dominance. Anderson supported the greater inclusion of Jews (who were often prominent financiers) such as Sampson Gideon in the body politic.[50] Gideon helped provide the funds that allowed Britain to put down the Jacobite rebellion in 1745. For opponents of the "Jew Bill," however, Jews represented the dangers of this new addiction to finance, being associated in customary antisemitic discourse with rootless unpatriotic modernity and cosmopolitanism. These anti-Semites emphasized the "autonomy that could only be acquired by stable property that made its owner independent of the men in government and thus able to resist the corruptive power of patronage, wrought to a great degree by the new orders of finance."[51] Disputes over the cultural and social meanings of a developing financial system that brought new kinds of people unexplained wealth demonstrate how the commercial growth of Britain, especially London and its more dynamic ports, such as Bristol and Liverpool—not coincidentally the centers of slave trading to the Americas and places with many merchants comfortable with complicated transatlantic trade—established an effective mercantilist strategy that provided a commercializing economy with an extraordinary share of profits from providing services to an expanding global economy.[52]

VI

For early Americanists, what is revealing about the intensive scholarship on the dimensions of economic growth in eighteenth-century England is how little attention is paid to how it was part of an empire. There is lots of synecdochal thinking, in which England comes to represent all of Britain and its empire. Breen identified this synecdochal approach to how the English viewed its empire in the mid-eighteenth century as a fundamental underlying cause of the American Revolution. He noted how insistently British Americans observed that they were Englishmen transplanted overseas.[53] Colonists argued that English settlers colonized America, bringing great benefits to Britain, overcoming Indigenous American resistance in the process, and had done so as Britons, not as a separate people. Charles Prior, however, has drawn on settler colonial theory to modify Breen's acceptance of colonial ideas of sovereignty by arguing that we might think of colonies as quasi-states situated among both European and Indigenous empires, with settlement based more on conquest than on peaceful migration, ideas Prior traces to Thomas Jefferson's *A Summary View of the Rights of British America* (1774).[54]

A few Englishmen (and some Scots) acknowledged the idea of a "Greater Britain," William Pitt most prominently.[55] But most did not, and even Pitt believed that Americans needed to submit to the supremacy of Parliament. Most British statesmen were less generous to their American kin. They saw a divide between the English and the rest of the empire that made British Americans and Irish Protestants as much the "other" as were French Canadian and Irish Catholics, Jamaican slaves, and Bengali peasants. P. J. Marshall's trenchant comment summarizes well the exclusionary view the English had about national identity: "The eighteenth-century experience ... revealed that 'imagined communities' of Britishness were parochial. English people could perhaps envisage a common community with the Welsh and, often with much difficulty, with the Scots, but they failed to incorporate the Irish or colonial Americans into their idea of nation."[56] Colonial British North Americans reacted to their exclusion from notions of Britishness with anger and then with rage, pushing them into revolt. As Thomas Jefferson bittersweetly commented, if Britain had not stood upon its dignity and had treated Americans as fellow countrymen rather than unruly foreigners, then "we might have been a free and a great people together."[57]

Breen's summary of the implications of an exclusionary idea of Britishness for the coming of the American Revolution still stands, especially as interest in what comprised being "British" and clarion calls that the object of study for historians of England should be how England fitted into a "Greater Britain" have declined.[58] British historians are mostly uninterested in either "Greater Britain" or in the Atlantic world, except in the study of transatlantic humanitarianism and medicine.[59] As Keith Brown wryly comments, in a survey of trends in Scottish historiography, invitations to Scottish historians to be part of conferences and edited collections on the theme of "Britishness" quickly dropped off around 2011. Surveys of the idea of the British world suggest that it has proven to be a busted flush.[60] What J. G. A. Pocock argued in 1982 about the parochialism of English history—that it was an insular history of English exceptionalism that maintained a willful amnesia about England's outlying dependencies—remains as true now as then.[61]

What happened outside England is hardly accounted for in how England became prosperous and politically stable after the Hanoverian succession had been confirmed by the final defeat of Jacobitism in 1745. This impression of a prosperous and peaceful Britain looks different, however, if famines in Ireland in the 1720s and especially in 1740–41 are included in debates about rising standards of living. The success of Britain from the second half of the eighteenth century in combining a rapidly growing population with sufficient food resources also looks less impressive if the immense losses of life in the Atlantic slave trade and annual decreases in enslaved British Caribbean populations (between 3 and 8 percent per annum) are considered. And if the disastrous man-created famine in Bengal of 1770, for which the East India Company was largely responsible and in which many million people died—called by David Arnold "one of the great catastrophes of the eighteenth century, and indeed, of modern times"—is factored into accounts of eighteenth-century Britain, then Britain appears to be one of the principal villains of that century, especially when we add to famine Prasannan Parthasarti's analysis of the effects of imperialism on the Indian economy, in which a prosperous part of the world was brought to poverty through deliberate deindustrialization.[62]

Such parochialism within English historiography is a missed opportunity, especially in a contemporary Britain in which the extent to which Britain has a responsibility to acknowledge its imperial past is an urgent political concern.[63] It is instructive to examine Britain as a settler colonial state and to ponder whether the price of metropolitan harmony was paid by the colonies that served as a "safety valve" whereby ordinary people in Britain (less in metropolitan England, where rates of immigration to

British North America were at a low ebb in the first half of the eighteenth century, but more common in the Scottish highlands and in Ulster) migrated to colonial British North America and established remarkably egalitarian and prosperous societies, at least for White populations.[64] The importance of settler colonialism in eighteenth-century Britain has been demonstrated by Matthew Dziennik, who shows how the presence of America was essential to integrating Scotland into the empire following the pacification of the Highlands after 1745. Highlanders were incorporated into the British Army and following service in the Seven Years' War were given land taken from Native Americans in the colony of New York and in the Ohio valley. The promise of land as a reward for enlisting in the military helped reconcile residents of the most troublesome region of Hanoverian Britain to their subordination to England within Great Britain.[65]

VII

Settler colonialism might be combined with greater attention to the concept of region within the early eighteenth-century British Empire. Location is important.[66] Before the 1760s, British statesmen understood the vital distinctions that needed to be made between different parts of the empire. It was only in the 1760s and 1770s that British rulers made the calamitous decision to try and treat all the different parts of the empire as if each region was the same.[67] Indeed, the most distinctive part of the empire was London—a place apart in all sorts of ways from everywhere else in the empire. It was thus less normal than exceptional, and attempts in the 1760s to make the viewpoint from London the only perspective that mattered in the empire were thus doomed to failure. We can see the difference between London and everywhere else clearly in the application of the "Bloody Code," the series of laws designed to protect property rights that greatly increased the number of offences that attracted capital punishment.[68] The study of executions and crime continues to be a vibrant feature of eighteenth-century British history, helped by the completion of one of the great historical digital projects, the transcription of the criminal records of the Old Bailey in London from the seventeenth to the nineteenth centuries.[69]

Rulers and ruled in regions far away from London and its environs did not exhibit the commitment to the Bloody Code evident in the nation's capital. Rulers refused, in particular, to accept that people should hang for property crimes, and they did not accept or follow London judges' understanding of the dread authority of the law. Peter King and Richard Ward utilize the work of the political scientist James C. Scott to show how there were substantial limits—"friction of the terrain"—on the ability of the British state to govern distant and inaccessible regions with low population density, pastoral agriculture, and mountainous or upland geographies.[70] Unlike Scott, however, King and Ward do not see the more distant regions of the realm as ungovernable. They argue that distant regions were governed differently, and in many ways were governed with more responsiveness to community feeling. It fits with a long-standing, though not uncontested, tendency in the study of continental America to question the assumptions of eighteenth-century governors and of most historians that the "frontier" was wilder and more anarchic than more settled regions. Matthew Ward, for example, an expert on settler society in the borderlands of Pennsylvania and the Ohio valley, disputes older understandings of this region as lawless and violent due to its large population of Ulsterman accustomed to conflict in their homelands. He shows that historians have consistently overestimated levels of crime in this region and especially how much crime was committed by the Scots-Irish. He notes that "overall frontier settlers embraced the legal system, even as they insisted it be applied in ways that accorded with local conditions."[71]

King and Ward's interpretation of how serious crime was managed in what they term, following Scott, "zones of relative autonomy" fits with assumptions well-known in early American historiography: that governance was negotiated between powerful local elites and an imperial state that had to manage within the limits of its authority. In the main, the state managed affairs successfully in the first half of the eighteenth century and in the Seven Years' War.[72] King and Ward show that the Bloody Code and its provisions for capital punishment for relatively minor, trivial property crimes was not enforced in northern England and Celtic Britain. As King and Ward argue, these findings "require us to rethink not only some of our core assumptions about the foundations of the elite's hegemony ... but also our understandings of the geographical limitations of the reach of the fiscal-military state in the long eighteenth century."[73] Possibly we need to have a binary rather than a unitary understanding of the fiscal-military state as it operated in the empire—a state that was becoming stronger in the center over time but was becoming less so in the peripheries, where a "less regulatory" "multi-centered institutional framework" made the state's reach in distant areas ineffective.[74]

Eighteenth-century British North America, a deurbanizing place that was expanding into the American interior, fits within the second version of the state, as do the Scottish Highlands and southern Ireland outside the Pale of Settlement around Dublin. Governance may have been less repressive in these areas than in the seemingly harmonious and well-ordered metropolitan England. Compare the brutal repression of the Hawkhurst smuggling gang in Sussex between 1747 and 1750—seventy-five men were hanged or transported, with fourteen suffering the ultimate indignity of being hung in chains—with smuggling in southern Ireland, where local opinion was generally sympathetic to smugglers and opposed to revenue men, and punishments, as Timothy Watt shows, were generally light.[75]

The viciousness of the response to the Hawkshurst gang, despite smuggling not only being generally tolerated by local communities on the southern coast of England and despite it being a vital cog in international commerce in which major London merchants played a central role, arose largely because a local grandee, the Duke of Richmond, was so appalled at smugglers committing murder in Chichester, a town he believed was under his control, that he mobilized the resources of the state to hunt down the gang. He could do so because Sussex was close enough to London that Richmond and the government could try smugglers at the Old Bailey in front of judges who believed that the Bloody Code should be enforced. As the reach of government retreated, the ability of the state to control smuggling receded. Indeed, when it came to tea marketed in Britain and the colonies by the East India Company, smuggling was endemic and incorporated into existing business practices.[76] David Chan Smith finds a similar pattern of judicial difference between London and the provinces. He analyses a court case from 1731 where a London merchant was prosecuted for tax evasion when he tried to make out that French Brandy had been sourced from Dunkirk and thus should attract lower custom duties as being Flemish goods. The merchant was tried in London, which was unfortunate for him because "while the central courts in London typically enforced the law, benches of JPs and juries in the provinces might prefer mitigation."[77]

Thus, V. A. C. Gatrell's statement that "the sanction of the gallows and the rhetoric of the death sentence were central to all relations of authority in Georgian England" needs to be tempered by an acknowledgement that in ordinary times Leviathan in the form of a strong and repressive state did not operate outside places such as Sussex, where powerful dukes were in control of local politics.[78] Of course, the state had enormous potential powers. It never hesitated in exercising such powers in times of emergency, resulting in recalibrations of the relationship between the general community, local elites, and the imperial state that often increased the power of the state over the others. When the British state was threatened—as it was by the Jacobite rebellions of 1715 and 1745, by Tacky's Revolt in Jamaica in 1760–61, and by the Whiteboys agricultural revolts in southern Ireland in the early 1760s—it lashed out and responded to attacks on its authority with the gallows and sometimes, as in Jamaica, with worse methods of execution than the gallows.[79]

In general, however, the state refrained from removing its iron fist from its glove, preferring, especially when dealing with strategically important people embedded within ruling political structures, to use its increasingly impressive bureaucratic functions to keep people in line. Aaron Graham demonstrates this in a study of James Brydges, Duke of Chandos (1673–1744), paymaster of the army in Europe between 1702 and 1713. Graham shows that even in the case of an extremely powerful politician through whose hands vast amounts of money passed and whose opportunities for corruption, often taken, were immense, there was an audit system that made Chandos subject to examination by a wide range of public bodies. The efficiency of such auditing systems, however, depended less on bureaucratic rigor than on politics. Graham argues that "insofar as effective auditing structures emerged during the eighteenth century, they were the outcomes of political rather than administrative developments, and reflected contingent sets of highly charged political circumstances which served to energize even unpromising formal institutions." Corruption, consequently, was a significant issue but arose less as a topic of public concern in this period than in the later Victorian age because of "the uncompromising political, cultural and intellectual attitudes of its audit officials or political overseers rather than what it did to the excellence or 'modernity' of its new auditing institutions."[80]

VIII

The Hanoverians were especially concerned about controlling potential revolt in Scotland, the most troublesome region of the British empire between 1603 and 1745. Casting an eye on what the British state did in Scotland is instructive for early Americanists trying to understand changes in imperial policy after the end of the Seven Years' War. Scotland, Christopher Whatley asserts, was a "deeply fissured" region where politics was fiercely contested among Presbyterians who were strong supporters of the Union and the Whig government and determined adversaries of Jacobites; a pro-Union but antigovernment Patriot Whig population; and a smaller but volatile Jacobite section of the population that tended toward Anglicanism and sometimes to Catholicism and that had its strongest support in the Highlands.[81]

Scotland was a tinderbox, in short. Or it should have been. Britain employed a mixture of carrots and sticks to deal with it, and, overall, the current scholarship suggests it did so with considerable success. Its success in Scotland in the time of Walpole and the Pelhams should temper an early American scholarship that sees these politicians as incompetent and indifferent to events outside metropolitan England, arguing that the political successes of the period and the expansion of imperial rule in the Americas, Asia, and Africa were due to "salutary neglect" and luck.[82] Hanoverian ineptitude can be largely discounted, as can be seen in a survey of Scottish history between the Union and the 1745 rebellion. A now-discarded view of the Scottish ruling elite saw it as "a beleaguered native oligarchy, dependent on the final analysis on English armed force to keep them in power."[83] Historians now see this elite as surprisingly skillful and relatively independent of English power. It was popular in Scotland, with considerable support among Presbyterians committed to the Union and to the dominance of a Presbyterian ascendancy that they believed had suffered terribly under late Stuart despotism. The rule of the Campbells, dukes of Argyll, was greatly enhanced among the Presbyterian majority in Scotland by their travails in the seventeenth century, when both the 8th and the 9th earls of Argyll had been executed by an English crown.[84]

Anti-Catholicism, in particular, was a potent force, making many Scots, both those supporting the Whig ministry and also those favoring the patriot opposition, fervent upholders of the Hanoverian dynasty and of George II, in particular.[85] Scots were also reconciled to the Union not just out of Whig ideological belief but for practical financial reasons.[86] Julian Hoppit shows that the British used tax policy judiciously in Scotland after the Union in 1707 in ways that brought lots of benefits to its northern neighbor. Scots were not keen on the increased tax burden they were given after 1707, especially as the economy before the 1730s was not robust. But they got more back from this enhanced tax regime than they gave away. English opposition politicians grumbled about this, noting (and foreshadowing similar arguments about Americans in the 1760s) that Scots did not pay a fair share of their defense needs and that they were better at tax evasion than their English counterparts. This grumbling, however, was low level, and antagonism to Scots declined to a vanishing point, especially toward upper-class Scots, who increasingly integrated themselves into a cohesive British aristocracy. Increased

Scottish taxation went toward large-scale infrastructure spending on such things as roads. That spending helped make Scotland secure, but it also opened up the English economy to Scottish goods and people. Scotland became a relatively prosperous and peaceful society, as can be seen in low rates of homicide, which W. W. J. Knox attributes to tight policing in a state with a powerful ruling class and great conformity to a rigorously enforced religious morality.[87]

The British state, however, never relaxed its grip on Scotland, acutely aware that Scotland could easily explode, as it did in 1715 and 1745. When Scots exhibited resistance to British state policies, they were put down firmly, even violently. The most obvious instance of this, of course, was the fierce repression that followed the Jacobite rebellions.[88] But the strong hand of the state to quell popular opposition had already been shown to Scots before 1745, after riots resulting from the imposition of a disliked tax on malt made in 1724 and after a smuggling-related popular protest in Edinburgh called the Porteous crisis of 1736–37. As Amy Watson argues regarding the malt-tax crisis, the Walpolean Whig ministry's aggressive attitude toward Scottish popular uprisings showed that "it treated the nation more as a rebellious colony than as a co-equal partner in British governance."[89] The Porteous crisis was especially revealing: a Scottish officer was sentenced to death for ordering troops to fire into a crowd protesting the execution of smugglers; he was then pardoned by the Crown and then lynched by a mob (in other words, a protest about the Bloody Code being extended into the town). It was a local dispute in Edinburgh that could have been dealt with by local magistrates in ways that reflected local concerns—that is certainly how Scottish authorities in Edinburgh thought the affair should have been addressed. The central government, however, came down very hard on Edinburgh, subjecting it to the sort of harsh measures, including military occupation, that Boston was to experience in 1773. Watson notes that the government's actions were disproportionate, as no English city ever suffered the same punishment for the actions of a minority of its citizens. Many Scots were irate because the government action showed that the British government did not respect the political autonomy of local elites and used force to make Scots submit to English authority. It "demonstrated that the Whig ministry would never consider Scotland's rights and institutions as equal to England's" and "encouraged Scots to see their fight for Scottish autonomy as part of a larger imperial struggle for a non-hierarchical British state."[90]

The heavy-handed actions of Walpole's government to Scottish protest between 1724 and 1737 illustrate that such actions, combined with incentives such as increased public spending and better access to English markets, were largely successful. Scotland simmered but mostly stayed loyal, with the majority of Scots in 1745 resisting the siren call of the bonnie prince across the seas. Articles on Hanoverian politics, such as that on petitioning by Mark Knights, show that the Whig regime navigated skillfully between insisting on its authority and allowing people to protest using traditional forms of complaint, such as petitions.[91] Moreover, Walpole and his ministers were masterful in using crises such as the Jacobite Atterbury conspiracy of 1723 to cement the loyalty of the middling and upper orders to the Hanoverian regime, including many women, through a public campaign of oath-taking of support for the rule of George I.[92]

The Whig regime was fortunate in its enemies—neither Jacobites nor Tories were impressive. But it also made its own fortune, drawing on widespread Francophobia and anti-Catholicism to cultivate an intense nationalism focused in particular around the unlikely figure of George II. The personal attributes and character deficiencies of the monarch have always been central in eighteenth-century British historiography, but most attention has been paid to George III, and how he "lost" America rather than to his dull and rigid grandfather.[93] George II is starting to get his due. Sally Holloway and Lucy Worsley, for example, dissect George II's court as a "multivalent emotional space with a practiced grammar of emotional concealment and display" that was "less dull than a marker of predictability, routine and stability." It was mostly important as a place of symbolic meaning, upholding the royal "brand," and was a comfortable reminder of British adherence to custom and Protestant allegiances rather than an area where politics was brokered.[94] George II was a soldier from a militant Protestant background that encouraged emotional reserve and strict regimentation, making him a stark contrast to the still-hated Stuarts and to the excesses of French absolutist monarchs. Holloway and Worsley assert that his insistence on order and disavowal of charisma "helped to contribute to a 'stable' Whig Britain, grounded in a political system more secure than England has ever known."[95]

George II was more respected in the colonies than at home, where his detestation of his popular son was held against him.[96] In Britain, J. C. D. Clark notes, "popular affection for monarchy," which was "prominent under Queen Anne," was "disastrously forfeited under George I and II, [and] came back with George III."⁹⁷ This was not the case in Atlantic America. George II's victory at Dettingen in 1743, where he was the last British monarch to lead troops into battle, was met with euphoria in British North America, raising him to the sort of hero status that was given sixteen years later to James Wolfe. Daniel Robinson argues that British settlers in North America were enamored of George II and the government that ruled in his name, sharing their monarch's and his ministry's obsession with securing the balance of power in Europe and in thwarting French pretensions to universal monarchy.⁹⁸

The second quarter of the eighteenth century was when settlers in the Atlantic world were most satisfied with the imperial regime and the Whig ruling class who ran that regime. It was a time of especially competent governors, well-run legislatures, minimal Toryism, and a moment where colonists were extremely concerned over growing French imperial power.⁹⁹ It raises an important question: If settlers were so comparatively happy with their imperial position in the 1730s and 1740s, can we continue to see this period as a prelude to revolution, where the problems that later caused revolt were steadily brewing? Was it not instead an example of how a dynamic, effective, and powerful empire managed its possessions and settlers in ways that deserve study for its own sake than merely as a preliminary to more important events leading to revolution?

Protestantism, monarchism, and Francophobia were a potent triad that was used to great advantage by the Whig oligarchy to secure assent to their uncontested political dominance. That oligarchy is treated with a surprising amount of respect in recent journal literature.¹⁰⁰ Great attention is paid to one person—the monarch—and the middling sort is covered well, as are the criminal poor, but the 85 percent of the population who were tradespeople, farmers, workers, and cottagers are ignored. There is only one article on workers in this sample, by Beverley Lemire, and that article refers to workers in the maritime world, a world to an extent removed from the society that existed on land. Lemire sees seamen as inhabiting a highly distinctive masculine subculture whose travels outside England connected them to the kinds of globalized patterns of consumption usually associated with the middling sort.¹⁰¹ It is hardly surprising that Hanoverian England is depicted as remarkably politically stable and united under oligarchical rule when the people most likely to be antagonistic to elite rule do not feature in contemporary historiography.

If this period was a time of good governance and imperial harmony, was there much colonial opposition to the Whig oligarchy? Ian

McBride's article about the greatest satire in the eighteenth-century British world, Jonathan Swift's *A Modest Proposal*, suggests not, as even in this biting criticism of Irish politics Swift indulged in little denunciation of British imperialism. *A Modest Proposal* was not, McBride asserts, a bitter anticolonial polemic. Swift's anger over dearth and death from hunger among the Irish population in the 1720s was directed not at British imperialists but at a backward Irish ruling elite that had failed to remake in their own image the society they ruled over by adopting English ideas of agricultural "improvement." Instead, Swift argued, the Irish elite was not only complicit in its own subjection but had "sabotaged" the larger project of transforming Irish society by wasteful practices of pastoralism designed for short-term profit taking and woefully deficient in turning Ireland into the more productive and happier England of agricultural reform.

In short, what was wrong with Ireland, Swift thought, was that England did not intervene enough into Irish affairs. Swift, McBride notes, "subverted the moral claims made for the Protestant Ascendancy" without challenging an existing social order, an order he thought needed to solidify its rule through taxing backward landlords, through the promotion of homegrown textiles, and by reducing pastoralism and wasteful Irish agricultural practices. It was not settler colonialism that was problematic in *A Modest Proposal*. The problem was settlers who went native (*Hiberniores Hibernis ipsis*) and thus failed to bring civilization and a just and progressive social order to a benighted island.[102]

IX

Eighteenth-century British historians are extremely committed to the idea of a long eighteenth century and are indifferent to the idea of an age of revolution in the last quarter of the eighteenth century.[103] Even the one revolution that did occur in eighteenth-century Britain, the Industrial Revolution, slowly evolved rather than occurring in the rapid way that is usually considered essential for an event to be thought of as revolutionary. This unwillingness to consider Britain as part of a global revolutionary moment is astonishing given the profound changes taking place in a short period after 1750, transforming English society and economy as rapid urbanization and industrial growth occurred. The American Revolution in particular is virtually ignored. Indeed, Paul Stock suggests in an article on how geographers thought of America that the American Revolution was epiphenomenal insofar as it was an event that was easily incorporated into existing conceptual frameworks.[104] The inattention to the American Revolution by historians of eighteenth-century Britain may arise from the difficulty in seeing how it could occur in a powerful and prosperous empire where imperial issues were usually expertly managed and where America was hardly a troublesome part of the empire prior to the 1760s. Britain continues to be seen by historians of the eighteenth century as a place where revolution was unimaginable.[105]

Eighteenth-century British historiography in the second decade of the twenty-first century is rich but unstartling—a historiography that in its essentials resembles the dynamic yet settled society of the eighteenth century. Its virtues lie in the diversity of subjects studied; the empirical heft of findings derived from assiduous archival research; and the imaginative ways in which scholars approach new topics and themes. Its weakness is its parochialism and lack of interest in the wider world. It is a stable and content historiography for a stable and content country and century—that century being the eighteenth century, not the more contentious one we now inhabit. This unadventurous approach to the period diminishes its appeal to early Americanists. But lessons can still be learned. As David Waldstreicher notes (in praising Andrew O'Shaughnessy for writing "a classical imperial history"), an imperial history that emphasizes the longue durée and the importance of institutions and settler colonialism in understanding mid-eighteenth-century America has returned from the dusty irrelevance into which it was cast by Morgan in 1957.[106] One lesson that emerges from this sample is that historians of Britain and America would profit from paying more attention to an imperial history that takes Britain as part of a wider world centrally into consideration.

8

The American Revolution

I

This field report into the writing of early American history, with a sideways glance to British history, is not a story of transformative historiographical change. The historiographical currents of the last decade have been evolutionary rather than revolutionary, with few significant interpretative leaps. The places it describes, from the future Canada and the United States to the British Caribbean colonies of Jamaica, Barbados, and Antigua and the Atlantic colony of Bermuda in many important ways had the same socioeconomic characteristics in 1784, or even in 1800, as they had done in 1713.

Indeed, the seventy years of the eighteenth century covered in this study probably saw less dramatic change than in the century before or the century after, notwithstanding the major event that occurred near the end of this period, the American Revolution. White elite men remained dominant everywhere, except when Indigenous people were in control, meaning that men of high lineage and charismatic power were in control. Patriarchy remained the overriding principle in household government. Slavery had been ended in a few places where it had not been dominant, and abolitionism was gathering steam in Britain, the northern United States, and Canada. Nevertheless, slavery remained a fundamental institution throughout the Americas as the eighteenth century came to a close, shaping the lives of almost all Black people and remaining essential to American prosperity, with slaveholders in control of the West Indian colonies and the newly independent nation of the United States.[1] The position of Indigenous Americans relative to settlers was deteriorating, but their presence in much of the North American continent remained determinative, with Indigenous Americans able to shape imperial and then national outcomes well into the nineteenth century. Traditional areas of disputation such as the Ohio country remained out of reach to European expansionist desires at least until the defeat of Native American forces at the Battle of Fallen Timbers in 1794.[2]

That little of real substance changed during the eighteenth century is a major theme in this book with its emphasis on enduring continuities rather than on transformative change.[3] That same emphasis on evolution, not revolution—which is such a feature of the imperial turn and which is apparent also in treatments of subjects as diverse as slavery, religion, Indigenous American history, economics, and politics—has meant that even the American Revolution is not always depicted as a watershed moment. Instead, it is sometimes depicted as just one in a series of political changes in the Western Hemisphere and easily the least revolutionary of the great revolutions, notably compared to the French and Haitian ones. Nevertheless, opinion remains divided about the long-term influence of the American Revolution. Many historians continue to see the American Revolution as marking a significant break between one kind of society and another. Mark Peterson, for example, argues that "the American Revolution must be considered as a critical moment in the transformation of North America's populations, economies, societies, cultures, and perhaps most importantly environmental conditions," and contends that the revolution was a major contributor, along with the "peopling of America," that has brought the world to the precipice of ongoing climate disaster.[4]

Edward Gray and Jane Kamensky summarize the current consensus as follows in their introduction to their coedited *The Oxford Handbook of the American Revolution*. They argue that "contemporary scholars are inclined to see the American Revolution less in terms of a series of discreet, momentous turning points and more in terms of the *longue durée*: a swatch of historical time, lasting half a century or more, characterized by many of the phenomena and processes commonly attributed to a much narrower Revolutionary time line." They suggest that "many of the changes scholars once made synonymous with the Revolution started much earlier, or were completed much later, or both."[5] Where scholars see change as most apparent comes from the War of American Independence between 1775 and 1783 rather than the American Revolution itself. In short, placing the American Revolution in a longer and more global context reduces the long-term impact of the revolution and emphasizes instead the destabilizing effects of war, some of which were only temporary. As Woody Holton notes in a review of this important collection of essays, "Widening the lens to take in the rest of the world . . . makes the

War of Independence seem smaller." "Almost inevitably," he concludes, "placing the War of Independence in global context diminishes it."[6]

Few of the authors in *The Oxford Handbook of the American Revolution*, and in the journal literature on the American Revolution, follow the once-paradigmatic argument of Gordon Wood that the American Revolution was a radical experiment in popular democracy, though Wood's argument is one, scholars such as Alan Taylor, Michael McDonnell, and David Waldstreicher agree, that authors define themselves against.[7] One exception is Allan Kulikoff, who agrees with Wood, though he comes to Wood's conclusions from a different direction, stressing the destructive effects of the war on poor peoples' material well-being. Kulikoff argues that the War for American Independence "radicalized slaves, Indians, many white women, and a multitude of small property holders, all seeking freedom and liberty and protection of their property often in conflict with their betters."[8] He provides figures that show that poorer White southerners faced a dramatic decline in wealth and living standards as the result of the war and contends that the South's position as the wealthiest part of British North America ended in this period, with its economic decline relative to the North a determining factor in American history that was in place well before a further dramatic decline that occurred after the Civil War.[9] Like Kulikoff, those writers who see the American Revolution as having "profound long term consequences," as Michael McDonnell argues, cast such consequences to be largely negative, with the tumults of the war leading to "residual resentments" and "new divisions" between states and peoples. Jane Merritt stresses the negative impact of the American Revolution on Indigenes, advancing "dispossession and dislocation" among many Native peoples previously accustomed to autonomy. The only two writers who describe positive changes are Gary Nash, who celebrates African American quests for freedom in the War for American Independence, which he argues set in motion more emancipatory quests by African Americans in the American North after the war ended; and Stephen Mihm, who sees the American Revolution as a watershed moment in the invention and elaboration of finance and administration.[10]

Otherwise, historians in the *Oxford Handbook of the American Revolution* support propositions that the American Revolution saw limited change. Michael Zuckerman denies that manners between different classes of Americans altered as a result of the revolution. And although Terry Bouton, Ray Raphael, and Christopher Tomlins argue for a "democratic moment" during the war, they each insist that such a moment was temporary, with elite rule reasserted after the war was finished. Moreover, the United States did not achieve its most desired aim from winning independence, which was to be recognized as an equal nation by the great European powers of France, Spain, and especially Britain. Paul Mapp notes that "what the United States did not gain was status and rights in international affairs commensurate with the self-image of its leaders and publicists."[11] Nor did the American Revolution initiate great changes in either the position of slavery or in how slavery was viewed in Britain and America. Christopher Brown notes that the revolution "inspired a shift in moral perception sufficient to unsettle the place of slavery in American life but insufficient to dislodge it from the social order or to force the formation of a new one."[12]

II

Yet, of course, the inescapable fact of early American history is that it included a major political and cultural event, the American Revolution, which the people who lived through it thought was an event that separated everything that went before it from what followed. They thought it a radical event, even if modern historians are less inclined to see it that way. Contemporaries' views of what they lived through highlighted the revolutionary implications of the event. John Adams, for example, argued in 1818, nearly two decades after he completed a term as US president, that the American Revolution saw "radical" changes in people's "principles, opinions, sentiments and affections" and that it marked a decisive caesura between old assumptions and a modern, liberal, and democratic world. Historians are unlikely to see the shift between an ancien régime and new models of sovereignty as transformative as Adams argued. Nevertheless, it is probably too soon to contend once more that the American Revolution was as unimportant as Hannah Arendt argued it was nearly sixty years ago. Arendt thought the American Revolution was so successful because it changed so little. "The sad truth of the matter," she declared, "is that the French Revolution, which ended in disaster, has made world history, while the American Revolution, so triumphantly successful, has remained an event of little more than local importance."[13]

It might be the case that the new nation that emerged in the 1780s in the thirteen colonies was remarkably similar to what went before—an empire masquerading as a nation-state—but that did not mean that the "local importance" of what happened between 1776 and 1787 was not significant in shaping and changing future national or imperial trajectories. As Eliga Gould argues, American settlers moving westward "drew on notions of sovereignty that were new and innovative, re-enacting in each territory the home rule proclaimed in 1776 and asserting rights of conquest and self-government that went well beyond those of American settlers still subject to the British Crown."[14] The American Revolution remains central to how the history of early American history is written, even if the vision of the American Revolution that arises from recent literature is, in the views of Serena Zabin, who concluded the most recent overview of the topic, "not a proud story." The revolution laid, in her view, "the foundation for the creation of a neo-imperial United States, and we live today in the long shadow of that history."[15] That theme is constantly present in most recent writings on the American Revolution.

At its most basic level, the American Revolution had an immediate political impact, whatever its social and cultural resonances. It divided British America into several parts—thirteen colonies that became the USA; another set of colonies in the Caribbean and Canada that stayed within the British Empire, eventually becoming independent countries at various times in the nineteenth and twentieth centuries; as well as numerous unincorporated Indigenous American nations who were in power in large parts of the North American continent until well into the nineteenth century. The biggest geopolitical effect was probably within the plantation colonies and on slavery. The empire of slavery was divided in two, meaning that a near-majority of enslaved people in British America stayed part of the empire, even though the proportion of Blacks in the US population reached a height in the 1780s it was never to attain again.[16] Nevertheless, the power of enslavers in both North America and the West Indies took a long time to decline. After all, the majority of US presidents until the American Civil War were enslavers. Planters remained dominant in the Caribbean at least until the Morant Bay rebellion in Jamaica in 1865, even if emancipation in 1834 severely clipped their wings.

The trend in recent writing on early American history, which emphasizes continuity over change, means that the American Revolution is not seen as either an end (to the colonial period) or a beginning (the start of the United States of America) but as an event that happened in the middle of a longer flow of change. That is the approach taken, for example, in the most authoritative recent overviews of the American Revolution, the single-volume treatment by Alan Taylor and the set of essays on the American Revolution edited by Edward Gray and Jane Kamensky.[17]

Michael McDonnell and David Waldstreicher trace the origins of this movement to the mid-1990s when early American historians were unconvinced in a forum on Gordon Wood's Pulitzer Prize–winning *The Radicalism of the American Revolution* (1992) of his thesis that the American Revolution was truly radical and transformative in introducing ideas of liberal democracy and enhanced representation of White men within the body politic. They suggest that the articles published during the first half of the 1990s that most accurately pointed to the future of research into the American Revolution were ones by Edward Countryman on Indian history and by Carole Shammas on household government. Countryman urged scholars to think of the American Revolution within the context of continental history, integrating the recent findings historians had made on Indigenous history into new narratives. He argued that new accounts should note the shift across the revolutionary period from external colonialism under the British to US internal colonialism. Shammas wrote about comparative household governance, arguing that any consideration of revolutionary transformations needs to consider changes and continuities (the latter more notable than the former) in patriarchal household government.[18]

Scholars of the American Revolution writing in the 2010s are more convinced about what they dislike than about what they like. Rosemarie Zagarri, for example, looking at the American Revolution from the viewpoint of the early republic, notes that academic historians have no truck with the standard celebratory narrative account so dominant in popular histories of the American Revolution. That story is indifferent to much of Indigenous American history and the history of enslaved people and continues to be oriented around Edmund Morgan's birth-of-the-republic chronology of the revolutionary era, which describes the North American British colonies as richer and freer than anywhere else in the world. In this chronology the colonies responded to what a large number of settlers considered to be the outrageous acts of a tyrannical British government through legally and morally justified colonial rebellion and ended up even richer and freer than before, while introducing radical new principles of democracy, equality, and natural rights that transformed American society and made the infant nation of the United States an example to the world. There is not even an echo of such a narrative in recent writings on the American Revolution in academic journal literature.

Zagarri also notes two other themes to which historians writing recently on the American Revolution are allergic. One is perpetuating the myth of American exceptionalism or reducing the history of early America to a quest to build a viable nation-state. She argues that traces of exceptionalist narrative in the writing of the history of the American Revolution are difficult to avoid, whether seeing the American Revolution ushering in positive changes or demonstrating that the United States is uniquely immoral or exceptionally dangerous. She states that "both forms of exceptionalism result from the same premise: an approach that emphasizes the country's separateness and distinctiveness as a nation-state rather than its connections to and similarities with the rest of the world."[19] She also warns of accounts that reify the hegemony of the nation-state as being inevitable and useful. "Whatever one thinks of the morality of the nation-state in the past," she argues, "or of their viability for the future, there is no doubt that nation-states have represented an important historical form of social and political organization."[20]

Alan Taylor and Serena Zabin, introducing and concluding a joint special issue on the American Revolution between *WMQ* and *Journal of the Early Republic* (*JER*), are equally uncertain about the direction of current scholarship on the American Revolution.[21] Taylor stresses the ways in which scholarship is limited by the desire to place the American Revolution in the kind of global perspective for which Zagarri advocated in 2011 so that historians can resist the teleology of the territorial nation-state. He notes that scholars write of the American Revolution without acknowledging any part of it as revolutionary in any meaningful sense and argues that they are resistant to examining either the causes or the consequences of the conflict.[22] The American Revolution, in short, has been reduced to the War for American Independence, and even that war is seen in limited ways, as being mostly about senseless violence, orchestrated, in Taylor's view, by elites who seldom had ordinary people's interests at the forefront of their attention. The emphasis in current scholarship, Taylor argues, is on continuity rather than ruptures or transformations, with writers describing the American Revolution as operating within prior cultural forms rather than in creating new context.[23] Indeed, Taylor concludes, the new standard interpretation is that the only change resulting from the American Revolution is that White Americans forming a nation acted just like the British imperialists they replaced, except worse. The American Revolution, per Taylor, escalated and empowered westward migration and Indian dispossession: it was "a republican Union committed simultaneously to breaking down trade barriers overseas and dispossessing Indians."[24]

Taylor, like most historians writing about the American Revolution, sees the war itself as a disaster. It devastated the economy; caused turmoil and destruction, including severe mortality for enslaved people; generated massive debts for the new nation; and was an unmitigated catastrophe for Indigenous peoples. His American Revolution is less globally focused than Zagarri's. Reflecting the North American–centric composition of the eight essays in the twinned special issues he was commentating on, Taylor does not place the American Revolution in a global context, not mentioning France, Spain, Canada, or the Caribbean.[25] Rather, he sees the American Revolution as "a hard-fought, close-run, and long-lasting civil war."[26] His view echoes that of McDonnell and Waldstreicher, whose review of recent scholarship on the American Revolution suggests that it "illuminates a revolution that gave rise to a virulent empire in which war's disruption followed by the quickening pace of colonialism outweighed gains made by subaltern groups during the revolutionary settlement."[27]

Taylor struggles to see many transformations coming out of the American Revolution, but he outlines three changes that occurred after the revolution had finished, all of which were essentially negative features about the impact of this event. The revolution, he notes, generated racial distinctions that associated freedom with whiteness; it regularized state formation that secured the rule of strategic elites; and it accelerated westward expansion and the seizing of Indian land.[28] Taylor's view is echoed by Zabin. She thinks that "in every direction, the view is bleak." If the revolution made any difference at all, she states, it intensified unfortunate trends similar to those Taylor identifies—more racial chattel slavery; enhanced westward expansion and Indigenous dispossession; and greater inequality as elites consolidated their economic and political power in the early republic.[29]

III

The literature on the American Revolution is shaped by special issues, collections of essays, and many monographs. It is a frequent theme, as you would expect, in the journal literature of the last decade. Articles on the American Revolution are numerous in comparison with the weight of articles on earlier periods, with articles on the 1770s and 1780s being fivefold as numerous as articles on the 1710s and 1720s, which remains the dark age of American history.[30] Yet although the articles are numerous, their perspective is narrow. The war itself is depicted as pointless, messy, and violent. Holger Hoock, for example, focuses on narratives of the war in which American revolutionaries successfully mobilized atrocity narratives that describe in horrifying detail British violence against

American civilians, obsessing about mangled bodies in voyeuristic and semipornographic fashion.[31]

American patriots were good at controlling how the American Revolution was discussed in revolutionary wartime narratives, including turning British taunts against Americans back against the British and appropriating those taunts as a point of pride.[32] Friederike Baer shows another side of this practice in an article on how Americans viewed the British use of foreign auxiliaries, mostly German, in its army. She argues that patriots were able to show an outraged American public that the British monarch's use of such foreign auxiliaries demonstrated that George III and his ministers saw Americans as foreign enemies more than dissatisfied British subjects.[33] Similar outrage occurred, Christopher Magra argues, over British impressment of Americans into their armies and merchant marines.[34]

A frequent topic in recent literature concerns the formation of revolutionary and Loyalist allegiances in a war of independence that was also a civil war. These articles draw from Michael McDonnell's pioneering examination of wartime allegiances in Virginia, which he argued were fluctuating and contingent on events in a society that was less committed to patriotic rebellion for ideological reasons than it was concerned with personal interest and local and state politics.[35] Joshua Canale, Matthew Dziennik, and Christopher Minty each look at committees of public safety—how they were formed and how they operated so as to make supporting American rebels the default option in local communities in the fraught battleground of New York, where both patriots and loyalists were present in almost equally large numbers. They show how vicious the War for American Independence was in this contested battleground and how gaining the support of the public was vital for military success. Canale terms New York as a civil war space, while Minty argues that the lived reality of the American Revolution in New York involved people in the region learning how to exist under forms of institutionalized surveillance that increased in scope and ferocity over time. Dziennik concludes that the American Revolution depended as much on the exercise of authority as on the exercise of liberty, a common theme in recent writings that focus on power and local politics as shaping events more than deeper ideological currents.[36]

This interpretation fits with a developing argument, most forcefully put forward by Linda Colley in a global history of constitution-making but also addressed in articles on the making of the American constitution by Christopher Flanagan and Thomas G. Rodgers: that the making of such documents was done in the crucible of war and depended on understandings of coercion, military violence, and empire more than they did on Enlightenment principles of liberty, equality, and fraternity. Herbert Johnson, in an article with a more traditional backgrounding in constitutional history, stresses how the War for American Independence shaped constitution-making, an institutional arrangement that evolved out of practical experience as much as it was a governmental system that was in part established by significant documents.[37] This stress on contingency within the pressures of war also accords with a general neoimperial understanding of the coming of the American Revolution that sees it as emerging from an imperial set of crises that were badly handled by British leaders with limited experiences and perspectives, who could not understand, let alone control, the pressures emanating from a large, complex, and interrelated empire. Contingency has taken on a new importance in a war alternately thought of as a civil war and as a global conflict as much as a struggle for America's future.

The contingency argument stresses that the causes of the America Revolution arose from Britain's problems with empire rather than as an outgrowth of the emergent maturation of settler societies in North America. It also has led—unsurprisingly, given the drift of historiography toward paying attention to Indigenous people as active actors in imperial and revolutionary events—to greater emphasis on problems in the interior as provoking revolt. In short, the Royal Proclamation of 1763 has taken on as much significance as the Stamp Act of 1765 in lighting the spark of rebellion. The inability of Britain to control events in the Ohio valley and Illinois country shows how the American Revolution was as much about the fate of the American West as the condition of the American East. François Furstenberg, for example, claims that the fate of the West represented "the great problem of North American, and perhaps even Atlantic, history from 1754 to 1815." This perspective also encourages a view of the American Revolution that does not see it finished until well into the nineteenth century, as Furstenberg hints at in this formulation.[38]

A crucial issue to determine is who supported rebellion, who were Loyalists, and who preferred neutrality. It makes the matter of allegiance very important. Donald Johnson, for example, writes explicitly about matters of allegiance, focusing on South Carolina, another greatly contested place during the revolution. He shows that many Americans did not have fixed views about which side in the conflict they would support and insists that revolutionary allegiances were fluid, contingent, and often contradictory. Loyalty or patriotism depended on how people saw themselves treated, more than any constellation of beliefs that people held, in this interpretation. American patriots were far better at this person management than were the British, he suggests. Indeed, the British showed a rare ability to behave in ways that turned loyalists into patriots. As with other accounts in a similar vein, such as two recent books by T. H. Breen on how ordinary people during the war channeled popular rage against the British into effective if authoritarian committees of public safety, Johnson largely ignores ideological undercurrents in favor of close political analysis of local issues, in this case the governance of South Carolina, especially Charleston in the early 1780s.[39] Lauren Duval adds a gender dimension to the discussion of British occupation of Charleston. She shows how the British alienated White women in their confiscation strategies designed to punish patriots and reward loyalists because they were unable to recognize that women had rights to family property and were important in managing such property. The British put themselves forward as the protectors of White womanhood, but their policies, which took houses and other property away from women in the belief that property was a White male right alone in which White women were not involved, made them the enemies of White women, keeping them firmly on the side of the husbands that the British wanted to punish for treasonous behavior.[40]

IV

One significant tendency in academic as opposed to popular accounts of the American Revolution is to see it as an unfortunate interruption of an otherwise reasonably effective imperial system of governance. The American Revolution is thus less an advance in human freedom than a step toward unjust racial capitalism and rapacious settler colonialism. Such a view is a logical outcome of an imperial turn in which imperialism is seen in mostly positive ways. Imperialism was a means of managing diversity, with imperial authority forming an effective stop to the depredations of White settlers. That process ended with the creation of the American republic in 1787. All roads, it seems, led past George Washington and James Madison to Thomas Jefferson and most of all to Andrew Jackson—the president whose stock has sunk lowest of the major presidential figures in the writing of the last generation. That the Bancroft Prize in American History in 2021 went to Claudio Saunt's excoriating condemnation of the Indian policies of the early republic and antebellum

America resulting in Indian removal in the 1830s is an indication of how the American Revolution is increasingly seen as a significant moment in the degradation of non-Whites more than an advance in freedom.[41]

The American Revolution is an event that is increasingly viewed within imperial parameters and as part of larger processes of global evolutionary change affecting empires everywhere in a "world crisis" that mirrors the older concept of a seventeenth-century "general crisis."[42] The logical next step for revolutionary studies is to lessen the connection to America and make the American Revolution an event within British and European history. Yet, as noted in the previous chapter, there is no sign that most eighteenth-century British historians are interested in seeing the American Revolution as an important part of British history. But within early American history, the Britishness of the American Revolution is increasingly obvious. Edward Gray and Jane Kamensky argue that "America's Revolution was Britain's American War: a series of fateful moves in the high-stakes chess game of the European great powers, and chapter in the entangled history of a vast and growing empire."[43]

One starting point, as Johann Neem argues, is to recognize that colonial British America was not colonial proto-American; that most settlers saw themselves before 1776 as unproblematically British; that few colonists identified with a nascent American identity; and that the country that a proportion of British American colonists founded as a result of breaking away from Britain remained indebted to British cultural values and was embedded within a powerful British economic orbit.[44] As P. J. Marshall notes, "The pre-revolutionary British Atlantic World was able to survive the upheavals of war and American independence" because Britain and the United States continued to have many common links. "The strength of the links holding together the British Atlantic world," he writes, "ensured its rapid recovery from the ultimate failure of politics that had led to a fratricidal war." The American republic remained an economic and cultural vassalage of the British Empire well into the nineteenth century, as Henry Clay lamented when he stated that the United States was "a sort of set of independent colonies of England—politically free, commercially slaves."[45] The Britishness of the American Revolution brings us back to T. H. Breen's argument in 1997 that American nationalism was a response to exclusive forms of English nationalism that refused to include Americans and most of the Irish as being British and thus part of a British nation.[46]

There is, however, a problem to this approach, which tends toward the view that the British held of themselves in the eighteenth century: namely, that while they were a conquering people, they were also a beneficent and humanitarian people, and that their empire was one that brought peace and harmony to the majority of peoples under its rule. In short, this view of empire, one still held in some conservative circles and to an extent in the historiography of eighteenth-century Britain (but not generally accepted as being the best way to view British imperialism) is a view that sees Britain's imperial elites as a polite and generous people, motivated by humanitarianism in their dealings with the outside world.[47]

They were a people, in this reading, who after the Glorious Revolution had established a stable polity, devised a harmonious social order, established mechanisms of effective wealth creation, and created an empire that was responsive, reflexive, in the main well-run, and adept at incorporating polyglot populations into its strong cultural matrix under a sensible monarchical system of government.[48] The preceding sentence tends toward caricature but is, somewhat surprisingly, a view of British imperialism that often comes out of contemporary American scholarship, in which a determination to see White Americans as bad translates into an odd tendency to see the British as good. Michael Mann, for example, praising the British empire in a backhanded way from a leftist perspective, argues that democracy in settler communities tends to increase genocidal tendencies, noting that while settler societies were "distinctly democratic ... their ethnic cleansing of the natives was usually worse than that committed by ... less democratic imperial authorities."[49]

That lets the British very much off the hook. It would have surprised contemporaries as much as it does modern British historians. As Linda Colley succinctly states about the eighteenth-century British empire, Britain's modest size and its aggressive colonialism went together, since "domestic smallness and a lack of self-sufficiency made up for continuous British extroversion, not to say global house-breaking, violence and theft."[50] It makes little sense to engage in national comparisons of which nation was worse to Indigenes, the enslaved, and the poor when each nation involved in the British Atlantic world as well as the empire that sustained this world did its fair share of bad things. This "curse on both houses" approach reflects the conclusions emphasized by Gregory Dowd in his consideration of counterfactuals in regard to Indigenous history if the American Revolution had not turned out the way that it did. The British Empire in the nineteenth century was not a noticeably kind and generous entity, especially to people outside normal conceptions of who could be said to be properly British, which conceptions were usually associated with Whiteness. Canadian historians are also resistant to notions that somehow their imperial history makes them a more historically worthy nation than the United States.⁵¹ They have been assiduous, for example, in destroying old ideas that somehow New France did not enslave both Indigenous and African people and in countering lingering nostalgia for a French Empire that behaved better than the British Empire.⁵² It fits even more badly with the historiography of the Caribbean, where the French and British built ferociously inhumane systems of slavery that made them places of death for the unfortunate Africans forced to labor to make Europeans rich. The multitude of works on places like Jamaica that are included in this sample destroy any lingering notion of European imperialism being at all gentle.⁵³

V

The treatment of the American Revolution, given its outsized importance in American and British imperial history—as the previous discussion of imperialism as being better than settler colonialism suggests—has always drawn historians to speculate about its importance as a guide to both revolutionary and contemporary politics. In a survey of papers presented at the Huntington Library on narrating the age of revolution, Sarah Knott was exasperated by what she saw as historians' avoiding bold interpretations of the American Revolution that might have a political impact. She asked historians of the American Revolution to respond to constant calls in American public life for outlines of what the American Revolution might mean in the present. Historians, she argues, concentrate so overwhelmingly on empirical findings and engaging stories from the past, with little interest in making modern parallels, that their accounts of the American Revolution are politically disengaged.⁵⁴

But accounts of the revolution that downplay its disruptive or transformative possibilities can themselves have a political dimension. Alan Taylor argues in his summary of articles published in 2017 jointly in *WMQ* and the *JER* that authors "balk at finding much explanatory and transformative power in the revolution," with changes occurring "at their own pace before, as well as after, the violent rupture of the British Empire in North America." He declares himself doubtful about "how revolutionary the revolution truly was" except in being economically disastrous and in forcing leaders "to make concessions to common people," which lasted not much longer than the revolution itself but had some long-lasting legacies about the potential of the revolutionary war to effect transformation. His conclusion is downbeat: "The patriot victors reaped freedom and prosperity, but that success contained contradictions that would provoke a new civil war, even bloodier and more destructive than the revolution."[55] The implicit political position Taylor suggests here is that the American past is not one to celebrated, or at least not to be celebrated uncritically.

Taylor has been criticized for developing such a position by Gordon Wood. Wood argues that Taylor has an animus against the Founding Fathers and against White Americans in general, with Thomas Jefferson a person of especial disdain. He notes that "Taylor never fails to point out the discrepancies between the ideals of white Americans and the sordid realities of their behavior" and quips that "it is startling to witness how much the Thomas Jefferson Foundation Professor at Jefferson's own university dislikes its patron, Thomas Jefferson."[56] McDonnell and Waldstreicher's conclusion that "the colonists' truly revolutionary act was to break away from Europe in order to set up their own virulent empire, à la Edward Countryman" has a clear political impact, akin to what has been termed "Black Armband history," in the conflicts over early Australian history that were an early manifestation of the cultural wars over history that have been increasingly common throughout the English-speaking world.[57]

Knott has a point when she accuses historians of the American Revolution of refusing to place their work within larger contexts, even though her objections to scholarship that is empirical and politically quiescent comes from a different position than where Wood is politically located. Such scholars currently resist being placed in schools of interpretation. McDonnell and Waldstreicher fashion their survey of trends in writing about the revolution since the 1950s around competition between several schools of interpretation—neo-Whig, neoprogressive, and neoimperial—and conclude that the neoimperial is now in the historiographical ascendant. But the neoimperial school they describe is defined less by what its proponents hold to be true than by what they are against. McDonnell and Waldstreicher see the contemporary neoimperial school as arguing against interpreting the American Revolution in exceptionalist terms or as a major and incomparable historical event. Adherents of the neoimperial approach, in this telling, show little interest in seeing the American Revolution as building a nation or in thinking that the American Revolution had a distinctive character. Edward Gray and Jane Kamensky are blunt about what is implied by arguing that what revolutionary Americans created was an empire—"not a colonizing, oceanic empire like its British counterpart, but an empire nonetheless."

This empire was a continuation of older patterns, much to the chagrin of opponents of the Constitution who thought a nation intent on war, settlement, and trade in order to increase territorial claims across North America was incompatible with republican government.[58] New imperialism was like old imperialism, characterized by "land hunger, profit seeking and eagerness to exploit new resources."[59] Such a view accords with the understanding of historians of imperialism, where empire is a destructive process, rather than with the views of writers on the American Revolution, many of whom see imperialism as being at least better than the alternative that replaced it.[60]

Other historians are less willing than McDonnell and Waldstreicher to sort historians into interpretive schools. Patrick Spero, for example, in an introduction to an important collection of essays on the American Revolution, argues that "the new paradigm is that there is no single paradigm." He is unconvinced that McDonnell and Waldstreicher's three schools of interpretation have much to offer historians of the American Revolution today, except in providing an implicit teleology that "obscured more than clarified the true nature of the American Revolution." He rejects the idea that the duty of the historian is "to clarify the past," and he welcomes more complicated narratives and applauds historians' "willful quest for messiness."[61] This does not mean that Spero thinks there is no pattern whatsoever to American revolutionary scholarship, but he insists that these perspectives are narrow and limited. Spero sees the American Revolution as primarily a civil war that foreshadowed, in the words of Gray and Kamensky, "future conflict between natives, settlers, and rulers."[62]

None of these authors follow traditional ideas of what caused the American Revolution. Spero sees the event "as a failed imperial project as much as a moment of nation-building," while Gray and Kamensky deny that the conflict was about taxation and representation and stress instead territorial sovereignty and territorial dispossession. Spero underplays ideology in favor of long-term environmental factors, and all authors are resistant to monocausal interpretations of the coming of the revolution. "The Glorious Cause was many causes," Gray and Kamensky argue, showing the complexity, fluidity, and polyglot nature of the period, which makes it difficult to pin down specific turning points: "Many of the changes scholars once made synonymous with the Revolution started much earlier, or were completed much later, or both."[63]

Nevertheless, the American Revolution is hard to treat as just another event in early American history. Americans have always believed that the revolution presented principles animating contemporary life in multiple ways. There is a strong tension in the literature about the need for the American Revolution to be transformative or another event to be fitted into international reconfigurations in the late eighteenth century. For some historians, it is important that their version of the American Revolution is meaningful for current generations given that, as Michael Zuckerman expounds, the revolution "has been the scripture that we share that binds us together as a nation." We might note the exclusive language used, assuming that the meaning of the American Revolution is mostly for Americans. We can also see in current literature the dismissal of any idea that the American Revolution has any real meaning for today, with Zuckerman declaring that "the transformative, even the transgressive, time of the American Revolution is over."[64]

Not all historians are so willing to see the American Revolution as having no transformative elements. Aaron Fogleman, for example, argues that one major transformation from the American Revolution was that migration to America moved from being mostly unfree, with people traveling coerced to British North America, to being movement that was overwhelmingly of free people, going willingly to the United States of America.[65] Rosemarie Zagarri insists that the long-term effect of the American revolutionary political settlement was only really effected with the election of Thomas Jefferson and his Democratic-Republican Party in 1800, which she argues was a transformative moment, even if the election had been bitterly contested. She argues that, despite internal contradictions, "by enshrining equality, natural right and individual liberty as the nation's foundational principles, [the Republicans] delegitimized a politics based on hierarchy, privilege and status."[66] Eliga Gould makes the nuanced point that "although we like to think of the American Revolution as the moment when Americans began to make their own history, it would be more accurate to see the Revolution as the moment when Americans began to make their own history that other nations and people were prepared to let them make."[67] Tom Cutterham returns to the older debate about the origins of capitalism in the United States and posits that the American Revolution was a critical event in this formation, less because it changed the world of labor than because it reconstructed capital. He notes the destructive nature of the war ruined some of the wealthiest families in colonial America, leading to their replacement by a new capitalist elite who owed their prominence to revolutionary agitation and disturbance—men such as Jeremiah Wadsworth of Connecticut, who was one of the three wealthiest capitalists in the country and who made his money through supplying French soldiers.[68]

One area where historians are eager to see transformational change is in the new nation's international dimensions. The creation of a new nation founded on republican principles and arising from a colonial revolt meant recourse to public international law when Americans interacted with other polities. That meant Americans immersing themselves in the law of nations. David Golove and Daniel Hulsebosch declare that revolutionary Americans committed themselves to the law of nations with "the faith of new, sometimes, desperate converts." They note that "from the Declaration of Independence and the writing of state constitutions, to the forging of a confederation to wage war and make treaties, the institutions, forms and doctrines of the law of nations structured the quest to escape the British Empire and create new republican governments."[69]

Yet even when we see authors arguing for the revolution as showing that "Americans obviously did make history in 1776," historians have tended to stand back from the implications of such bold statements. No one, for example, has followed Fogleman in exploring different migration patterns after 1787 as resulting from the ideology enunciated in the American Revolution, and even Fogleman backs away from the implications of his argument, stating that the American Revolution did not began "an ongoing, contrapuntal set of cultural and social changes," but rather that "the age of revolution must be treated as a single long-going upheaval, lasting from 1760s to the 1860s, whose history needs a single, organic, dramatic portrayal."[70]

Zagarri also walks back from her argument that the long-term political implications of the American Revolution included a national commitment to foundational principles of equality by comparing British India to the American early republic. She comes to the "sobering possibility" that in practice the American Revolution made little difference in the crucial area of establishing White supremacy, something that "developed in a startingly similar fashion in both places." The United States of America was decidedly not exceptional either in a positive sense of celebrating America's commitment to equality and natural rights or in a negative sense that "points to the country's unique moral culpability." She concludes that "if a discourse of white racial solidarity extended across the globe, and similar racial practices emerged in India and the U.S. at about the same time, then American ideas of white racial superiority may have gained greater legitimacy and force precisely because they were not unique to the United States."[71]

Gould, too, qualifies his belief that the American Revolution had several transformative aspects by turning colonies into states and subjects into ostensibly equal citizens by noting that new changes fed on old impulses of colonialism and that what was transformative was how old patterns resulted in the assertion of "rights of conquest and self-government that went well beyond those of their own predecessors, let alone those of American settlers still subject to the British Crown." He wryly concludes that the revolution was transformative "only because of the uses to which contemporaries put it."[72] He stresses, too, that Americans—no matter their bombast about independence and the reality that they had removed themselves from the political, if not the economic influence of Britain—were still constrained by their tenuous position in international politics. He concludes that "to focus on the history that Americans made without mentioning the constraints by which they were bound is to risk falling once again into the trap of American exceptionalism, and in so doing to miss the many ways in which the history of the American people . . . remained entangled with the histories of other nations and people."[73]

VI

The study of the American Revolution is thus in transition, more so than is the case for other areas of early American history, in part because more is at stake for studies of the American Revolution than for the rest of early American history. We can see this in controversies over the *New York Times* 1619 Project, a Pulitzer Prize–winning initiative that has proved a lightning rod in the culture wars that periodically roil the United States. The premise behind the 1619 Project is similar to that which animates recent work on the American Revolution, which is to insist on continuity in US history from the earliest colonial time to the present. For the *New York Times*, the thesis advanced is that the real founding of America was in 1619 when the first enslaved people from Africa arrived in Virginia (though, of course, Africans had arrived in other parts of the North American continent that later became part of the United States in the sixteenth century) rather than 1776, the date usually considered the start of the United States. The year 1619 should be considered the start of the US nation because American history should be written around the establishment of slavery and persisting racial inequality and discrimination from 1619 to 2019. As Patrick Griffin comments, the

1619 Project wants to replace 1776 with 1619 because it insists that "to understand the United States meant rooting its birth in the seventeenth, not the eighteenth century," and to do so means to concentrate this narrative on "the oppression of the marginalized, particularly the enslaved."[74]

For most early American historians, a historical trajectory of American history that starts with slavery in the seventeenth century (an alternative would be Indigenous dispossession) is unproblematic. It is generally unproblematic for other historians and for the general public, too. To my knowledge, few of the complaints about supposed inaccuracies in the 1619 Project concern the telling of early American history. Indeed, the 1619 Project, despite wanting to stress the ongoing continuities between seventeenth-century and later America history until the present, does not spend much time on the colonial period, and none of the historical advisors employed by the New York Times are experts on colonial history. The controversies over the 1619 Project have been largely around supposed misinterpretations and errant facts about the causes of the American Revolution and about what is seen as a lack of respect for the Founding Fathers and to customary understandings of the American Revolution as a revolution about liberty and establishing America as a haven of freedom rather than about going to war to preserve slavery. The controversies are sufficiently arresting as to move outside of academia into quality journals like The Atlantic, the New Republic, and the New York Review of Books and into statements by important historians defending traditional interpretations of the American Revolution in which the role of slavery as a cause of the American Revolution and the constitution as proslavery document are strongly contested.[75] The fierce arguments show, inter alia, that the moral meaning of the American Revolution for the present-day citizens of the United States still matters.

As Patrick Griffin notes, the year "1776 is one totemic date among many for an Atlantic-wide moment of nation-building, all emerging from the age of revolution. Symbols from the age and the dates that go along with them ... underwrite both long-held and evolving understandings of liberty and order." He concludes that "1776 is premised on the idea of redemption" and "should call forth humility, not certainty or celebration: the nation that is the United States is ever failing but also ever striving. It therefore gestures to aspirations, just as it sustains peace."[76] The evocation of such sentiments shows the American Revolution to be in a special historical category, an event that speaks to the present as much as to the past. It might be true that scholars "of a new generation" "disdain to take a heroic stance" when presenting research on the American Revolution, spurning nation-building exercise with an aim to "blur boundaries and heighten contingency." They may be intent on "decentering and destabilizing" schoolbook verities and the "epic grandeur" of traditional accounts. But these efforts to demystify the American Revolution occur while historians are still participating in "a civic conversation that began with the birth of the republic and has never abated."[77] It is impossible to entirely decenter and downplay the significance of the American Revolution when it plays such an important role in America's mythic past. Scholars may comment that the current historiography of the American Revolution revolves around decentering it from the bombastic themes of the past that are used to explain the American present and future, but they also tend to insist that, as Gould and Zagarri write, "the revolution has lost none of its disruptive force."[78] Early American history has thus not yet entirely merged into, or taken over, the historiography of the American Revolution, even if scholars tend toward stressing continuities between what happened in the British imperial Atlantic before the American Revolution and what went after. The American Revolution matters as part of civic discourse. It matters more, for early American historians at least, in how it helps define the boundaries of their subject. At present those boundaries are spatially wide but also temporally capacious—the American Revolution is less an event sufficient into itself but is one that has global repercussions, even if these repercussions are in an early stage of being worked out. It is very much placed within the context of an age of revolutions, in which the American Revolution is neither a start nor an end but an event that is part of a wider transformation of the world in the late eighteenth and early nineteenth centuries.[79]

Conclusion

I

In the last decade early American historians (and eighteenth-century British historians) have written a great deal of fascinating empirical work on early America, the long eighteenth century in Britain, and the American Revolution. The empirical understanding of this period, in both its Continental and Atlantic frameworks, has been spectacularly advanced. The amount of data produced about early America in the eighteenth century is astounding—as it is, of course, for the writing on almost any historical period. It does sometimes seem as if there are nearly as many historians of this period writing today as there have been in the 150 years or so of professional writing on early America and the American Revolution. And what they write about has undergone a shift in the last decade, at least a shift in the topics covered and in the geographical scope of what constitutes early America, while there have been less obviously important shifts in the interpretative schemas and in the methodological and theoretical foundations of the field.

The expansion in geographical scope is truly remarkable. Early America is no longer the thirteen colonies of traditional historiography. In geographical terms, the reach of the field is notably large, meriting the hashtag #VastEarlyAmerica, which has been successfully applied to early Americanists' spatial horizons by one of the leading research institutions shaping scholarship, the Omohundro Institute, located in Williamsburg, Virginia, where the leading journal in the field, *WMQ*, has been published since 1943.

If anything, the traditional colonies where most early American writing in the past has been located—New England and the Chesapeake—have become marginalized in a more expansive spatial understanding of early America in which Jamaica and New France might be more conspicuous than New York or Pennsylvania. The choice of such places as suitable for investigation indicates just how far early Americanists have moved away from seeing eighteenth-century British America as merely a prologue to the American Revolution and the creation of a new nation called the United States of America. If the period were about nation-building (which increasingly it is not), it is about the creation of several nations, such as Canada, the United Kingdom, and island nations in the Caribbean, and about the development of the British Empire into the Leviathan it became in the nineteenth century. What has replaced the thirteen colonies in the early American lexicon? To a large extent, the topics and areas that have attracted most interest among early American historians fit outside the normal boundaries of the thirteen colonies: Indigenous America; slavery and plantation societies, especially in the West Indies; and the various permutations of empire, including the idea of gender frontiers within imperial frameworks.

The range and quality of the work I have read in the journal literature of the 2010s is of a very high standard. This book is thus a mixture of admiration for good work and concern that the field is not moving fast enough toward new paradigms. Early American history is less impressive when viewed collectively than when it is read as individual pieces of work. Early American historians have taken to heart the imperative to find connections between places and themes, in what Johann Neem has criticized as an historiography built around the politics of exchange. They have considered this finding of connections as an inherently good thing without putting much effort into examining why they think studying connections and processes of exchange is so important.[1] Early American historians seemingly want to "only connect," in the words of E. M. Forster, in *Howard's End* (1910). But it is the modifier "only" rather than the imperative to "connect" that impresses. The effort at finding connections has resulted in a great deal of linkages between topics, themes, and places but fewer grand interpretative advances than might have been expected.

Early American historians have been better at *describing* than they have been in *explaining*. At least as it emerges from their journal publications, they are relentless empiricists devoted to archival research and accustomed to working within a narrow historiography developed by like-minded experts on aspects of early American history rather than aspiring to be expansively minded scholars trying to transform the field through new ways of envisioning how to understand and write about early America. For all the achievements of early American historians as noted in this survey of recent journal literature, early American history—probably like other historical fields in cognate areas, and certainly like practitioners in the relatively conservative field of eighteenth-century British history—can be remarkably insular and parochial, seldom moving outside well-worn pathways and, at least in the last decade, tending toward the unadventurous finding rather than the controversial approach.

A harsh view of the majority of the articles I have read for this study is that they are "worthy": nice and unproblematic additions to scholarship in an evolving but seldom revolutionary field. Such a critical view of the field may, of course, derive from the research strategy used—the process of getting research findings published as an article and the fierce peer review involved in turning a thought into a published article might mitigate against theoretical originality and the promulgation of controversial views. Not surprisingly, given the methodological and theoretical conservatism in the field—the devotion to empirical research and the lack of interest or knowledge of work done in cognate fields of history outside the narrow bounds of what happened in the eighteenth century, let alone in disciplines other than in history such as in the social sciences or literary criticism—the emphasis throughout my reading is on the importance of continuity over the significance of change.

II

So where does this leave us in regard to an evaluation of the writing of early American history today? I won't venture where the field is going—it is difficult enough to assess where we are now and what are the major themes that animate early American historians without doing what historians are not good at, which is predicting the future. The 1993 special issue in *WMQ* where the confident predictions of where the field was likely to go in the near and medium future were often wide of the mark suggests that gazing into the crystal ball of future historiographical directions for early American history is a fool's errand. Moreover, my aim in this book is to report as fairly and without prejudice where I see the principal topics that historians are interested in rather than to try and direct where I think scholarship should be heading. I have tried to report on what I have found and occasionally on what I have not found less to align this work to what I think historians should or should not be interested in than to report on the state of the field as I have found it.

Some conclusions do present themselves, however. Early American history is in good shape although it is unlikely that in 2022 we can repeat

Fred Anderson and Drew Cayton's claim in 1992 that there has "never a better time to be an early American historian than now."[2] The advances in historical scholarship in early American history have been less pronounced and less dramatic since 1992 than in the previous three decades when early Americanists' embrace of social science history made them methodologically advanced and a model of scholarship that proved influential in other fields. The horizons of the field have shrunk. It is a subdiscipline in history that is remarkably insular and self-regarding; generally uninterested in perspectives from other fields of history, let alone from other disciplines; surprisingly parochial in its relative indifference to works in other languages and in nations other than the United States; and with a tendency to engage in unwitting exclusionary language when thinking about the audience for research findings in which that audience is presumed to be residents of the current American republic.

The field of early American history can be very narrowly focused, as revealed by a short list of important topics that one would think early American historians would be interested in, but are not. Early Americanists urge their fellow historians to take a wider view of early American history than occurred in the period in which they were enamored of social science and in exploring in enormous detail the small-scale societies of relatively isolated people living in New England towns or Chesapeake parishes. Their new, outward-looking histories intersect the global history beginning in 1750 that John McNeill and Kenneth Pomeranz chronicle in their introduction to the modern volumes of the *Cambridge World History* (2015), which they describe as "@1750: destruction, connection, and a world of colliding empires." But early American history in the last decade has contributed little to the three developments that McNeill and Pomeranz consider the most extraordinary changes in this period. They note that the eighteenth-century world was a world on the move. It was a time of great population growth, following the last period (1610–80) in which the global population grew very little and perhaps not at all. In the eighteenth century the global population grew by 50 percent, a phenomenon that had never happened before. An even more remarkable change was the energy transition from plant fuels to fossil fuels and the crucial first act to the modern drama of continuing economic growth that we term industrialization, which has led to global GDP increasing by about 100 times since 1750—the start of the uniquely creative and uniquely destructive Anthropocene. And the final change connected economics to geopolitics, which was the shift of global economic and political power from the great landed empires of Asia, especially China, where the center of world history had resided for millennia, to the seaborne empires of western Europe and the neo-Europes created by the settlers from Europe in many parts of the world. Recent studies in early American history show a profession that is not notably interested in questions of population and migration nor in the transition to industrialization; nor is it concerned about the arresting thesis that has been of considerable interest to Asian and European scholars of what Kenneth Pomeranz has called the Great Divergence, a momentous global change in the distribution of wealth and power that signaled a shift in geopolitical power, from east to west and away from what later became conceptualized as the global south towards the global north.[3]

III

Moreover, the leading journal literature on early America in the last eight or nine years can be surprisingly limited in what subjects are covered, especially when it comes to previously dominant topics. There is nothing recently published in journals about the eighteenth-century Great Awakening and relatively little written overall on aspects of religion; traditional topics of interest such as the causes of the American Revolution, the nature of the Chesapeake elite and the Chesapeake in general are neglected; and the impact of the subaltern school and other developments in the historiographies of cognate areas of colonialism and postcolonialism, with the significant exception of settler colonialism, is notable by its absence. Nor is there interest in the Founding Fathers and their role in creating an American nation, despite how important that topic is within popular history. The Enlightenment is hardly mentioned. Most importantly, interest in the historical subjects that were so important in the social science inflected scholarship of the generation before the current one—ordinary men and women as workers, farmers, and members of households (history from below, in short)—has virtually disappeared. Accounts of these people seem to have been the principal casualties of the move first to cultural history and then to imperial and global history. Tony Hopkins noted this tendency to ignore ordinary people early on in the move, which he promoted, to a more capacious history oriented around the twin themes of imperialism and globalization. He commented, a tad waspishly, that "an analysis of the titles published in journals specializing in the history of the world outside Europe and North

America shows that peasants and proletarians and class vanished in 1989 and were replaced thereafter by asylums, knowledge (especially science and medicine) and a plenitude of representations."[4]

Thus, early American history has narrowed its perspectives in the last thirty years, with scholarship being overwhelmingly focused on the twin subjects of race and racial relations—whether between Europeans and Indigenous people or Europeans and Africans, African Americans and Afro-Caribbeans—and the ramifications of European and Native American imperialism in an early America defined by empire. It engages less with antebellum history and European history than one would expect and hardly at all with other historical fields. Yet other fields also neglect early Americanists' findings, as we have seen in this account in a summary of recent trends in the writing of eighteenth-century British history. This would also be true if we looked at mainstream French history, where, Cécile Vidal has lamented, French historians have seldom paid much attention to what early American historians have been writing or to placing the history of France in Atlantic or global perspectives.[5]

Such indifference by other historians about the findings made by early American historians is unfortunate because the study of early America is rewarding in itself for the details that have been discovered about a dynamic, fascinating, and meaningful period in the history of the Americas and the Atlantic world by a host of talented historians. One sign of the vitality of early American history as a historical subfield is how the agenda that drives scholarship in this area—notably the importance of Indigenes in American history; the centrality of racial chattel slavery to Atlantic history from the Columbian encounter to the death of George Floyd in Minneapolis in 2020; and the ways in which colonialism and imperialism continue to shape the modern world long after the particular features of these early American staples had supposedly ended—has been taken up by scholars in other fields, without much knowledge of what happened in eighteenth-century British America. It is remarkable how the topics of interest in eighteenth-century British American history are those that now shape historical discourse in later periods of American history, more than the other way around, a trend especially noticeable in scholarship on the American Revolution and the early republic. It is scholarship on early America that conditions work in these later historical periods, rather than the opposite.

IV

The most surprising feature of recent early American history writing is that the period before the American Revolution is viewed in such favorable ways. J. H. Elliott, for example, notes about America in the second quarter of the eighteenth century that the shortcomings of British imperialism in the Americas were less important than its vibrancy and success.[6] And the general message that the literature on the long eighteenth century in Britain presents is one that would have delighted the leaders of the Whig oligarchy who ran that country—eighteenth-century Britain in current historiography shows a wealthy, prosperous, generally happy country moving with great success into both modernity and global predominance.

The enthusiasm for empire in accounts of this period runs counter to most of the assumptions in the writing of early American history from the 1940s to the 1980s, when British venality was stressed and the rightness of the patriot complaints against authoritarian and liberty-denying British imperialism—the Glorious Cause, in effect—was fundamental. The historiography of the present in regard to understanding the nature of British (and French) imperialism from the Treaty of Utrecht to the end of the Seven Years' War is not whiggish (early American historians repeatedly argue that we need to avoid exceptionalist accounts of American history and that we should work hard to escape the trap of teleological interpretations whereby all roads lead to the American Revolution and to the creation of the US republic), but it favors Whig history, insofar as the Whig oligarchy that ran British politics in this period and the imperial officials that represented that oligarchy in the empire are seen, in new ways, as remarkably effective, presiding over settler societies that operated essentially in harmonious ways.

The beneficence of the ancien régime might not seem so apparent, however, to some of those who experienced life at the margins of the prerevolutionary world, whether they were the London criminal poor dying on the gallows or the modal migrant to eighteenth-century America—a Biafran enslaved women transported in the horrific Middle Passage to work and to die producing sugar for the European sweet tooth while living in the brutal conditions of a Jamaican sugar plantation. But the advantages of living in an ancien régime that was dynamic, modernizing, and able to manage diversity and that was surprisingly inclusive may have seemed more apparent to the urban merchant in Kingston, Philadelphia,

Montreal, Detroit, or Bristol, who is the ideal imperial type getting most attention in the literature covered in this book.

This relatively positive view of the ancien régime of imperial Britain and France in a growing and increasingly flourishing colonial world is the aspect of recent writings on early America with which my own work is most at odds, especially when combined with a position on the American Revolution that stresses how it intensified the less pleasant aspects of eighteenth-century imperial life in new, more authoritarian and exploitative ways and posits that what came before the American Revolution was better than what happened after. There is no shortage of articles in this book's sample that demonstrate how the vitality of eighteenth-century early America before the American Revolution came about through mistreating the less fortunate, especially Indigenous people and the enslaved. An overall impression of eighteenth-century British America is that it was an improvement on the horrors of colonization, war, and violence of seventeenth-century British America and on the depredations carried out by strategically important White elites in the early republic and afterward. Nevertheless, determining whether the American Revolution saw an improvement or a decline in the quality of American and British imperial life is a line of inquiry that does not lead to historically useful conclusions but merely responds to a seemingly insistent need to evaluate whether the American Revolution was a *novus ordus seclorum*, a new order of the ages. I am not sure we get anywhere trying to work out whether the colonial period was a good thing or not, an interlude of relative harmony when Enlightenment values prevailed as opposed to the war, violence, and tumult of a calamitous "Little Ice Age" seventeenth century or the harsher nineteenth-century world of Andrew Jackson and Manifest Destiny.[7] We have yet to see the close attention paid to change over time in eighteenth-century British, British imperial, and early American scholarship—decades tend to merge into one another with little appreciation of decadal differences—that has been manifest in the close attention paid to similarities and differences over space that is fundamental to a vision of a capacious early America.

Such a view of relative imperial beneficence followed by a harsher political regime fits poorly both with how the British Empire is viewed outside American perspectives and with the reality of empire in Jamaica. I have not included my work in the last decade published in journals in this analysis, but if I did, the eleven articles, mostly on Jamaican themes, that I have published in this period would portray a British Empire that fostered an especially brutal slave regime in which enslaved people were treated with almost unbelievable contempt and where the culture of White enslavers was contemptible. My work shows, inter alia, how the plantation system brought such wealth to imperial coffers that people turned a blind eye until the late 1780s to how terrible slavery was in Jamaica.

The late seventeenth and early eighteenth century saw in British America a "terrible transformation," as Peter Wood has argued, and marked the eighteenth-century British Empire as being founded on many examples of extreme injustice.[8] The "terrible transformation" was not just a harsher form of Black slavery but involved a fresh repression of Indigenous societies and a determination to keep poorer White Americans and West Indians in their place. Neither Black slaves, Indigenous Americans, nor ordinary workers accepted how they were treated, meaning that beneath the surface of "improved" American society in the eighteenth century lay the barbarous instincts that characterized the seventeenth century.[9]

The notion of a relatively beneficent British Empire also does not fit well with the history of Quebec, as reenvisioned in recent literature influenced by work on early American history. Nancy Christie and Michael Gauvreau have been especially active in this respect. They show that British rule was very contested, with their work bringing Quebec into close dialogue with similar contestations during and after the American Revolution in the thirteen colonies and United States. Christie argues against an orthodox narrative of benign and nonauthoritarian British rule in postconquest Quebec. It might be that in 1763 British officials in Quebec did not repeat the barbarity of 1755, when thousands of French Acadians were expelled from Acadia to other parts of the French Empire, but, Christie insists, this did not presage a new era of humanitarianism or lead to a peaceful integration of French-Canadian subjects into British imperial social and political orders. She sees Quebec not through the accommodationist lens that was promulgated by British governors with a self-interest in seeing the province as tranquil and in good order, but as a place of intense ethnic conflict, a colony "simmering with multiple axes of discontent, riven by tensions between the civil and military authorities, between the ambitions of French and English merchants, and the differing outlooks of people of different rank and ethnicities." She notes that French Canadians may have been less obviously oppressed by Britain than Indigenous or Black populations, but they were denigrated all the same, never considered fully British or fully civilized. British rule and Anglicization as French Canadians experienced it was far from benign, as it was founded upon a xenophobic Britishness that privileged the rights of freeborn Englishman and was predicted upon eradicating French culture and political rights.[10]

If we want to see how the British Empire acted in reality, not in the theoretical ways that might be imagined in counterfactuals in which British America never experienced revolution, let's look at British imperialism in the Windward Islands, which were returned (except for Tobago) to Britain in the Peace of Paris in 1783. Britain showed there that they had learned lessons from the settler revolt in North America, mainly that the "soft" hand of imperialism did not work and that everyone except for White elites needed to be treated with the "hard" fist of Britain's powerful armed forces. Even White elites needed to become subservient to imperial rule, and their political autonomy was severely decreased in the 1780s and 1790s. The British abandoned policies of assimilation and accommodation in this imperial meridian. After 1783 they took away the political rights of Catholics and restricted their right to worship; they subjected people of color to increasingly rigid legal procedures that tested these people's legal status; they acted in repressive ways toward the enslaved; and they ordered Kalinagos to remain behind a boundary line established in 1773.

When the Haitian Revolution erupted in the early 1790s, as the French Revolution created civil war in the eastern Caribbean, and as war between France and Britain started in 1794, tensions became unbearably high and one of the greatest, though little known, Caribbean slave revolts—Fedon's Revolt, led by a free man of color, Julien Fedon—broke out in Grenada between March 1795 and June 1796. It signaled Britain's worst fears—a coalition of Kalinagos, French Catholics, free people of color (the leaders of the revolt), and thousands of enslaved people taking up arms against imperial power. When it finished, damages were over £3 million sterling; the plantation economy was irretrievably damaged; and almost half of the colony's enslaved population of 25,000 had been killed in battle, executed, or had deserted the colony for other places. The brutality was on the level of the Haitian Revolution, both from insurgents and even more from the British government and British planters. Slave rebellion was accompanied by Indigenous war, in the Second Carib War, a war of extreme violence that resulted in the defeat of the Kalinagos in St Vincent and the end of their centuries-long resistance to imperial rule. Most of the Kalinagos were forcibly removed, at great cost of lives, first to a dismal island prison near St. Vincent and then to Spanish island of Roatan in the Bay of Honduras, where they established a culture that remains today. Few episodes in the history of the infant United States, including Indian removal in the 1830s, can match the viciousness of how the British Empire acted toward its opponents in 1795–96 in the eastern Caribbean.[11] We should not assume, therefore, that if the course of history had run differently and America had remained part of the British Empire that some of the less appealing features of Jacksonian America would have been mitigated.

These counterfactual musings also show how early American historians still struggle with the concept of the "global." For early Americanists studying seventeenth- and eighteenth-century North America, placing early America in global context seems both obvious and necessary. Philip Morgan and Molly Warsh sum up the obviousness and necessity of placing early America in global perspective with succinctness and clarity. They suggest that the impulses shaping early North America (and this is also true for the British West Indies) "came from both within the continent and from beyond its borders" and that "regardless of their origins ... these disparate impulses were all internal to a world in transformation."[12] But the extent to which early American history and American history is truly global is problematic. Early America is only occasionally involved in general surveys of global history and world history. North America is hardly mentioned in the early modern volumes of the *Cambridge World History*, and the one essay on the United States in world history in a later volume hardly deals with the colonial period, although the author contends that America was always embedded in global affairs, noting that in the colonial period North America was "a major theatre for the working out of imperial ambitions between France, Spain and Britain, and the various Amerindian tribes." The Caribbean, by contrast, is much more integrated into global processes in this multivolume undertaking, including two essays with the Caribbean as important featuring in the early modern volume: one by Alan Karras highlights the Caribbean as a principal region of global interactions.[13]

It is instructive that when scholars move temporally from writing about a capacious seventeenth- and eighteenth-century early America that includes not just the Caribbean and Canada but in some cases Europe and Africa, they narrow their horizons to the United States and to those places that become part of the United States. Books such as Jamie Belich's *Replenishing the Earth*, which places the nineteenth-century United States within the context of transnational British migration patterns, remain rare.[14] When Alan Taylor wrote about the legacies of the American Revolution in his survey from 2016, he confined his attention to how the American Revolution changed life for residents of the United

States without dealing with what staying in the British Empire meant for the residents of the Caribbean, Ireland, or Canada. This US-centric approach is noticeable in a book that promises that it will end with the creation of a new nation never part of either the USA or to British America—Haiti—in 1804.[15]

This US-centric approach continues, even though there are many advocates in favor of an early American section of that history that consciously tries to avoid the teleological tendency that early American history is only about the history of those parts of the Americas that became the United States. *WMQ*, for example, has been determined to publish articles about places in the Americas that were never occupied by the British and that did not become part of the United States, such as Rebecca Earle's examination of *casta* paintings in Spanish America.[16] There are, of course, counter currents to a strong tendency to see the American Revolution as a strictly American event of interest only to US residents. Eliga Gould has been especially active in noting that the American Revolution had strong international repercussions and argues for it to be an event in British history as much as American history, though few British historians have taken up this challenge—possibly because, as Harry Dickinson notes, the political effects of the American Revolution on Britain were limited. The loss of the American colonies, Dickinson notes, did not cause the economic and political stress that had been feared. Britain retained economic hegemony in the English-speaking Americas, and its empire elsewhere only expanded after the American Revolution.[17]

The novelty of American constitutional changes resulting in a new workable system of government in 1787–88 were more consequential than the geopolitical effects on Britain of the loss of the thirteen colonies, and the American Constitution had greater impact on how legislators thought about constitution-making in many parts of the world, even if few people outside the United States thought the American precedent worth copying.[18] The publication in 2021 of the first volume of the *Cambridge History of America and the World* shows the extent to which many early American historians want to situate early America within a global context, although the volume—which does not include any author working outside Anglophone university systems and which takes a perspective that is intended to alert scholars of American history of the extent to which early America had an international dimension rather than trying to place early America as part of a developing global world—could have considered how people who were not residents of early America might have viewed America in the early modern period.[19] More to the point, editors of early American journals continue to publish articles that deal with the histories of places that did not become part of the United States as they evolved into the nineteenth century. *WMQ*, for example, has published articles in recent years by Shauna J. Sweeney, Nicholas Radburn, Simon Newman, and Elizabeth A. Dolan and Ahmed Idressi Alami on Jamaica in the late eighteenth and early nineteenth century, articles by Nancy Christie and Elspeth Martini that deal with Quebec and the Canadian part of the Great Lakes, respectively, and, in 2022, an article by Natasha Lightfoot on Antigua in the 1830s.[20]

Yet a tendency remains to see the American Revolution in parochial terms, as an event whose meaning is mostly for residents and citizens of the United States. We can see the parochialism in a variety of ways. One is in the limited coverage of writings on early America and the American Revolution in languages other than English, which is a problem not confined to this period but to American history as a whole. It is noticeable that there is not yet a single reference to a secondary source not written in English in the entirety of the multivolume *Oxford History of the United States*, though this will be remedied in the forthcoming volume on pre-1681 origins by Peter Mancall.[21]

Another is the exclusionary language that scholars revert to when assessing the contemporary relevance of the American Revolution. In the conclusion to the joint *WMQ-JER* special issue on the American Revolution in 2017, Serena Zabin starts by stating that "we are living though our own unlooked-for American Revolution, thanks to an election that revealed an America quite different from what many had thought." She attempts to qualify this exclusionary language in the next sentence, noting that this is a concern for citizens and noncitizens alike, but at least for this non-American the "we" in the previous sentence confined the people interested in the past American Revolution to those living in a United States of America who participated in the 2016 election. Zabin notes that we need more information about the American Revolution because a range of "us" in America—neighbors, students, media pundits, and people in public life ill-informed about American history—are eager to learn all about it. She ends her article with a plea for a "fully inclusive history," which is at odds with the exclusionary language used to set boundaries around the audience for work on the American Revolution.[22]

Annette Gordon-Reed and Peter Onuf also make clear that the audience for work on the American Revolution is primarily American in their concluding remarks on a 2021 forum on situating the American

Revolution within #VastEarlyAmerica. Indeed, they are explicit about their use of exclusionary language, starting and ending their article with invocations of what the meaning of the American Revolution might be to "early Americanists from the US" thinking about democracy in uncertain, fog-bound days in the twenty-first century when this institution in the United States is under "genuine threats." They argue that work on the American Revolution has to "bring the world back in" for a "chastened, demythologized, post-exceptionalist national narrative," in which US citizens participate. They don't ask what lessons might come from fresh studies on the American Revolution that place it in global context for people who are residents or citizens of other countries.[23]

The question of audience for work on the American Revolution raises the question of audience for an early America conceived of as capacious and not coterminous with the history of the United States. There is a mismatch between subject matter and audience. The point of #VastEarlyAmerica is that it is geographically expansive and determinedly not put in teleological frameworks that were common in the past in which, as David Armitage notes, the history of early America was "reduced ... to the long drawn out prelude to independent nationhood ... [that] consigned the colonies in North America and the Caribbean that did not rebel to the histories of Canada, the Caribbean, and the British empire." Yet once the revolution is over, the intersection of places previously in early America largely ends, with each area moving into its own national or imperial histories, only coming together again when there are international disputes or transnational social and political movements, such as abolitionism.[24]

Alan Karras has complained about the implications of such narrowing of perspective in a dyspeptic essay (it starts with the headline "musing from the irritated"), a process that he sees as the colonization of Atlantic history by North American historians of mainland British America. He urges historians to adopt a broader Atlantic history that explores *all* of the societies that bordered the Atlantic's shores in a genuinely world history.[25] Karras's points are worth considering: how Atlantic history as written by early Americanists limits the field's "promising internationalist tendencies" by fashioning the field so much around British North America that it "minimize[es] the role that more distant societies" had in world history. He calls for the more capacious kind of early American history done in the last decade. There is still an ambivalence toward looking at connections between places in a geographically expansive early America outside a particular historical literature that leads into the history of the United States.[26]

V

The overall finding from this field report into the journal literature of the last decade written about early American history is that the idea of #VastEarlyAmerica is more than just a form of savvy social media branding; it is also a working definition of the things that early American historians and historians of the American Revolution generally find institutionally and intellectually appealing. Eliga Gould and Rosemarie Zagarri, in their introduction to their forum on situating the United States of America within early American history take as axiomatic that #VastEarlyAmerica is now "the main story, challenging the certainties with which historians once wrote about the revolution and the early republic."[27] Significantly, Michael Hattem takes up this challenge in seeking to understand how historians should incorporate the insights of scholarship on #VastEarlyAmerica, with its assumptions (seldom challenged) that the proper subject of study for early Americanists ought to be how the vast geographic scope and chronological breadth of the field allow for histories characterized by open-endedness and diversity—both unexamined and self-obviously good things.[28]

Hattem sees a commitment to the idea of #VastEarlyAmerica as automatic among historians of his generation—the early career historians of the 2010s who did their undergraduate studies in the wake of 9/11; were graduate students around the years of the economic crash of 2008; and who have been trying, not always successfully, to get positions in the grim academic job market during the presidency of Donald Trump (2017–21) and the pandemic of 2020–21. He argues that the contemporary world influences this generation of historians in their scholarship as much as do the invocations from people from my generation of historians that a more capacious, diverse, and inclusive scholarship is desirable. Yet, Hattem's contemporary world is the opposite of that suggested by #VastEarlyAmerica, as it is bounded by an unthinking assumption that only events that happen in the United States of America matter. He accepts, however, that seeing early America as vast in geographical scope and broad in chronological extent is now paradigmatic among early career historians, citing many of these scholars' first books to show how the concept of #VastEarlyAmerica is invoked often in studies that examine cultural power, state formation, institution building, and the intersection of race and capitalism.[29]

He argues that new scholarship inspired by #VastEarlyAmerica avoids tedious "reductionist" binaries centered around the nebulous notion of "meaning," which he posits as an unfortunate characteristic of early American history writing done in the second half of the twentieth century. It is scholarship, he suggests, that is intensely pragmatic in its intentions. It contains "no essentializing impulse, no pretense toward an all-encompassing or overarching interpretation," a scholarship what works with, rather than trying to replace, previous historiographical paradigms. The ambitions, if there are any in scholarship that so strenuously avoids taking confrontational positions, is integrative and evolutionary and is determinedly nonpolitical both in its consideration of the past and in how it sees what is written about in being relevant to the present. The contemporary world informs scholarship; but that scholarship is disconnected from trying to explain or change modern politics or society.

Whether Hattem speaks for his generation of scholars is not for someone from my generation, or for people from generations older than mine, to judge. But his analysis rings true based on the hundreds of articles I have read in order to write this book. The last decade of writing on early American history has seen certain themes emerge—more on race as central to the early American experience; Indigenes as central actors in most aspects of early American life; the ubiquity of empire as a mode of analysis and as a structure conditioning how early America worked; and, most of all, a belief that early America was dynamic, complex, globally connected and, in particular, "vast" in regard to both space and time. These themes have emerged within existing paradigms rather than outside them or in contradiction of them. It will be a great surprise, however, if the scholarship surveyed here, which tends toward the evolutionary and non-confrontational (indeed rather gentle), persists in a world that now seems troubled by ongoing crises, whether they arise from approaching climate catastrophe, the challenges of transformative technology; the return of nation-states with hard borders and authoritarian leaders; or the end of what has been a relatively short global period of the Great Divergence.[30] It will be interesting to see whether these challenges make what I have written about an evolving early American scholarship in this book seem as quaint and out of touch as other surveys when authors make the mistake of trying to predict future trends and suggest ways that scholarship could be improved. I would be pleased if that is the case.

APPENDIX A
EARLY AMERICAN HISTORY IN ACADEMIC JOURNALS

Where do scholars publish; which kinds of people publish in academic journals; and what geographic areas, themes, and perspectives are frequent? Table 1 lists the places of publication of 393 articles in 52 journals. It shows both concentration and diffusion. Articles in eighteenth-century British history can be found in all sorts of journals, but they tend to be concentrated in a few venues, such as *P&P* and the *Journal of British Studies*. Unsurprisingly, early Americanists tend to publish in their specialist journals: 75 publishing in *WMQ*, 61 in *EAS*, and 18 in *JEAH*. Nearly one in five early American history articles was published in *WMQ*, and 43 percent of articles were published either in that journal or in *EAS*. If we add the third most popular place of publication, *S&A*, then 53 percent of articles in these two fields were published in the three most popular journals. Nevertheless, a substantial number of articles on early American history or eighteenth-century British history were published in other journals than the principal three journals. There were fourteen journals with five or more articles in this field published and nine journals that published ten or more articles. *WMQ* remains a dominant force in the field, but it is now more *primus inter pares* than the sun around which everything else revolves.

Scholars from all stages of their careers published articles in journals between 2012 and 2020, even if there was a slight bias toward younger scholars placing their work in journals. That bias toward early-career scholars is unsurprising, since having an article published in a good journal is an important career step for scholars in academia and is an excellent venue for testing out major ideas and interpretations before developing them into larger book projects. But senior and midcareer scholars also published in journals on a regular basis. Table 2 notes the professional status of 92 authors publishing in *WMQ* and *EAS* in 2019 and 2020. It shows that while 42 percent of authors were early career, with assistant professors the single most likely group of people to publish in journals, there were 13 authors at professorial rank and 25 who were associate professors. The great majority of authors were employed within the academy. Only 10 percent of authors in these two journals worked outside the academy. There is an unsurprising tendency for people at the professorial level to be asked to write for journals on commission rather than going through the competitive process of review, submission, and resubmission, but enough professors and professors with named chairs choose to submit themselves to this sometimes-ferocious process of peer review to suggest that publishing in journals is what active researchers do on a regular basis.

Tables 3–5 break down the sample of articles for the 251 articles that can be assigned safely to region (86 percent of early American articles). They demonstrate clearly the impact of #VastEarlyAmerica on the field, notably the growing importance of the West Indies within the field of early America. Fewer than half of articles now deal with British North America, and even if the 25 articles (10 percent of all articles) on Africa or Britain are excluded from analysis, the percentage of articles on British North America only increases to 52 percent. Nearly a third of articles (31 percent) concentrate on the West Indies with 31 articles (12 percent) dealing with either the history of the interior outside European influence or with French Canada, either in New France/Quebec or in Louisiana. The dominance of New England and the Chesapeake in the field, which was so apparent a generation ago, has weakened to the point of disappearance. Just under a quarter of articles deal with New England and Canada, but that is still less than the 28 percent that are concerned with the West Indies or Bermuda. Each broad region of early America has a substantial number of articles written about it.

Within these figures, however, are some startling changes in the spatial orientation of early America. The most remarkable rise has been in interest in Jamaica, which has considerably more articles that focus on it than for any other part of North America including New England and, most surprisingly, the Chesapeake. That once-mighty field of research has only 7 articles, or 5 percent of research in early American history.[1] Moreover, the longstanding indifference of early Americanists to the history of Canada has disappeared.[2] The interest in Canada, the West Indies and Bermuda, and the unincorporated parts of early America—amounting to 74 articles, or 49 percent of the 152 articles that can be assigned to particular early American regions—shows that early American history has achieved what Joyce Appleby and others advocated in 1993, which is to move away from a US-centric historiography concentrated on what happened in the thirteen colonies. Atlantic and Continental history has made a real difference to the choice of topics that early American historians now choose to study.[3]

TABLE 1. Principal journals of article publication in early American and eighteenth-century British history, 2012–2020

Name of journal	Number of articles	Percentage
William and Mary Quarterly	75	19.1
Early American Studies	61	15.5
Slavery & Abolition	32	8.1
Past & Present	24	6.1
Journal of Early American History	18	4.5
Journal of British Studies	16	4.0
Atlantic Studies	14	3.5
Historical Journal	12	3.0
English Historical Review	11	2.8
Parliamentary History	9	2.2
Economic History Review	9	2.2
Journal of the History of Ideas	7	1.7
Journal of the Early Republic	8	2.0
Journal of Imperial and Commonwealth History	7	1.7
Journal of Eighteenth-Century History	6	1.4
Scottish Historical Review	6	1.4
Gender History	5	1.2
Other (35 journals)	73	18.6
Total	393	

Table 2. Professional status of authors of articles in *William and Mary Quarterly* and *Early American Studies*, January 2019–January 2021

Academic status	WMQ		EAS		Total	
	Number of articles	Percentage	Number of articles	Percentage	Number of articles	Percentage
Senior	10	25	9	17.3	19	20.7
Named Professor	4	10	2	3.8	6	6.5
Professor	6	15	7	13.5	13	14.1
Middle	10	25	15	28.8	25	27.2
Associate Professor	10	25	15	28.8	25	27.2
Junior	17	42.5	22	42.3	39	42.4
Assistant Professor	14	35	14	26.9	28	30.4
Post-doc/lecturer	3	7.5	6	11.5	9	9.8
Pre PhD	0	0	2	3.8	2	2.2
Other	3	7.5	6	11.5	9	9.8
Total	40	100	52	100	92	100

Table 3. Early American history topics in journal literature by general geographic area

Location	Number of articles (N = 252)	Percentage
British North America	118	47.0
West Indies	78	31.0
Continental America	16	6.4
French America	15	6.0
Africa	10	4.0
Britain	15	6.0

TABLE 4. Early American history topics in
journal literature by general region of early America

Location	Number of articles (N = 163)	Percentage
Northern colonies and Canada	39	23.9
Middle colonies	28	17.2
South	32	19.6
West Indies or Bermuda	46	28.2
Continental America	18	11.0

TABLE 5. Early American history in
journal literature by specific region of early America

Location	Number of articles (N = 163)	Percentage
Canada	17	10.4
New England	22	13.5
New York and New Jersey	12	7.4
Pennsylvania and Delaware	16	9.8
Chesapeake	7	4.3
Lower South	25	15.3
Jamaica	34	20.9
Eastern Caribbean	11	6.7
Bermuda	1	0.6
Continental America	18	11.0

APPENDIX B
CITATIONAL PRACTICES IN EARLY AMERICAN HISTORY

One way of ascertaining the influence of individual historians within the historiography of early America is through citations. Unlike other disciplines, citational practices are ill-developed within history as a discipline, with relatively few journals providing information about who is cited and how often in journal articles. Thus, working out which historians have been cited by other historians in early American journal articles is a laborious process of counting by hand mentions (excluding self-citations and not counting multiple citations to an author in a single article) in each article. The list below of those authors most cited is from the 322 articles in this sample on early American history. It lists 94 authors cited 10 or more times in these articles, 69 men and 25 women. It is biased, unsurprisingly, toward senior scholars, as younger scholars have both published less than their elders and, more important, have published more recently than works that may be many decades old and thus are less likely to get cited by other historians. Consequently, 7 of the top 8 and 12 of the top 18 most-cited authors are emeritus professors, and the great majority of the 70 most-cited authors are full professors, either emeritus or not far from that status. I have tried to be as accurate as possible in tracking these citations, but as it is done by hand there will inevitably be mistakes, though the basic patterns are quite clear.

What is noticeable about the list is the large number of people who are cited with some regularity and the democratic nature of such citations, with little concentration on a few historians and even less on central books as shaping the field. It is hard to see that individual historians have such disciplinary power that they shape the field through important works that a majority of scholars in early America read and cite. The citational practices of early American historians indicate that there are virtually no paradigm-shifting books in early American history to which early American historians feel they need to respond. The top cited author, Jack Greene, is cited 50 times, meaning that he is cited in 15.5 percent of all early American articles in this sample. Only 6 authors are cited in 10 percent or more of all articles. Moreover, the most highly cited authors are cited not just for one publication but for many works—that is notably true for very highly cited authors such as Greene, Bernard Bailyn, Philip Morgan, T. H. Breen, Gary Nash, and David Waldstreicher. The only canonical work that appears with some regularity is *The Middle Ground* by Richard White, with 23 citations. My strong impression is that authors are, in the main, cited for the empirical information that they provide rather than as authors against whose theses other scholars test their arguments. Thus, there is an overrepresentation of authors who work on Jamaica and Barbados, mainly, I suspect, because the recent turn toward more article production on these colonies means a heavy reliance on the relatively few scholars who have written in the past on these areas. There are 14 highly cited authors on Jamaica and Barbados, including 8 cited twenty or more times.

Also noticeable in the citation list noted below is the overwhelming dominance of authors resident in the United States and a pronounced masculine bias in authors cited. Only 16 highly cited authors are based outside of the United States—2 in Australia; 10 in the United Kingdom; 2 in Canada; and 2 (Eric Williams and Kamau Braithwaite), from a previous generation of scholars in the Caribbean. Reflecting how seldom early American historians look at literature not written in English, just 3 French scholars—Cécile Vidal, Bertrand Van Ruymbeke, and Gilles Havard—are cited 4 times each, and no scholar resident in any other non-English speaking country is cited more than twice each. Citations to books written by historians now working in the field but writing in languages other than English are so few (no more than half a dozen citations) as to be irrelevant to current scholarship. The most well-cited Canadian-based author is Michael Craton, with 21 citations, then Ian Steele, with 14 citations, followed by Allan Greer with 8 citations.

There are 12 authors who are deceased, as of June 2022, only one of whom—Eric Williams—who has been dead for a long time. Early American historians are not in thrall to long-gone authority or very interested in historiographical debates that predate the present. References to such major twentieth-century historians as Charles Beard, Charles Andrews, Lawrence Gipson, Benjamin Quarles, Richard Morris, or Carl Bridenbaugh are remarkable in their paucity. I don't think there are more than one or two references, for example, to Samuel Eliot Morison in this sample and virtually none to any female scholar writing in the first half of the twentieth century.

Most authors cited are men, especially among the most highly cited authors, with only Kathleen Wilson and Kathleen Duval being among the 28 authors with 20 or more citations. Women are also overrepresented among leading historians whose citations are surprisingly low: Jill Lepore with 10 citations, Mary Beth Norton and Joyce Appleby with 9 citations, Maya Jasanoff and Linda Kerber with 6 citations, and Annette Gordon-Reed with 3 citations. Some other highly lauded historians who are only seldom cited include John Demos (whose work tends to be on seventeenth-century early American history) with 7 citations, J. R. McNeill (whose work ranges very widely over time, including major works on the twentieth century) with 10 citations, and, perhaps most remarkably, given the centrality of his work to early American history in the 1980s, Rhys Isaac, who is mentioned in just 7 articles. This low citation rate indicates just how much scholarship has moved away this century from the study of the eighteenth-century Chesapeake.

High Citation authors:

30 or more citations: Jack P. Greene (50), Trevor Burnard (45), Philip D. Morgan (37), Bernard Bailyn (36), John J. McCusker (33), David Eltis (33), T. H. Breen (31), Gary Nash (30)

27 citations: B. W. Higman, David Waldstreicher

25 citations: Eliga Gould, Andrew Jackson O'Shaughnessy, Richard White

24 citations: Vincent Brown, Richard S. Dunn, P. J. Marshall, Kathleen Wilson, Gordon S. Wood

23 citations: David Hancock

22 citations: Alan Taylor

21 citations: David Armitage, Michael Craton, Kathleen DuVal, Eric Hinderaker, Steven Pincus, Marcus Rediker, Daniel K. Richter, John Thornton

20 citations: Ira Berlin

19 citations: Joyce Chaplin, Gregory Dowd, Jennifer Morgan

18 citations: Fred Anderson, Christopher L. Brown, Colin Calloway, Linda Colley, Russell R. Menard

17 citations: Jacob Price, P. David Richardson, Richard B. Sheridan

16 citations: Kathleen Brown, Pekka Hämäläinen, Kenneth Morgan, Peter Wood

15 citations: Lauren Benton, Robin Blackburn, Jorge Canizares-Esguerra, Jerome Handler, J. H. Elliott, Cathy Matson, Edmund Morgan, Brett Rushforth, Simon Newman

14 citations: Marisa Fuentes, Pauline Maier, Ian Steele, Laurel Thatcher Ulrich

13 citations: Richard Bushman, Stephen Conway, Woody Holton, Joseph Inikori, Peter Mancall, Claudio Saunt, David Shields, Lorena S. Walsh, Eric Williams

12 citations: Juliana Barr, William Cronon, Michael A. McDonnell, Peter Onuf, Christopher Tomlins

11 citations: Kamau Braithwaite, Max Edelson, Sheryllynne Haggerty, Ellen Hartigan-O'Connor, Paul Kelton, Sidney Mintz, J. G. A. Pocock, Stephanie Smallwood, Karin Wulf

10 citations: Sharon Block, Aaron Fogleman, Richard Godbeer, Emma Hart, Susan Klepp, Jill Lepore, J. R. McNeill, Joshua Piker, Nancy Shoemaker, Peter Silver, David Silverman, Susan Sleeper-Smith, Serena Zabin

ACKNOWLEDGMENTS

This book is my pandemic project. When Britain decided that it would lockdown society as a result of the COVID-19 crisis on 24 March 2020, a lockdown that lasted, with occasional liftings, until 19 July 2021, I took the opportunity of forced working from home and the closure of archives to read widely in the journal literature of, first, eighteenth-century British history and second, early American history, concentrating on articles written in leading journals that were national or international in orientation, published mostly between 2012 and 2020. These are the areas of my expertise, and my interest and the initial objective was selfish—to acquire a greater knowledge of contemporary academic research in eighteenth-century American, Atlantic, Indigenous, African, and British history. The first results of my reading appeared in a paper on recent journal literature on eighteenth-century British history that I presented to the lively Zoom seminar convened by Steve Pincus of the University of Chicago. I thank Steve for the opportunity to test my findings in front of a large and argumentative audience and for being such a great scholar of this period. Following this largely positive experience, I approached Frank Cogliano of the University of Edinburgh and Patrick Griffin of the University of Notre Dame, editors of a book series in which I have been previously involved, a series on the age of revolution, published by University of Virginia Press. They encouraged me to look at a wider range of articles over a longer period and to survey the whole of the field of early American history between roughly the signing of the Treaty of Utrecht in 1713 and the signing of the Peace of Paris Treaty in 1783. This book is a result of this encouragement and a result of equally encouraging words from my editor at Virginia, Nadine Zimmerli.

My research strategy was simple: to read all the articles in the fields and years noted above and comment about what collectively they tell us about the state of early American historiography in the early 2020s. This book is thus not a complete survey of early American history writing, as Jack P. Greene did so brilliantly in *Pursuits of Happiness* (1988), which influenced a whole generation of graduate students in how they thought about early American history. I know that book well not just from extensive reading and rereading of it but from being employed to check its extensive footnotes. Greene, probably the best read of all early American historians working in the twentieth century, used his vast knowledge of the whole field of early American history in monographs, articles, and book chapters and his wonderful capacities for synthesis to outline a comprehensive survey of the field as a whole.

This book is less ambitious than Greene's masterpiece. It is not a complete survey of the field—the field has grown too large for that kind of comprehensive survey—nor is it designed to promulgate a certain vision of what I think early American history should be, though like any historian I know what I like. It summarizes 393 articles, outlining less where I want the field to go than where I think the writers of journal articles see the field evolving. I believe that if we are to understand any historical field and hope to contribute to it by our own research or by reading in the subject, we will be better placed if we appreciate how what we are writing about or reading fits within longstanding arguments, debates, and conversations. Moreover, to make a meaningful contribution to these conversations, it is a good thing to be literate in what assumptions lie behind such conversations and how those assumptions shape how arguments are expressed. My hope is that by the end of this book readers will have an appreciation of the journey that scholars in the field of early American history have been on since the 1990s. I hope that the contents in this book will enable readers to catch a historical field of analysis developing at a moment in time and be able to link that moment to research findings from the past as well as the swirl of events in the present.

As this description of this book suggests, this was a self-indulgent project. I wanted to get on top of recent secondary literature on early American, American revolutionary, and eighteenth-century British history so that I was as familiar in the early 2020s with such literature as I had been with the scholarship on these topics that I did in preparing for comprehensive exams for an MA at The Johns Hopkins University in 1985. My principal thanks therefore go to the 400 or so authors who wrote the articles that entertained, educated, and occasionally provoked me in my reading during that strange pandemic period in 2020 and 2021. I also leant on the advice of practitioners in the field in Britain, France, and the United States for their opinions, devising a series of Zoom sessions (thus meaning that the people I leaned on did not even get the small pleasure of a meal or drinks for doing what they did) to discuss aspects of the book. I also presented parts of the manuscript to colleagues in France, Germany, and Australia in Zoom seminars. I thank Paul

Betts, Claire Bouris-Mattioli, Glenn Burgess, Amanda Capern, Nancy Christie, Will Christie, Deirdre Coleman, Stephan Conermann, Vinita Damoradan, Saul Dubow, Rebecca Earle, Nicholas Evans, Anne-Claire Facquez, Karwan Fatah-Black, Anne Gerritsen, Pierre Gervais, Aaron Graham, Emma Hart, Marie Houllemare, Mark Knights, Michael McDonnell, Simon Middleton, Jennifer Milam, Jen Motter, Johann Neem, Simon Newman, Andrew O'Shaughnessy, Damian Pargas, Allan Potofsky, Charles Prior, Kristopher Ray, Giorgio Riello, Marie-Jeanne Rossignol, Bertrand van Ruymbeke, Garritt van Dyk, Elliott Warren, Sophie White, and Michael Zeuske for their advice and criticism, some of which I accepted. Particular thanks go to Paul Mapp and Katherine Carte Engel who each read the manuscript with great care and acuity for the University of Virginia Press and graciously provided their names to their anonymous reports suggesting revisions and recommending publication.

My wife, Deborah Morgan, does not concern herself with such minor matters as early American historiography, but her insistence on daily walks in our newly adopted city of Kingston-upon-Hull during the pandemic kept both of us sane and allowed welcome breaks from intensive reading. She remains bemused by another activity that kept me sane during lockdown and that continues to be an immense source of enjoyment for me, which is a weekly Zoom pub session with fellow early Americanists. She occasionally makes a show of asking what we talked about for an hour and half almost every Sunday and can't quite understand why we spend so much time in our bonding sessions on idle but animated chat on what we think good and (more often) not good about writing on the history of early America and the American Revolution. We sometimes drift into other topics, such as the arcane politics of Florida and California and what is wrong with the modern United States, little of which interests me, but we keep on coming back to matters of opinion about early American scholarship. Our Zoom group, which started almost the same time as I started work on this book in March 2020, is Edward Gray, Eliga Gould, Eric Hinderaker, Mark Peterson, and Peter Mancall. They have read the manuscript and disagree with a lot of it but have always been supportive of what I think they believe (but are too polite to say) is a quixotic project. I'd like to dedicate this quixotic project to Ed, Lige, Eric, Mark, and Peter, in part because their outstanding scholarship has greatly enriched the fields under consideration in this book. I dedicate this book to them, however, for the more substantial reason that their friendship and their views and opinions, as well as their good-natured (I think) joshing has sustained me in all sorts of ways in the last two-and-a-half years since our weekly Zoom sessions began.

TREVOR BURNARD
Kingston-on-Hull

NOTES

Abbreviations

AHR	American Historical Review
AS	Atlantic Studies
EAS	Early American Studies
EcHR	Economic Historical Review
EHR	English Historical Review
EEH	Explorations in Economic History
HJ	Historical Journal
HWJ	Historical Workshop Journal
JAH	Journal of American History
JEAH	Journal of Early American History
JER	Journal of the Early Republic
JEcH	Journal of Economic History
JGH	Journal of Global History
JICH	Journal of Imperial and Commonwealth History
S&A	Slavery and Abolition
P&P	Past & Present
WMQ	William and Mary Quarterly

Introduction

1. Three useful syntheses are Alan Taylor, *The American Colonies* (New York: Penguin, 2001); Daniel K. Richter, *Before the Revolution: America's Ancient Pasts* (Cambridge: Harvard University Press, 2011); and Bertrand Van Ruymbeke, *L'Amérique avant les États-Unis: Une histoire de l'Amérique anglaise, 1497–1776* (Paris: Flammarion, 2016).

2. Joyce Appleby, "A Different Kind of Independence: The Postwar Restructuring of the Historical Study of Early America," *WMQ* 50 (1993): 245–67; Gordon S. Wood, "A Century of Writing Early American History: Then and Now Compared; Or, How Henry Adams Got it Wrong," *AHR* 100 (1995): 687.

3. For early American history written in journals in other languages than English, see, inter alia, *XVII–XVIII: Revue de la Société d'études anglo américaines des XVIIe et XVIIIe siècles*; *Revue d'histoire de l'Amérique française*; *Nuevo mundo mundos nuevos*.

4. Why choose as a comparator British history in the long eighteenth century? Understanding the British roots of the American experience has been important for most colonial British American historians with periodic attempts by historians from Edmund Morgan in 1957 to T. H Breen in 1997 to Steven Pincus, Tiraana Bains, and A. Zuercher Reichardt in 2019 to try and relate what is happening in British history to the historiography of early America. Morgan, "The American Revolution: Revisions in Need of Revising," *WMQ* 14 (1957): 14–15; Breen, "Ideology and Nationalism on the Eve of the American Revolution: Revisions Once More in Need of Revising," *JAH* (1997): 13–39; Steven Pincus, Tiraana Bains, and A. Reichardt, "Thinking the Empire Whole," *History Australia* 16 (2019): 610–37. For a survey of Britain and British America, see Trevor Burnard, *Britain in the Wider World, 1603–1800* (London: Routledge, 2020), chs. 6–9. For the importance of English and British historiography to early Americanists (though "colonialists arguable read more about England than historians of England read about colonial history"), see Joyce E. Chaplin, "Expansion and Exceptionalism in Early American History," *JAH* 89 (2003): 1438.
5. David L. Ammerman and Philip D. Morgan, comps., *Books about Early America: 2001 Titles* (Williamsburg, VA: Institute of Early American History and Culture, 1989).
6. Chaplin, "Expansion and Exceptionalism," 1431.
7. Omohundro Institute of Early American History and Culture, "'Joshua Piker' Is a Problem: The Cost of Our Invisible Labors," *Uncommon Sense* (blog), 12 April 2019, https://blog.oieahc.wm.edu/joshua-piker-is-a-problem-the-cost-of-our-invisible-labors/.
8. Edmund S. Morgan, "Slavery and Freedom: The American Paradox," *JAH* 59 (1972): 5–29; Morgan, *American Slavery, American Freedom: The Ordeal of Colonial Virginia* (New York: W. W. Norton, 1975).
9. *WMQ*, https://oieahc.wm.edu/publications/wmq/.
10. Michael A. McDonnell and David Waldstreicher, "Revolution in the Quarterly? A Historiographical Analysis," *WMQ* 74 (2017): 633–66.
11. Ibid., 635.
12. Cécile Vidal, "Pour une histoire globale du monde atlantique ou des histoires connectées dans au-delà du monde atlantique," *Annales* 67 (2012): 391–413.
13. See Appendix A.
14. But see Woody Holton, *Liberty Is Sweet: The Hidden History of the American Revolution* (New York: Simon & Schuster, 2021); and Mary Beth Norton, *1774: The Long Year of Revolution* (New York: Random House, 2020).
15. Keith B. Berwick, "A Peculiar Monument: The Third Series of WMQ," *WMQ* 21 (1964): 13–14.

16. McDonnell and Waldstreicher, "Revolution in the *Quarterly?*"; Jack P. Greene, *The Constitutional Origins of the American Revolution* (Cambridge: Cambridge University Press, 2011), 2–3. For books against this trend, see Robert Parkinson, *The Common Cause: Creating Race and Nation in the American Revolution* (Chapel Hill: University of North Carolina Press, 2016); T. H. Breen, *The Will of the People: The Revolutionary Birth of America* (Cambridge, MA: Harvard University Press, 2019); and Gerald Horne, *Counter-revolution of 1776: Slave Resistance and the Origins of the United States of America* (New York: New York University Press, 2014).
17. Staughton Lynd and David Waldstreicher, "Free Trade, Sovereignty, and Slavery: Toward an Economic Interpretation of American Independence," *WMQ* 68 (2011): 597–630, with responses from Barbara Clark Smith, Jack Rakove, Robert G. Parkinson, and Michael A. McDonnell, 631–48.
18. Jack Rakove, "Get Nexus," *WMQ* 68 (2011): 636.
19. Karl Koth and John Serieux, "Sugar, Slavery, and Wealth: Jamaica Planter Nathaniel Phillips and the Williams Hypothesis," *Capitalism: A Journal of History and Economics* 1 (2019): 59–91; and Laura Sandy, "Slave Owning Overseers in Eighteenth-Century Virginia and South Carolina," *S&A* 38 (2017): 459–74.
20. Jessica Choppin Roney, "Introduction: Distinguishing Port Cities, 1500–1800," *EAS* 15 (2017): 657–58. For merchants, see Emma Hart and Cathy Matson, "Situating Merchants in Late Eighteenth-Century British Atlantic Port Cities," *EAS* 15 (2017): 660–82; Trevor Burnard, "Towns in Plantation Societies in Eighteenth-Century British America," *EAS* 15 (2017): 835–59; Nancy Christie, "Merchant and Plebeian Commercial Knowledge in Montreal and Quebec, 1760–1820," *EAS* 13 (2015) 856–80; Robert J. Gamble, "'For Lucre of Gain and in Contempt of the Laws': Itinerant Traders and the Politics of Mobility in the Eighteenth-Century Mid-Atlantic," *EAS* 13 (2015): 836–55.
21. Shantel George, "Tracing the Ethnic Origins of Enslaved Africans in Georgia," *AS* 17 (2020): 160–83; J. David Hacker, "From '20. And odd' to 10 Million: The Growth of the Slave Population in the United States," *S&A* 41 (2020): 840–55; Simon Newman et al., "The West African Ethnicity of the Enslaved in Jamaica," *S&A* 34 (2013): 410–24; Russell R. Menard, "Making a 'Popular Slave Society' in Colonial British America," *Journal of Interdisciplinary History* 43 (2013): 377–95; Gregory E. O'Malley, "Slavery's Converging Ground: Charleston's Slave Trade and the Black Heart of the Lowcountry," *WMQ* 74 (2017): 271–302; Timothy Shannon, "A 'Wicked Commerce': Consent, Coercion and Kidnapping in Aberdeen's Servant Trade," *WMQ* 74 (2017): 437–66.
22. Diana Paton, "The Driveress and the Nurse: Childcare, Working Children and Other Work on Caribbean Slavery," *P&P* 246 (2020), supplement 15, 27–53. See also Mark Hailwood, "Time and Work in Rural England,

1500–1700," *P&P* 248 (2020): 87–121; Anne L. Murphy, "'Clock-Watching': Work and Working Time at the Late Eighteenth-Century Bank of England," *P&P* 236 (2017): 99–132; Karen Harvey, "Rabbits, Whigs, and Hunters: Women and Protest in Mary Toft's Monstrous Births of 1726," *S&A* 238 (2018): 43–83; and Carolyn Steedman, "Threatening Letters: E. E. Dodd, E. P. Thompson, and Making of 'the Crime of Anonymity,'" *HWJ* 82 (2016): 50–82.

23. Renee C. Romano and Clare Bond Potter, eds., *Historians on Hamilton: How a Blockbuster Musical Is Restaging America's Past* (Brunswick, NJ: Rutgers University Press, 2018).

24. Kieran J. O'Keefe, "Faith before Creed: The Private and Public Religion of George Washington," *Journal of Religious History* 43 (2019): 400–418; Sophus A. Reinart, "The *Way to Wealth* around the World: Benjamin Franklin and the Globalization of American Capitalism," *AHR* (2015): 61–97; Vivian Bruce Conger, "Reading Early American Women's Political Lives: The Revolutionary Performance of Deborah Read Franklin and Sarah Franklin Bache," *EAS* 16 (2018): 317–52; Alan Houston, "'A Difference in Opinion Is Inevitable': Franklin, Hemphill, and Modern Toleration," *Eighteenth-Century Studies* 50 (2017): 401–16. Gordon Sayre, "Jefferson Takes On Buffon: The Polemic on American Animals in *Notes on the State of Virginia*," *WMQ* 78 (2021): 79–116, was published too late for this study. See also the special issue with essays by Gregory Claeys, Yannich Bosc, Carine Louinas, Allan Potofsky, and Thomas C. Walker, "Thomas Paine: A Transatlantic Republican between Two Revolutions," *JEAH* 6 (2016): 101–51. This special issue mainly deals with Paine and the French Revolution rather than the American Revolution.

25. Vaughn Scribner, "Transatlantic Actors: The Intertwining Stages of George Whitefield and Lewis Hallam, Jr., 1739–1756," *Journal of Social History* 49 (2016): 1–27; Wilson H. Kimnach and Kenneth P. Minkeman, "The Material and Social Practices of Intellectual Work: Jonathan Edward's Study," *WMQ* 69 (2012): 683–730; David Waldstreicher, "Ancients, Moderns and Africans: Phillis Wheatley and the Politics of Empire and Slavery in the American Revolution," *JER* 37 (2017): 701–33; and Ryan Hanley, "Calvinism, Proslavery, and James Albert Ukawsaw Gronniosaw," *S&A* 36 (2015): 360–81.

26. Carl I. Hammer, "'Being Old and Dayly Finding the Symptoms of Mortality': The Troubled Last Years of Hannah Beamon of Deerfield and the Law of 1726," *EAS* 17 (2029): 151–82; Pernille Ipsen, "'The Christened Mulatresses': Euro-African Families in a Slave-Trading Town," *WMQ* 70 (2013): 371–98; Kathleen S. Murphy, "Collecting Slave Traders: James Petiver, Natural History, and the British Slave Trade," *WMQ* 70 (2013): 637–70; Douglas Hamilton, "'A Most Active, Enterprising Officer':

Captain John Perkins, the Royal Navy and the Boundaries of Slavery and Liberty in the Caribbean," *S&A* 39 (2018): 89–100.
27. Wilcomb E. Washburn, "Samuel Eliot Morison," *WMQ* 26 (1979): 325–52; Richard R. Johnson, "Charles McLean Andrews and the Invention of American Colonial History," *WMQ* 43 (1986): 519–41; David T. Courtwright, "Fifty Years of American History: An Interview with Edmund S. Morgan," *WMQ* 44 (1987): 336–69; A. Roger Ekirch, "'Sometimes an Art, Never a Science, Always a Craft': A Conversation with Bernard Bailyn," *WMQ* 51 (1994): 625–58.
28. For an exception, see John M. Dixon, "Henry F. May and the Revival of the American Enlightenment: Problems and Possibilities for Intellectual and Social History," *WMQ* 71 (2014): 255–80.
29. "Appreciations," *EAS* 17 (2019): 610–21.
30. Jonathan Israel "J. G. A. Pocock and the 'Language of Enlightenment' in His *Barbarism and Religion*," *Journal of the History of Ideas* 77 (2016): 107–27; Pierre Force, "The 'Exasperating Predecessor': Pocock on Gibbon and Voltaire," *Journal of the History of Ideas* 77 (2016): 129–45; and Helena Rosenblatt, "On Context and Meaning in Pocock's *Barbarism and Religion* and on Gibbon's 'Protestantism' and His Chapters on Religion," *Journal of the History of Ideas* 77 (2016): 147–55.
31. Incivility may have just been transferred to other fora. Periodic "Twitterstorms" and angry communications in the correspondence sections of journals, as well as in magazines and newspaper opinion pieces are the places where fierce debate and polemic, sometimes ad hominem, assertions are most commonly made today.
32. Blair Worden, "Hugh Redwald Trevor-Roper, 1914–2003," *Proceedings of the British Academy* 60 (2007): 247–84.
33. Martin Ridge, "An Exile in Eden," *Pacific Historical Review* 66 (1997): 1–20.
34. Daniel Rogers, "Republicanism: The Career of a Concept," *JAH* 79 (1992): 11–38; Allan Kulikoff, "The Transition to Capitalism in Rural America," *WMQ* 46 (1989): 120–44.
35. Jesse Lemsich, "Bailyn Besieged in His Bunker," *Radical History Review* 3 (1976): 72–83; Marcus Rediker, "The Old Guard, the New Guard, and the People at the Gates: New Approaches to the Study of American History in the U.S.S.R.," *WMQ* 48 (1991): 580–97.
36. Keith Mason, "The Absentee Planter and the Key Slave: Privilege, Patriarchalism and Exploitation in the Early Eighteenth-Century Caribbean," *WMQ* 70 (2013): 79–102; James Dator, "Frank Travels: Space, Power and Slave Mobility in the British Leeward Islands, c. 1700–1730," *S&A* 36 (2015): 360–81; Daniel I. O'Neill, "Edmund Burke on Slavery and the Slave Trade: A Response to Gregory M. Collins," *S&A* 41 (2020): 816–27, Collins's response, 828–39. See also Heather V. Vermeulen, "Thomas

Thistlewood's Libidinal Linnaean Project: Slavery, Ecology, and Knowledge Production," *Small Axe* 22 (2018), for an article designed to respond to other interpretations.

37. The major exception is continued interest in the work of Eric Williams on the relationship between capitalism and slavery. See Koth and Serieux, "Sugar, Slavery and Wealth"; Ahmed Reid, "Sugar, Slavery, and Productivity in Jamaica, 1750–1807," *S&A* 37 (2016): 159–82; Reid and David B. Ryden, "Sugar, Land, Markets and the Williams' Thesis: Evidence from Jamaica's Property Sales, 1750–1810," *S&A* 34 (2013): 401–24; and Nuala Zahediah, "Eric Williams and William Forbes: Copper, Colonial Markets and Commercial Capitalism," *EcHR* 74 (2021): 784–808. For an examination of another important late twentieth-century historian, see Peter C. Mancall, "Pigs for Historians," *WMQ* 67 (2010): 347–75. See also Susan Sleeper Smith, ed., "Forum: Richard White's *The Middle Ground* Revisited," *WMQ* 63 (2006): 3–96.

38. Asheesh Kapur Siddique, "The Archival Epistemology of Political Economy in the Modern British Atlantic World," *WMQ* 77 (2020): 641–74; Siddique, "Governance through Documents: The Board of Trade, Its Archive, and the Imperial Constitution of the Eighteenth-Century British Atlantic World," *JBS* 59 (2020): 264–90.

39. Marie Houllemare, "La fabrique des archives colonials et la conscience impériale France," *Revue d'Histoire Moderne et Contemporaine* 61 (2014): 7–31; Houllemare, "Seeing the Empire through Lists and Charts: Colonial Records in the 18th Century," *Journal of Early Modern History* 22 (2018): 1–21; Houllemare, "Procedures, Jurisdictions and Records: Building the French Empire in the Early Eighteenth-Century," *Journal of Colonialism and Colonial History* 21 (2020), https://muse-jhu-edu.hull.idm.oclc.org/article/761128/pdf.

40. Saidiya Hartman, "Venus in Two Acts," *Small Axe* 12 (2008): 1–2; Nicola Aljoe, "Reading the 'Memoirs of the Life of Florence Hall' through the *Long Song* of the Caribbean Colonial Archive," *American Literary History* 32 (2020): 623–44; Ann Laura Stoler, "Archival Disease: Thinking through Colonial Ontologies," *Communication and Critical/Cultural Studies* 7 (2010): 215–19; Jennifer Morgan, "Accounting for 'The Most Excruciating Torment': Gender, Slavery, and Trans-Atlantic Passages," *History of the Present* 6 (2016): 184–207; Sasha Turner, "The Nameless and the Forgotten: Maternal Grief, Sacred Protection, and the Archive of Slavery," *S&A* 38 (2017): 232–50; and Ashley Glassburn Falzetti, "Archival Absence: The Burden of History," *Settler Colonial Studies* 5 (2014): 1–17.

41. Joshua Piker and Karin Wulf, "NAIS Is Central to Early American Scholarship," *Uncommon Sense* (blog), 23 July 2020, Omohundro Institute of Early American History & Culture, https://blog.oieahc.wm.edu/nais-is-central-to-early-american-scholarship/.

42. Alyssa Mt. Pleasant, Caroline Wigginton, and Kelly Wisecup, "Materials and Methods in Native American and Indigenous Studies: Completing the Turn," *WMQ* 75 (2018): 207–36; and Christian Ayne Crouch, "Surveying the Present, Projecting the Future: Revaluating Colonial French Plans of Kanesatake," *WMQ* 75 (2018): 323–42. See also Christine DeLucia, "Fugitive Collections in New England Indian Country: Indigenous Material Culture and Early American History Making of Ezra Stiles's Yale Museum," *WMQ* 75 (2018): 109–50.
43. See, for example, Peter M. Solar and Karl Rönnback, "Copper Sheathing and the British Slave Trade," *EcHR* 68 (2015): 805–29; Zahedieh, "Eric Williams and William Forbes"; and David Chan Smith, "Fair Trade and the Political Economy of Brandy Smuggling in Early Eighteenth-Century Britain," *P&P* 251 (2021): 75–111. Few economic history articles, however, in this sample employ more than basic methodologies and techniques drawn from economics. For literature, see, for example, Dorothy Couchman, "'Mingo Everywhere': How Anglophones Hear Chattel Slavery," *S&A* 36 (2005): 704–20.
44. Chris Evans, "The Plantation Hoe: The Rise and Fall of an Atlantic Commodity, 1650–1850," *WMQ* 69 (2012): 71–100.
45. Reinart, "Way to Wealth"; John E. Crowley, "Sugar Machine: Picturing Industrialized Slavery," *AHR* 121 (2016): 403–36; Margaret Williamson, "Africa or Old Rome? Jamaican Slave Naming Practices Revisited," *S&A* 38 (2017): 117–34; Scott Zukowski, "Language Ideology in the Paxton Pamphlet War," *EAS* 18 (2020): 32–60; Stefanie Hunt-Kennedy, "'Had his nose cropt for being formerly runaway': Disability and the Bodies of Fugitive Studies in the British Caribbean," *S&A* 41 (2020): 212–33; Cornelia H. Dayton, "'The Oddest Man that I Ever Saw': Assessing Cognitive Disability on Eighteenth-Century Cape Cod," *Journal of Social History* 49 (2015): 77–99; and Georgia Canley, "Cost, Commodity and Gift: The Board of Trade's Conceptualization of British-Native American Gift Giving during Pontiac's War," *EAS* 14 (2016): 203–24.
46. Newman, "West African Ethnicity"; Zachary Dorner, "'No one here knows half so much of this matter as yourself': The Deployment of Expertise in Silvester Gardiner's Surgical, Druggist and Land Speculation Networks," *WMQ* 72 (2015): 287–322; Simon P. Newman, "Hidden in Plain Sight: Escaped Slaves in Late Eighteenth- and Early Nineteenth-Century Jamaica," *WMQ* (OI Reader App) (June 2018): 1–53; Robert Michael Morrissey, "Kaskaskia Social Networks: Kinship and Assimilation in the French-Illinois Borderlands, 1695–1735," *WMQ* 70 (2013): 103–46; Turk McCleskey and James C. Squire, "Knowing When to Fold: Litigation on a Writ of Debt in Mid-Eighteenth-Century Virginia," *WMQ* 76 (2019): 509–44; Tinni Sen, Turk McCleskey, and Atin Basuchoudhary, "When Good Little Debts Went Bad: Civil Litigation

on the Virginia Frontier, 1745–1755," *Journal of Interdisciplinary History* 46 (2015): 60–89.

47. Johann N. Neem, "From Polity to Exchange: The Fate of Democracy in the Changing Fields of Early American Historiography," *Modern Intellectual History* 17 (2020): 867–88; Nathan Perl-Rosenthal, "Atlantic Cultures and the Age of Revolution," *WMQ* 74 (2017): 667–96; and Ian Chambers, "The Empire Visits the Metropolis: The Red Atlantic, Spatial Habitus, and the Cherokee," *AS* 12 (2015): 67–89. For the use of linguistic theory derived from the work of Richard Baumon and Andrew Newman, see Scott Zukowski, "Language and Ideology in the Paxton Pamphlet War," *EAS* 18 (2020): 32–60; and for the use of Bourdieu, see Ipsen, "The Christened Mulatresses."
48. Maggie Blackhawk, "Federal Indian Law as Paradigm within Public Law," *Harvard Law Review* 132 (2019): 1787–877.
49. Ned Blackhawk, "The Iron Cage of Erasure: American Indian Sovereignty in Jill Lepore's *These Truths*," *AHR* 125 (2020): 1755.
50. Ibid., 1763.
51. Boyd Cotheran, *Remembering the Modoc War: Redemptive Violence and the Making of American Innocence* (Chapel Hill: University of North Carolina Press, 2014), 16.
52. Alicia Cox, "Settler Colonialism," in *Oxford Bibliographies Online: Literary and Critical Theory*, 26 July 2017, https://www.oxfordbibliographies.com/view/document/obo-9780190221911/obo-9780190221911-0029.xml; Patrick Wolfe, "Settler Colonialism and the Elimination of the Native," *Journal of Genocide Research* 8 (2006): 387–409.
53. Frederick E. Hoxie, "Retrieving the Red Continent: Settler Colonialism and the History of American Indians in the United States," *Ethnic and Racial Studies* 31 (2008): 1153–67; Walter L. Hixson, *American Settler Colonialism: A History* (New York: 2013).
54. Allan Greer, "Settler Colonialism and Empire in Early America," *WMQ* 76 (2019): 384. See also Daniel Richter, "His Own, Their Own: Settler Colonialism, Native Peoples, and Imperial Balances of Power in Eastern North America, 1660–1715," in Ignacio Gallup-Diaz, *The World of Colonial America: An Atlantic Handbook* (New York: Routledge, 2017).
55. Jennifer M. Spear, "Beyond the Native/Settler Divide in Early California," *WMQ* 76 (2019): 427–34.
56. Charles Prior, "Beyond Settler Colonialism: State Sovereignty in Early America," *JEAH* 9 (2019): 1–25.
57. Jeffrey Ostler, "Locating Settler Colonialism in Early American History," *WMQ* 76 (2019): 443.
58. For Black settlers and migrants in the 2019 forum, see Stephanie Smallwood, "Reflections on Settler Colonialism, the Hemispheric Americas and Chattel Slavery," *WMQ* 76 (2019): 407–16; and Tiya Miles, "Beyond

a Boundary: Black Lives and the Settler-Native Divide," *WMQ* 76 (2019): 417–26.
59. Nancy Shoemaker, "Settler Colonialism: Universal Theory or English Heritage?," *WMQ* 76 (2019): 369–74.
60. Michael Witgen, "A Nation of Settlers: The Early American Republic and the Colonization of the Northwest Territory," *WMQ* 76 (2019): 391–98.
61. Ibid., 398. See also Bethel Saler, *The Settlers' Empire: Colonialism and State Formation in America's Old Northwest* (Philadelphia: University of Pennsylvania Press, 2014).
62. Jeffrey Ostler, "'To Extirpate the Indians': The Indigenous Consciousness of Genocide in the Ohio Valley and Lower Great Lakes, 1750s–1810s," *WMQ* 72 (2015): 587–622; Ostler, *Surviving Genocide: Native Nations and the United States from the American Revolution to Bleeding Kansas* (New Haven, CT: Yale University Press, 2019); Gregory Evans Dowd, "Indigenous People without the Republic," *JAH* 104 (2017): 19–41.
63. Dylan Ruediger, "'Neither Utterly to Reject Them, Nor Yet to Drawe Them to Come In': Tributary Subordination and Settler Colonialism in Virginia," *EAS* 18 (2020): 1–31; Whitney Barlow Robles, "The Rattlesnake and the Hibernaculum: Animals, Ignorance, and Extinction in the Early American Underworld," *WMQ* 78 (2021): 3–44.
64. For an exemplary use of settler colonialism in this respect, see Bethel Saler, *The Settlers' Empire: Colonialism and State Formation in America's Old Northwest* (Philadelphia: University of Pennsylvania, 2019).
65. Nikole Hannah-Jones, ed. *The 1619 Project: A New American Origin Story* (New York: W. H. Allen, 2021).
66. Karin Wulf, "Vast Early America," *The Humanities* 40 (2019), https://www.neh.gov/article/vast-early-america.

1. The Historiography of Early America

1. For surveys that show the tensions between contemporary accounts of settler success and the ways in which that success had some basis in Indigenous dispossession and the mistreatment of the enslaved, see Alan Taylor, *American Revolutions: A Continental History, 1750–1804* (New York: W. W. Norton, 2016); Holton, *Liberty Is Sweet*.
2. Jack P. Greene, "Britain's Overseas Empire before 1780: Overwhelmingly Successful and Bureaucratically Challenged," in Greene, *Creating the British Atlantic: Essays on Transplantation, Adaptation, and Continuity* (Charlottesville: University of Virginia Press, 2013), 116.
3. For a similar understanding of recent trends in the early republic period, see Rosemarie Zagarri, "The Significance of the 'Global Turn' for the Early American Republic: Globalization in the Age of Nation-Building," *JER* 31 (2011): 1–37.

4. Carl Bridenbaugh, "The Neglected First Half of American History," *AHR* 53 (1948): 506–17.
5. Jack P. Greene and J. R. Pole, "Reconstructing British-American Colonial History: An Introduction," in Greene and Pole, eds., *Colonial British America: Essays in the New History of the Early Modern Era* (Baltimore: Johns Hopkins University Press, 1984), 4.
6. Appleby, "Different Kind of Independence."
7. Fred Anderson and Andrew R. L. Cayton, "The Problem of Fragmentation and the Prospects for Synthesis in Early American Social History," *WMQ* 50 (1993): 299–310. The four books are John Demos, *A Little Commonwealth: Family Life in Plymouth Colony* (New York: Oxford University Press, 1970); Philip Greven, *Four Generations: Population, Land, and Family in Colonial Andover, Massachusetts* (Ithaca, NY: Cornell University Press, 1970); Kenneth Lockridge, *A New England Town: The First Hundred Years: Dedham, Massachusetts, 1636–1736* (New York: W. W. Norton, 1970); and Michael Zuckerman, *Peaceable Kingdoms: New England Towns in the Eighteenth Century* (New York: Knopf, 1970).
8. Jack P. Greene, *Pursuits of Happiness: The Social Development of Early Modern British Colonies and the Formation of American Culture* (Chapel Hill: University of North Carolina Press, 1988); Bernard Bailyn, *Voyagers to the West: A Passage on the Peopling of America on the Eve of Revolution* (New York: Knopf, 1986); John J. McCusker and Russell R. Menard, *The Economy of British America, 1607–1789* (Chapel Hill: University of North Carolina Press, 1985).
9. She had a stake in this very debate: Joyce Appleby, "The New Republican Synthesis and the Changing Political Ideas of John Adams," *American Quarterly* 25 (1973); Appleby, "Liberalism and the American Revolution," *New England Quarterly* 49 (1976); Appleby, "Republicanism in Old and New Contexts," *WMQ* 43 (1986). In the same year as her *WMQ* article in 1992, she published *Liberalism and Republicanism in the Historical Imagination* (Cambridge, MA: Harvard University Press, 1992) and an article that extended her historiographical analysis beyond the field of early American history: Appleby, "Recovering America's Historical Diversity: Beyond Exceptionalism," *JAH* 79 (1992): 419–31.
10. Appleby, "Different Kind of Independence."
11. Wood, "Century of Writing Early American History," 687.
12. Wood's criticisms of the current direction of the field are subtle and betray easy generalization, but in essence he thinks the field has lost its way for three interrelated reasons: an obsession with diversity and in chronicling the lives of the marginal rather than the important; an unwillingness to consider the issue of national origins as a primary reason for writing early American history; and abdicating the field of interpretation of the colonial and revolutionary period from historians in the academy to

popular historians. Wood, "History in Context: The American Vision of Bernard Bailyn," *Weekly Standard*, February 23, 2015.
13. Wood, "Century of Writing Early American History."
14. Appleby, "Different Kind of Independence," 247.
15. Ibid., 267.
16. Anderson and Cayton, "Problem of Fragmentation."
17. Saul Connell, "Early Modern History in a Postmodern Age," *WMQ* 50 (1993): 329–41; Michael Meranze, "'Even the Dead Will Not Be Safe': An Ethics of Early American History," *WMQ* 50 (1993): 367–78; Darren Marcus Staloff, "Intellectual History Naturalized: Materialism and the 'Thinking Class,'" *WMQ* 50 (1993): 406–17.
18. Daniel K. Richter, "Whose Indian History?," *WMQ* 50 (1993): 381–82. The question of intellectual ownership of research and the responsibilities of researchers to Indian communities has become ever more prominent in the writing of Indian history. "Forum: Historians and Native Americans and Indigenous Studies," *AHR* 125 (2020): 517–51.
19. James H. Merrell, *The Indians' New World: Catawbas and Their Neighbors from European Contact through the Era of Indian Removal* (Chapel Hill: University of North Carolina Press, 1989); Daniel H. Usner, *Indians, Settlers, and Slaves in a Frontier Indian Economy: The Lower Mississippi Valley before 1783* (Chapel Hill: University of North Carolina Press, 1992); Daniel K. Richter, *The Ordeal of the Longhouse: The Peoples of the Iroquois League in the Era of European Colonization* (Chapel Hill: University of North Carolina, 1992); Timothy Silver, *A New Face on the Countryside: Indians, Colonist, and Slaves in South Atlantic Forests, 1500–1800* (Cambridge: Cambridge University Press, 1990); and Richard White, *The Middle Ground: Indians, Empires and Republics in the Great Lakes Region, 1656–1815* (Cambridge: Cambridge University Press, 1991).
20. Ned Blackhawk, "Look How Far We've Come: How American Indian History Changed the Study of American History in the 1990s," *Organization of American Historians' Magazine of History* 19, no. 6 (November 2005): 13–17.
21. Richter, "Whose Indian History?," 380, 393. For similar negative predictions, see James H. Merrell, "Some Thoughts on Colonial Historians and American Indians," *WMQ* 46 (1989): 94–119; and Richter, "Second Thoughts on Colonial Historians and American Indians," *WMQ* 69 (2012): 451–512.
22. Kathleen Brown, "Brave New Worlds: Women and Gender History," *WMQ* 50 (1993): 311–28; Jon Sensbach, "Charting a Course in Early African-American History," *WMQ* 50 (1993): 394–405.
23. For a "golden age," see Lois Green Carr and Lorena S. Walsh, "The Planter's Wife: The Experience of White Women in Seventeenth-Century Maryland," *WMQ* 34 (1977): 542–71.

24. Brown, "Brave New Worlds," 328; and Brown, *Good Wives, Nasty Wenches, and Anxious Patriarchs: Gender, Race, and Power in Colonial Virginia* (Chapel Hill: University of North Carolina Press, 1996), 33.
25. Brown, "Brave New Worlds," 325.
26. Peter Wood, "'I Did the Best I Could for My Day': The Study of Early Black History during the Second Reconstruction, 1960 to 1976," *WMQ* 35 (1978): 185–225; and Philip D. Morgan, "British Encounters with Africans and African-Americans circa 1600–1780," in Bernard Bailyn and Morgan, eds, *Strangers within the Realm: Cultural Margins of the First British Empire* (Chapel Hill: University of North Carolina Press, 1991): 157–219.
27. Sensbach, "Charting a Course," 397.
28. Barbara Solow, Introduction to *Slavery and the Rise of the Atlantic System* (Cambridge: Cambridge University Press, 1991), 1.
29. Joseph E. Inikori, "Africa and the Globalization Process, 1450–1850," *JGH* 2 (2007): 63–86; Burnard and Vidal, "Location and the Conceptualization of Historical Frameworks: Early North American History and Its Multiple Reconfigurations in the US and in Europe," in Nicolas Barreyre, Michael Heale, Stephen Tuck, and Cécile Vidal, eds., *You, the People: Historical Writing about the United States in Europe* (Berkeley: University of California Press, 2014), 141–64.
30. Sensbach, "Charting a Course," 405.
31. Alex Lichtenstein, "From the Editor's Desk: 1619 and All That," *AHR* 125 (2020): xv–xxi; Sean Wilentz, "A Matter of Facts," *The Atlantic*, January 22, 2020; Hazel Carby, "The Limits of Caste," *London Review of Books*, 21 January 2021.
32. Ira Berlin, *Many Thousands Gone: The First Two Centuries of Slavery in North America* (Cambridge, MA: Harvard University Press, 1998); and Philip D. Morgan, *Slave Counterpoint: Black Culture in the Eighteenth-Century Chesapeake and Lowcountry* (Chapel Hill: University of Carolina Press, 1998).
33. Daniel Vickers, "Beyond Jack Tar," *WMQ* 50 (1993): 418–24.
34. Simona Cerutti, "Who Is Below? E. P. Thompson, historien des societies modernes: une relecture," *Annales* 70 (2016): 943–53. For an exception, see Katherine Egner Gruber, "'By Measures Taken by Men': Clothing the Classes in William Carlin's Alexandria, 1763–1782," *EAS* 13 (2015): 931–53.
35. The classic work on seamen as class warriors is Jesse Lemisch, "Jack Tar in the Streets: Merchant Seamen in the Politics of Revolutionary America," *WMQ* 25 (1968): 371–407. See also "*AHR* Review Roundtable: Julius S. Scott's *The Common Wind: Afro-American Currents in the Age of the American Revolution*," *AHR* 125 (2020): 915–47. For recent works on seamen, see Nathan Perl-Rosenthal, *Citizen-Sailors: Becoming American in the*

Age of Revolution (Cambridge, MA: Harvard University Press, 2015); and Niklas Frykman, *The Bloody Flag: Mutiny in the Age of Atlantic Revolutions* (Berkeley: University of California Press, 2020).

36. Allan Kulikoff, "Households and Markets: Toward a New Synthesis of American Agrarian History" *WMQ* 50 (1993): 342–55.
37. Naomi Lamoureaux, "Rethinking the Transition to Capitalism in the Early American Northeast," *JAH* 90 (2003): 437–621. For social and economic networks, see David Hancock, *Oceans of Wine: Madeira and the Emergence of American Trade and Taste* (New Haven, CT: Yale University Press, 2009). For illegal trade, see Wim Klooster, "Inter-Imperial Smuggling in the Americas, 1600–1800," in Bernard Bailyn, ed., *Soundings in Atlantic History: Latent Structures and Intellectual Currents, 1500–1825* (Cambridge, MA: Harvard University Press, 2009), 141–80; and Casey Schmitt, "Virtue in Corruption: Privateers, Smuggler and the Shape of Empire in the Eighteenth-Century Caribbean," *EAS* 13 (2015): 80–110. For a useful summary, see Emma Hart, "From Field to Plate: The Colonial Livestock Trade and the Development of an American Economic Culture," *WMQ* 73 (2016): 112–14.
38. Trevor Burnard and Giorgio Riello, "Slavery and the New History of Capitalism," *JGH* 15 (2020): 225–44.
39. Vickers and Kulikoff were among the last early American historians to treat farmers as a social group. Daniel Vickers, *Farmers and Fishermen: Two Centuries of Work in Essex County, Massachusetts, 1630–1850* (Chapel Hill: University of North Carolina Press, 1994); Allan Kulikoff, *From British Peasants to Colonial American Farmers* (Chapel Hill: University of North Carolina Press, 2000). For an important study, see Richard Bushman, *The American Farmer in the Eighteenth Century: A Social and Cultural History* (New Haven, CT: Yale University Press, 2018).
40. Hart, "From Field to Plate." For commodity studies, see Jennifer Anderson, *Mahogany: The Costs of Luxury in Early America* (Cambridge, MA: Harvard University Press, 2012); Frank Trentemann, *Empire of Things: How We Became a World of Consumers, from the Fifteenth Century to the Twenty-First* (London: Allen Lane, 2016); and Ben Marsh, *Unrivalled Dreams: Silk and the Atlantic World, 1500–1800* (Cambridge: Cambridge University Press, 2020).
41. Russell R. Menard, "Whatever Happened to Early American Population History?" *WMQ* 50 (1993): 356–66.
42. This neglect is surprising, given his future work, heavily reliant on population history, on the origins and nature of the plantation system in seventeenth-century Barbados. Russell R. Menard, *Sweet Negotiations: Sugar, Slavery, and Plantation Agriculture in Early Barbados* (Charlottesville: University of Virginia Press, 2006).
43. David S. Jones, "Virgin Soils Revisited," *WMQ* 60 (2003): 703–42.

44. Russell R. Menard, *Migrants, Servants, and Slaves: Unfree Labor in Colonial British America* (Ashgate: London, 2001).
45. Hacker, "From '20. And odd' to 10 million."
46. A forum in 2022 would be unlikely to have nine men and one woman as contributors and have no one who was not White or American.
47. Meranze, "Even the Dead Will Not Be Safe."
48. *In Search of Early America* (Williamsburg: Institute of Early American History and Culture, 1993); James A. Henretta, "Families and Farms: Mentalité in Pre-Industrial America," *WMQ* 35 (1978): 3–32.
49. Christopher Grasso and Peter Mancall, "World and Ground," *WMQ* 74 (2017): 195–202. For an enthusiastic endorsement of Atlantic history, see Alison F. Games, "Atlantic History: Definitions, Challenges, and Opportunities," *AHR* 111 (2006): 741–57.
50. Eric Hinderaker and Rebecca Horn, "Territorial Crossings: Histories and Historiographies of the Early Americas," *WMQ* 67 (2010): 395–432.
51. Grasso and Mancall, "World and Ground."
52. Joyce Chaplin, "Expansion and Exceptionalism in Early American History," *JAH* 89 (2003): 1431–55; Claudio Saunt, "Go West: Mapping Early American Historiography," *WMQ* 65 (2008): 745–78; Christopher Grasso and Karin Wulf, "Nothing Says 'Democracy' Like a Visit from the Queen: Reflections on Empire and Nation in Early American Histories," *JAH* 95 (2008): 764–81; Johann N. Neem, "From Polity to Exchange: The Fate of Democracy in the Changing Fields of Early American Historiography," *Modern Intellectual History* 17 (2020): 867–88; Fred Anderson and Andrew Cayton, "The Problem of Authority in the Writing of Early American History," *WMQ* 66 (2009): 467–94; Hinderaker and Horn, "Territorial Crossings"; Grasso and Mancall, "World and Ground."
53. "It is essential that an historian, when dealing with our colonial beginnings, know English history and be competent to determine the place that England occupied as part of our colonial background." Andrews, "On Writing Colonial History," 27.
54. Chaplin, "Expansion and Exceptionalism."
55. For the United States as postcolonial, see Jack P. Greene, "Colonial History and National History: Reflections on a Continuing Problem," *WMQ* 64 (2007): 235–50.
56. Grasso and Wulf, "Nothing Says 'Democracy,'" 770.
57. Saunt, "Go West." See also James A. Hijayi, "Why the West Is Lost," *WMQ* 51 (1994): 276–92.
58. Wulf, "Vast Early America"; Steven Sarson, "'Breadth and Depth': Some Remarks on Empire, Atlantic History and Vast Early America (Roundtable II)," *XVII–XVIII* 74 (2017), https://doi.org/10.4000/1718.820.
59. Wood, "History in Context." See Josh Piker, "Getting Lost," *Uncommon Sense* (blog), 21 January 2016, https://blog.oieahc.wm.edu/getting-lost/.

60. Wood, "History in Context."
61. Neem "From Polity to Exchange," 888.
62. Pierre Bourdieu, *The Field of Cultural Production: Essays on Art and Literature*, rev. ed., trans. Randal Johnson (New York: Columbia University Press, 1993), 30–1.
63. Edward P. Pompeian, "Mind the Global U-Turn: Reorienting Early American History in a Global Context," *JER* 36 (2016): 715–52. Despite the title, the subject matter is the early republic rather than colonial British America.
64. Saskia Sassen, *Losing Control? Sovereignty in an Age of Globalization* (New York: Columbia University Press, 1996); Nicholas G. Onuf, "Sovereignty: Outline in a Conceptual History," *Alternatives* 16 (1991): 425–66.
65. For an early appreciation of empire and early American history, see Trevor Burnard, "Empire Matters? The Historiography of Imperialism in Early America, 1492–1830," *History of European Ideas* 33 (2007): 87–107. See also Ladan Niayesh and Marie-Jeanne Rossignol, "Whither the Empire in the Seventeenth and Eighteenth Centuries? Taking Stock of a Vibrant Field in English and American Studies," *XVII–XVIII* 74 (2017), https://doi.org/10.4000/1718.860; Bertrand Van Ruymbeke, "L'Empire au prisme de l'histoire atlantique: le cas des Treize Colonies (Round-table I)," *XVII–XVII* 74 (2017), https://doi.org/10.4000/1718.826; and Emmanuelle Saada, "More than a Turn? The 'Colonial' in French Studies," *French Politics, Culture and Society* 32 (2014): 34–39.
66. Neem, "From Polity to Exchange," 881.
67. Ibid., 878–79. Jeffers Lennox, "A Time and a Place: The Geography of British, French, and Aboriginal Interactions in Early Nova Scotia," *WMQ* 72 (2015): 423–60; Lisa Ford, *Settler Sovereignty: Jurisdiction and Indigenous People in America and Australia, 1788–1836* (Cambridge, MA: Harvard University Press, 2010), 2. For empires as complex and fragile, see Joshua Piker, "Lying Together: The Imperial Implications of Cross-Cultural Untruths," *AHR* 116 (2011): 964–86.
68. Krishnan Kumar, *Visions of Empire: How Five Imperial Regimes Shaped the World* (Princeton, NJ: Princeton University Press, 2017), 3, 475.
69. Neem, "From Polity to Exchange," 879.
70. Ibid., 877.
71. Ibid.
72. Allan Greer sees Taylor as open to considering that different national historiographies might emerge out of the study of early America but argues that he cannot really envision being outside the physical boundaries of the present-day United States, whether in Havana or Montreal. Allan Greer, "National, Transnational, and Hypernational Historiographies: New France Meets Early American History," *Canadian Historical Review* 91 (2010): 699–700.

73. Ibid., 884–86. Alan Taylor, *Liberty Men and Great Proprietors: The Revolutionary Settlement on the Maine Frontier, 1760–1820* (Chapel Hill: University of North Carolina Press, 1990); Taylor, *American Colonies* (New York: Penguin, 2001); Taylor, *American Revolutions*.
74. My publications that might worry Neem include Trevor Burnard, *The Atlantic in World History, 1492–1830* (London: Bloomsbury, 2020); "America the Good, America the Brave, America the Free: Reviewing the *Oxford History of the United States*," *Journal of American Studies* 45 (2011): 401–41; and "The Founding Fathers in Early American Historiography: A View from Abroad," *WMQ* 62 (2005): 745–64.
75. Neem, "From Polity to Exchange," 887.
76. Sarah Knott, who also places early American historiography within a neoliberal framework, thinks that early American historians adopting a history of exchange approach are politically quietist. Sarah Knott, "Narrating the Age of Revolution," *WMQ* 73 (2016): 3–36. Neem sees darker undertones to that quietism, believing that Knott is hesitant to recognise the political implications of such work. Neem, "From Polity to Exchange," 880–81. For contemporary work on neoliberalism influencing Neem, see Quinn Slobodian, *Globalists: The End of Empire and the Birth of Neoliberalism* (Cambridge, MA: Harvard University Press, 2018). For problems with using neoliberalism given the tendency for it to be used for polemical abuse, see Daniel Rodgers, "The Uses and Abuses of 'Neoliberalism,'" *Dissent* 65 (Winter 2018): 78.
77. Trevor Burnard, "The British Atlantic World," in Jack P. Greene and Philip D. Morgan, eds., *Atlantic History: A Critical Appraisal* (New York: Oxford University Press, 2009), 111–36.
78. Sarson, "Breadth and Depth."

2. Wealth, Commerce, Environment

1. Benjamin Franklin, *Observations on the Increase of Mankind*, in *The Papers of Benjamin Franklin*, ed. Leonard W. Labaree et al. (New Haven, CT: Yale University Press, 1959–): 4:225–34; James Otis, *The Rights of the British Colonies Asserted and Proved* (Boston, 1764), in Bernard Bailyn, ed., *Pamphlets of the American Revolution, 1750–1776* (Cambridge, MA: Harvard University Press, 1965): 1:435–36, 439–40.
2. Franklin, *Observations*.
3. Benjamin Franklin to Sir William Johnson, 12 September 1766, *Papers of Benjamin Franklin*, 13:416.
4. Pekka Hämäläinen, "The Shapes of Power: Indians, Europeans, and North American Worlds from the Seventeenth to the Nineteenth Centuries," in Juliana Barr and Edward Countryman, eds., *Contested Spaces of Early America* (Philadelphia: University of Pennsylvania Press, 2014), 37.

5. John Murrin, "Beneficiaries of Catastrophe: The English Colonies in America," in Eric Foner, ed., *The New American History* (Philadelphia: Temple University Press, 1997), 4.
6. Gordon Sayre, "Jefferson Takes on Buffon: The Polemic on American Animals in *Notes on the State of Virginia*," *WMQ* 78 (2021): 79–116.
7. James Belich, *Replenishing the Earth: The Settler Revolution and the Rise of the Anglo-World, 1783–1939* (Oxford: Oxford University Press, 2009).
8. Saul Dubow, "How British was the British World? The Case of South Africa," *JICH* 37 (2009): 4.
9. Robert Lee, "Accounting for Conquest: The Price of the Louisiana Purchase of Indian Country," *JAH* 103 (2017): 921–42; William A. Darity Jr. and A. Kirsten Mullen, *From Here to Equality: Reparations for Black Americans in the Twenty-First Century* (Chapel Hill: University of North Carolina Press, 2020).
10. Trevor Burnard, "Terror, Horror, and the British Atlantic Slave Trade in the Eighteenth Century," in Robert Antony, Stuart Carroll, and Caroline Dodds Pennock, eds., *The Cambridge World History of Violence*, vol. 3: *AD 1500–AD 1800* (Cambridge: Cambridge University Press, 2020), ch. 1.
11. Peter H. Lindert and Jeffrey G. Williamson, "American Colonial Incomes, 1650–1774," *EcHR* 69 (2016): 54–77.
12. Robert C. Allen, Tommy E. Murphy, and Eric B. Schneider, "The Colonial Origins of the Divergence in the Americas: A Labor Market Approach," *JEcH* 72 (2012): 863–94. For the importance of high American wages in colonial politics, see Thomas Agostini, "'The Provincials Will Work Like Giants': British Imperialism, American Colonial Troops, and Transatlantic Labor Economics during the Seven Years' War," *EAS* 15 (2017): 64–98.
13. Lindert and Williamson, "American Colonial Incomes," 55, 57, 74. See also Philip D. Morgan, "The Poor: Slaves in Early America," in David Eltis, Frank D. Lewis, and Kenneth L. Sokoloff, eds., *Slavery in the Development of the Americas* (Cambridge: Cambridge University Press, 2004), 288–323.
14. J. R. Ward, "The Amelioration of British West Indian Slavery: Anthropological Evidence," *EcHR* 71 (2018): 1223.
15. Richard S. Dunn, *A Tale of Two Plantations: Slave Life and Labor in Jamaica and Virginia* (Cambridge, MA: Harvard University Press, 2014).
16. Peter C. Mancall and Thomas Weiss, "Was Economic Growth Likely in Colonial British North America?," *JEcH* 59 (1999): 34. See also Pekka Hämäläinen, "The Politics of Grass: European Expansion, Ecological Change, and Indigenous Power in the Southwest Borderlands," *WMQ* 67 (2010): 173–208.
17. Joshua L. Rosenbloom and Thomas Weiss, "Economic Growth in the Mid-Atlantic Region: Conjectural Estimates for 1720 to 1800," *EEH* 51 (2014): 41–59.

18. Trevor Burnard, Laura Panza, and Jeffrey G. Williamson, "Living Costs, Real Incomes and Inequality in Colonial Jamaica," *EEH* 71 (2019): 55–71.
19. Trevor Burnard, *Planters, Merchants, and Slaves: Plantation Societies in British America, 1650–1820* (Chicago: University of Chicago Press, 2015).
20. Trevor Burnard and John Garrigus, *The Plantation Machine: Atlantic Capitalism in French Saint-Domingue and British Jamaica* (Philadelphia: University of Pennsylvania Press, 2016). The gap in wealth between Whites and Blacks in Saint-Domingue was probably even greater than in Jamaica, with the enslaved continually on the verge of starvation. John Garrigus, "'Like an epidemic one could stop only with the most violent of remedies': Poison versus Livestock Disease in Saint Domingue, 1750–1788," *WMQ* 78 (2021): 617–52.
21. Vincent Geloso, "Predation, Seigneurial Tenure, and Development in French Colonial America," *Social Science History* 44 (2020): 747–70.
22. Trevor Burnard and Giorgio Riello, "Slavery and the New History of Capitalism," *JGH* 15 (2020): 225–44; Burnard, *Jamaica in the Age of Revolution* (Philadelphia: University of Pennsylvania Press, 2020): 229–30; Louis P. Nelson, *Architecture and Empire in Jamaica* (New Haven, CT: Yale University Press, 2016); Mark Peterson, "Capitalism," in Joseph C. Miller, ed., *The Princeton Companion to Atlantic History* (Princeton, NJ: Princeton University Press, 2015): 71–75.
23. Eric Williams, *Capitalism and Slavery* (Chapel Hill: University of North Carolina Press, 1944).
24. Ahmed Reid, "Sugar, Slavery and Productivity in Jamaica, 1750–1807," *S&A* 37 (2016): 159–82; Ahmed Reid and David Beck Ryden, "Sugar, Land Markets, and the Williams' Thesis: Evidence from Jamaica's Property Sales, 1750–1810," *S&A* 34 (2013): 401–24.
25. David Eltis, Frank D. Lewis, and David Richardson, "Slave Prices, the African Slave Trade, and Productivity in the Caribbean, 1674–1807," *EcHR* 4 (2005): 673–700; Eltis, Lewis, and Richardson, "Slave Prices, the African Slave Trade and Productivity in Eighteenth Century South Carolina," *JEcH* 66 (2006): 1054–65; Peter C. Mancall, Joshua L. Rosenbloom, and Thomas Weiss, "Slave Prices and the South Carolina Economy, 1722–1809," *JEcH* 61 (2001): 616–39; Mancall, Rosenbloom, and Weiss, "Agricultural Labor Productivity in the Lower South, 1720–1800," *EEH* 39 (2002): 390–424; Mancall, Rosenbloom, and Weiss, "Slave Prices, the African Slave Trade, and Productivity in Eighteenth-Century South Carolina: A Reply," *JEcH* 66 (2006): 1066–71.
26. Klas Rönnbäck estimates that plantation trade, including production on American plantations and industries dependent on the American plantation complex, accounted for an annual value-added average of 3.5 percent of GDP in 1700–10, rising to 11 percent of GDP in 1800–10. Rönnbäck, "On the Economic Importance of the Slave Plantation Complex to the

British Economy during the Eighteenth Century: A Value-Added Approach," *JGH* 13 (2018) 308–27.
27. Ira Berlin and Philip D. Morgan, eds., *Cultivation and Culture: Labor and the Shaping of Slave Life in the Americas* (Charlottesville: University of Virginia Press, 1993), 1.
28. Neil Oatsvall and Vaughn Scribner, "'The Devil Was in the Englishman that He Makes Everything Work': Implementing the Concept of 'Work' to Re-evaluate Sugar Production and Consumption in the Early Modern British Atlantic World," *Agricultural History* 92 (2018): 463–64.
29. John E. Crowley, "Sugar Machines: Picturing Industrialized Slavery," *AHR* 121 (2016): 403–36.
30. Britt Rusert, "Plantation Ecologies: The Experimental Plantation in and against James Grainger's *The Sugar Cane*," *EAS* 13 (2015): 341–73; Tristan Schweiger, "Grainger's West Indian Planter: Property and Authority in *The Sugar Cane*," *Eighteenth-Century Studies* 50 (2017): 401–16.
31. Sarah Yeh, "Colonial Identity and Revolutionary Loyalty: The Case of the West Indies," in Stephen Foster, ed., *The Oxford History of the British Empire: British North America in the Seventeenth and Eighteenth Centuries* (Oxford: Oxford University Press, 2013), 204.
32. Matthew Mulcahy and Stuart Schwartz, "Nature's Battalions: Insects as Agricultural Pests in the Early Modern Caribbean," *WMQ* 75 (2018): 433–64.
33. Katherine Johnston, "Endangered Plantations: Environmental Change and Slavery in the British Caribbean, 1631–1807," *EAS* 18 (2020): 259–86.
34. Paton, "Driveress and Nurse," supplement 15, 27–53; Nicholas Radburn and Justin Roberts, "Gold versus Life: Jobbing Gangs and British Caribbean Slavery," *WMQ* 76 (2019): 223–56; Justin Roberts, "The 'Better Sort' and the 'Poorer Sort': Wealth Inequalities, Family Formation and the Economy of Energy on British Caribbean Sugar Plantations, 1750–1800," *S&A* 35 (2014): 458–73. See essays by Roberts, Radburn, and Inge Dornan in Trevor Burnard, ed., "Special Issue: The Management of Enslaved People on Anglo-American Plantations, 1700–1860," *Journal of Global Slavery* 6 (2021): 1–178.
35. Cited in Radburn and Roberts, "Gold versus Life," 255n38.
36. Roberts, "The Better Sort."
37. Justin Roberts, "The Whip and the Hoe: Violence, Work and Productivity on Anglo-American Plantations," *Journal of Global Slavery* 6 (2021): 108–30.
38. Sidney Mintz, "Enduring Substances, Trying Theories: The Caribbean Region as Oikumene," *Journal of the Royal Anthropological Institute* 2 (1996): 295, 298.
39. Karl Koth and John Serieux, "Sugar, Slavery, and Wealth: Jamaica Planter Nathaniel Phillips and the Williams Hypothesis," *Capitalism: A Journal of History and Economics* 1 (2019): 59–91.

40. Catherine Hall et al., eds., *Legacies of British Slave-Ownership: Colonial Slavery and the Formation of Victorian Britain* (Cambridge: Cambridge University Press, 2016); Sheryllynne Haggerty and Susanna Seymour, "Imperial Careering and Enslavement in the Long Eighteenth Century: The Bentinck Family, 1710–1830s," *S&A* 39 (2018): 642–62.
41. Chris Evans, "The Plantation Hoe: The Rise and Fall of an Atlantic Commodity, 1650–1850," *WMQ* 69 (2012): 71–100.
42. Nuala Zahedieh, "Colonies, Copper, and the Market for Inventive Activity in England and Wales, 1680–1730," *EcHR* 66 (2013): 805–25; Zahedieh, "Eric Williams and William Forbes."
43. Nuala Zahedieh, "Regulation, Rent-Seeking, and the Glorious Revolution in the British Atlantic Economy," *EcHR* 63 (2010): 865–90; Klas Rönnbäck, "Governance, Value-Added and Rents in Plantation Slavery-Based Value Chains," *S&A* 42 (2021): 130–50.
44. Jonathan Barth, "Reconstructing Mercantilism: Consensus and Conflict in British Imperial Economy in the Seventeenth and Eighteenth Centuries," *WMQ* 73 (2016): 257–90.
45. Steven Pincus, "Rethinking Mercantilism: Political Economy, the British Empire, and the Atlantic World in the Seventeenth and Eighteenth Centuries," *WMQ* 69 (2012) 28; Pincus, "Reconfiguring the British Empire," *WMQ* 69 (2012): 69. For support, see Jacob Soll, "For a New Economic History of Early Modern Empire: Anglo-French Imperial Co-development beyond Mercantilism and Laissez-Faire," *WMQ* 77 (2020): 525–50; and Julian Hoppit, *Britain's Political Economies: Parliament and Economic Life, 1600–1800* (Cambridge: University of Cambridge Press, 2017). For opposition, see Jonathan Eacott, "Leverage: Foreign Strength in British Economic Thinking," *WMQ* 77 (2020): 551–80.
46. Barth, "Reconstructing Mercantilism," 258; Hannah Farber, "The Political Economy of Marine Insurance and the Making of the US," *WMQ* 77 (2020): 581–612; Katherine Smoak, "The Weight of Necessity: Counterfeit Coins in the British Atlantic World, circa 1760–1800," *WMQ* 74 (2017): 467–502; Simon Middleton, "William Fishbourn's 'Misfortunes': Public Accounting and Paper Money in Early Pennsylvania," *EAS* 19 (2021): 64–99.
47. [William Wood], *A Survey of Trade in Four Parts . . .* (London, 1718).
48. Sophus A. Reinart, "The *Way to Wealth* around the World: Benjamin Franklin and the Globalization of American Capitalism," *AHR* (2015): 64.
49. Ibid., 64–65.
50. For urban early America, see Aaron Graham, "Towns, Government, Legislation and the 'Police' in Jamaica and the British Atlantic," *Urban History* 47 (2020): 41; Andrew Wells, "Global Cities, Local Fauna: Animals and the Urban British Atlantic, 1660–1800," *Urban History* 47 (2020): 1–20; Emma Hart, "City Government and the State in Eighteenth-Century

South Carolina," *Eighteenth-Century Studies* 50 (2017): 195–211; Trevor Burnard, "Towns in Plantation Societies in Eighteenth-Century British America," *EAS* 15 (2017): 837–57; and Paul Musselwhite, "'This Infant Borough': The Corporate Political Identity of Eighteenth-Century Norfolk," *EAS* 15 (2017): 801–34.

51. Emma Hart, "From Field to Plate: The Colonial Livestock Trade and the Development of an American Economic Culture," *WMQ* 73 (2016): 104–40; Ellen Hartigan-O'Connor, "Public Sales and Public Values in Eighteenth-Century North America," *EAS* 13 (2015): 749–73.

52. Radburn, "Keeping 'Wheels in Motion'"; Hannah Farber, "Political Economy of Marine Insurance"; Farber, "Sailing on Paper: The Embellished Bill of Lading in the Material Atlantic, 1720–1864," *EAS* 17 (2019): 37–83; Farber, "State-Building after War's End: A Government Financier Adjusts His Portfolio for Peace," *JER* 38 (2018): 67–76.

53. David Hancock, *Citizens of the World: London Merchants and the Integration of the British Atlantic Community, 1735–1785* (Cambridge: Cambridge University Press, 1995), 25; S. Max Edelson, *Plantation Enterprise in Colonial South Carolina* (Cambridge, MA: Harvard University Press, 2006), 180–81.

54. Nancy Christie, "Merchant and Plebeian Commercial Knowledge in Montreal and Quebec, 1760–1820," *EAS* 13 (2015): 856–80.

55. Emma Hart and Cathy Matson, "Situating Merchants in Late Eighteenth-Century British Atlantic Port Cities," *EAS* 15 (2017): 660–82; Cathy Matson, "Putting the Lydia to Sea: The Material Economy of Shipping in Colonial Philadelphia," *WMQ* 74 (2017): 303–32.

56. Walker, "Pursuing Her Profits"; Gamble, "For Lucre of Gain."

57. Hart and Matson, "Situating Merchants," 663, 681.

58. Claudio Saunt, "Population Counts," *WMQ* 78 (2021): 251–60.

59. J. R. McNeill, "Energy, Population, and Environmental Change since 1750: Entering the Anthropocene," in McNeill and Kenneth Pomeranz, eds., *The Cambridge World History*, vol 7.1, *Production, Destruction and Connection, 1750–Present* (Cambridge: Cambridge University Press, 2015), 80.

60. Joyce E. Chaplin, "The Other Revolution," *EAS* 13 (2015): 285–308; Kenneth Pomeranz, *The Great Divergence: China, Europe, and the Making of the Modern World* (Princeton, NJ: Princeton University Press, 2002); Tirthankar Roy and Giorgio Riello, eds., *Global Economic History* (London: Bloomsbury, 2019), 19–136.

61. Trevor Burnard, "Plantations and the Great Divergence," in Roy and Riello, *Global Economic History*, 102–17; Maxine Berg, "Sea Otters and Iron: A Global Microhistory of Value and Exchange at Nootka Sound, 1774–1792," *P&P* (2019): supplement 14.

62. For Britain, see David Zylberberg, "Fuel Prices, Regional Habits and Cooking Habits in the English Industrial Revolution," *P&P* 229 (2015):

91–122; and Giorgio Riello, "Cotton Textiles and the Industrial Revolution," *P&P* 255 (2022): 87–139.
63. Chaplin, "Other Revolution," 286.
64. Paul Warde, "Trees, Trade and Textiles: Potash Imports and Ecological Dependence in British Industry, ca. 1550–1770," *P&P* 240 (2018): 47–82; E. A. Wrigley, *The Path to Sustained Growth: England's Transition from an Organic Economy to an Industrial Revolution* (Cambridge: Cambridge University Press, 2016).
65. For historiographical evaluations, see Peter C. Mancall. "Pigs for Historians," *WMQ* 67 (2010): 347–75; and David S. Jones, "Virgin Soils Revisited," *WMQ* 60 (2003): 703–42.
66. Here, the monograph literature is richer than the journal literature. For a sampling of recent books just on the American North, see Christopher M. Parsons, *A Not-So-New World: Empire and Environment in French Colonial America* (Philadelphia: University of Pennsylvania Press, 2018); Sam White, *A Cold Welcome: The Little Ice Age and Europe's Encounter with North America* (Cambridge, MA: Harvard University Press, 2017); Strother Roberts, *Colonial Ecology, Atlantic Economy: Transforming Nature in Early New England* (Philadelphia: University of Pennsylvania, 2019); and Thomas M. Wickman, *Snowshoe County: An Environmental and Cultural History of Winter in the Early American Northeast* (Cambridge: Cambridge University Press, 2018).
67. Chaplin, "Other Revolution," 297.
68. Ibid., 286.
69. Joyce E. Chaplin, "Ogres and Omnivores: Early American Historians and Climate History," *WMQ* 72 (2015): 25–32. For important articles about climate in other periods, see Sam White, "'Shewing the difference betweene their conjuration, and our invocation on the name of God for rayne': Weather, Prayer, and Magic in Early American Encounters," *WMQ* 72 (2015): 33–56; Wickman, *Snowshoe County*; Peter C. Mancall, "The Raw and the Cold: Five English Sailors in Sixteenth-Century Nunavut," *WMQ* 70 (2013): 3–40; and Tony C. Perry, "'In Bondage When Cold was King': The Frigid Terrain of Slavery in Antebellum Maryland," *S&A* 38 (2017): 23–36.
70. Jean-François Mouhot, "Past Connections and Present Similarities in Slave Ownership and Fossil Fuel Usage," *Climatic Change* 105 (2011): 329–55; Oatsvall and Scribner, "The Devil Was in the Englishman," 463–64.
71. Natale Zappia, "Revolutions in the Grass: Energy and Food Systems in Continental North America, 1763–1848," *Environmental History* 21 (2016): 30–53.
72. Chaplin, "Other Revolution," 308. See also Frederik Albrotten Jonsson, "Climatic Change and the Retreat of the Atlantic: The Cameralist Context of Peter Kalm's Voyage to North America, 1748–51," *WMQ* 72 (2015):

99–126; and Anya Zilberstein, "Inured to Empire: Wild Rice and Climate Change," *WMQ* 72 (2015): 127–58.

73. James D. Rice, "Early American Environmental Histories," *WMQ* 75 (2018): 410–32.

74. Ibid., 429. See also Molly A. Warsh, "A Political Ecology in the Early Spanish Caribbean," *WMQ* 71 (2014): 517–48; and Keith Pluymers, "Atlantic Iron: Wood Scarcity and the Political Ecology of Early English Expansion," *WMQ* 73 (2018): 389–426.

75. Adam R. Hodge, "'In Want of Nourishment for to Keep Them Alive': Climate Fluctuations, Bison Scarcity and the Smallpox Epidemic of 1780–82 on the Northern Great Plains," *Environmental History* 17 (2012): 365–403; Robert Michael Morrissey, "The Power of the Ecotone: Bison, Slavery and the Rise and Fall of the Kaskaskia," *JAH* 102 (2015): 667–92; Morrissey, "Climate, Ecology and History in North America's Tallgrass Prairie Borderlands," *P&P* 245 (2019): 40–77; Morrissey, "Bison Algonquians: Cycles of Violence and Exploitation in the Mississippi Valley Borderlands," *EAS* 13 (2015): 309–40; and Thomas M. Wickman, "'Winters Embittered with Hardships': Severe Cold, Wabanaki's Power and English Adjustments, 1690–1710," *WMQ* 72 (2015): 57–98.

76. Morrissey, "Kaskaskia Social Networks."

77. Stephen Aron, *American Confluence: The Missouri Frontier from Borderland to Border* (Bloomington: Indiana University Press, 2006).

78. For a counternarrative, see Hämäläinen, "Politics of Grass."

79. Morrissey, "Bison Algonquians," 329.

80. On alcohol and guns, see Michael Goode, "Dangerous Spirits: How the Indian Critique of Alcohol Shaped Eighteenth-Century Quaker Revivalism," *EAS* 14 (2016): 258–83.

3. Slavery

1. Charles McLean Andrews, "Colonial Commerce," *AHR* 20 (1914): 43; Thomas M. Truxes, *The Overseas Trade of British America: A Narrative History* (New Haven, CT: Yale University Press, 2021), 7.

2. The 1619 Project, nytimes.com.

3. For Jamaica, see Trevor Burnard, "Tropical Hospitality, British Masculinity, and Drink in Late Eighteenth-Century Jamaica," *HJ* 64 (2021): 1–22; Christine Walker, "As Though She 'Was a Virtuous Woman': Colonial Changes to Gender Roles, Marital Practices, and Family Formation in Atlantic America, 1720–1760," *Journal of Colonialism and Colonial History* 21 (Summer 2020), http://doi.org/10.1353/cch.2020.0016; Walker, "Pursuing Her Profits: Women in Jamaica, Atlantic Slavery and a Globalising Market, 1700–60," *Gender and History* 26 (2014): 478–501; David Beck Ryden, "Manumission in Late Eighteenth-Century Jamaica," *New West India*

Guide 92 (2018): 211–44; Stanley Mirvis, "Between Assembly and Crown: The Debate over Jewish Taxation in Jamaica (1692–1740)," *JEAH* 6 (2016): 196–219; Aaron Graham, "Jamaican Legislation and the Transatlantic Constitution, 1664–1839," *HJ* 61 (2018): 327–55; Graham, "Towns, Government, Legislation"; Williamson, "Africa or Old Rome?"; Helen McKee, "From Violence to Alliance: Maroons and White Settlers in Jamaica, 1739–1795," *S&A* 39 (2018): 27–52; Erin Trahey, "Among Her Kinswomen: Legacies of Free Women of Color in Jamaica," *WMQ* 76 (2019): 257–88; Daniel Livesay "Privileging Kinship: Family and Race in Eighteenth-Century Jamaica," *EAS* 14 (2016): 688–711; and Katherine Gerbner, "'They call me Obea': German Moravian Missionaries and Afro-Caribbean Religion in Jamaica, 1754–1760," *AS* 12 (2015): 160–78.

4. Barbara L. Solow, "Capitalism and Slavery in the Exceedingly Long Run," *Journal of Interdisciplinary History* 17 (1987): 732, 735; Sven Beckert, "Revisiting Europe and Slavery," *S&A* 42 (2021): 166.

5. Russell R. Menard, "Making a 'Popular Slave Society' in Colonial British America," *Journal of Interdisciplinary History* 43 (2013): 377–95.

6. Jared Ross Hardesty, "Disappearing from Abolitionism's Heartland: The Legacy of Slavery in Boston," *International Review of Social History* 65 (2020): 145–68; Hardesty, "An Angry God in the Home of Sinners: Enslaved Africans and the Uses of Protestant Christianity in Prerevolutionary Boston," *S&A* 35 (2014): 66–83; Hardesty, "Creating an Unfree Hinterland: Merchant Capital, Bound Labor, and Market Production in Eighteenth-Century Massachusetts," *EAS* 15 (2017): 37–63; Gloria McCahon Whiting, "Emancipation without the Courts or Constitution: The Case of Revolutionary Massachusetts," *S&A* 41 (2020): 458–78; Whiting, "Power, Patriarchy, and Provision: African Families Negotiate Gender and Slavery in New England," *JAH* (2016): 583–605; Whiting, "Race, Slavery, and the Problem of Numbers in Early New England: A View from Probate Court," *WMQ* 77 (2020): 405–40; Wendy Warren, "'Thrown upon the World': Valuing Infants in the Eighteenth-Century North American Slave Market," *S&A* 39 (2018): 623–41.

7. Jared Hardesty, *Black Lives, White Worlds: A History of Slavery in New England* (Amherst, MA: Bright Leaf, 2019); and Wendy Warren, *New England Bound: Slavery and Colonization in Early America* (Boston: Liveright, 2016). For the wider context of Boston, see Mark A. Peterson, *The City-State of Boston: The Rise and Fall of an Atlantic Power, 1630–1865* (Princeton, NJ: Princeton University Press, 2019).

8. Hardesty, "Disappearing from Abolitionism's Heartland," 161.

9. Whiting, "Race, Slavery in Early New England," 407. See Margaret Ellen Newell, *Brethren by Nature: New England Indians, Colonists, and the*

Origins of American Slavery (Ithaca, NY: Cornell University Press 2015); and essays by Newell, Linford Fisher, and Brett Rushforth in Sophie White and Trevor Burnard, eds., *Hearing Enslaved Voices: African and Indian Slave Testimony in British and French America, 1700–1848* (New York: Routledge, 2020), 81–142. For Indian slavery, see Christian Ayne Crouch, "The Black City: African and Indian Exchanges in Pontiac's Upper Country," *EAS* 14 (2016): 284–318; M. Scott Heerman, "Beyond Plantations: Indian and African Slavery in the Illinois Country, 1720–1780," *S&A* 38 (2017): 489–509; and D. Andrew Johnson, "Displacing Captives in Colonial South Carolina: Native American Enslavement and the Rise of the Colonial State after the Yamasee War," *JEAH* 7 (2017): 115–40.

10. Stephanie Smallwood, "The Politics of the Archive and History's Accountability to the Enslaved," *History of the Enslaved* 6 (2016): 126.
11. Kelly Wisecup, "Panel Introduction: Slavery in the Caribbean—Archives and Representations," *Studies in Eighteenth-Century Culture* 49 (2020): 66.
12. Saidiya Hartman, *Lose Your Mother: A Journey along the Atlantic Slave Route* (New York: Farrar, Strauss and Giroux, 2007); Jennifer Morgan, "Accounting for 'The Most Excruciating Torment': Gender, Slavery, and Trans-Atlantic Passages," *History of the Present* 6 (2016): 188.
13. Douglas Hamilton, "'A most active, enterprising officer': Captain John Perkins, the Royal Navy, and the Boundaries of Slavery and Liberty in the Caribbean," *S&A* 39 (2018): 89–100. For the links between maritime service and Black freedom, see Julius Scott, *The Common Wind: Afro-American Currents in the Age of the American Revolution* (New York: Verso, 2018).
14. Maria Alessandra Bollettino, "'Of equal or of more service': Black Soldiers and the British Empire in the Mid-Eighteenth-Century Caribbean," *S&A* 38 (2017): 510–33.
15. Marisa J. Fuentes, *Dispossessed Lives: Enslaved Women, Violence, and the Archive* (Philadelphia: University of Pennsylvania Press, 2016): 144–47.
16. Carolyn Steedman, *Dust* (Manchester: Manchester University Press, 2002); Trevor Burnard and John Lean, "Hearing Slave Voices: The Fiscal's Reports of Berbice and Demerara-Essequibo," *Archives* 27 (2002): 37–50; Cornelia Hughes Dayton, "Rethinking Agency, Recovering Voices," *AHR* 109 (2004): 827–43; Sue Peabody, "Microhistory, Biography, Fiction: The Politics of Narrating the Lives of People Under Slavery," *Transatlantica* 2 (2012): consulted 24 September 2022, http://journals.openedition.org/transatlantica/6184; and Natalie C. Zacek, "Voices and Silences: The Problem of Slave Testimony in the English West Indian Law Court," *S&A* 24 (2003): 24–39. See also Miles Ogburn, *The Freedom of Speech: Talk and Slavery in the Anglo-Caribbean World* (Chicago: University of Chicago Press, 2019); and Nancy Christie, Michael Gauvreau, and Matthew Gerber, eds., *Voices in the Legal Archives in the French Colonial World: "The King Is Listening"* (New York: Routledge, 2021). For French colonial archives,

see Marie Houllemare, "La fabrique des archives colonials et la conscience impériale France," *Revue d'Histoire Moderne et Contemporaine* 61 (2014): 7–31; Laurent Dubois, "Maroons in the Archives: The Uses of the Past in the French Caribbean," in Frais Bloom and William Rosenberg, eds., *Archives, Documentation, and Institutions of Social Memory* (Ann Arbor: University of Michigan Press, 2005); Loïc Charles and Paul Cheney, "The Colonial Machine Dismantled: Knowledge and Empire in the French Atlantic," *P&P* 219 (2013): 127–63; Matthew Gerber, "Bastardy, Race, and Law in Eighteenth-Century French Atlantic: The Evidence of Litigation," *French Historical Studies* 36 (2013): 571–600; and Sophie White, *Voices of the Enslaved; Love, Labor, and Longing in French Louisiana* (Chapel Hill: University of North Carolina Press, 2019).

17. Essays by White, Vidal, Rogers, and Clark, in White and Burnard, *Hearing Enslaved Voices*.
18. Sasha Turner, "The Nameless and the Forgotten: Maternal Grief, Sacred Protection, and the Archive of Slavery," *S&A* 38 (2017): 232.
19. Keith Mason, "The Absentee Planter and the Key Slave: Privilege, Patriarchalism and Exploitation in the Early Eighteenth-Century Caribbean," *WMQ* 70 (2013): 79–102.
20. James Dator, "Frank Travels: Space, Power and Slave Mobility in the British Leeward Islands, c. 1700–1730," *S&A* 37 (2016): 159–82; James H. Sweet, *Domingos Álvares, African Healing and the Intellectual History of the Atlantic World* (Chapel Hill: University of North Carolina Press, 2011).
21. Radburn and Roberts, "Gold versus Life"; Roberts, "The 'Better Sort' and the 'Poorer Sort.'"
22. Simon P. Newman, "Freedom-Seeking Slaves in England and Scotland, 1700–1870," *EHR* 134 (2019): 1136–68; Newman, "Rethinking Runaways in the British Atlantic World: Britain, the Caribbean, West Africa and North America," *S&A* 38 (2017): 49–75; Newman, "Hidden in Plain Sight."
23. Simon Middleton, "Runaways, Rewards and the Social History of Money," *EAS* 15 (2017): 612–47; Jordan E. Taylor, "Enquire of the Printer: Newspaper Advertising and the Moral Economy of the North American Slave Trade, 1704–1807," *EAS* 18 (2020): 287–323.
24. Hunt-Kennedy, "Had his nose cropt for being formerly runaway." For normalisation of Caribbean violence, see Dallin Lewis, "Domesticating the Plantation: The Politics and Tragedy of Slave Kinship in the British Atlantic World," *Eighteenth Century* 60 (2019): 201–30.
25. Yong Hwi Yoon, "The Spread of Antislavery Sentiment through Proslavery Tracts in the Transatlantic Evangelical Community, 1740s–1770s," *Church History* 81 (2012): 348–77; Philippa Koch, "Slavery, Mission and the Perils of Providence in Eighteenth-Century Christianity: The Writings of Whitefield and the Halle Pietists," *Church History* 84 (2015):

369–93. For transatlantic connections, see Elizabeth Bouldin, "In Search of 'Fellow Pilgrims': Radical Protestants and Trans-confessional Exchanges in Europe and the British Atlantic, c. 1670–1730," *Church History* 83 (2014): 590–617.

26. John Coffey, "Tremble, Britannia! The Fear of God and the Abolition of the Slave Trade, 1758–1807," *EHR* 127 (2012): 846, 881; Nicholas Guyatt, *Providence and the Invention of the United States* (Cambridge: Cambridge University Press, 2007); Christopher Leslie Brown, *Moral Capital: The Foundations of British Abolitionism* (Chapel Hill: University of North Carolina Press, 2006); Roger Anstey, "A Re-interpretation of the Abolition of the British Slave Trade, 1806–07," *EHR* 87 (1972): 313; Boyd Hilton, *The Age of Atonement: The Influence of Evangelicalism on Social and Economic Thought* (Oxford: Oxford University Press, 1988), 209.

27. Ryan Hanley, "Calvinism, Proslavery and James Albert Ukowsaw Gronniosaw," *S&A* 36 (2015): 360–81.

28. Devin Leigh, "The Origins of a Source: Edward Long, Coromantee Slave Revolts, and *The History of Jamaica*," *S&A* 40 (2019): 295–320; Matilde Cazzola and Lorenzo Ravano, "Plantation Society in the Age of Revolution: Edward Long, Pierre-Victor Malouet and the Problem of Slave Government," *S&A* 41 (2020): 234–55.

29. Jeffrey Glover, "Witnessing African War: Slavery, the Laws of War, and Anglo-American Abolitionism," *WMQ* 74 (2017): 503–32; Nicole K. Dressler, "'Enimies to Mankind': Convict Servitude, Authority and Humanitarianism in the British Atlantic World," *EAS* 17 (2019): 343–76.

30. Coffey, "Tremble, Britannia!," 845–46. For a guide to debates about the causes of abolition in the past, see Brown, *Moral Capital*; and David Richardson, *Principles and Agents: The British Slave Trade and Its Abolition* (New Haven, CT: Yale University Press, 2022).

31. Beckert, "Revisiting Europe and Slavery," 166–67. For misreadings and underappreciation of Williams in American historical studies, see H. Reuben Neptune "Throwin' Scholarly Shade: Eric Williams in the New History of Capitalism and Slavery," *JER* 39 (2019): 299–326. For reverence for Williams's text by postcolonial radicals, who seldom shared Williams's nationalistic and often conservative politics, see "Eric Williams and the Postcolonial Caribbean: A Special Issue," *Callaloo* 20 (1997). For Williams and early American slavery, see Russell R. Menard, "Reckoning with Williams: 'Capitalism and Slavery' and the Reconstruction of Early American History," *Callaloo* 20 (1997): 791–99.

32. Burnard and Riello, "Slavery and the New History of Capitalism"; Nicolas Barreyre and Alexia Blin, "À la redécouverte du capitalisme américain," *Revue d'histoire du XIXe siècle* 54 (2017): 135–48; Kenneth Lipartito, "Reassembling the Economic: New Departures in Historical Materialism," *AHR* 121 (2016): 115–16.

33. Nathan Friend, "Inventing Revivalist *Millennialism*: Edwards and the Scottish Connection," *Journal of Religious History* 42 (2018): 52–71. But see a magnificent treatment of the Great Awakening in Douglas L. Winiarski, *Darkness Falls on the Land of Light: Experiencing Religious Awakenings in Eighteenth-Century New England* (Chapel Hill: University of North Carolina Press, 2017).
34. Catherine A. Brekus, "Contested Words: History, America, Religion," *WMQ* 75 (2018): 3–36.
35. Janet Moore Lindman, "'This Union of the Soul': Spiritual Friendship among Early American Protestants," *Journal of Social History* 50 (2017): 680–700. For commerce and religion, see, inter alia, Kristen Beales, "Commercial Theologians and the Problem of Bubbles: The Pennsylvania Land Company and the Quaker Debate on Financial Ethics," *Eighteenth-Century Studies* 54 (2020): 121–41. For commerce and medicine, see Susan Brandt, "'Getting into a Little Business': Margaret Hill Morris and Women's Medical Entrepreneurship during the American Revolution," *EAS* 13 (2015): 774–807.
36. Brekus, "Contested Words," 15; Katherine Gerbner, *Christian Slavery: Conversion and Race in the Protestant Atlantic World* (Philadelphia: University of Pennsylvania Press, 2018); Gerbner, "They call me Obea"; Kristen Block, "Slavery and Inter-Imperial Leprosy Discourse in the Atlantic World," *AS* 14 (2017): 243–62; Christopher M. Parsons, "The Natural History of Colonial Science: Joseph-François Lafitau's Discovery of Ginseng and Its Afterlives," *WMQ* 72 (2015): 587–622.
37. SlaveVoyages.org, http://www.slavevoyages.org. David Eltis and David Richardson, "A New Assessment of the Transatlantic Slave Trade," in Eltis and Richardson, eds., *Extending the Frontiers: Essays of the New Transatlantic Slave Trade Database* (New Haven, CT: Yale University Press): 1–60; Henry B. Lovejoy et al., "Redefining African Regions for Linking Open-Source Data," *History in Africa* 46 (2019): 5–36.
38. Rönnbäck, "Governance, Value-Added and Rents," 133–34. For France, see Guillaume Daudin, "Profitability of Slave and Long-Distance Trading in Context: The Case of Eighteenth-Century France," *JEcH* 64 (2004): 144–71. For Portugal, see Filipa Ribiera da Silva, "The Profits of the Portuguese-Brazilian Transatlantic Slave Trade: Challenges and Possibilities," *S&A* 42 (2021): 77–104. For the Dutch trade, see Karwan Fatah-Black and Matthias van Rossum, "Beyond Profitability: The Dutch Transatlantic Slave Trade and Its Economic Impact," *S&A* 36 (2015): 63 and 83, with criticism from David Eltis, Pieter C. Emmer, and Frank D. Lewis, "More than Profits? The Contributions of the Slave Trade to the Dutch Economy: Assessing Fatah-Black and van Rossum," *S&A* 37 (2016): 724–35.
39. "Towns are like electric transformers. They increase tension, accelerate the rhythm of exchange and constantly recharge human life." Fernand

Braudel, *The Structures of Everyday Life: The Limits of the Possible*, trans. Sian Reynolds (New York: Harper and Row, 1981), 479; Jacob Price, "Economic Functions and the Growth of American Port Towns in the Eighteenth Century," *Perspectives in American History* 8 (1974): 123–86.

40. Nicholas Radburn, "Keeping 'the Wheel in Motion': Transatlantic Credit Terms, Slave Prices, and the Geography of Slavery in the British Americas, 1755–1807," *JEcH* 75 (2015): 660–89.

41. See also K. Tawny Paul, "Credit and Ethnicity in the Urban Atlantic World: Scottish Associational Culture in Colonial Philadelphia," *EAS* 13 (2015): 661–91; Sen, McCleskey, and Basuchoudhary, "When Good Little Debts Went Bad"; McCleskey and James C. Squire, "Knowing When to Fold: Litigation on a Writ of Debt in Mid-Eighteenth-Century Virginia," *WMQ* 76 (2019): 509–44.

42. Nicholas Radburn, "Guinea Factors, Slave Sales, and the Profits of the Transatlantic Slave Trade in Eighteenth-Century Jamaica: The Case of John Tailyour," *WMQ* 72 (2015): 243–86; Radburn, "Keeping 'the Wheel in Motion.'"

43. Gregory O'Malley, "Slavery's Converging Ground: Charleston's Slave Trade and the Black Heart of the Lowcountry," *WMQ* 74 (2017): 271–302; Trevor Burnard, "Slaves and Slavery in Kingston, 1770–1815," *International Review of Social History* 65 (2020): 39–65.

44. Sean M. Kelley, "Scrambling for Slaves: Captive Sales in Colonial South Carolina," *S&A* 34 (2013): 1–21. See also Trevor Burnard, "'A Pack of Knaves': The Royal African Company, the Development of the Jamaican Plantation Economy and the Benefits of Monopoly, 1672–1708," *Journal of Colonialism and Colonial History* 21 (2020).

45. Peter Pelizzari, "Supplying Slavery: Jamaica, North America, and British Intra-Imperial trade, 1752–1769," *S&A* 41 (2020): 528–54.

46. Sean Kelley, "New World Slave Traders and the Problem of Slave Goods: Brazil, Barbados, Cuba and North America in Comparative Perspective," *EHR* 134 (2019): 302–33; Riello, "Cotton Textiles and the Industrial Revolution"; Kazuo Kobayashi, *Indian Cotton Textiles in West Africa: African Agency, Consumer Demand and the Making of the Global Economy, 1750–1850* (London: Palgrave Macmillan, 1991).

47. Ty M. Reese, "Controlling the Company: The Structures of Fante-British Relations on the Gold Coast, 1750–1821," *JICH* 41 (2013): 104–19.

48. Anne Ruderman, "Intra-European Trade in Atlantic Africa," *WMQ* 77 (2020): 228.

49. Joseph E. Inikori, "The Development of Capitalism in the Atlantic World: England, the Americas and West Africa, 1450–1900," *Labor History* 58 (2017): 138–53.

50. Matthew Dziennik, "'Till These Experiments be Made': Senegambia and British Imperial Policy in the Eighteenth Century," *EHR* 130 (2015): 1132–61.

51. Jan de Vries, "The Limits of Globalization in the Early Modern World," *EcHR* 63 (2010): 710–33.
52. Randy J. Sparks, "Gold Coast Merchant Families, Pawning, and the Eighteenth-Century British Slave Trade," *WMQ* 70 (2013): 317–40; Ipsen, "The Christened Mulatresses"; Bronwen Everill, "'All the baubles that they needed': 'Industriousness' and Slavery in Saint-Louis and Gorée," *EAS* 15 (2017): 714–39.
53. C. L. R. James, *The Black Jacobins: Toussaint L'Ouverture and the San Domingo Revolution*, 2d ed. (New York: Vintage Books, 1963), 392. See also David Scott, "Modernity that Predated the Modern: Sidney Mintz's Caribbean," *HWJ* 58 (2004): 191–210.
54. For American slavery, capitalism, and the development of White supremacy, see Walter Johnson, *The Broken Heart of America: St. Louis and the Violent History of the United States* (New York: Basic Books, 2020). The term "racial capitalism" was first coined in 1976 in antiapartheid writings in South Africa and was taken up and popularized by Cedric Robinson. Ken Olende, "Cedric Robinson, Racial Capitalism and the Return of Black Radicalism," *International Socialism* 169 (2021), http://isj.org.uk/cedric-robinson-racial-capitalism/, accessed 6 June 2022.
55. For plantations as being particular sites of creative destruction—creating wealth but destroying people and place—see Philip D. Morgan, J. R. McNeill, Matthew Mulcahy, and Stuart B. Schwartz, *Sea and Land: An Environmental History of the Caribbean* (Oxford: Oxford University Press, 2022).
56. White, *Voices of the Enslaved*.
57. Peterson, *City-State of Boston*; David Waldstreicher, "Ancients, Moderns, and Africans: Phillis Wheatley and the Politics of Empire and Slavery in the American Revolution," *JER* 37 (2017): 701–33; and Coffey, "Tremble, Britannia!"

4. Indigenous Peoples

1. Hämäläinen, "Politics of Grass."
2. Tai S. Edwards and Paul Kelton, "Germs, Genocides, and America's Indigenous Peoples," *JAH* 107 (2020): 52–76.
3. Melanie J. Newton, "Returns to a Native Land: Indigeneity and Decolonization in the Anglophone Caribbean," *Small Axe* 17 (2013): 108; David Noble Cook, *Born to Die: Disease and New World Conquest, 1492–1650* (Cambridge: Cambridge University Press, 1998); and Scott M. Fitzpatrick, "The Pre-Columbian Caribbean: Colonization, Population Dispersal and Island Adaptations," *PaleoAmerica* 1 (2015): 301–31.
4. Michael Witgen, *An Infinity of Nations: How the Native New World Shaped Early North America* (Philadelphia: University of Pennsylvania Press, 2012), 320–21.

5. Richter, "Whose Indian History?"
6. Susan Sleeper-Smith et al., *Why You Can't Teach United States History without American Indians* (Chapel Hill: University of North Carolina Press, 2015).
7. Jean M. O'Brien, *Firsting and Lasting: Writing Indians Out of Existence in New England* (Minnesota: University of Minneapolis Press, 2010), xiii.
8. Juliana Barr, "The Red Continent and the Cant of the Coastline," *WMQ* 69 (2012): 521.
9. Christine DeLucia, *Memory Lands: King Philip's War and the Place of Violence in the Northeast* (New Haven, CT: Yale University Press, 2018); Lisa Brooks, *Our Beloved Kin: A New History of King Philip's War* (New Haven, CT: Yale University Press, 2018).
10. James Merrell, "Second Thoughts on Colonial Historians and American Indians," *WMQ* 69 (2012): 451–512; Ann Marie Plane, *Colonial Intimacies: Indian Marriage in Early New England* (Ithaca, NY: Cornell University Press, 2000), 10.
11. Merrell, "Second Thoughts"; Scott Zukowski, "Language and Ideology in the Paxton Pamphlet War," *EAS* 18 (2020): 32–60; Sean P. Harvey and Sarah Rivett, "Colonial Indigenous Language Encounters in North America in the Intellectual History of the Atlantic World," *EAS* 15 (2017): 442–73.
12. Lisa Brooks, "Awikhigawôgan to Pildowi Ôjmowôgan: Mapping a New History," *WMQ* 75 (2018): 259–94; John DuVal and Kathleen DuVal, "Writing Translations, Writing History: Colonial American Voices and the Problem of Verticality," *Early American Literature* 53 (2018): 153–68; Edward G. Gray, *New World Babel: Languages and Nations in Early America* (Princeton, NJ: Princeton University Press, 1999).
13. Merrell, "Second Thoughts"; Mt. Pleasant, Wigginton, and Wisecup, "Materials and Methods in Native American Studies"; Pekka Hämäläinen and Samuel Truett, "On Borderlands," *JAH* 98 (2011): 338–61.
14. Gilles Havard, *La Grande Paix de Montréal de 1701: Les voies de la diplomatie franco-amérindienne* (Montreal, 1992); Havard, *Empire et métissages: Indiens et Français dans le pays d'en haut, 1660–1715* (Quebec, 2003); Havard with Cécile Vidal, *Histoire de l'Amerique française* (Paris, 2003); Havard, *Histoire des Coureurs de bois: Amérique du Nord, 1600–1840* (Paris: Les Indes savants, 2016).
15. Merrell, "Second Thoughts," 512.
16. Andrew Cayton, "Not the Fragments but the Whole," *WMQ* 69 (2012): 513, 515–16.
17. Charles W. A. Prior, *Settlers in Indian Country* (Cambridge: Cambridge University Press, 2020).
18. Michael A. Blaakman, "'Haughty Republicans': Native Land, and the Promise of Preemption," *WMQ* 78 (2021): 244.

19. Andrew Fitzmaurice, *Sovereignty, Property, and Empire, 1500–2000* (Cambridge: Cambridge University Press, 2014); Stuart Banner, *How the Indians Lost Their Land: Law and Power in the Frontier* (Cambridge, MA: Harvard University Press, 2005); Allan Greer, *Property and Dispossession: Natives, Empires and Land in Early Modern North America* (Cambridge: Cambridge University Press, 2018); and Claudio Saunt, *Unworthy Republic: The Dispossession of Native Americans and the Road to Indian Territory* (New York: W. W. Norton, 2020).
20. Stephen Aron, "Once Upon a Time . . . in Ohio: David McCullough's *The Pioneers* as History and Wishstory," *JER* 41 (2021): 233–38.
21. Mt. Pleasant, Wigginton, and Wisecup, "Materials and Methods"; Michael Witgen, "Rethinking Colonial History as Continental History," *WMQ* 69 (2012): 527–30; Hämäläinen and Truett, "On Borderlands."
22. Lauren Coats and Steffi Dippold, "Beyond Recovery: An Introduction," *Early American Literature* 55 (2020): 297–319.
23. Barr, "No Such Thing as Prehistory"; Pekka Hämäläinen, *The Comanche Empire* (New Haven, CT: Yale University Press, 2009); Hämäläinen, *Lakota America: A New History of Indigenous Power* (New Haven, CT: Yale University Press, 2019).
24. Mt. Pleasant, Wigginton, and Wisecup, "Material and Methods," 223–25.
25. Juliana Barr, "Geographies of Power: Mapping Indian Borders in the 'Borderlands' of the Early Southwest," *WMQ* 68 (2011): 5–46.
26. Barr, "Red Continent," 524.
27. Matthew R. Bahar, "People of the Dawn, People of the Door: Indian Pirates and the Theft of the Atlantic World," *JAH* 101 (2014): 401–26.
28. Evan Nooe, "Common Justice: Vengeance and Retribution in Creek Country," *Ethnohistory* 62 (2015): 241–61.
29. Chad Anderson, "Rediscovering Native North America: Settlements, Maps, and Empires in the Eastern Woodlands," *EAS* 14 (2016): 478–505.
30. Ibid., 481; Juliana Barr and Edward Countryman, eds., *Contested Spaces of Early America* (Philadelphia: University of Pennsylvania Press, 2014): 18–20.
31. Alejandra Dubcovsky, *Informed Power: Communication in the American South* (Cambridge, MA: Harvard University Press, 2016), 11–41. See also Paul W. Mapp, *The Elusive West and the Contest for Empire, 1713–1763* (Chapel Hill: University of North Carolina Press, 2011).
32. Hämäläinen, "Shapes of Power."
33. Georgia Canley, "Cost, Commodity, and Gift: The Board of Trade's Conceptualization of British-Native American Gift-Giving during Pontiac's War," *EAS* 17 (2016): 203–24.
34. Carla Cevasco, "Hunger Knowledges and Cultures in New England's Borderlands," *EAS* 16 (2018): 255–81.

35. Bradley J. Dixon, "'His One Netev ples': The Chowans and the Politics of Native Petitions in the Colonial South," *WMQ* 76 (2019): 41–74.
36. Elizabeth Ellis, "The Natchez War Revisited: Violence, Multinational Settlements and Indigenous Diplomacy in the Lower Mississippi Valley," *WMQ* 77 (2020): 441–72.
37. Gregory D. Smithers, "'Our Hands and Hearts Are Joined Together': Friendship, Colonialism and the Cherokee People in Early America," *Journal of Social History* 50 (2017): 609–29.
38. D. Andrew Johnson, "Displacing Captives in Colonial South Carolina: Native American Enslavement and the Rise of the Colonial State after the Yamasee War," *JEAH* 7 (2017): 115–40.
39. Alejandra Dubcovsky, "Defying Indian Slavery: Apalachee Voices and Spanish Sources in the Eighteenth-Century Southwest," *WMQ* 75 (2018): 321–22.
40. Christian Ayne Crouch, "Surveying the Present, Projecting the Future: Reevaluating Colonial French Plans of Kanesatake," *WMQ* 75 (2018): 323–42. For how Europeans used native informants, see Kelly Wisecup, "Medicine, Communications, and Authority in Samson Occom's Herbal," *EAS* 10 (2021): 540–65; and Parsons, "Natural History of Colonial Science."
41. Jeffers Lennox, "A Time and a Place: The Geographies of British, French and Aboriginal Interactions in Early Nova Scotia, 1726–44," *WMQ* 72 (2015): 423–60; Elizabeth Mancke, "Spaces of Power in the Early Modern Northeast," in Stephen J. Hornsby and John G. Reid, eds., *New England and the Maritime Provinces: Connections and Comparisons* (Montreal: McGill-Queens University, 2005), 32–49; Eliga H. Gould, "Zones of Law, Zones of Violence: The Legal Geography of the British Atlantic," *WMQ* 60 (2003): 471–510.
42. Witgen, "Rethinking Colonial History," 528–29.
43. For the seventeenth century, see Michael Witgen, "The Rituals of Possession: Native Identity and the Invention of Empire in Seventeenth-Century Western North America," *Ethnohistory* 54 (2007): 639–68. For "Native New World," see Colin Calloway, *New Worlds for All: Indians, Europeans, and the Remaking of Early America*, 2nd ed. (Baltimore: Johns Hopkins University Press, 2013).
44. James Sidbury and Jorge Canizares-Esguerra, "Mapping Ethnogenesis in the Early Modern Atlantic," *WMQ* 68 (2011): 181–208; and Hämäläinen and Truett, "On Borderlands."
45. Robin Blackburn, *The Making of New World Slavery: From the Baroque to the Modern, 1492–1800* (London: Verso, 1997), 5.
46. Sidbury and Canizares-Esguerra, "Mapping Ethnogenesis,"
47. Pekka Hämäläinen, "Lost in Transition: Suffering, Survival, and Belonging in the Early Modern Atlantic World," *WMQ* 68 (2011): 219–23.

48. Jeremy Adelman and Stephen Aron, "From Borderlands to Borders: Empires, Nation-States, and the Peoples in Between in North American History," *AHR* 104 (1999): 814–41.
49. Hämäläinen and Truett, "On Borderlands," 348–49.
50. Ibid., 352.
51. Ibid.; William Cronon, "Revisiting the Vanishing Frontier: The Legacy of Frederick Jackson Turner," *Western Historical Quarterly* 18 (1987): 157–76; David Weber, "Turner, the Boltonians, and the Borderlands," *AHR* 91 (1986): 66–81; Frederick Jackson Turner, "The Significance of the Frontier in American History," in *The Frontier in American History* (New York: Holt, 1920), 1–38.
52. Herbert Bolton, *The Spanish Borderlands: A Chronicle of Old Florida and the Southwest* (New Haven, CT: Yale University Press, 1921).
53. Jessica Choppin Roney, "Containing Multitudes: Time, Space, the United States and Vast Early America," *WMQ* 78 (2021): 264.
54. Frederick E. Hoxie, "Retrieving the Red Continent: Settler Colonialism and the History of American Indians in the US," *Ethnic and Racial Studies* 31 (2008): 1154.
55. Blaakman, "Haughty Republicans," 250.
56. Max M. Edling, *A Hercules in the Cradle: War, Money, and the American State, 1783–1867* (Chicago: University of Chicago Press, 2014); Bethel Saler, *The Settlers' Empire: Colonialism and State Formation in America's Old Northwest* (Philadelphia: University of Pennsylvania Press, 2015); Gautham Rao, "The New Historiography of the Early Federal Government: Institutions, Contexts, and the Imperial State," *WMQ* 77 (2020): 97–128; Trevor Burnard and Aaron Graham, "Security, Taxation and the State in Jamaica, 1721–1782," *EAS* 18 (2020): 461–89; and Patrick A. Walsh, "The Fiscal State in Ireland, 1691–1769," *HJ* 56 (2013): 629–56.
57. Hoxie, "Retrieving the Red Continent."
58. Eran Zelnik, "Self-Evident Walls: Reckoning with Recent Histories of Race and Nation," *JER* 41 (2021): 30.
59. Roney, "Containing Multitudes," 268.
60. Paul Kelton, "The British and Indian War: Cherokee Power and the Fate of Empire in North America," *WMQ* 69 (2012): 763–92; Michael A. McDonnell, "Maintaining a Balance of Power: Michilimackinac, the Anishinaabe Odawas, and the Anglo-Indian War of 1763," *EAS* 13 (2015): 38–79; and Jeffrey D. Kaja, "'Sometimes bad people take the liberty of stragling into your Country': The Struggle to Control Mobility during Pontiac's War," *EAS* 14 (2016): 225–57.
61. Peter Silver, *Our Savage Neighbors: How Indian War Transformed Early America* (New York: W. W. Norton, 2008); Patrick Griffin, *American Leviathan: Empire, Nation, and Revolutionary Frontier* (New York: Hill and Wang, 2007); Patrick Spero, *Frontier Rebels: The Fight for American*

Independence in the American West, 1765–1776 (Philadelphia: University of Pennsylvania Press, 2016); Rob Harper, *Unsettling the West: Violence and State Building in the Ohio Valley* (Philadelphia: University of Pennsylvania Press, 2018).

62. For a hardening of racial thinking and laws in the 1760s, see David Silverman, "Racial Walls: Race and the Emergence of American White Nationalism," in Ignacio Gallup-Diaz, Andrew Shankman, and David J. Silverman, eds., *Anglicizing Americans: Empire, Revolution, Republic* (Philadelphia: University of Pennsylvania Press, 2015), 181–204.

63. While the 250th anniversaries of the Pontiac War and Paxton Boys' Rebellion in 2013 were commemorated, the anniversary of the Stamp Act went by without notice in 2015. Patrick Spero, "1763: Pontiac and Paxton," *EAS* 14 (2016): 202.

64. Scott Paul Gordon, "The Paxton Boys and Edward Shippen: Defiance and Deference on a Collapsing Frontier," *EAS* 14 (2016): 319–47; Zukowski, "Language and Ideology in the Paxton Pamphlet War"; John Smolenski, "Embodied Politics: The Paxton Uprising and the Gendering of Civic Culture in Colonial Pennsylvania," *EAS* 14 (2016): 377–407; Judith A. Ridner, "Unmasking the Paxton Boys: The Material Culture of the Pamphlet War," *EAS* 14 (2014): 348–76; and Matthew C. Ward, "Laws, Courts and Communities in the Pennsylvania Backcountry, ca. 1750–1800," *JEAH* 6 (2016): 196–219.

65. Rob Harper, "Looking the Other Way: The Gnadenhutten Massacre and the Contextual Interpretation of Violence," *WMQ* 64 (2007): 621–44.

66. Jeffrey Ostler, "'To Extirpate the Indians': The Indigenous Consciousness of Genocide in the Ohio Valley and Lower Great Lakes, 1750s–1810s," *WMQ* 72 (2015): 587–622 (quote 622); Tom Arne Midtrød, "'Calling for More than Human Vengeance': Desecrating Human Graves in Early America," *EAS* 17 (2019): 281–314; and Justin Pope, "Inventing an Indian Slave Conspiracy on Nantucket, 1738," *EAS* 15 (2017): 505–38.

67. Samuel Fisher, "Fit Instruments in a Howling Wilderness: Colonists, Indians, and the Origin of the American Revolution," *WMQ* 73 (2016): 647–80.

68. Ibid.; Samuel Fisher, "Atlantic '45: Gaels, Indians and the Origins of Imperial Reform in the British Atlantic," *EHR* 136 (2021): 85–116.

69. Eliga H. Gould, *Among the Powers of the Earth: The American Revolution and the Making of a New World Empire* (Cambridge, MA: Harvard University Press, 2012), 42; and Griffin, *American Leviathan*, 154, 171, 254–56.

70. Gregory Evans Dowd, "Indigenous Peoples without the Republic," *JAH* (2017): 19–41.

71. Johann N. Neem, "From Polity to Exchange: The Fate of Democracy in the Changing Fields of Early American Historiography," *Modern Intellectual History* 17 (2020): 867–88.

72. Dowd, "Indigenous Peoples without the Republic," 35.
73. Zelnik, "Self-Evident Walls," 17–18; Robert Parkinson, *The Common Cause: Creating Race and Nation in the American Revolution* (Chapel Hill: University of North Carolina Press, 2016); Silverman, "Racial Walls"; Nicholas Guyatt, *Bind Us Apart: How Enlightened Americans Invented Segregation* (Cambridge: Cambridge University Press, 2016).
74. George Van Cleve, "*Somerset's Case* and Its Antecedents in Imperial Perspective," *Law and History Review* 24 (2006): 601–45; and Matthew Mason, "North American Calm, West Indian Storm: The Politics of the *Somerset* Decision in the British Atlantic," *S&A* 41 (2020): 723–47.
75. Matilde Cazzola and Lorenzo Ravano, "Plantation Society in the Age of Revolution: Edward Long, Pierre-Victor Malouet and the Problem of Slave Government," *S&A* 41 (2020): 234–55.
76. Brooke Newman, "Gender, Sexuality, and the Formation of Racial Identities in the Eighteenth-Century Anglo-Caribbean World," *Gender and History* 22 (2010): 585–602; Andrew Wells, "Race Fixing: Improvement and Race in Eighteenth-Century Britain," *History of European Ideas* 36 (2010): 134–38; James Delbourgo, "The Newtonian Slave Body: Racial Enlightenment in the Atlantic World," *AS* 9 (2012): 185–207. For the late emergence of abolitionism, see Seymour Drescher, "The Shocking Birth of British Abolitionism," *S&A* 33 (2012): 572–89.
77. Pernille Røge, *Economistes and the Reinvention of Empire: France in the Americas and Africa, 1750–1802* (Cambridge: Cambridge University Press, 2019); P. J. Marshall, *Edmund Burke and the British Empire in the West Indies: Wealth, Power and Slavery* (Oxford: Oxford University Press, 2019); Marion Godfrey, *Kourou, 1763, la dernier rêve de l'Amerique française* (Paris: Edition Vendemaire, 2012); Tessa Murphy, *Creole Archipelago: Race and Borders in the Colonial Caribbean* (Philadelphia: University of Pennsylvania Press, 2021), chs. 3–4; Elena Schneider, "African Slavery and Spanish Empire; Imperial Imaginings and Bourbon Reform," *JEAH* 5 (2015): 3–29; Heather Freund, "'Who Should Be Treated with Every Degree of Humanity?': Debating Rights for Planters, Soldiers, and Caribs/Kalingo on St. Vincent, 1763–1773," *AS* 13 (2015): 125–43; and Melanie J. Newton, "Counterpoints of Conquest: The Royal Proclamation of 1763, the Lesser Antilles, and the Ethnocartography of Genocide," *WMQ* 79 (2022): 241–82.

5. The Imperial Turn

1. John Shovlin, "Selling American Empire on the Eve of the Seven Years' War: The French Propaganda Campaign of 1755–1756," *P&P* 206 (2010): 121–149; Helen Dewar, "Canada or Guadeloupe? French and British Perceptions of Empire, 1760–1763," *Canadian Historical Review* 91 (2010):

637–60; Anna Brinkman-Schwartz, "The *Antigallican* Affair: Public and Ministerial Responses to Anglo-Spanish Maritime Conflict in the Seven Years' War, 1756–1758," *English Historical Review* 135 (2020): 1132–64; Philippe Castejón *"Colonia,* entre appropriation et rejet: la naissance d'un concept (de la fin des années 1750 aux révolutions hispaniques)," *Mélanges de la Casa de Velázquez* 43 (2013): 251–71; Christian Hausser and Horst Pietschmann, "Empire: The Concept and Its Problems in the Historiography on Iberian Empires in the Early Modern Period." *Culture & History Digital Journal* 3 (2014), http://dx.doi.org/10.3989/chdj.2014.002. Marie Houllemare, "La fabrique des archives coloniales et la naissance d'une conscience impériale (France, XVIIIe siècle)," *Revue d'Histoire Moderne et Contemporaine* 61 (2014): 7–31; Pablo Ortega-Del-Cerro, "Retos de la monarquía española en contexto global: La expedición a Guinea (1777–1779)," *Revista de Historia Moderna. Anales de la Universidad de Alicante* 38 (2020): 360–96; Francois-Joseph Ruggiu, "Des nouvelles France aux colonies—Une approche comparée de l'histoire impériale de la France de l'époque modern," *Nuevo Mundo Mundos Nuevos* (2018), accessed 6 June 2022, http://journals.openedition.org.janus.bis-sorbonne.fr/nuevomundo/72123. See also Pernille Røge, *Economistes and the Reinvention of Empire: France in the Americas and Africa, 1750–1802* (Cambridge: Cambridge University Press, 2019); John Shovlin, *Trading with the Enemy: Britain, France, and the Eighteenth-Century Quest for a Peaceful World Order* (New Haven, CT: Yale University Press, 2021); and François Ternat, *Partager le monde: Rivalités impériales franco-britanniques (1748–1756)* (Paris: Presses Universitaires de Paris-Sorbonne, 2015).
2. Jack P. Greene, *Negotiated Authorities: Essays in Colonial Political and Constitutional History* (Charlottesville: University of Virginia Press, 1994), 12–24.
3. François-Joseph Ruggiu, "Extraction, Wealth and Industry: The Ideas of Nobles and of Gentility in the English and French Atlantic (17th and 18th centuries)," *History of European Ideas* 34 (2008): 444–55; Ruggiu, "Une noblesse atlantique? Le second ordre français de Ancien au Nouveau Mondes," *Outre-Mer* 96 (2009): 39–63; Eric Nelson, "Hebraism and the Republican Turn of 1776: A Contemporary Account of the Debate over Common Senses, 2," *WMQ* 70 (2013): 781–812.
4. Paul A. Kramer, "Power and Connection: Imperial Histories of the United States in the World," *AHR* 116 (2011): 1348–91.
5. Kramer, "Power and Connection," 1348.
6. Ibid., 1353.
7. Karen Ordahl Kupperman, "International from the Creation: Early Modern American History," in Thomas Bender, ed., *Rethinking American History in a Global Age* (Berkeley: University of California Press, 2002); Jane Burbank and Frederick Cooper, *Empires in World History: Power and the Politics of Difference* (Princeton, NJ: Princeton University Press, 2010), 3.

8. Patrick O'Brien, "Historiographical Traditions and Modern Imperatives for the Restoration of Global History," *JGH* 1 (2006): 3–39.
9. Danielle Kinsey, "Assessing Imperialism," in McNeill and Pomeranz, *Cambridge World History* 7:1, 359–60.
10. Trevor Burnard, "Empire Matters? The Historiography of Imperialism in Early America, 1492–1830," *History of European Ideas* 33 (2007): 87–107.
11. Kramer, "Power and Connection," 1348.
12. Charles M. Andrews, "On the Writing of Colonial History," *WMQ* 1 (1944): 27–48; Richard R. Johnson, "Charles McLean Andrews and the Invention of American Colonial History," *WMQ* 43 (1986): 519–41; Lawrence Henry Gipson, *The British Empire before the American Revolution*, 15 vols. (New York: Knopf, 1936–70); Patrick Griffin, "In Retrospect: Lawrence Henry Gipson's *The British Empire before the American Revolution*," *Reviews in American History* 31 (2003): 171–83; Richard B. Morris, "The Spacious Empire of Lawrence Henry Gipson," *WMQ* 24 (1967): 169–89.
13. Edmund S. Morgan, "Colonial Ideas of Parliamentary Power, 1764–1766," *WMQ* 5 (1948): 311–41.
14. McDonnell and Waldstreicher, "Revolution in the *Quarterly?*"
15. Edmund S. Morgan, *The Birth of the Republic, 1763–89*, rev. ed. (Chicago: University of Chicago Press, 2015); Jackson Turner Main, *The Upper House in Revolutionary America, 1763–1788* (Madison: University of Wisconsin Press, 2002); Merrill Jensen, *The Founding of a Nation: A History of the American Revolution, 1763–1776* (New York: Oxford University Press, 1968); Gordon S. Wood, *The Creation of the American Republic, 1776–87* (Chapel Hill: University of North Carolina Press, 1970); Jack P. Greene, ed., *The Reinterpretation of the American Revolution, 1763–89* (New York: Harper and Row, 1968); Robert Middlekauf, *The Glorious Cause: The American Revolution, 1763–89* (Oxford: Oxford University Press, 1992).
16. Jeremy Adelman, "Empires, Nations and Revolution," *Journal of the History of Ideas* 79 (2018): 73–88.
17. C. A. Bayly, *The Birth of the Modern World, 1780–1914* (Oxford: Blackwell, 2004).
18. John Darwin, *After Tamerlane: The Rise and Fall of Global Empire* (London: Bloomsbury, 2007).
19. Jeremy Adelman, "An Age of Imperial Revolutions," *AHR* 113 (2008): 319–40; Janet Polasky, *Revolutions without Borders: The Call to Liberty in the Atlantic World* (New Haven, CT: Yale University Press, 2015); Wim Klooster, *Revolutions in the Atlantic World: A Comparative History*, rev. ed (New York: New York University Press, 2018); Klooster, ed., *The Cambridge History of the Age of Atlantic Revolutions*, 3 vols. (Cambridge: Cambridge University Press, forthcoming).
20. Lauren Benton, *Law and Colonial Cultures: Legal Regimes in World History, 1400–1900* (Cambridge: Cambridge University Press, 2002).

21. Caitlin Fitz, "Nation, Continent, Hemisphere: Situating the United States in the Vast Early Americas," *WMQ* 78 (2021): 207–14.
22. For wider perspectives, see Jonathan Israel, *The Expanding Blaze: How the American Revolution Ignited the World, 1775–1848* (Princeton, NJ: Princeton University Press, 2017); and Eliga H. Gould, *Among the Powers of the Earth: The American Revolution and the Making of a New World Empire* (Cambridge: Cambridge University Press, 2012). For comparative history, see Michael Werner and Bénédicte Zimmerman, "Beyond Comparison: Histoire Croisée and the Challenges of Reflexivity," *History and Theory* 45 (2006): 30–50.
23. Wim Klooster, "Making Comparisons in Atlantic History: Representation in the Age of Revolution," in Jürgen Gebhardt and Stefan Fröhlich, eds., *New Perspectives on Transatlantic Relations: Multidisciplinary Approaches* (Heidelberg: Universitätserlag, 2021), 19–38.
24. Wim Klooster, "Slave Revolts, Royal Justice, and a Ubiquitous Rumor in the Age of Revolution," *WMQ* 71 (2014): 401–24. See also Laurent Dubois, "An Enslaved Enlightenment: Rethinking the Intellectual History of the French Atlantic," *Social History* 31 (2006): 1–14.
25. Robin Blackburn, *The American Crucible: Slavery, Emancipation, and Human Rights* (London: Verso, 2011), 362.
26. Nathan Perl-Rosenthal, "Atlantic Cultures and the Age of Revolution," *WMQ* 74 (2017): 667–96.
27. O'Brien, "Historiographical Traditions," 4–7.
28. Eliga H. Gould, "Entangled Histories, Entangled Worlds: The English-Speaking Atlantic as a Spanish Periphery," *AHR* 112 (2007): 764–86.
29. Jack P. Greene, "The American Revolution," *AHR* 105 (2000): 93–102.
30. Pierre Bourdieu, *Outline of a Theory of Practice*, trans. Richard Nice (Cambridge: Cambridge University Press, 1977); Michel de Certeau, *L'invention du quotidian, t.1, Arts de faire* (Paris: Gallimard, 1999).
31. Sarah Knott, *Sensibility and the American Revolution* (Chapel Hill: University of North Carolina Press, 2009); Sarah Pearsall, *Atlantic Families: Lives and Letters in the Later Eighteenth Century* (New York: Oxford University Press, 2008).
32. Rosenthal, "Atlantic Cultures," 681.
33. Ibid., 696.
34. Michael McDonnell, "Rethinking the Age of Revolution," *AS* 13 (2016): 301–14.
35. Eric Hobsbawm, *The Age of Revolutions: Europe, 1789–1848* (London: Weidenfeld and Nicholson, 1962).
36. Adelman, "Age of Imperial Revolutions," 320–21; R. R. Palmer, *The Age of the Democratic Revolution: A Political History of Europe and America, 1760–1800*, 2 vols. (Princeton, NJ: Princeton University Press, 1959, 1964).

37. Burbank and Cooper, *Empires in World History*; Antoinette Burton, ed., *After the Imperial Turn: Thinking with and Through the Nation* (Durham, NC: Duke University Press, 2003).
38. Griffin, "In Retrospect: Gipson's *British Empire*."
39. J. G. A. Pocock, "British History: A Plea for a New Subject," *Journal of Modern History* 47 (1975): 601–21; Pocock, "The Limits and Divisions of British History: In Search of the Unknown Subject," *AHR* 87 (1982): 311–36; Pocock, "Deconstructing Europe," *London Book Review* 13 (December 1991).
40. D. K. Fieldhouse, "Can Humpty-Dumpty Be Put Together Again? Imperial History in the 1980s," *JICH* 12 (1984): 9–23.
41. Bill Schwarz, "Subaltern Histories," *HWJ* 89 (2020): 90–107; Ranajit Guha, *Elementary Aspects of Peasant Insurgency in Colonial India* (Delhi: Oxford University Press, 1983). The lack of attention to subaltern studies in early American history is remarkable. I have not found any significant discussion of subaltern studies in *WMQ* or *EAS*.
42. A. G. Hopkins, "Back to the Future: From National History to Imperial History," *P&P* 164 (1999): 198–243.
43. Bernard Bailyn, *Atlantic History: Concept and Contours* (Cambridge, MA: Harvard University Press, 2005), 6; Alison F. Games, "Atlantic History: Definitions, Challenges, Opportunities," *AHR* 111 (2006): ft. 41.
44. J. H. Elliott, *Empires of the Atlantic World: Britain and Spain in America, 1492–1830* (New Haven, CT: Yale University Press, 2006); P. J. Marshall, *The Making and Unmaking of Empires: Britain, India and America, c. 1750–1783* (Oxford: Oxford University Press, 2005); Hämäläinen, *Comanche Empire*.
45. Jorge Cañizares-Esguerra, *Puritan Conquistadors: Iberianizing the Atlantic, 1550–1700* (Stanford, CA: Stanford University Press, 2006); Pedro Cardim, Tamar Herzog, Ruiz Ibáñez, José Javier, and Gaetano Sabatini, *Polycentric Monarchies: How Did Early Modern Spain and Portugal Achieve and Maintain a Global Hegemony?* (Brighton, UK: Sussex Academic Press, 2012); and J. H. Elliott, "A Europe of Composite Monarchies," *P&P* 137 (1992): 48–71.
46. Sathnam Sanghera, *Empireland: How Imperialism Shaped Modern Britain* (London: Penguin, 2021).
47. Robert Saunders, "Brexit and Empire: 'Global Britain' and the Myth of Imperial Nostalgia," *JICH* 48 (2020): 1140–74.
48. Eric Hinderaker, "The 'Four Indian Kings' and the Imaginative Construction of the British Empire," *WMQ* 53 (1996): 486.
49. Kathleen Wilson, Introduction to *A New Imperial History: Culture, Identity, and Modernity in Britain and the Empire, 1660–1840* (Cambridge: Cambridge University Press, 2004), 3.
50. For works on early American history with "empire" in the title, see Michael A. McDonnell, *Masters of Empire: Great Lakes Indians and the Making*

of America (New York: Hill and Wang, 2017); Amanda B. Moniz, *From Empire to Humanity: The American Revolution and the Origins of Humanitarianism* (New York: Oxford University Press, 2016); Maya Jasanoff, *Liberty's Exiles: The Loss of America and the Remaking of the British Empire* (New York: HarperCollins, 2011); Peter S. Onuf, *Jefferson's Empire: The Language of American Nationhood* (Charlottesville: University of Virginia Press, 2000); Joseph M. Fradera, *The Imperial Nation: Citizens and Subjects in the British, French, Spanish and American Empires*, trans. Ruth MacKay (Princeton, NJ: Princeton University Press, 2018).

51. A. G. Hopkins, *American Empire: A Global History* (Princeton, NJ: Princeton University Press, 2018); Charles Maier, *Among Empire: American Ascendancy and its Predecessors* (Cambridge, MA: Harvard University Press, 2006).
52. Wilson, *A New Imperial History*, 3–5.
53. Krishnan Kumar, *Visions of Empire: How Five Imperial Regimes Shaped the World* (Princeton, NJ: Princeton University Press, 2017), 3, 475. See also Adam Getachew, *World-Making after Empire: The Rise and Fall of Self-Determination* (Princeton, NJ: Princeton University Press, 2019); and Robert Gildea, *Empires of the Mind: The Colonial Past and the Politics of the Present* (Cambridge: Cambridge University Press, 2019).
54. Jack P Greene, "Colonial History and National History: Reflections on a Continuing Problem," *WMQ* 64 (2007): 225–50.
55. Andrew Shankman, "Toward a Social History of Federalism: The State and Capitalism To and From the American Revolution," *JER* 37 (2014): 617, 623–24.
56. Gautham Rao, "The New Historiography of the Early Federal Government: Institutions, Contexts and the Imperial State," *WMQ* 77 (2020): 97–128.
57. S. Max Edelson, *The New Map of Empire: How Britain Imagined America before Independence* (Cambridge, MA: Harvard University Press, 2017), 17–18.
58. Annette Gordon-Reed and Peter Onuf, "The Nation-State in a Changing World: Epilogue," *WMQ* 78 (2021): 276–77.
59. Max Edling, *A Hercules in the Cradle: War, Money, and the American State, 1783–1867* (Chicago: University of Chicago Press, 2014); Peter S. Onuf, "American Exceptionalism and National Identity," *American Political Thought* 1 (2012): 77–100.
60. Shankman, "Toward a Social History of Federalism," 620–22.
61. John Craig Hammond, "Slavery, Settlement, and Empire: The Expansion and Growth of Slavery in the North American Continent," *JER* 32 (2012): 205–6.
62. Steven Pincus, *The Heart of the Declaration: The Founders' Case for an Activist Government* (New Haven, CT: Yale University Press 2016); Justin

du Rivage, *Revolution against Empire: Taxes, Politics, and the Origins of American Independence* (New Haven, CT: Yale University Press, 2017); Bethel Saler, *The Settlers' Empire: Colonialism and State Formation in America's Old Northwest* (Philadelphia: University of Pennsylvania Press, 2015); Ned Blackhawk, *Violence over the Land: Indians and Empires in the Early American West* (Cambridge, MA: Harvard University Press, 2006); and Brian Phillips Murphy, *Building the Empire State: Political Economy in the Early Republic* (Philadelphia: University of Pennsylvania Press, 2015).

63. Robert T. Aggorworth, "'One Chief Letter Office at New York': Packet Ships, Imperial Administration, and the Geography of the American Post," *JICH* 48 (2020): 199–229.
64. Agostini, "The Provincials Will Work Like Giants."
65. Aaron Graham, "Corruption and Contractors in the Atlantic World, 1754–1763," *EHR* 134 (2019): 1136–68; Trevor Burnard and Aaron Graham, "Security, Taxation and the State in Jamaica, 1721–1782," *EAS* 18, 4 (Fall 2020): 461–89; Aaron Graham, "Jamaican Legislation and the Transatlantic Constitution, 1664–1839," *HJ* 61 (2018): 327–55; Graham, "Towns, Government, Legislation"; Graham, "Legislatures, Legislation, and Legislating in the British Atlantic, 1692–1820," *Parliamentary History* 37 (2018): 369–88.
66. Jessica Choppin Roney, "1776, Viewed from the West," *JER* 37 (2017): 655–700.
67. McDonnell and Waldstreicher, "Revolution in the *Quarterly?*," 635, 651, 665–66.
68. Katherine Carté Engel, "Connecting Protestants in Britain's Eighteenth-Century Atlantic Empire," *WMQ* 75 (2018): 37–70.
69. Engel, "Connecting Protestants," 64, 65, 69, 70; Rhys Isaac, *The Transformation of Virginia, 1740–1790* (Chapel Hill: University of North Carolina Press, 1982); Patricia Bonomi, *Under the Cope of Heaven: Religion, Society and Politics in Colonial America* (New York: Oxford University Press, 1986). See also Jon Butler, *Awash in a Sea of Faith: Christianizing the American People* (Cambridge, MA: Harvard University Press 1990). Protestantism had the potential to include within its ranks more Africans than usually thought. See Patricia Bonomi, "'Swarms of Negroes Comeing about My Door': Black Christianity in Early Dutch and English North America," *JAH* (2016): 34–58.
70. Gabriel Glickman, "Catholic Interests and the Politics of English Overseas Expansion, 1660–1689," *JBS* 55 (2016): 680–708.
71. Jessica L. Harland-Jacobs, "Incorporating the King's New Subjects: Accommodation and Anti-Catholicism in the British Empire, 1763–1815," *Journal of Religious History* 39 (2015): 203–23; Aaron Wallis, "The Standing of New Subjects: Grenada and the Protestant Constitution after the Treaty of Paris," *JICH* 42 (2014): 1–21.

72. Carys Brown, "Militant Catholicism, Interconfessional Relations and the Rookwood Family of Stanningfield, Suffolk, c. 1689–1737," *HJ* 60 (2017): 21–45.
73. Nancy Christie, "'He is the master of this house': Families and Political Authority in Counterrevolutionary Montreal," *WMQ* 70 (2013): 341–70.
74. Michael D. Breidenback, "Conciliarism and the American Founding," *WMQ* 73 (2016): 487–500.
75. David Waldstreicher, "Ancients, Moderns, and Africans: Phillis Wheatley and the Politics of Empire and Slavery in the American Revolution," *JER* 37 (2017): 701–33; Burnard, *Jamaica in the Age of Revolution*, ch.6.
76. Mason, "North American Calm, West Indian Storm."
77. Matthew Mason, "A Missed Opportunity? The Founding Postcolonial Realities, and the Abolition and Slavery," *S&A* 35 (2014): 199–213; Gary B. Nash, "Sparks from the Altar of '76: International Repercussions and Reconsiderations of the American Revolution," in David Armitage and Sanjay Subrahmanyam, eds., *The Age of Revolutions in Global Context, c. 1760–1840* (London: Palgrave Macmillan, 2010), 1–19.
78. Hacker, "From '20. And odd' to 10 Million."
79. Mason, "A Missed Opportunity?," 203.
80. Paul A. Gilje, "Commerce and Conquest in Early American Foreign Relations, 1750–1850," *JER* 37 (2017): 735–70.
81. Jonathan Eacott, "Leverage: Foreign Strength in British Economic Thinking and Policy, 1600–1763," *WMQ* 77 (2020): 551–80.
82. Jacob Soll, "For a New Economic History of Early Modern Empire: Anglo-French Imperial Co-Development beyond Mercantilism and Laissez Faire," *WMQ* 77 (2020): 529.
83. C. A. Bayly, *Imperial Meridian: The British Empire and the World, 1780–1830* (London: Longman, 1989), 5.
84. Arthur Young, *Political Essays Concerning the Present State of the British Empire* (London, 1772), 552; Jack P. Greene, "Britain's Overseas Empire before 1780: Overwhelmingly Successful and Bureaucratically Challenged," in Greene, *Creating the British Atlantic: Essays on Transplantation, Adaptation, and Continuity* (Charlottesville: University of Virginia Press, 2013), 113–39.
85. Steven Pincus, Tiraana Bains, and A. Zuercher Reichardt, "Thinking the Empire Whole," *History Australia* 16 (2019): 610–11.
86. Patrick Griffin, *The Townshend Moment: The Making of Empire and Revolution in the Eighteenth Century* (New Haven, CT: Yale University Press, 2017), 25.
87. For the French empire, see Marie Houllemare, "Law, Jurisdictions, and Paperwork: Building the French Empire in the Early Eighteenth Century," *Journal of Colonialism and Colonial History* (2020), http://doi.org/10.1353/cch.2020.0015; Scott Berthelette, "New France and the Hudson Bay

Watershed: Transatlantic Networks, Backcountry Specialists and French Imperial Projects in Post-Utrecht North America," *Canadian Historical Review* 101 (2020): 1–26.

88. Amy Watson, "The New York Patriot Movement: Partisanship, the Free Press, and Britain's Imperial Constitution, 1731–39," *WMQ* 77 (2020): 33–64; and Daniel Robinson, "Giving Peace to Europe: European Geopolitics, Colonial Political Culture, and the Hanoverian Monarchy in British North America, ca. 1740–1763," *WMQ* 73 (2016): 291–332.
89. Peter Way, "Militarizing the Atlantic World: Army Discipline, Coerced Labor, and Britain's Commercial Empire," *AS* 13 (2016): 346.
90. Ibid., 359.
91. Asheesh Kapur Siddique, "Governance through Documents: The Board of Trade, Its Archive and the Imperial Constitution of the British Atlantic World," *JBS* 59 (2020): 264–90; Siddique, "The Archival Epistemology of Political Economy in the Early Modern British Atlantic World," *WMQ* 77 (2020): 641–74; Will Slauter, "The Paragraph as Information Technology: How News Traveled in the Eighteenth-Century Atlantic World," *Annales* 67 (2012): 253–78.
92. Marie Houllemare, "Seeing the Empire through Lists and Charts: French Colonial Records in the Eighteenth Century," *Journal of Early Modern History* 22 (2018): 1–21; and Houllemare, "Silencing Madmen: The Legal Process of Interdiction, Saint-Domingue, Eighteenth Century," in Christie, Gauvreau, and Gerber, eds., *Voices in the Legal Archives in the French Colonial World*, 115–27.
93. Edward Cavanaugh, "The Imperial Constitution of the Law Officers of the Crown: Legal Thought on War and Colonial Government, 1719–1774," *JICH* 47 (2019): 619–51.
94. David Chan Smith, "The Hudson's Bay Company: Social Legitimacy and the Political Economy of the Eighteenth-century Empire," *WMQ* 75 (2018): 71–108; Marie Peters, "State, Parliament and Empire in the Mid-Eighteenth Century: Hudson's Bay and the Parliamentary Enquiry of 1749," *Parliamentary History* 29 (2010): 171–91.
95. Sophus A. Reinert and Pernille Røge, eds. *The Political Economy of Empire in the Early Modern World* (Basingstoke: Palgrave Macmillan, 2013).
96. Philip J. Stern, "Early Eighteenth-Century British India: Antimeridian or Antemeridian?," *Journal of Colonialism and Colonial History* 21 (2020), https://doi.org/10.1353/cch.2020.0014.
97. Dziennik, "Till These Experiments Be Made."
98. For recent examples of studies of European movement to the Americas placed within imperial context, see Cécile Vidal, *Caribbean New Orleans: Empire, Race, and the Making of a Slave Society* (Chapel Hill: University of North Carolina Press, 2019); Wim Klooster and Gert Oostindie, *Realms between Empires: The Second Dutch Atlantic, 1680–1815* (Ithaca, NY:

Cornell University Press, 2018); and Gabriel Paquette, *The European Seaborne Empires: From the Thirty Years' War to the Age of Revolutions* (New Haven, CT: Yale University Press, 2019).

99. Allan Greer, "National, Transnational, and Hypernational Historiographies: New France Meets Early American History," *Canadian Historical Review* 91 (2010): 724.

6. Gender

1. Morrissey, "Kaskaskia Social Networks"; Paton, "Driveress and Nurse," supplement 15, 27–53; Sasha Turner, "The Nameless and the Forgotten: Maternal Grief, Sacred Protection, and the Archive of Slavery," *S&A* 38 (2017): 232–50; Nancy Christie, "Merchant and Plebeian Commercial Knowledge in Montreal and Quebec, 1760–1820," *EAS* 13 (2015): 856–80.
2. Wilson, *A New Imperial History*, 20.
3. Terri L. Snyder, "Refiguring Women in Early American History," *WMQ* 69 (2012): 421.
4. T. H. Breen, "Persistent Localism: English Social Change and the Shaping of New England institutions," *WMQ* 32 (1975): 4–28.
5. Trevor Burnard and Ann Little, "Where the Boys Aren't: Women as Reluctant Migrants but Rational Actors in Early America," in Jay Kleinberg, ed., *Revisioning Women's History* (New Brunswick, NJ: Rutgers University Press, 2007), 12–29.
6. Ritchie Robertson, *The Enlightenment: The Pursuit of Happiness, 1680–1790* (London: Allen Lane, 2020).
7. Snyder, "Refiguring Women in Early American History."
8. Amy Dru Stanley, "Histories of Capitalism and Sex Difference," *JER* 36 (2016): 343; Ellen Hartigan-O'Connor, "The Personal Is Political Economy," *JER* 36 (2016): 337.
9. Greta La Fleur, "Sex and 'Unsex': Histories of Gender Trouble in Eighteenth-Century North America," *EAS* 12 (2014): 492–93.
10. Lois Green Carr and Lorena S. Walsh, "The Planter's Wife: The Experience of White Women in Seventeenth-Century Maryland," *WMQ* 34 (1977): 542–71. The idea of a golden age was thoroughly demolished in Mary Beth Norton, "The Evolution of White Women's Experience in Early America," *AHR* 89 (1984): 593–619.
11. Erin Trahey, "Among Her Kinswomen: Legacies of Free Women of Color in Jamaica," *WMQ* 76 (2019): 257–88.
12. Walker, "Pursuing Her Profits"; Robert J. Gamble, "'For Lucre of Gain and in Contempt of the Laws': Itinerant Traders and the Politics of Mobility in the Eighteenth-Century Mid-Atlantic," *EAS* 13 (2015): 836–55; Walker, "As Though She 'Was a Virtuous Woman.'"

13. Sharon Block, "Reconstituting Archives of Violence and Silence in Early American Women's History," *Journal of Women's History* 30 (2018): 154–62; Ashley Glassburn Falzetti, "Archival Absence: The Burden of History," *Settler Colonial Studies* 5 (2015): 1–17.
14. Lois Green Carr and Lorena S. Walsh, "The Standard of Living in the Colonial Chesapeake," *WMQ* 45 (1988): 135–59.
15. Jan de Vries, *The Industrious Revolution: Consumer Behavior and the Household Economy, 1650 to the Present* (Cambridge: Cambridge University Press, 2008); Jane Humphries and Jacob Weisdorf, "The Wages of Women in England, 1260–1850," *JEcH* 75 (2015); Humphries and Weisdorf, "Unreal Wages? Real Income and Economic Growth in England, 1260–1850," *Economic Journal* 129 (2019); Sara Horrell and Humphries, "Children's Work and Wages in Britain, 1280–1860," *EEH* 73 (2019), https://doi.org/10.1016/j.eeh.2019.04.001; and Horrell, Humphries, and Weisdorf, "Family Standards of Living over the Long Run, England, 1280–1850," *P&P* 250 (2021): 87–134.
16. Horrell, Humphries and Weisdorf, "Family Standards of Living," 99.
17. Ibid., 130–32.
18. Klas Rönnback, "Living Standards in the Pre-colonial Gold Coast: A Quantitative Estimate of African Laborers' Welfare Ratios," *European Economic History Review* 18 (2014): 185–202.
19. Trevor Burnard, Laura Panza, and Jeffrey Williamson, "Living Costs, Real Incomes and Inequality in Colonial Jamaica," *EEH* 71 (2019): 55–71; Kenneth Morgan, "Slave Women and Reproduction in Jamaica, c. 1776–1834," *History* 91 (2006): 231–53; Katherine Paugh, "The Politics of Childbearing in the British Caribbean and in the Atlantic World during the Age of Abolition," *P&P* 221 (2013): 119–60.
20. Bronwen Everill, "'All the baubles that they needed': 'Industriousness' and Slavery in Saint-Louis and Gorée," *EAS* 15 (2017): 718.
21. Ibid., 736–37.
22. Morrissey, "Kaskaskia Social Networks"; Kate Gibson, "Marriage Choice and Kinship among the English Catholic Elite, 1680–1730," *Journal of Family History* 41 (2016): 144–64.
23. Sara T. Damiano, "Agents at Home: Wives, Lawyers, and Financial Competence in Eighteenth-Century New England Port Cities," *EAS* 13 (2015): 808–35; Carole Shammas, "Household Formation, Lineage and Gender Relations in the Early Modern Atlantic World," in Nicholas Canny and Philip D. Morgan, eds., *The Oxford Handbook of the Atlantic World* (Oxford: Oxford University Press, 2011), 372–74.
24. Vivian Bruce Conger, "Reading Early American Women's Political Lives: The Revolutionary Performances of Deborah Read Franklin and Sally Franklin Bache," *EAS* 19 (2016): 284–318.

25. Brandt, "Getting into a Little Business"; and Inge Dornan, "'Whoever takes her up, gives her 50 good lashes, and delivers her to me': Women Slaveowners and the Politics of Slave Management in South Carolina," *Journal of Global Slavery* 6 (2021): 131–55.
26. Sharon Block, "Making Meaningful Bodies: Physical Appearances in Colonial Writings," *EAS* 12 (2014): 524–47.
27. Paul Langford, *A Polite and Commercial People: England, 1727–1783* (Oxford: Oxford University Press, 1989); Elaine Chalus and Perry Gauci, eds., *Revisiting the Polite and Commercial People* (Oxford: Oxford University Press, 2019), 4–6.
28. Jonah Miller "The Touch of the State: Stop and Search in England, c.1660–1750," *HWJ* 87 (2019): 52–71.
29. Garthine Walker, "Rape, Acquittal and Culpability in Popular Crime Reports in England, c. 1670–c.1750," *P&P* 220 (2013): 115–42; Walker, "Imagining the Unimaginable: Parricide in Early Modern England and Wales, c. 1600–1760," *Journal of Family History* 41 (2016): 271–93.
30. Lisa Wynne Smith, "Resisting Silences: Gender and Family Trauma in Eighteenth-Century England," *Gender and History* 32 (2020): 30–53.
31. Soile Ylivuori, "Rethinking Female Chastity and Gentlewomen's Honour in Eighteenth-Century England," *HJ* 59 (2016): 71–97.
32. Bernard Capp, "The Double Standard Revisited: Plebeian Women and Male Sexual Reputation in Early Modern England," *P&P* 162 (1999): 70–100.
33. Hannah Greig and Amanda Vickery, "The Political Day in London, c. 1697–1834," *P&P* 252 (2021): 101–37. See also Elaine Chalus, *Elite Women in English Political Life, c. 1754–1790* (Oxford: Oxford University Press, 2005); Judith S. Lewis, *Sacred to Female Patriotism: Gender, Class, and Politics in Late Georgian Britain* (London: Taylor and Francis, 2003); Peter Mandler, "Namier in Petticoats," Reviews in History online, accessed 18 September 2022, https://www.history.ac.uk/reviews/review/63.
34. Karen Harvey, "Epochs of Embodiment: Men, Women and the Material Body," *JBS* 42 (2019): 455–69.
35. Dror Wahrman, *The Making of the Modern Self: Identity and Culture in Eighteenth-Century England* (New Haven, CT: Yale University Press, 2007).
36. Harvey, "Epochs of Embodiment."
37. Karen Harvey, "What Mary Toft Felt: Women's Voices, Pain, Power and the Body," *HWJ* 80 (2015): 33–51; Harvey, "Rabbits, Whigs and Hunters: Women and Protest in Mary Toft's Monstrous Births of 1726," *P&P* 238 (2018): 43–83.
38. Kathleen Brown, "Brave New Worlds: Women and Gender History," *WMQ* 50 (1993): 311–28.

39. Kathleen Wilson, "Rethinking the Colonial State: Family, Gender, and Governmentality in Eighteenth-Century British Frontiers," *AHR* 116 (2011): 1294–1322.
40. Ibid.
41. Daniel Livesay, "Privileging Kinship: Family and Race in Eighteenth-Century Jamaica," *WMQ* 75 (2018): 323–42.
42. Wilson, "Rethinking the Colonial State," 1317.
43. Trevor Burnard, "'Rioting in Goatish Embraces': Marriage and Improvement in Early British Jamaica, 1660–1780," *History of the Family* 11, 4 (2006): 185–97; Burnard, "Tropical Hospitality, British Masculinity, and Drink in Late Eighteenth-Century Jamaica," *HJ* 65 (2022): 202–23.
44. Wilson, "Rethinking the Colonial State," 1321.
45. Ibid.; Walker, "As Though She 'Was a Virtuous Woman.'"
46. Dallin Lewis, "Domesticating the Plantation: The Politics and Tragedy of Slave Kinship in the British Atlantic World," *Eighteenth Century* 60 (2019): 201–30.
47. Walker, "As Though She 'Was a Virtuous Woman.'"
48. Daniel Livesay "Privileging Kinship: Family and Race in Eighteenth-Century Jamaica," *EAS* 14 (2016): 693.
49. Ibid., 708–9.
50. Trahey, "Among Her Kinswomen."
51. Vermeulen, "Thomas Thistlewood's Libidinal Linnaean Project." See also Jenny Shaw, "In the Name of the Mother: The Story of Susannah Mingo, a Woman of Color in the Early English Atlantic," *WMQ* 77 (2020): 177–210.
52. Jane Whittle and Mark Hailwood, "The Gender Division of Labour in Early Modern England," *EcHR* 73 (2019): 19.
53. For the politics of motherhood, see Paugh, "Politics of Childbearing"; Turner, "Nameless and Forgotten"; and Diana Paton, "Maternal Struggles and the Politics of Childlessness under Pronatalist Caribbean Slavery," *S&A* 38 (2017): 251–68.
54. Paton, "Driveress and the Nurse."
55. Susan Sleeper-Smith, "Eighteenth-Century Indian Trading Villages in the Wabash River Valley," *Ethnohistory* 62 (2015): 241–61; Sleeper-Smith, *Indigenous Prosperity and American Conquest; Indian Women of the Ohio River Valley* (Chapel Hill: University of North Carolina Press, 2018).
56. Felicity Donohue, "To Beget a Tame Breed of People: Sex, Marriage, Adultery and Indigenous North American Women," *EAS* 10 (2012): 101–31.
57. Sophie White, "Massacre, Mardi Gras, and Torture in Early New Orleans," *WMQ* 70 (2013): 533–34.
58. Ibid., 537.
59. Toby L. Ditz, "The New Men's History and the Peculiar Absence of Gendered Power: Some Remedies from Early American History," *Gender and History* 16 (2004): 1–35.

60. Elizabeth Mancke and Colin Grittner, "From Communal to Independent Manhood in Liverpool, Nova Scotia, ca. 1760–1820," *Histoire Sociale/Social History* 52 (2019): 257–80; Richard Butterwick-Pawlickowski, "'In the Greatest Wildness of My Youth': Sir Charles Hanbury Williams and Mid-Eighteenth-Century Libertinism," *Journal of Eighteenth-Century Studies* 41 (2018): 3–23; Joanne Bailey, "Paternal Power: The Pleasures and Perils of 'Indulgent' Fathering in Britain in the Long Eighteenth Century," *History of the Family* 17 (2012): 326–42; and Alvar Blomgren, "'Shew Yourselves as Men': Gender, Citizenship, and Political Propaganda in the 1773 and 1774 Worcester Election Contests," *Parliamentary History* 36 (2017): 346–60. See also Evan Zelnik, "Yankees, Doodles, Fops and Cuckolds: Compromised Manhood and Provincialism in the Revolutionary Period, 1740–1781," *EAS* 16 (2018): 514–44.
61. Linda Colley, "Gendering the Globe: The Political and Imperial Thought of Philip Francis," *P&P* 209 (2010): 117–48; Michèle Cohen, "'Manners Make the Man': Politeness, Chivalry and the Construction of Masculinity, 1750–1830," *JBS* 54 (2005): 312–29.
62. Carole Pateman, *The Sexual Contract* (Cambridge: Cambridge University Press, 1988), 3.
63. Paton, "Driveress and the Nurse." See also Whittle and Hailwood, "Gender Division of Labour in Early Modern England."
64. Troy Bickham, "Preparing for an Imperial Inheritance: Children, Play, and Empire," *JBS* 60 (2021): 658–88; J. R. Oldfield, "Anti-Slavery Sentiment in Children's Literature," *S&A* 10 (1989): 44–59.
65. Carole Shammas, *A History of Household Government in America* (Charlottesville: University of Virginia Press, 2002).
66. R. W. Connell, *Masculinities* (Cambridge: Cambridge University Press, 1975). For masculinity, see Thomas A. Foster, *Long before Stonewall: Histories of Same-Sex Sexuality in Early America* (New York: New York University Press, 2007); Foster, ed., *New Men: Manliness in Early America* (New York: New York University Press, 2011); Foster, *Sex and the Founding Fathers: The American Quest for a Relatable Past* (Philadelphia: Temple University Press, 2014); and Foster, *Rethinking Rufus: Sexual Violations of Enslaved Men* (Athens: University of Georgia Press, 2019). See also Richard Godbeer, *The Overflowing of Friendship: Love Between Men and the Creation of the American Republic* (Baltimore: Johns Hopkins University Press, 2009); and Daina Ramey Berry and Leslie M. Harris, eds., *Sexuality and Slavery: Reclaiming Intimate Histories in the Americas* (Athens: University of Georgia Press, 2018). For early American history as heteronormative, see Jennifer Mannion, "Historic Heteroessentialism and Other Orderings in Early America," *Signs* 34 (2009): 981–1003.
67. Heather Miyano Kopelson, "Sinning Property: The Legal Transformation of Abominable Sex in Early Bermuda," *WMQ* 70 (2013): 459–76.

68. John D'Emilio, afterword in Foster, *Long before Stonewall*, 384. See also Rachel Hope Cleves, "Beyond the Binaries in Early America," *EAS* 12 (2004): 459–68; and Jen Manion, *Female Husbands: A Trans History* (Cambridge: Cambridge University Press, 2020). For early American sexuality, see Brooke N. Newman, *A Dark Inheritance: Blood, Race, and Sex in Colonial Jamaica* (New Haven, CT: Yale University Press, 2018). For surveys of early American sexuality, see Sharon Block and Kathleen M. Brown, "Clio in Search of Eros: Redefining Sexualities in Early America," *WMQ* 60 (2003): 5–12; and Clare A. Lyons, "Mapping an Atlantic Sexual Culture: Homoeroticism in Eighteenth-Century Philadelphia," *WMQ* 60 (2003): 119–54. See also Kopelson, "Sinning Property."
69. Karen Harvey, "Ritual Encounters, Punch Parties, and Masculinity in the Eighteenth Century," *S&A* 214 (2012): 165–203. For rum, see Nuala Zahedieh, "A Copper Still and the Making of Rum in the Eighteenth-Century Atlantic World," *HJ* (2022): 149–66.
70. Burnard, "Tropical Hospitality," 20.
71. Colley, "Gendering the Globe."

7. Eighteenth-Century British History

1. Penelope J. Corfield, "British History: The Exploding Galaxy," *Journal of Eighteenth-Century Studies* 34 (2011): 524–26.
2. For an excellent recent survey of Georgian history, adopting traditional forms of interpretation, see Penelope J. Corfield, *The Georgians: The Deeds and Misdeeds of Eighteenth-Century Britain* (New Haven, CT: Yale University Press, 2022).
3. Edmund S. Morgan, "The American Revolution: Revisions in Need of Revising," *WMQ* 14 (1957): 14–15.
4. Edmund Morgan, "The Puritan Ethic and the American Revolution," *WMQ* 24 (1967): 3–43.
5. Morgan, "American Revolution," 13; Benjamin L. Carp, "Retrospective: Edmund S. Morgan and the Urgency of Good Leadership," *Reviews in American History* 44 (2016): 1–18.
6. McDonnell and Waldstreicher, "Revolution in the *Quarterly?*," 649. See also Edmund S. Morgan, *The Birth of the Republic, 1763–89* (Chicago: University of Chicago Press, 1956).
7. Breen, "Ideology and Nationalism."
8. Langford, *A Polite and Commercial People*, 364; Kathleen Wilson, *The Sense of the People: Politics, Culture and Imperialism in England, 1715–1785* (Cambridge: Cambridge University Press, 1995): 4.
9. Langford, *Polite and Commercial People*; John Brewer, *The Sinews of Power: War, Money and the English State, 1688–1763* (Cambridge, MA: Harvard University Press, 1989); Linda Colley, *Britons: Forging the Nation, 1707–1837*

(New Haven, CT: Yale University Press, 1989); Jan de Vries, "The Industrial Revolution and the Industrious Revolution," *JEcH* 54 (1994): 249–70; Colin Kidd, "North Britishness and the Nature of Eighteenth-Century British Patriotisms," *HJ* 39 (1996): 361–82; Roy Porter, "Seeing the Past," *S&A* 118 (1988): 186–205. Three books that Breen did not mention are Peter Borsay, *The English Urban Renaissance: Culture and Society in the Provincial Town, 1660–1760* (Oxford: Oxford University Press, 1989); C. A. Bayly, *Imperial Meridian: The British Empire and the World, 1780–1830* (London: Routledge, 1989); and Patrick K. O'Brien, *Power with Profit: The State and the Economy, 1688–1815* (London: University of London, 1991).

10. A dig at what Breen considers a parochial account in Middlekauf, *The Glorious Cause*, 14, 21.
11. Breen, "Ideology and Nationalism," 16.
12. J. C. D. Clark, *English Society, 1688–1832* (Cambridge: Cambridge University Press, 1985); Clark, *Revolution and Rebellion: State and Society in England in the Seventeenth and Eighteenth Centuries* (Cambridge: Cambridge University Press, 1986). For negative reviews, see Joanna Innes, "Jonathan Clark, Social History and England's Ancien Regime," *P&P* 115 (1987): 165–200; with a response by Jonathan Clark, "On Hitting the Buffers: The Historiography of England's Ancien Regime," *P&P* 117 (1987): 195–207. See also H. T. Dickinson in "Symposium: Revolution and Revisionism," *Parliamentary History* 7 (1988): 36–38.
13. Breen, "Ideology and Nationalism," 17.
14. Excellent textbooks are Frank O'Gorman, *The Long Eighteenth Century*, 2nd ed. (London: Bloomsbury, 2016); and Jeremy Black, *Eighteenth-Century Britain, 1688–1763* (Basingstoke: Palgrave Macmillan, 2001).
15. Giorgio Riello, *Cotton: The Fabric that Made the Modern World* (Cambridge: Cambridge University Press, 2013); John Darwin, *Unfinished Empire: The Global Expansion of Britain* (London: Allen Lane, 2012).
16. Outstanding works in eighteenth-century British history include Maxine Berg, *Luxury and Pleasure in Eighteenth-Century Britain* (Oxford: Oxford University Press, 2005); Stephen Conway, *War, State, and Society in Mid-Eighteenth-Century Britain and Ireland* (Oxford: Oxford University Press, 2006); Robert Shoemaker, *London Mob Violence and Disorder in Eighteenth-Century England* (London: Bloomsbury, 2007); Joanna Innes, *Inferior Politics: Social Problems and Social Policies in Eighteenth-Century Britain* (Oxford: Oxford University Press, 2009); Erin Mackie, *Rakes, Highwaymen, and Pirates: The Making of the Modern Gentleman in the Eighteenth Century* (Baltimore: Johns Hopkins University Press, 2009); Mark Knights, *The Devil in Disguise: Deception, Delusion, and Fanaticism in the Early English Enlightenment* (Oxford: Oxford University Press, 2011); Knights, *Trust and Distrust: Corruption in Office in Britain and its Empire, 1600–1850* (Oxford: Oxford University Press, 2021); Julian Hoppit, *Britain's*

Political Economies: Parliament and Economic Life, 1600–1800 (Cambridge: University of Cambridge Press, 2017); Jane Humphries, *Childhood and Child Labour in the British Industrial Revolution* (Cambridge: Cambridge University Press, 2010); and Helen Berry, *Orphans of Empire: The Fate of London's Foundlings* (Oxford: Oxford University Press, 2019).

17. The strongest argument for a political revolution in Britain is Steve Pincus, *1688: The First Modern Revolution* (New Haven, CT: Yale University Press, 2009). For strenuous denial of Pincus's claims, see Scott Sowerby, "Pantomime History," *Parliamentary History* 30 (2011): 236–58.

18. Ian McBride, "The Politics of *A Modest Proposal*: Swift and the Irish Crisis of the Late 1720s," *P&P* 244 (2019): 89–122.

19. "The most fundamental weakness of the Hanoverian regime was neither its corruption, nor the exclusiveness of its elite nor its antiquated representative system, Rather, it was its assertion of imperial control over its Celtic sub-nations, Chauvinistic self-regard disabled the rulers of Hanoverian England from identifying the reasonable and objective grievances of Scotland and Ireland." Frank O'Gorman, "The Recent Historiography of the Hanoverian Regime," *HJ* 29 (1986): 1014.

20. "Irish nationalism arose from Ireland's perceived exclusion from empire, not her inclusion in it." Bayly, *Imperial Meridian*, 12. John Murrin notes that the American Revolution was a crisis of imperial *integration* that the British state could not handle. Murrin, *Rethinking America: From Empire to Republic* (New York: Oxford University Press, 2018), 162–3.

21. Ashley Walsh, "The Saxon Republic and Ancient Constitution in the Standing Army Controversy, 1697–1699," *HJ* 62 (2019): 663–84; and Edward Taylor, "John Tutchin's *Observator*, Comment Serials, the 'Rage of Party' in Britain, 1678–c1730," *HJ* 63 (2020): 862–84.

22. Brodie Waddell, "The Politics of Distress in the Aftermath of the Glorious Revolution," *EHR* 130 (2015): 318–351; and Lionel Glassey, "In Search of the Mot Juste: Characterizations of the Revolution of 1688–89," in Tim Harris and Stephen Taylor, eds., *The Final Crisis of the Stuart Monarchy: The Revolutions of 1688–91 in Their British, Atlantic and European Contexts* (Cambridge: Cambridge University Press, 2013), 1–32.

23. E. A. Wrigley and R. S. Schofield, *The Population History of England: A Reconstruction* (Cambridge: Cambridge University Press, 1981).

24. Stephen Broadberry, Bruce M. S. Campbell, Alexander Klein, Mark Overton, and Bas van Leeuwen, *British Economic Growth, 1270–1870* (Cambridge: Cambridge University Press, 2015). See also Robert C. Allen, "Class Structure and Inequality during the Industrial Revolution: Lessons from England's Social Tables, 1688–1867," *EcHR* 72 (2019): 88–125; Jane Humphries and Jacob Weisdorf, "Unreal Wages? Real Income and Economic Growth in England, 1260–1850," *Economic Journal* 129 (2019): 2867–87; Judy Z. Stephenson, "'Real' Wages? Contractors, Workers and

Pay in London Building Trades, 1650–1800," *EcHR* 71 (2018): 106–32; Patrick Wallis, Justin Colson, and David Chilosi, "Structural Change and Economic Growth in the British Economy before the Industrial Revolution, 1500–1800," *JEcH* 78 (2018): 862–903; and Sara Horrell, Jane Humphries, and Jacob Weisdorf, "Family Standards of Living over the Long Run, England 1280–1850," *P&P* 250 (2021): 87–134.

25. Gregory Clark, "Growth or Stagnation? Farming in England, 1200–1800," *EcHR* 71 (2018): 55–81; and Stephen Broadberry et al., "Clark's Malthusian Delusion: Response to 'Farming in England 1200–1800,'" *EcHR* 71 (2018): 639–64.

26. Jonathan Scott, *How the Old World Ended: The Anglo-Dutch American Revolution 1500–1800* (New Haven, CT: Yale University Press, 2020).

27. Trevor Burnard, "Plantations and the Great Divergence," in Giorgio Riello and Tirthankur Roy, eds., *Economic Change in Global History* (London: Bloomsbury, 2018), ch.6.

28. Eric Williams, *Capitalism and Slavery* (Chapel Hill: University of North Carolina Press, 1944); Joseph Inikori, *Africans and the Industrial Revolution in England: A Study of International Trade and Development* (Cambridge: Cambridge University Press, 2003).

29. Burnard and Riello, "Slavery and the Industrial Revolution." See essays by Robin Blackburn, Pat Hudson, and Chris Evans, in Catherine Hall, Nick Draper, and Keith McClelland, eds., *Emancipation and the Remaking of the British Imperial World* (Manchester: Manchester University Press, 2014); and Sheryllynne Haggerty, Anthony Webster, and Nicholas White, eds., *The Empire in One City: Liverpool's Inconvenient Imperial Past* (Manchester: Manchester University Press, 2008).

30. Mark Harvey, "Slavery, Indenture and the Development of British Industrial Capitalism," *HWJ* 88 (2019): 66–88.

31. Rönnbäck, "On the Economic Importance of the Slave Plantation Complex"; Gregory Clark, Kevin H. O'Rourke, and Alan M. Taylor, "Made in America? The New World, the Old, and the Industrial Revolution," *American Economic Review* 98 (2008): 523–28; and C. Knick Harley, "Slavery, the British Atlantic, and the Industrial Revolution," in Adrian Leonard and David Pretel, eds., *The Caribbean and the Atlantic World Economy: Circuits of Trade, Money and Knowledge, 1650–1914* (Basingstoke: Palgrave Macmillan, 2015), 161–83.

32. Zahedieh, "Colonies, Copper, and the Market for Inventive Activity"; and Pat Hudson, "Slavery, the Slave Trade and Economic Growth: A Contribution to the Debate," in Hall, Draper, and McClelland, *Emancipation and the Remaking of the British Imperial World*, 51.

33. Chris Evans, "Slavery and Welsh Industry before and after Emancipation," in Hall, Draper, and McClelland, *Emancipation and the Remaking of the British Imperial World*, 61; and Evans, "'Voyage Iron': An Atlantic Slave

Trade Currency, Its European Origins, and West African Impact," *P&P* 239 (2018): 41–70.
34. Jon Stobart, "Making the Global Local? Overseas Goods in English Rural Shops, c. 1600–1760," *Business History* 59 (2017): 1136–53.
35. Stephen Conway, *War, State, and Society in Mid-Eighteenth-Century Britain and Ireland* (New York: Oxford University Press, 2006); Patrick A. Walsh, "The Eighteenth-Century Fiscal Military State: A Four Nations' Perspective," in Naomi Lloyd-Jones and Margaret Scull, eds., *Four Nations Approaches to Modern British History: A Disunited Kingdom* (Basingstoke: Palgrave Macmillan, 2017), 85–109; Walsh, "The Fiscal State in Ireland, 1691–1769," *HJ* 56 (2013): 629–56; and Aaron Graham and Walsh, *The British Fiscal-Military States, 1660–c. 1783* (Farnham: Taylor and Francis, 2016). For the fiscal-military state in early America, see Stephen Mihm, "Funding the Revolution: Monetary and Fiscal Policy in Eighteenth-Century America," in Edward G. Gray and Jane Kamensky, eds., *The Oxford Handbook of the American Revolution* (New York: Oxford University Press, 2013). For welfare and the Seven Years' War, see Erica Charters, "The Caring Fiscal-Military State during the Seven Years War, 1756–1763," *HJ* 52 (2009): 921–41.
36. Graham, "Corruption and Contractors"; Anne L. Murphy, "Performing Public Credit at the Eighteenth-Century Bank of England," *JBS* 58 (2019): 58–78.
37. Patrick K. O'Brien, "The Nature and Historical Evaluation of an Exceptional Fiscal State and Its Possible Significance for the Precocious Commercialization and Industrialization of the British Economy from Cromwell to Nelson," *EcHR* 64 (2011): 437.
38. Ibid., 438. See also Saumitra Jha, "Financial Asset Holdings and Political," *Quarterly Journal of Economics* (2015): 1485–1545. For the primacy of the Glorious Revolution, see Gary W. Cox, "Was the Glorious Revolution a Constitutional Watershed?," *JEcH* 72 (2012): 567–600.
39. Martin Daunton, "The Politics of Taxation in Britain from the Glorious Revolution to the Great War," in Bartolome Yun-Casalilla and Patrick. K. O'Brien, eds., *The Rise of Fiscal States: A Global History, 1500–1914* (Cambridge: Cambridge University Press, 2013), 111–44; Burnard, *Planters, Merchants, and Slaves*.
40. O'Brien, "Nature and Historical Evolution of an Exceptional Fiscal State," 420.
41. Stephen Broadberry et al., "Clark's Malthus Delusion: Response to 'Farming in England, 1200–1800,'" *EcHR* 71 (2018): 639–40. See Gregory Clark, "Growth or Stagnation? Farming in England, 1200–1800," *EcHR* 71 (2018): 55–81.
42. Allen, "Class Structure and Inequality."
43. Ibid.; Broadberry et al., *British Economic Growth*.

44. Peter Lindert and Jeffrey Williamson, "American Colonial Incomes, 1650–1774," *EcHR* 69 (2016): 54–77. See also Robert Allen et al., "The Colonial Origins of the Divergence in the Americas: A Labor Market Approach," *JEcH* 72 (2012): 863–94.
45. Calculations of average income and GDP and living standards for the different component parts of the British Empire outside England and North America are in their infancy. For Ireland, some calculations suggest an average GDP per annum of just £0.6 in the mid-eighteenth century, suggesting that the great majority of Irish people were either destitute or were subsistence peasants, living outside the market economy. For Jamaica, White per capita wealth was enormous, but enslaved people lived at the verge of destitution even at the best of times. Burnard, Panza, and Williamson, "Living Costs, Real Incomes and Inequality in Colonial Jamaica."
46. Julian Hoppit, "Scotland and the Taxing Union, 1707–1815," *Scottish Historical Review* 98 (2019): 45–70; Hoppit, "Petitions, Economic Legislation and Interest Groups in Britain, 1660–1800," *Parliamentary History* 37 (2018): 52–71; and Hoppit, "Taxing London and the British Fiscal State, 1660–1815," in Hoppit et al., eds., *Money and Markets: Essays in Honour of Martin Daunton* (Melton: Boydell Press, 2019).
47. John Beckett, "The Glorious Revolution, Parliament and the Making of the First Industrial Nation," *Parliamentary History* 33 (2014): 53.
48. Emma Hart, *Trading Spaces: The Colonial Marketplace and the Foundations of American Capitalism* (Chicago: University of Chicago Press, 2019).
49. Mark Latham, "'The City has been Wronged and Abused!': Institutional Corruption in the Eighteenth Century," *EcHR* 68 (2015): 1038–61; Jonathan Barth, "Reconstructing Mercantilism: Consensus and Conflict in the British Imperial Economy in the Seventeenth and Eighteenth Centuries," *WMQ* 73 (2016): 257–90; and du Rivage, *Revolution against Empire*, 26–52.
50. Paul Tonks, "British Union and Empire in *The Origin of Commerce*: Adam Anderson as Eighteenth-Century Historian and Scottish Political Economist," *History* 105 (2020): 60–81.
51. Yuval-Naeh, "The 1753 'Jew Bill,'" 468. See also J. G. A. Pocock, *Virtue, Commerce, and History: Essays on Political Thought and History, Chiefly in the Eighteenth Century* (Cambridge: Cambridge University Press, 1994).
52. O'Brien, "Nature and Historical Evolution of an Exceptional Fiscal State," 439.
53. Breen, "Ideology and Nationalism," 26–34. For concerns over empire, see Jack P. Greene, *Evaluating Empire and Confronting Colonialism in Eighteenth-Century Britain* (Cambridge: Cambridge University Press, 2013); and P. J. Marshall, *The Making and Unmaking of Empires: Britain, India and America, c. 1750–1783* (Oxford: Oxford University Press, 2005).
54. Charles W. A. Prior, "Settlers among Empires: Conquest and the American Revolution," in Edward Vallance, ed., *Remembering Early Modern*

Revolutions: England, North America, France and Haiti (London: Routledge, 2018): 81; Prior, "Beyond Settler Colonialism: State Sovereignty in Early America," *JEAH* 9 (2019): 1–25.
55. Marie Peters, "The Myth of William Pitt, Earl of Chatham, Great Imperialist Part I: Pitt and Imperial Expansion 1738–1763," *JICH* 21 (1993): 54–55.
56. P. J. Marshall, "A Nation Defined by Empire, 1755–1776," in Alexander Grant and Keith J. Springer, eds., *Uniting the Kingdom? The Making of British History* (London: Routledge, 1995), 221.
57. Cited in Breen, "Ideology and Nationalism," 34.
58. David Armitage, "Greater Britain: A Useful Category of Historical Analysis?," *AHR* 104 (1999): 427–45; and Eliga H. Gould "A Virtual Nation: Greater Britain and the Imperial Legacy of the American Revolution," *AHR* 104 (1999): 476–89.
59. Amanda B. Moniz, "Reforming Expectations: Parliamentary Pressure and Moral Reform," *Parliamentary History* 37 (2018): 102–18; David Parrish, "A Party Contagion: Party Politics and Inoculation in the British Atlantic World, c. 1721–1723," *Journal of Eighteenth-Century Studies* 39 (2016): 41–58; Sarah Irving Stonebraker, "Disease and Civilization: A Scottish Atlantic Network of Physicians in the Enlightenment," *British World* 10 (2017): 197–216.
60. Keith M. Brown, "Early Modern Scottish History—a Survey," *Scottish Historical Review* 92 (2013): 5–24. See also "Roundtable: Britain and the World: A New Field?," *JBS* 57 (2018): 677–708; Rachel K. Bright and Andrew R. Dilley, "After the British World," *HJ* 60 (2017): 547–58; and Stephen Howe, "British Worlds, Settler Worlds, World Systems and Killing Fields," *JICH* 40 (2012): 691–725.
61. J. G. A. Pocock, "The Limits and Divisions of British History: In Search of the Unknown Subject," *AHR* 87 (1982): 311–14.
62. James Kelly, "Coping with Crisis: The Response to the Famine of 1740–41," *Eighteenth-Century Ireland* 27 (2012): 93–122; David Arnold, "Hunger in the Garden of Plenty: The Bengal Famine of 1770," in Alessa Johns, ed., *Dreadful Visitations: Confronting National Catastrophe in the Age of Enlightenment* (London: Routledge, 1999), 86; Prasannan Parthasarti, *Why Europe Grew Rich and Asia Did Not: Global Economic Divergence, 1600–1850* (Cambridge: Cambridge University Press, 2011); and William Dalrymple, *The Anarchy: The Relentless Rise of the East India Company* (London: Bloomsbury, 2019). In global terms, the most historically important event in the 1760s may have been the failed investigation in 1766–67 into the East India Company's actions in India, which was the last opportunity for Britain to envision a different future for India than subjection to a rapacious private company. Spencer A. Leonard, "'The Capital Object of the Public': The 1766–7 Parliamentary Inquiry into the East India Company," *EHR* 132 (2017): 1110–48.

63. Amelia Gentleman, *The Windrush Betrayal: Exposing the Hostile Environment* (London: Faber and Faber, 2019). See also James Vernon, "The Worlding of Britain," *JBS* 57 (2018): 10–17; and Catherine Hall, "Gendering Property, Racing Capital," *HWJ* 78 (2014): 22–38; and Newman, "Freedom-Seeking Slaves."
64. Aaron Fogleman, "From Slaves, Convicts, and Servants to Free Passengers: The Transformation of Immigration in the Era of the American Revolution," *JAH* 88 (1998): 43–76.
65. Matthew Dziennik, *The Fatal Land: War, Empire and the Highland Soldier in British America* (New Haven, CT: Yale University Press, 2015).
66. Trevor Burnard and Cécile Vidal, "Location and the Conceptualization of Historical Frameworks: Early North American History and Its Multiple Reconfigurations in the US and in Europe," in Nicolas Barreyre, Michael Heale, Stephen Tuck, and Cécile Vidal, eds., *You, the People: Historical Writing about the United States in Europe* (Berkeley: University of California Press, 2014), 141–64.
67. Andrew O'Shaughnessy, "British Imperial Policy and the American Revolution," in Elaine Chalus and Perry Gauci, eds., *Revisiting the Polite and Commercial People* (Oxford: Oxford University Press, 2019), ch. 10; Stephen Conway, "Moral Economy, Contract, and Negotiated Authority in American, British and German Militaries, ca. 1740–1783," *Journal of Modern History* 88 (2016): 34–59; Burnard, "Empire Matters?"
68. E. P. Thompson, *Whigs and Hunters: The Origins of the Black Act* (London: Pantheon, 1975); Douglas Hay et al., *Albion's Fatal Tree: Crime and Society in Eighteenth-Century England* (New York: Pantheon, 1975). For the role of property in English society and politics for the "middling sort," see Paul Langford, *Public Life and the Propertied Englishman, 1689–1798* (Oxford: Oxford University Press, 1991).
69. Robert Shoemaker, "Worrying about Crime: Experience, Moral Panics and Public Opinion in London, 1600–1800," *P&P* 234 (2017): 71–100; Shoemaker, "Print and Female Voice: Representations of Women's Crime in London, 1690–1755," *Gender and History* 22 (2012): 75–91; Garthine Walker, "Rape, Acquittal, and Culpability in Popular Crime Reports in England c. 1670–c. 1750," *P&P* 220 (2012): 115–42; Peter King and Richard Ward, "Rethinking the Bloody Code in Eighteenth-Century Britain: Capital Punishment at the Centre and on the Periphery," *P&P* 228 (2018): 159–205; See also Timothy Hitchcock and Robert Shoemaker, *London Lives: Poverty, Crime, and the Making of a Modern City, 1690–1800* (Cambridge: Cambridge University Press, 2015).
70. James C. Scott, *The Art of Not Being Governed: An Anarchist Upland Southeast Asia* (New Haven, CT: Yale University Press, 2009); King and Ward, "Rethinking the Bloody Code"; Matthew C. Ward, "Laws, Courts,

and Communities in the Pennsylvania Backcountry, ca. 1750–1800," *JEAH* 6 (2016): 40–67.
71. Ward, "Laws, Courts, and Communities in the Pennsylvania Backcountry"; Robert Harper, *Unsettling the West: Violence and State Building in the Ohio Valley* (Philadelphia: University of Pennsylvania, 2018).
72. Greene, *Creating the British Atlantic*; and J. H. Elliott, *Empires of the Atlantic World: Britain and Spain in America, 1492–1830* (New Haven, CT: Yale University Press, 2006).
73. King and Ward, "Rethinking the Bloody Code," 205.
74. Joanna Innes, "What Would a 'Four Nations' Approach to the Study of Eighteenth-Century British Social Policy Entail?," in S. J. Connolly, ed., *Kingdoms United? Great Britain and Ireland Since 1500: Integration and Diversity* (Dublin: Four Courts, 1999), 183–95.
75. Zoe Dyndor, "The Gibbet in the Landscape: Locating the Criminal Corpse in Mid-Eighteenth Century England," in Richard Ward, ed., *A Global History of Execution and the Criminal Corpse* (Basingstoke: Palgrave Macmillan, 2015), 102–25; Timothy D. Watt, "Taxation Riots and the Culture of Popular Protest in Ireland, 1714–1740," *EHR* 130 (2015): 1418–41. See also the classic account in Cal Winslow, "Sussex Smugglers," in Hay et al., *Albion's Fatal Tree*.
76. H. V. Bowen, "Privilege and Profit: Commanders of East Indiamen as Private Traders, Entrepreneurs and Smugglers, 1760–1813," *International Journal of Maritime History* 19 (2007): 1–46; Alan Karras, *Smuggling: Contraband and Corruption in World History* (New York: Rowman and Littlefield, 2010).
77. David Chan Smith, "Fair Trade and the Political Economy of Brandy Smuggling in Early Eighteenth-Century Britain," *P&P* 251 (2021): 75–111.
78. V. A. C. Gatrell, *The Hanging Tree: Execution and the English People* (Oxford: Oxford University Press, 1994), 32.
79. Vincent Brown, *Tacky's Revolt: The Story of an Atlantic Slave War* (Cambridge, MA: Harvard University Press, 2020); Alan I. MacInnes and Douglas J, Hamilton, eds., *Jacobitism, Enlightenment and Empire, 1680–1820* (London: Taylor and Francis, 2014); S. J Connolly, "Jacobites, Whiteboys and Republicans: Varieties of Disaffection in Eighteenth-Century Ireland," *Eighteenth-Century Ireland* 18 (2003): 63–79.
80. Aaron Graham, "Auditing Leviathan: Corruption and State Formation in Early Eighteenth-Century Britain," *EHR* 128 (2013): 806–38.
81. Chris Whatley, "Reformed Religion, Regime Change, Scottish Whigs and the Struggle for the 'Soul' of Scotland c. 1688–c. 1788," *Scottish Historical Review* 92 (2013): 66–99; Amy Watson, "Patriotism and Partisanship in Post-Union Scotland, 1724–37," *Scottish Historical Review* 97 (2018): 57–84.
82. D. H. Robinson, *The Idea of Europe and the Origins of the American Revolution* (Oxford: Oxford University Press, 2020).

83. Daniel Szechi, "The Hanoverians in Scotland," in Mark Greengrass, ed., *Conquest and Coalescence: The Shaping of the State in Early Modern Europe* (London: E. Arnold, 1991), 123.
84. Andrew Mackillop, "Subsidy State or Drawback Province? Eighteenth-Century Scotland and the British Fiscal-Military Complex," in Aaron Graham and Patrick Walsh, eds., *The British Fiscal-Military States, 1660–c. 1783* (London: Routledge, 2016), 182.
85. Watson, "Patriotism and Partisanship."
86. Whatley, "Reformed Religion."
87. Julian Hoppit, "Scotland and the Taxing Union, 1707–1815," *Scottish Historical Review* 98 (2019): 45–70; W. W. J. Knox, "Homicide in Eighteenth-Century Scotland: Numbers and Theories," *Scottish Historical Review* 94 (2015): 48–73; Keith M. Brown and Allan Kennedy, "Land of Opportunity? The Assimilation of Scottish Migrants in England, 1603–c.1762," *JBS* 57 (2018): 709–35; T. M. Devine, "Scotland," in Roderick Floud, Jane Humphries, and Paul Johnson, eds., *The Cambridge Economic History of Modern Britain*, vol. 1, *Industrialization, 1700–1870*, 2nd ed. (Cambridge: Cambridge University Press, 2018), 65.
88. MacInnes and Hamilton, *Jacobitism, Enlightenment and Empire*; Geoffrey Plank, *Rebellion and Savagery: The Jacobite Rising of 1745 and the British Empire* (Philadelphia: University of Pennsylvania Press, 2006); Allan I. MacInnes, "Jacobitism in Scotland: Episodic Cause or National Movement?," *Scottish Historical Review* 86 (2007): 225–52.
89. Watson, "Patriotism and Partisanship," 67.
90. Ibid., 83, 84.
91. Mark Knights, "'The Lowest Degree of Freedom': The Right to Petition Parliament, 1640–1800," *Parliamentary History* 37 (2018): 18–34.
92. Edward Vallance, "Women, Politics and the 1723 Oaths of Allegiance to George I," *HJ* 59 (2016): 975–99.
93. Richard Pares, *King George III and the Politicians* (Oxford: Oxford University Press, 1954); Herbert Butterfield, *George III and the Historians* (London: Collins, 1957); Jeremy Black, *George III: America's Last King* (New Haven, CT: Yale University Press, 2006); Linda Colley, "The Apotheosis of George III: Loyalty, Royalty and the British Nation, 1760–1820," *P&P* 102 (1984): 94–129; and Andrew Jackson O'Shaughnessy, *The Men Who Lost America: British Leadership, the American Revolution, and the Fate of Empire* (New Haven, CT: Yale University Press, 2013). For George II: Jeremy Black, *George II: Puppet of the Politicians?* (Exeter: University of Exeter Press, 2007); Andrew C. Thompson, *George II: King and Elector* (New Haven, CT: Yale University Press, 2011); and Hannah Smith, *The Georgian Monarchy: Politics and Culture, 1714–1760* (Cambridge: Cambridge University Press, 2006). For an enthusiastic rehabilitation of George III as a modern monarch in which he is seen, surprisingly, as intellectually

curious and even as Britain's earliest abolitionist, see David Armitage, "George III and the Law of Nations," *WMQ* 79 (2022): 3–30.

94. Sally Holloway and Lucy Worsley, "'Everybody took notice of the scene in the drawing room': Performing Emotions at the Early Georgian Court, 1714–60," *Journal of Eighteenth-Century Studies* 40 (2017): 443–64; Hannah Smith, "The Court in England, 1714–1760: A Declining Political Institution?," *History* 90 (2005): 23–41; and Stephanie Koscak, "The Royal Sign and Visual Literacy in Eighteenth-century London," *JBS* 55 (2016): 24–56.

95. Holloway and Worsley, "Everybody took notice," 447, citing J. H. Plumb, *The Growth of Political Stability in England, 1675–1825* (London: Palgrave, 1967), 188.

96. Hannah Smith and Stephen Taylor, "Hephaestion and Alexander: Lord Hervey, Frederick, Prince of Wales and the Royal Favourite in England in the 1730s," *EHR* 124 (2009): 283–312.

97. J. C. D. Clark, "The Re-Enchantment of the World? Religion and Monarchy in Eighteenth-Century Europe," in Michael Schaich, ed., *Monarchy and Religion* (Oxford: Oxford University Press, 2007), 67.

98. Daniel Robinson, "Giving Peace to Europe: European Geopolitics, Colonial Political Culture, and the Hanoverian Monarchy in British North America, ca. 1740–1763," *WMQ* 73 (2016): 291–332.

99. Ibid., 325; John Shovlin, *Trading with the Enemy: Britain, France, and the Eighteenth-Century Quest for a Peaceful World Order* (New Haven, CT: Yale University Press, 2021), ch. 4.

100. E. P. Thompson, "The Moral Economy of the English Crowd in the Eighteenth Century," *P&P* 50 (1971): 76–136.

101. Beverley Lemire, "'Men of the World': British Mariners, Consumer Practice and Material Culture in an Era of Global Trade, c. 1660–1800," *JBS* 54 (2015): 288–319.

102. McBride, "Politics of *A Modest Proposal*," 120–22.

103. Joanna Innes and Mark Philp, *Re-imagining Democracy in the Age of Revolutions: America, France, Britain, Ireland, 1750–1850* (Oxford: Oxford University Press, 2015).

104. Paul Stock, "America and the American Revolution in British Geographical Thought, c. 1760–1830," *EHR* 131 (2016): 64–91.

105. Ian Christie, *Stress and Stability in Late Eighteenth-Century Britain: Reflections on the British Avoidance of Revolution* (Oxford: Clarendon Press, 1984).

106. David Waldstreicher, "The Revolutions of Revolution Historiography: Cold War Contradance, Neo-Imperial Waltz, or Jazz Standard?," *Reviews in American History* 42 (2014): 23–35; O'Shaughnessy, *The Men Who Lost America*.

8. The American Revolution

1. Christer Petley, "Slaveholders and Revolution: The Jamaican Planter Class, British Imperial Politics, and the Ending of the Slave Trade, 1775–1807," *S&A* 39 (2018): 55–79.
2. Colin Calloway, "Red Power and Homeland Security: Native Nations and the Limits of Empire in the Ohio Country," in Michael A. McDonald and Kate Fullager, eds., *Facing Empire: Indigenous Experiences in a Revolutionary Age* (Baltimore: Johns Hopkins University, 2018), 145.
3. Kristine Bruland, Anne Gerritsen, Pat Hudson, and Giorgio Riello, eds., *Reinventing the Economic History of Industrialisation* (Montreal: McGill-Queens University Press, 2020); Zylberberg, "Fuel Prices, Regional Habits and Cooking Habits."
4. Mark Peterson, "The Social Origins of *Ideological Origins*: Notes on the Historical Legacy of Bernard Bailyn," *Reviews in American History* 49 (2021): 383.
5. Edward Gray and James Kamensky, "Introduction: American Revolutions," in Gray and Kamensky, eds., *The Oxford Handbook of the American Revolution* (New York: Oxford University Press, 2013), 6.
6. Woody Holton, "The World Is Not Enough," *Reviews in American History* 43 (2015): 33.
7. Gordon S. Wood, *The Radicalism of the American Revolution* (New York: Knopf, 1992); Alan Taylor, "Introduction: Expand or Die: The Revolution's New Empire," *WMQ* 74 (2017): 621; McDonnell and Waldstreicher, "Revolution in the *Quarterly?*," 665–66.
8. Allan Kulikoff, "The War in the Countryside," in Gray and Kamensky, *Oxford Handbook of the American Revolution*, 231.
9. Ibid., 223.
10. Essays by Michael McDonnell, Gary B. Nash, Jane Merritt, and Stephen Mihm, in Gray and Kamensky, *Oxford Handbook of the American Revolution*, 116, 245, 267 345–46.
11. Paul Mapp, "The Revolutionary War and Europe's Great Powers," in Gray and Kamensky, *Oxford Handbook of the American Revolution*, 324.
12. Christopher Leslie Brown, "The Problem of Slavery," in Gray and Kamensky, *The Oxford Handbook of the American Revolution*, 428.
13. Hannah Arendt, *On Revolution* (New York: Viking Press, 1963), 49.
14. Eliga H. Gould, "The Question of Home Rule," *WMQ* 64 (2007): 258.
15. Serena Zabin, "Conclusion: Writing To and From the Revolution," *WMQ* 74 (2017): 783.
16. US Bureau of the Census, *Historical Statistics of the United States, Colonial Times to 1970* (Washington, DC, 1975), II. 1168 (Ser. Z 1–19).
17. Alan Taylor, *The American Revolution: A Continental History, 1750–1804* (New York: W. W. Norton, 2016); Gray and Kamensky, *Oxford Handbook of the American Revolution*.

18. McDonnell and Waldstreicher, "Revolution in the *Quarterly?*," 664; "Forum: How Revolutionary was the Revolution? A Discussion of Gordon S. Wood's *The Radicalism of the American Revolution*," *WMQ* 51 (1994): 677–716; Edward Countryman, "Indians, the Colonial Order and the Social Significance of the American Revolution," *WMQ* 53 (1996): 342–62; and Carole Shammas, "Anglo-American Household Government in Comparative Perspective," *WMQ* 52 (1995): 104–44.
19. Rosemarie Zagarri, "The Significance of the 'Global Turn' for the Early American Republic: Globalization in the Age of Nation-Building," *JER* 31 (2011): 6.
20. Zagarri, "Significance of the 'Global Turn,'" 7. For the interplay between national and global history, see Johann N. Neem, "America in a Global Age," *History and Theory* 50 (2011): 41–70.
21. Taylor, "Introduction: Expand or Die"; and Zabin, "Conclusion: Writing To and From the Revolution."
22. Fisher, "Fit Instruments in a Howling Wilderness"; Mary Beth Norton, "The Seventh Tea Ship," *WMQ* 73 (2016): 681–710.
23. Tom Cutterham "Class, State and Revolution in the History of American Capitalism," *Journal of the History of Sociology* 33 (2020): 26–38.
24. Taylor, "Introduction: Expand or Die," 624.
25. For the American Revolution elsewhere in the Western Hemisphere: Nicholas G. Dipucchio, "Conquest for Commerce: American Policymakers, Bermuda and the War for Independence, 1775–83," *EAS* 18 (2020): 61–89; Ross Nedervelt, "Caught between Realities: The American Revolution, the Continental Congress and Political Turmoil in the Bahamian Islands," *JICH* 43 (2015): 747–69.
26. Taylor, "Introduction: Expand or Die," 626.
27. McDonnell and Waldstreicher, "Revolution in the *Quarterly?*," 664.
28. Taylor, "Introduction: Expand or Die," 631.
29. Zabin, "Conclusion: Writing To and Fom the Revolution," 763.
30. Mason, "The Absentee Planter and the Key Slave," 80.
31. Holger Hoock, "Mangled Bodies: Atrocity in the American Revolutionary War," *S&A* 230 (2016): 123–59.
32. Zelnik, "Yankees, Doodles, Fops and Cuckolds."
33. Friederike Baer, "The Decision to Hire German Troops in the War of American Independence: Reactions in Britain and North America, 1774–1776," *EAS* 13 (2015): 111–50.
34. Christopher P. Magra, "Anti-Impressment Riots and the Origins of the American Revolution," *International Review of Social History* 58 (2013): 131–51.
35. Michael A. McDonnell, *The Politics of War: Race, Class and Conflict in Revolutionary Virginia* (Chapel Hill: University of North Carolina Press, 2007).
36. Joshua Canale, "'When a State Abounds in Rascals': New York's Revolutionary Era Committees for Public Safety, 1775–1783," *JER* 39 (2019):

203–38; Christopher Minty, "'Of One Hart and One Mind': Local Institutions and Allegiance during the American Revolution," *EAS* 15 (2017): 99–132; Matthew P. Dziennik, "New York's Refugees and Political Authority in Revolutionary America," *WMQ* 77 (2020): 65–96.

37. Linda Colley, *The Gun, the Ship, and the Pen: Warfare, Constitutions and the Making of the Modern World* (London: Profile, 2021); Christopher Flanagan, "A Revolutionary Empire: Ideas of Empire and the Making of the Constitution, 1787–8," *JEAH* 8 (2018): 153–77; Thomas G. Rodgers, "Reconciling Coercion in the Constitution of the American Republican State," *JEAH* 8 (2018): 207–30; Herbert A. Johnson, "American Constitutionalism and the War for Independence," *EAS* 14 (2016): 140–73.

38. François Furstenberg, "'The Significance of the Trans-Appalachian Frontier in Atlantic History," *AHR* 113 (2008): 647–77; Claudio Saunt, *West of the Revolution: An Uncommon History of 1776* (New York: W. W. Norton, 2014); Colin Calloway, *The Indian World of George Washington: The First President, the First Americans, and the Birth of the Nation* (New York: Oxford University Press, 2018).

39. Donald F. Johnson, "The Failure of British Rule in Revolutionary Charleston, South Carolina," *JICH* 42 (2014): 22–40; Johnson, "Ambiguous Allegiances: Urban Loyalties during the American Revolution," *JAH* (2017): 610–31; T. H. Breen, *American Insurgents, American Patriots: The Revolution of the People* (New York: Hill and Wang, 2010); and Breen, *The Will of the People: The Revolutionary Birth of America* (Cambridge, MA: Harvard University Press, 2019).

40. Lauren Duval, "Mastering Charleston: Property and Patriarchy in British-Occupied Charleston," *WMQ* 75 (2018): 589–622.

41. Saunt, *Unworthy Republic*.

42. Geoffrey Parker, "Crisis and Catastrophe: The Global Crisis of the Seventeenth Century Reconsidered," *AHR* 113 (2008): 1053–79.

43. Gray and Kamensky, "Introduction: American Revolutions," in *Oxford Handbook of the American Revolution*, 3.

44. Neem, "America in a Global Age," 63.

45. P. J. Marshall, *Remaking the British Atlantic: The United States and the British Empire after American Independence* (Oxford: Oxford University Press, 2012), 321; Kinsley Brauer, "The United States and British Imperial Expansion, 1815–1860," *Diplomatic History* 12 (1988): 24.

46. Breen, "Ideology and Nationalism." Scots, however, were increasingly considered British. Linda Colley, *Britons: Forging the Nation, 1707–1837* (New Haven, CT: Yale University Press, 1989), 120–32.

47. Amanda B. Moniz, *From Empire to Humanity: The American Revolution and the Origins of Humanitarianism* (New York: Oxford University Press, 2016).

48. Robert Gildea, *Empires of the Mind: The Colonial Past and the Politics of the Present* (Cambridge: Cambridge University Press, 2019); Jeremy Paxman,

Empire: What Ruling the World Meant to the British (London: Viking, 2012); Dane Kennedy, *The Imperial History Wars: Debating the British Empire* (London: Bloomsbury, 2018); Stuart Ward and Astrid Rasch, eds., *Embers of Empire in Brexit Britain* (London: Bloomsbury, 2019); and Kwasi Kwarteng, *Ghosts of Empire: Britain's Legacies in the Modern World* (London: Bloomsbury, 2011).

49. Michael Mann, "The Dark Side of Democracy: The Modern Tradition of Ethnic and Political Cleansing," *New Left Review* 235 (1999): 26.
50. Linda Colley, *Captives: Britain, Empire and the World, 1600–1850* (London: Jonathan Cape, 2002), 10.
51. Phillip Buckner and John G. Reid, eds., *The Conquest of Canada in Historical Perspective* (Toronto: University of Toronto Press, 2012); Nancy Christie, *The Formal and Informal Politics of British Rule in Post-Conquest Quebec, 1760–1837: A Northern Bastille* (Oxford: Oxford University Press, 2020).
52. Harvey Amani Whitfield, "White Archives, Black Fragments: Problems and Possibilities in Telling the Lives of Enslaved Black People in the Maritimes," *Canadian Historical Review* 101 (2020): 323–45; Brett Rushforth, *Bonds of Alliance: Indigenous and Atlantic Slaveries in New France* (Chapel Hill: University of North Carolina Press, 2012); Houllemare, "La fabrique des archives colonials et la conscience impériale France"; Daniel Gilles, "La norme esclavagiste, entre pratique coutumière et norme étatique: les esclavages panis et leur condition juridique au Canada (XViie–XVIIIe siècles)," *Ottawa Law Review* 30 (2009): 495–536.
53. Trevor Burnard, "'Wi Lickle but Wi Tallawah': Writing Jamaica into the Atlantic World, 1655–1834," *Reviews in American History* 49 (2021): 168–86.
54. Sarah Knott, "Narrating the Age of Revolution," *WMQ* 73 (2016): 3–36.
55. Taylor, "Introduction: Expand or Die," 621, 625–26, 632.
56. Gordon S. Wood, "'American Republics' Review: A Patchwork Nation," *Wall St. Journal*, May 28, 2021.
57. Stuart Macintyre and Anna Clark, *The History Wars* (Melbourne: Melbourne University Press, 2004).
58. Gray and Kamensky, "Introduction: American Revolutions," in *Oxford Handbook of the American Revolution*, 8.
59. Greene, "Colonial History and National History," 247.
60. Krishnan Kumar, *Visions of Empire: How Five Imperial Regimes Shaped the World* (Princeton, NJ: Princeton University Press, 2017).
61. Patrick Spero, "Introduction: Origins," in Spero and Michael Zuckerman, eds., *The American Revolution Reborn* (Philadelphia: University of Pennsylvania Press, 2016), 4.
62. Gray and Kamensky, "Introduction: American Revolutions," in *Oxford Handbook of the American Revolution*, 5.
63. Ibid., 6.

64. Michael Zuckerman, "Conclusion: Beyond the Rebirth of the American Revolution: Coming to Terms with Coming of Age," in Spero and Zuckerman, *American Revolution Reborn*, 300, 318.
65. Aaron Fogleman, "From Slaves, Convicts, and Servants to Free Passengers: The Transformation of Immigration in the Era of the American Revolution," *JAH* 88 (1998): 43–76; Fogleman, "The United States and the Transformation of Transatlantic Migration during the Age of Revolution," in Spero and Zuckerman, *American Revolution Reborn*, 251–56.
66. Rosemarie Zagarri, "The American Revolution in New National Politics," in Gray and Kamensky, *Oxford Handbook of the American Revolution*, 496.
67. Eliga H. Gould, "The Empire that Britain Kept," in Gray and Kamensky, *Oxford Handbook of the American Revolution*, 466.
68. Cutterham, "Class, State, and Revolution in the History of American Capitalism."
69. David M. Golove and Daniel J. Hulsebosch, "The Federalist Constitution as a Project in International Law," *Fordham Law Review* 89 (2021): 1843.
70. Peterson, "Social Origins," 383; Fogleman, "Transformation of Transatlantic Migration," 269.
71. Zagarri, "Significance of the 'Global Turn,'" 36–37.
72. Eliga H. Gould, "The Question of Home Rule," *WMQ* 64 (2007): 257–58; Gould, *Among the Powers of the Earth: The American Revolution and the Making of a New World Empire* (Cambridge: Cambridge University Press, 2012).
73. Gould, "Empire that Britain Kept," 476.
74. Patrick Griffin, "De-Decentering the Narrative: The Case for a Vast 1776," *WMQ* 78 (2021): 229.
75. Sean Wilentz, "A Matter of Facts," *Atlantic*, January 22, 2020; William Hogeland, "Against the Consensus Approach to History: How Not to Learn about the American Past," *New Republic*, January 25, 2021; Letters from Noah Feldman and James Oakes, *New York Review of Books*, June 23, 2022, 62. For a particularly acrimonious exchange over this matter, see "Communications," *AHR* 125 (2020): 768–74.
76. Griffin, "De-Decentering the Narrative," 234.
77. Zuckerman, "Conclusion: Beyond the Rebirth of the American Revolution," in Spero and Zuckerman, *American Revolution Reborn*, 301–3.
78. Eliga H. Gould and Rosemarie Zagarri, "Situating the United States in Vast Early America: Introduction," *WMQ* 78 (2021): 91.
79. Janet Polasky, *Revolutions without Borders: The Call to Liberty in the Atlantic World* (New Haven, CT: Yale University Press, 2016); Klooster, *Cambridge History of the Age of Revolutions*; and Eliga Gould, Paul Mapp, and Carla Gardina Pestana, eds., *Cambridge History of America and the World*, vol. 1, 1500–1820 (Cambridge: Cambridge University Press, 2021).

Conclusion

1. Neem, "From Polity to Exchange."
2. Fred Anderson and Andrew R. L. Cayton, "The Problem of Fragmentation and the Prospects for Synthesis in Early American Social History," *WMQ* 50 (1993): 299–310.
3. J. R. McNeill and Kenneth Pomeranz, "Production, Destruction, and Connection: 1750–Present: Introduction," in McNeill and Pomeranz, eds., *Cambridge World History* 7.1, 51–82; Tirthankar Roy and Giorgio Riello, eds., *Global Economic History* (London: Bloomsbury, 2019).
4. Hopkins, "Back to the Future."
5. Cécile Vidal, "The Reluctance of French Historians to Address Atlantic History," *Southern Quarterly* 43 (2006): 153–89.
6. Elliott, *Empires of the Atlantic World*, 291.
7. Parker, "Crisis and Catastrophe."
8. Peter H. Wood, *Strange New Land: Africans in Colonial America* (New York: Oxford University Press, 2003), 23–35.
9. Peter C. Mancall, "Bernard Bailyn's Barbarous Modernity," *New England Quarterly* 95 (2022): 462–88.
10. Christie, *Formal and Informal Politics*, 5, 388.
11. Kit Candlin, "The Role of the Enslaved in the 'Fedon Rebellion' of 1795," *S&A* 39 (2018): 685–707; Tessa Murphy, "A Reassessment of Rights: Fedon's Rebellion, Grenada, 1795–96," *La Révolution française* 14 (2018), https://doi.org/10.4000/lrf.2017; Julie Chan Kim, "The Caribs of St. Vincent and Indigenous Resistance during the Age of Revolutions," *EAS* 11 (2013): 117–32; and Newton, "Counterpoints of Conquest."
12. Philip D. Morgan and Molly A. Warsh, *Early North America in Global Perspective* (London: Routledge, 2014), 4.
13. Ian Tyrrell, "The United States in World History since the 1950s," in McNeill and Pomeranz, *Cambridge World History* 7.1, *Production, Destruction and Connection, 1750–Present* (Cambridge: Cambridge University Press, 2015), 585; Alan Karras, "The Caribbean Region: Crucible for Modern World History," in Jerry H. Bentley, Sanjay Subrahmanyam, and Merry E. Wiesner-Hanks, *Cambridge World History* 6.1, *The Construction of a Global World, 1400–1800 CE: Foundations* (Cambridge: Cambridge University Press, 2015), 393–414; and Trevor Burnard, "Plantation Societies," in Bentley, Subrahmanyam, and Wiesner-Hanks, *Cambridge World History* 6.2, *Construction of a Global World, 1400–1800 CE: Patterns of Change* (Cambridge: Cambridge University Press, 2015), 263–82.
14. James Belich, *Replenishing the Earth: The Settler Revolution and the Rise of the Anglo-World, 1783–1939* (Oxford: Oxford University Press, 2009).
15. Taylor, *American Revolutions: A Continental History*.

16. Rebecca Earle, "The Pleasures of Taxonomy: Casta Paintings, Classification, and Colonialism," *WMQ* 73 (2016): 427–66.
17. Gould, *Among the Powers of the Earth*; Harry Dickinson, "The Impact of the War on British Politics," in Gray and Kamensky, *Oxford Handbook of the American Revolution*, 367; Daniel J. Hulschbosch, "The Revolutionary Portfolio: Constitution-Making and the Wider World in the American Revolution," *Suffolk University Law Review* 47 (2014): 759–822.
18. David Armitage, "1320, 1776, and All That: A Tale of Two 'Declarations,'" *Scottish Historical Review* 101 (2022): 512–31; Armitage, "'George III and the Law of Nations,'" *WMQ* 79 (2022): 3–30.
19. Gould, Mapp, and Pestana, *Cambridge History of America and the World*.
20. Shauna J. Sweeney, "Market Marronage: Fugitive Women and the Internal Marketing System in Jamaica, 1781–1834," *WMQ* 76 (2019): 197–222; Newman, "Hidden in Plain Sight," 1–53; Radburn, "Guinea Factors, Slave Sales"; Elizabeth A. Dolan and Ahmed Idressi Alami, "Muhammad Kabā Saghanughu's Arabic Address on the Occasion of Emancipation in Jamaica," *WMQ* 76 (2019): 289–312; Christie, "Merchant and Plebeian Commercial Knowledge in Montreal and Quebec"; Elspeth Martini, "'Visiting Indians,' Natural Fathers, and Anglo-American Empires in the Post-War of 1812 Western Lakes," *WMQ* 78 (2021): 459–90; Natasha Lightfoot, "'So Far to Leeward': Eliza Moore's Cosmopolitan Routes to Freedom in the Nineteenth-Century Caribbean," *WMQ* 79 (2022): 61–88.
21. Trevor Burnard, "America the Good, America the Brave, America the Free: Reviewing the *Oxford History of the United States*," *Journal of American Studies* 45, 3 (2011): 401–41.
22. Zabin, "Conclusion: Writing To and From the Revolution," 771.
23. Annette Gordon-Reed and Peter Onuf, "The Nation-State in a Changing World: Epilogue," *WMQ* 78 (2021): 276–77.
24. J. R. Oldfield, *Transatlantic Abolitionism in the Age of Revolution* (Cambridge: Cambridge University Press, 2013); and Oldfield, *The Ties that Bind: Transatlantic Abolitionism in the Age of Reform* (Liverpool: Liverpool University Press, 2020).
25. Alan Karras, "The Atlantic Ocean Basin," in Jerry Bentley, ed., *The Oxford Handbook of World History* (Oxford: Oxford University Press, 2011), 529–45.
26. Ibid., 530–31.
27. Gould and Zagarri, "Situating the United States in Vast Early America," 190–91.
28. Michael Hattem, "Revolution Lost? Vast Early America, National History, and the American Revolution," *WMQ* 78 (2021): 269–74.
29. Ibid., 270–71.
30. Mark Peterson, "Unschooling the Revolution," *JER* 40 (2020): 123.

Appendix A

1. "Forum: Transformations of Virginia: Tobacco, Slavery, and Empire," *WMQ* 68 (2011): 327–426.
2. Allan Greer, "National, Transnational, and Hypernational Historiographies: New France Meets Early American History," *Canadian Historical Review* 91 (2010): 695–724; Catherine Desbarats and Allan Greer, "North America from the Top Down: Visions from New France," *JEAH* 5 (2015): 109–36; Helen Dewar, "Agents, Institutions and French Empire/State Formation," *Canadian Historical Review* 102 (2021): 85–108; Gregory Kennedy, "Militaristic Visions of New France in the French Atlantic World, 1663–1763," *Canadian Historical Review* 102 (2021): 109–24; and Alexandra Havrylyshyn, "Troublesome Trials: How a Parisian Legal Practitioner Disrupted the Ordeal of New France," *WMQ* 78 (2021): 45–78.
3. Early American History remains biased toward work in the English language. Thomas Müller-Bahkle and Hermann Wellenreuther note in a complaint about an article indifferent to writing in German that "while American scholars seem to expect, for example, French, Danish, Dutch, or German scholars to use all relevant literature in English, they cheerfully ignore everything published in any other language but their own." Communication, *WMQ* 74 (2017): 815–17. Literature in other languages about early America is not entirely absent: *WMQ* has reviewed four works written in French since 2015. See also Burnard and Vidal, "Location and the Conceptualization of Historical Frameworks," in Barreyre, Heale, Tuck, and Vidal, *You, the People*, 141–64.

INDEX

Page numbers in italics indicate figures or tables.

abolitionism: overview, 173; Great Britain, 46, 63, 72, 73, 79, 101, 147; "just war" concept, 73–74; plantations and, 45–46, 50; religion, 72–73, 74–75, 82; slave trade and, 46, 63. *See also* proslavery movement

Adams, John, 65, 176

Adelman, Jeremy, 93, 107, 108, 111

advertisements, and runaway enslaved people, 66, 70–71

Africa/Africans: academic journals, 2; British imperialism, 79, 126–27; commerce, 79, 80, 81, 157; Creole people, 49, 55, 63, 92, 109, 124, 142; domestic slavery, 80, 136; living standards, 135–36; merchants, 50, 53–54, 76–77, 78, 79, 80; runaway enslaved people, 70–71; slave trade, 75–76, 78, 79, 80, 81, 127, 136; women's role, 80, 136

African Americans, 9, 27, 28–29, 42, 175. *See also* Blacks; enslaved children; enslaved men; enslaved people; enslaved women

agency, and Indigenous peoples, 21, 85, 88–89, 90, 102–3

age of revolutions: overview, 151, 171–72, 190; democracy, 108, 111; globalization, 107–11, 174, 180; imperialism, 105, 108, 110

Aggorworth, Robert T., 117

Agostini, Thomas, 117

Alami, Ahmed Idressi, 207

Allen, Robert C., 43, 159

American Constitution, 25, 34, 188, 192, 206

American Revolution (1776–83): overview, 8, 17; age of revolutions, 107, 109, 110, 174; capitalism, 183, 189; as civil war, 180, 181, 182, 188; critique, 179–80, 186–87; current themes, 7–8, 21, 177–78, 205–6, 207–8; democracy and, 175–76; elites and, 7, 37, 175–76, 179, 180, 189; free Blacks, 66, 101, 175; freedom, 175, 180, 181–82, 186–87, 192; globalization, 174–75, 177, 180, 207–8; imperialism, 119–20, 183–88; influence/significance of, 173–76; Loyalists, 181, 182–83; negative effects, 175–76, 178, 179–81; patriots, 181, 182–83, 186–87; plantations and, 45–46, 50, 51; politics, 37, 99, 174, 181, 186, 189; positive effects, 175–76, 178, 179; slavery, 66–67, 77, 101, 176, 177, 178–79; traditional themes, 3, 21, 24, 25, 31, 151, 171–72; #VastEarlyAmerica, 207–8; violence, 178–79, 180–81. *See also* Indigenous peoples, and American Revolution; United States; wars: War for/of American Independence

American Revolution (1776–83), and White people: race and, 8, 37, 101, 161–62, 180, 184; settlers, 8, 37, 101, 115, 118, 161–62, 184; whiteness, 17, 137, 180, 190; women, 17, 137, 183. *See also* American Revolution (1776–83)

American West (the West): current themes, 15; environment and, 56–58; historiography, 33, 34; Indigenous peoples, 57–58, 96–97; settler colonialism, 87, 96–97

Anderson, Adam, 160

Anderson, Chad, 88

Anderson, Fred, 23, 24, 26, 32, 197–98

Andrews, Charles MacLean, 10, 63, 106, 113

293

Anstey, Roger, 72
Anthropocene, 55, 56, 198
Appleby, Joyce, 23–26, 32–33, 34, 234n9
archives, 12, 67–71, 81, 90, 134
Arendt, Hannah, 176
Armitage, David, 208
Arnold, David, 162
Aron, Stephen, 57, 93
Atlantic world: age of revolutions, 108–9; current themes, 31–32; mercantilism, 51–52; merchants, 50, 53–54, 64, 78; scholarship, 4–5, 6, 113. *See also* Africa/Africans; British America; British North America; French America
Australia, 14–15, 41, 100–101
authority: British history, 165–66; imperialism, 104, 105, 115–18, 121, 122; Indigenous peoples and, 97, 177, 182

Bache, Sally Franklin, 137
Baer, Friederike, 181, 182–83
Bahar, Matthew R., 87–88
Bailyn, Bernard, 10, 23, 26, 113
Bains, Tiraana, 226n4
Barr, Juliana, 85, 87, 88
Barth, Jonathan, 51–52
Bayly, C. A., 107, 110, 124
Beamon, Hannah, 9
Beard, Charles, 10
Beckert, Sven, 64
Beckett, John, 159–60
Belich, James, 41, 205
Benezet, Anthony, 73–74
Benton, Lauren, 108
Berlin, Ira, 29
Berwick, Keith B., 7
Bickham, Troy, 147
Blaakman, Michael A., 95–96
Blackburn, Robin, 92, 109
Blackhawk, Maggie, 13–14
Blackhawk, Ned, 14, 27
Blacks: African Americans, 9, 27, 28–29, 42, 175; Black men, 9, 65, 67–68; Black women, 65–66, 80, 133, 136, 141, 142–43; French America, 133, 186; inheritance practices, 136, 143; marriage and, 65–66; wealth/plantation wealth, 42, 43, 44, 52, 242n20. *See also* enslaved children; enslaved men; enslaved people; enslaved women; free Blacks
Block, Kristen, 75
Block, Sharon, 137
Bloody Code, 163–64, 165, 166
Bollettino, Maria Alessandra, 68
borderlands, 87, 91–92, 93–95, 99, 164
Boston, Massachusetts. *See* Massachusetts
Bourdieu, Pierre, 13, 35, 109
Bouton, Terry, 175–76
Brandt, Susan, 137
Braudel, Fernand, 252n39
Breen, T. H.: American Revolution, 161–62, 183; Hanoverian era described, 151–52, 275nn9–10; historiography, 151, 152, 153, 226n4; national identity, 184
Breidenback, Michael D., 121
Brekus, Catherine A., 75
Brewer, John, 151, 152, 157–58
Bridenbaugh, Carl, 23
British America: authority, 115–16, 117–18; Catholics, 100, 120–21; imperialism and, 106, 113, 117–18, 123–24; marriage practices, 137, 147–48; merchants, 50, 53, 54; runaway enslaved people, 70–71; scholarship, 22–26; slavery, 30, 44, 46, 54, 63; wealth/plantation wealth, 45, 46–47, 63. *See also* British history; Canada; White settlers
British Empire: overview, 114, 124–25; Catholics, 43, 100, 120–21, 159; commerce, 63, 76, 123–24, 157; current themes, 202–5; enslaved people, 101, 102, 125; household governance, 140–41; Indigenous peoples and, 100–101, 102; living standards, 159, 279n45. *See also* British America
British history: overview, 1, 2, 17, 39, 150, 154, 171–72; academic journals, 2, 4, 6, 226n4; authority, 165–66; Bloody Code, 163–64, 165, 166; Catholics, 159, 161, 167, 169; crime, 163–64, 165, 168; elites, 153, 158, 164, 165–66, 168; Francophobia, 154, 169, 170; globalization, 78, 105–6, 152–53, 160, 170, 171;

historiography, 151, 152–53; identity, 151, 152, 153–54, 161, 185, 276nn19–20; living standards, 159, 162, 279n45; Protestants, 154, 159, 161, 167, 170, 171, 266n99; regions, 163–69; settler colonialism, 1, 161–63; traditional themes critiques, 32, 238n53; White settlers' identity, 26, 37, 152, 161–62, 184. *See also* British history, and economy; British history, and politics; Canada; fiscal-military state, and British history; Hanoverian (Georgian) era

British history, and economy: overview, 154–57; fiscal-military state, 157–59, 160; GDP, 153, 155, 156, 279n45; globalization, 160, 170, 171; market economy, 152, 159–60; slavery and capitalism, 155–57, 160. *See also* British history

British history, and politics: Jacobitism, 124, 152, 160, 162, 166–67; oligarchy, 152, 153, 154, 167, 170; Union, 100, 166–67; Whigs, 151, 153, 154, 166–67, 168, 169, 170. *See also* British history; British history, and economy

British imperialism: overview, 104; Africa/Africans, 79, 126–27; British America, 106, 113, 117–18, 123–24; globalization and, 105–6; (re)turn to, 111–12, 124. *See also* British Empire; Great Britain; imperialism

British North America: abolitionism, 46, 63, 72; authority, 115–16, 117, 118; commerce, 76, 123–24; free Blacks, 65, 66; French Catholics, 43, 121; GDP, 43, 44, 242n26; gender issues, 132, 133, 137, 148; geographies/settlements, 87, 88, 90–91; living standards, 135–36; politeness, 147–48; Protestants, 72, 75, 100, 119–20; regions, 164–65; settler colonialism, 1, 161, 162–63; slavery, 30, 44, 64–66, 76, 77–78, 80, 101, 122; space/spaces of power, 87, 90–91, 92, 94, 95, 96–97; traditional themes, 23–24, 27; wealth/plantation wealth, 43, 44, 45, 54, 158, 242n26. *See also* British America; Canada; White settlers

Broadberry, Stephen, 159

Brown, Carys, 121
Brown, Christopher L., 176
Brown, Kathleen, 27–28, 147
Brown, Keith M., 162
Brown, Vincent, 67
Burbank, Jane, 105

Canada: abolitionism, 173; American Revolution and, 177; current themes, 22, 127; environment and, 56; French Canadians, 53–54, 161; HBC and, 125–26; merchants, 53–54; White settlers' successes, 41

Canale, Joshua, 181
Cañizares-Esguerra, Jorge, 91, 92, 113
Canley, Georgia, 88

capitalism: American Revolution and, 183, 189; gender and, 132–33, 135, 144; historiography, 52–53; racial capitalism, 81, 183, 254n54; slavery and, 80–81, 155–57, 160, 230n37; slave trade and, 53, 74–75, 79, 160. *See also* commerce

Carby, Hazel, 29
Cardim, Pedro, 113–14

Caribbean islands: Afro-Caribbeans, 42, 279n45; American Revolution, 177; Black soldiers and, 68; Carib-European War, 102; Catholics, 120; Creole people, 92, 142; current themes, 1, 50; enslaved people, 46–47, 48, 50, 70–71, 76, 162; Haiti (Saint Domingue), 45, 80–81, 108, 109, 174, 204, 206; imperialism, 102, 186; Indigenous peoples, 83, 87, 102; living standards, 42, 159, 279n45; marriage practices, 137; violence and plantations, 48, 49–50, 64, 71, 143, 186; wealth/plantation wealth, 42, 46–47; White people, 50, 159, 279n45. *See also specific colonies and islands*

Carib-European War (1769–73), 102

Catholics: British Empire, 43, 100, 120–21, 159; British history, 159, 161, 167, 169; French Catholics, 43, 121

Cavanaugh, Edward, 125
Cayton, Andrew R. L., 23, 24, 26, 32, 86, 197–98
Cazzola, Matilde, 101–2

Cevasco, Carla, 88–89
Chambers, Ian, 13
Chaplin, Joyce, 4, 32–33, 34, 55, 56, 57
Chesapeake, 24, 64, 76
children: childcare practices, 50, 143–44, 147; slavery and, 50, 63, 66, 68–69, 143–44, 147; White children, 134–35, 144, 147, 148
Christie, Nancy, 53, 121, 203, 207
citational practices, 11, 217–20
Clark, Emily, 68
Clark, Gregory, 159
Clark, J. C. D., 152, 169–70
Coffey, John, 72–73, 82
Colley, Linda, 146–47, 151, 152, 181–82, 185
colonialism. *See* White settlers
commerce: overview, 41, 42, 51–52, 58–59; Africa/Africans, 79, 80, 81, 157; British Empire, 63, 76, 123–24, 157; historiography, 52–53; Indigenous peoples, 58–59, 125–26; mercantilism, 51–52, 123, 160; merchants, 53–54, 58–59; slavery, 28, 58–59, 63, 76, 78; traditional themes, 30, 31. *See also* capitalism
Conger, Vivian Bruce, 137
constitutional-making: overview, 181–82, 206; American Constitution, 25, 34, 188, 192, 206
Cooper, Frederick, 105
Cornell, Saul, 26
Cotheran, Boyd, 14
Countryman, Edward, 88, 178, 187
Cox, Alicia, 14
Creole people, 49, 55, 63, 92, 109, 124, 142, 143
crime: property crime, 163–64, 165; rape, 49, 64, 138, 143; smuggling, 165, 168
Cronon, William, 56
Crosby, Alfred W., 56
Crouch, Christian Ayne, 90
Crutzen, Paul, 55
current themes: overview, 1, 7–11, 21–22, 199–200, 229n31; academic journals, 2, 3, 4, 5, 6, 17; empiricism, 2, 11, 12, 17, 195, 197; interdisciplinary approach, 11–13, 26; literature critiques, 195–96, 198–99,

207–8, 292n3. *See also* traditional themes
Cutterham, Tom, 189

Damiano, Sara T., 137
Darwin, John, 170–71
Dator, James, 69–70
Daunton, Martin, 158
de Certeau, Michel, 109, 110
Delbourgo, James, 102
D'Emilio, John, 148
democracy: overview, 34, 35, 36, 37; age of revolutions, 108, 111; American Revolution and, 175–76; imperialism and, 116, 119, 185
demography: current themes, 9, 36, 37, 39; enslaved people, 28, 30, 44, 63; Indigenous peoples, 42; traditional themes, 30–31, 237n42
de Vries, Jan, 80, 134, 136, 151
Ditz, Toby L., 146
diversity, 26, 36–37, 39, 120–21, 122
Dixon, Bradley J., 89
Dolan, Elizabeth A., 207
Donohue, Felicity, 144–45
Dornan, Inge, 137
Dorner, Zachary, 13
Dowd, Gregory Evans, 100–101, 185
Dressler, Nicole, 74
Dubcovsky, Alejandra, 90
Dubois, Laurent, 92
Dubow, Saul, 41–42
Dunn, Mary Maples, 10
DuVal, Kathleen, 36, 37
Duval, Lauren, 183
Dziennik, Matthew, 79, 126, 163, 181

Eacott, Jonathan, 123
Earle, Rebecca, 208
early American history, 1, 2, 3, 6. *See also* current themes; historiography, and early America; traditional themes
East India Company, 126, 162, 165, 280n62
economy. *See* British history, and economy
Edelson, S. Max, 53, 116
Edling, Max M., 116

Edwards, Jonathan, 9, 75
elites: American Revolution and, 7, 37, 175–76, 179, 180, 189; British history, 153, 158, 164, 165–66, 168
Elliott, J. H., 113–14, 201
Ellis, Elizabeth, 89
Ellis, Joseph, 85
Eltis, David, 46
empires: overview, 1, 12, 16, 32, 33, 36–37; diversity, 36–37, 120–21, 122; globalization, 108; neoliberalism, 37, 105; research methodologies, 15; scholarship, 3, 32, 33, 113–15; settler colonialism and, 13–14, 15, 41, 95–97, 100, 101
Engel, Katherine Carté, 119–20, 223
enslaved children, 50, 63, 66, 68–69, 143–44, 147
enslaved men: American Revolution, 17, 101; archives, 69–70; family structures, 65–66; marriage, 65–66; plantations, 47, 49; slave trade data, 63; violence against, 49, 67, 68, 70; wealth/plantation wealth, 42, 43, 44, 242n20. *See also* enslaved women
enslaved people: advertisements for runaway enslaved people, 70–71; American Revolution, 17, 101; archives, 67–71, 81; British Empire, 101, 102, 125; demography, 28, 30, 44, 63; environmental impact, 58–59; living standards, 28, 58–59, 82, 136, 159, 186; revolts, 108–9; runaway enslaved people, 13, 66, 70–71; violence, 48, 49, 67, 68–69, 70, 71; wealth/plantation wealth, 42–44, 45–47, 48, 50, 242n20, 242n26. *See also* enslaved men; plantations; slavery
enslaved women: archives, 67, 68–69; childcare practices, 50, 143–44, 147; current themes, 9; family structures, 65–66; living standards, 136; rape, 49, 64, 138, 143; reproduction, 50, 136, 144; slave trade data, 63; violence against, 49–50, 68–69, 143. *See also* enslaved men; enslaved people; slavery
environment, 42, 48, 55–59, 83, 103
Europe. *See* Atlantic world; *and specific countries*

Evans, Chris, 12, 50–51, 157
Everill, Bronwen, 80, 136
exceptionalism: traditional themes, 29, 32–33, 34; US, 24, 29, 33, 34, 178–79, 191

Farber, Hannah, 53
farmers, White, 8, 29–30, 50, 66, 237n39. *See also* White settlers
Fieldhouse, D. K., 112
fiscal-military state, and British history: overview, 96, 107, 124, 152, 164; economy, 157–59, 160; taxes, 153, 158
Flanagan, Christopher, 181–82
Floyd, George, 200
Fogelman, Aaron, 189
Forbes, William, 51
Ford, Lisa, 36
France: archives, 12; British-French-Indigenous relationship, 90, 97–98; Francophobia and, 154, 169, 170; French Revolution, 108, 110–11, 176; imperialism, 102, 104, 123, 124, 170, 186; maps of North America, 88, 90; Seven Years' War, 21, 88, 90–91, 97–98, 107; slave trade, 76. *See also* French America (New France)
Frank (enslaved man), 69–70, 81
Franklin, Benjamin: Franklin state attempts, 118; materialism, 53, 54; White settlers' successes, 40, 41, 42, 52, 59, 98; White women and living standards, 134
Franklin, Deborah Reed, 137
free Blacks: American Revolution and, 66, 101, 175; British armed forces recruits, 9, 67–68; Creole people, 49, 55, 63, 92, 109, 124, 142; New England, 65, 66; women, 133, 142–43
freedom, and American Revolution, 175, 180, 181–82, 186–87, 192. *See also* free Blacks
French America (New France): Blacks, 133, 186; commerce, 125–26; enslaved people, 68, 186; French Louisiana, 13, 89, 145, 146; geographies/settlements, 89–90; identity, 145–46; Indigenous peoples, 86, 186; merchants and, 50, 53–54; slavery, 68, 80, 186;

French America (New France) (*continued*)
wealth/plantation wealth, 42–43, 45, 242n20. *See also* France; *and specific colonies and countries*
French Empire, 123, 124, 125, 186. *See also* France
French Revolution, 108, 110–11, 176. *See also* France
frontiers: borderlands, 87, 91–92, 93–95, 99, 164; gender frontiers, 28, 42, 132, 140, 142–43, 147–48
Fuentes, Marisa J., 68
Furstenberg, François, 182

Gainsborough, Thomas, 153
Gamble, Robert J., 54
Games, Alison F., 113
Gardiner, Silvester, 13
Gatrell, V. A. C., 165
Gauvreau, Michael, 203
GDP (Gross Domestic Product), and British history, 43, 44, 153, 155, 156, 242n26, 279n45
Geloso, Vincent, 45
gender: overview, 131–33; Black women, 133, 136, 141, 142–43; capitalism and, 132–33, 135, 144; femininity, 28, 131, 139; gender frontiers, 28, 42, 132, 140, 142–43, 147–48; gender relations, 137–38, 146–48; identity, 132, 139, 140, 146; imperialism, 132, 137, 147; inheritance practices, 131, 133, 136, 142, 143; politics, 137, 139, 140; rape, 138, 143. *See also* sexuality; White men; White women
George I, 169–70
George II, 153–54, 167, 169–70
George III, 99–100, 112, 154, 169–70, 181, 283n93
Georgian (Hanoverian) era. *See* Hanoverian (Georgian) era
Gerbner, Katherine, 75
Gibbon, Edward, 10
Gibson, Kate, 138–39
Gilje, Paul A., 123
Gipson, Lawrence Henry, 106, 111

globalization: age of revolutions, 107–11, 174, 180; American Revolution and, 174–75, 177, 180, 207–8; British history, 78, 105–6, 152–53, 160, 170, 171; current themes, 37, 196, 205–7, 208–9; imperialism, 105–6, 111, 127; merchants, 78, 79; traditional themes, 195–96
Golove, David, 190
Gordon-Reed, Annette, 116, 207–8
Gould, Eliga, 109, 177, 189, 191, 193, 206, 209
Graham, Aaron, 117, 160, 166
Grainger, James, 47–48
Grasso, Christopher, 31–32, 33, 34
Gray, Edward, 174, 177, 184, 187, 188
Great Britain: abolitionism, 46, 72, 73, 79, 101, 147; Blacks in armed forces and, 9, 67–68; British Army, 117, 124–25, 163, 166, 167, 181, 204; Catholics, 121, 159; Indigenous peoples' relations, 100–101, 102; industrialization, 46, 50–51, 156; living standards, 42, 43, 134–36, 159; marriage, 147–48; mercantilism, 51–52, 123, 160; merchants, 50, 53–54; patriarchy, 121, 137, 138; politeness, 137–38, 146–48, 151; Pontiac's War (1763), 88, 98, 259n63; proslavery movement, 73, 74; race, 101–2, 185; Royal Navy, 9, 67–68, 116; Royal Proclamation (1763), 100, 182; Seven Years' War, 21, 88, 90–91, 97–98, 107; sexuality, 138–39; *Somerset* case (1772), 101, 122; Stamp Act (1765), 98, 107, 182, 259n63; Wales, 50, 51, 153, 157; wealth/plantation wealth, 45, 46, 50–51; White children, 134–35, 147; White men, 28, 134–35, 138; White women, 134–35, 138, 139–40. *See also* British imperialism; British North America; Hanoverian (Georgian) era
Great Divergence, 55, 58, 155, 199
Greene, Jack P., 21, 23, 115, 116, 123, 124
Greenwood, John, 148–49
Greer, Allan, 14–15, 127, 239n72
Greig, Hannah, 139
Griffin, Patrick, 111, 124, 191–92
Gronniosaw, James Albert Ukawsaw, 9, 73

Gross Domestic Product (GDP), and British history, 43, 44, 153, 155, 156, 242n26, 279n45
Guha, Ranajit, 112
Guyatt, Nicholas, 72

Haggerty, Sheryllynne, 50
Haiti (Saint Domingue), 45, 80–81, 108, 109, 174, 204, 206
Hämäläinen, Pekka, 41, 83, 86, 91, 92–93, 94, 113
Hamilton, Douglas J., 67–68
Hancock, David, 53
Hanley, Ryan, 73
Hannah-Jones, Nikole, 29
Hanoverian (Georgian) era: described, 137–38, 151–52, 154, 275nn9–10; George I, 169–70; George II, 153–54, 167, 169–70; George III, 99–100, 112, 154, 169–70, 181, 283n93; identity, 154, 276nn19–20; traditional themes, 152. See also British history
Hardesty, Jared Ross, 65, 66
Harland-Jacobs, Jessica L., 120–21
Hart, Emma, 30, 53
Hartigan-O'Connor, Ellen, 53, 132–33
Hartman, Saidiya, 67
Harvey, Karen, 139–40, 148
Harvey, Mark, 156
Hattem, Michael, 209–10
Havard, Gilles, 86
HBC (Hudson's Bay Company), 125–26
Henretta, James, 31
Hinderaker, Eric, 32, 114
historiography, and early America: overview, 17, 21–22, 38–39; academic journals, 3, 4–6, 211–13, 213, 215, 292n3; citational practices, 11, 217–20; future scholarship, 17, 29, 39, 197, 210; research methodologies, 2–6, 195, 226n4. See also current themes
historiography described, 2–3. See also current themes; historiography, and early America; traditional themes
Hobsbawm, Eric, 110–11
Hogarth, William, 148, 153
Holloway, Sally, 169

Holton, Woody, 174–75
Hoock, Holger, 180–81
Hopkins, A. G., 113, 199–200
Hoppit, Julian, 52, 159, 167
Horn, Rebecca, 32
Horrell, Sara, 134–35
Houllemare, Mare, 12, 125
household governance, 137, 140–41, 173, 178
Hudson, Pat, 156–57
Hudson's Bay Company (HBC), 125–26
Hulsebosch, Daniel, 190
Humphries, Jane, 134–35
Hunt, Philip, 157–58
Hunt-Kennedy, Stefanie, 71

identity: overview, 92; British history, 151, 152, 153–54, 161, 185, 276nn19–20; French America and, 145–46; gender and, 132, 139, 140, 146; Ireland, 161, 184, 276n20; settler colonialism, 100, 161, 183, 184; US, 37; White settlers, 26, 37, 100, 161–62
imperialism: overview, 104–6; age of revolutions, 105, 108, 110; American Revolution and, 119–20, 183–88; authority, 104, 105, 115–18, 121, 122; Caribbean islands, 102, 186; democracy and, 116, 119, 185; France, 102, 104, 123, 124, 170, 186; gender and, 131, 132, 137, 147; globalization, 105–6, 111, 127; historiography, 106–7; Seven Years' War (1756–63), 115–16, 117–18; slavery and, 63, 82, 117, 122; (re)turn to, 111–15, 124, 127; US, 113, 115, 116, 117, 122; White settlers and, 100, 132, 137, 147, 183. See also British imperialism
India, 55, 112, 126, 147, 162, 165, 190, 280n62
Indigenous peoples: agency, 21, 85, 88–89, 90, 102–3; American West, 57–58, 96–97; autonomy, 14, 89, 118, 175; bound labor, 65, 66; Caribbean islands, 83, 87, 102; commerce, 58–59, 125–26; current themes, 7, 13–14, 16, 21, 22, 85–86, 102–3; demography, 42; disappearance myth, 83–84, 87, 95;

Indigenous peoples (*continued*)
environment and, 57–59, 83, 103; ethnogenesis, 91–93; French America, 86, 186; future scholarship, 91, 103; gender and, 131; genocide, 14, 16, 99; geographies/settlements of, 87, 88, 90–91; Great Britain's relations, 100–101, 102; historiography, 2, 84–86; imperialism, 113, 116; land appropriation from, 42, 52, 54, 63, 96, 163, 180; living standards, 14, 43, 58–59, 63, 159; maps, 88, 90–91; Middle Ground/s and, 89, 91–92, 93; race, 14, 98, 99, 101; recovery of history, 87–91, 96–97; replacement of, 55, 83–84; resources, 86, 88–89; settler colonialism and, 13–14, 87, 91–92, 161; slave trade, 59, 89–90; traditional themes, 3, 26–27, 30–31, 86, 235n18; violence, 16, 58, 89, 97, 98–99; wealth, 42, 44; women, 144–45. *See also* Indigenous peoples, and groups; Indigenous peoples, and power; Indigenous peoples, and wars

Indigenous peoples, and American Revolution: authority, 97, 177, 182; British-Indigenous peoples' relations, 89, 99–100; negative effects, 17, 175, 178, 179–80, 183–84. *See also* American Revolution (1776–83); Indigenous peoples; Indigenous peoples, and power; Indigenous peoples, and wars

Indigenous peoples, and groups: Anishinaabe Odawas, 98; Apaches, 87; Apalachees, 90; Cherokees, 89, 97–98, 118; Choctaws, 89, 144–45; Chowans, 89; Comanches, 87, 94; Conestogas, 99; Creek, 88, 90; Detroit, 98; Haudenosaunees (Six Nations of the Iroquois Confederacy), 90, 97–98; Hurons, 98; Kaskaskias, Illinois Nation, 57–58; Lakotas, 87, 94; Wabanakis, 87–88; Watangans, 118. *See also* Indigenous peoples; Indigenous peoples, and American Revolution; Indigenous peoples, and wars

Indigenous peoples, and power: overview, 40–41, 83, 84, 86–87, 173–74; authority, 97, 177, 182; borderlands, 87, 91–92, 93–95, 99; French America, 145–46; historiography, 84, 85, 86; recovery of history, 90, 96–97; settler colonialism versus, 95–97; space/spaces of power, 87, 90–91, 92, 94, 95, 96–97; time/temporality, 87, 88, 89, 93, 95, 96–97; women, 144. *See also* Indigenous peoples; Indigenous peoples, and American Revolution; Indigenous peoples, and groups

Indigenous peoples, and wars: Battle of Fallen Timbers (1794), 174; blood revenge custom, 88, 89; Carib-European War (1769–73), 102; Natchez War (1729), 89, 145; Paxton Boys' Rebellion (1763), 98, 99, 100, 259n63; Pontiac's War (1763), 88, 98, 259n63; Seven Years' War (1756–63), 97–98; Yamasee War (1715), 89–90. *See also* Indigenous peoples; Indigenous peoples, and American Revolution; Indigenous peoples, and groups; Indigenous peoples, and power

Indigenous Ways of Knowing, 12, 85–86, 90, 99

industrialization: overview, 42, 155, 177; American Revolution's effects, 45–46, 50, 51; childcare practices, 144; children's labor, 135; environment, 55–56; gender and, 132–33, 135, 144; Great Britain, 46, 51; living standards, 43; plantations and, 46, 51; women's labor, 135

Industrial Revolution, 55, 56, 134, 135, 154, 155–56. *See also* industrialization

inheritance practices, 131, 133, 136, 142, 143

Inikori, Joseph, 79, 155–56

internationalism, and United States, 114, 176, 189, 190, 191

Ipsen, Pernille, 80

Ireland: overview, 152, 170–71; identity, 161, 184, 276n20; Irish Catholics, 159, 161; living standards, 159, 162, 279n45; regions and, 164–65; Scots-Irish settlers, 21–22, 164

Jackson, Andrew, 183, 202
Jacobitism, 124, 152, 160, 162, 166–67
Jamaica: Black women, 141, 143; free Blacks, 133, 142–43; gender frontiers and, 142–43; household governance, 141; imperialism, 117, 133–34, 186; living standards, 44–45, 242n20, 279n45; merchants, 54, 78, 133; Morant Bay Revolt, 177; religion, 75, 142; sexuality, 141, 142; Tacky's Revolt, 67, 166; White men, 141, 143; White supremacy, 143; White women, 54, 64, 133–34, 141, 142, 143
Jamaica, and plantations: childcare practices, 50, 143–44, 147; reproduction, 136, 144; sugar plantations, 49, 50–51, 81, 136, 144, 201; violence, 49–50, 186; wealth, 45–46, 50, 242n26. *See also* Jamaica
Jamaica, and slavery: childcare practices, 143–44, 147; enslaved people, 13, 64, 70, 71; enslaved women, 49–50, 136, 143–44, 147; interdisciplinary approach, 13; living standards, 136; productivity, 46, 49; reproduction, 136, 144; runaway advertisements, 70–71; slave trade, 76–77; violence, 48, 49–50, 64, 71, 143, 186; White women as slaveholders, 133, 142. *See also* Jamaica; Jamaica, and plantations
James, C. L. R., 80–81
Jefferson, Thomas, 41, 161, 183, 187, 189
Johnson, Andrew, 89–90
Johnson, Donald, 182–83
Johnson, Herbert A., 182

Kamensky, Jane, 174, 177, 184, 187, 188
Karras, Alan, 205, 208–9
Kelley, Sean M., 78
Kelton, Paul, 97
Kidd, Colin, 151
King, Peter, 164
Kinsey, Danielle, 106
Klooster, Wim, 108–9
Knights, Mark, 169
Knott, Sarah, 186, 187, 240n76

Koch, Philippa, 72
Kopelson, Heather Miyano, 148
Koth, Karl, 50, 51
Kramer, Paul, 104–5, 106
Kühberg, Lene, 9, 80
Kulikoff, Allan, 29–30, 175, 237n39
Kumar, Krishnan, 36, 114
Kupperman, Karen Ordahl, 105

La Fleur, Greta, 133
Langford, Paul, 137, 151
Latour, Bruno, 13
Lemire, Beverley, 170
Lemisch, Jesse, 10, 236n35
Lennox, Jeffers, 38, 90
Lewis, Dallin, 142
Lewis, Frank D., 46
Lightfoot, Natasha, 207
Lindert, Peter H., 43–44, 45
Livesay, Daniel, 142–43
living standards: British history, 159, 162, 279n45; British North America, 135–36; enslaved people, 28, 58–59, 82, 136, 159, 186; Indigenous peoples, 14, 58–59, 63; Jamaica, 44–45, 242n20; White women, 134–35. *See also* wealth
Long, Edward, 73, 74, 101–2, 141
Lynd, Staughton, 7–8

Mancall, Peter C., 31–32, 44, 46, 207
Mandler, Peter, 139
Mann, Michael, 185
Mapp, Paul, 176
marriage: Blacks and, 65–66; British America, 137, 147–48
Marshall, P. J., 113, 161, 184
Martini, Elspeth, 207
masculinity, 28, 132, 146–49. *See also* White men
Mason, Keith, 69–70
Mason, Matthew, 122
Massachusetts, 8, 64–65, 76, 80, 81, 82, 117, 168
McBride, Ian, 170–71
McCleskey, Turk, 13
McCusker, John J., 23

McDonnell, Michael A.: age of revolutions, 110, 151; American Revolution, 7, 119, 175, 178, 180, 181, 187, 188; historiography, 6, 7; Indigenous peoples, 97, 98, 100
McGiffert, Michael, 26
McNeill, John (J. R.), 55, 198
Menard, Russell R., 23, 29, 30, 31, 64–65, 237n42
Meranze, Michael, 26, 31
mercantilism, 51–52, 123, 160
merchants: Africa/Africans, 50, 53–54, 76–77, 78, 79, 80, 136; Atlantic world, 50, 53–54, 64, 78; British America, 50, 53, 54; commerce and, 53–54, 58–59; current themes, 8–9, 30; French America, 50, 53–54; globalization, 78, 79; Jamaica, 54, 78; non-White laborers, 66; plantations, 50–51, 66; slavery and, 50; slave trade, 76–77, 78; urban life, 8–9, 53, 54, 76–77, 252n39
Merrell, James H., 85, 86, 91
Merritt, Jane, 175
Middle Ground/s, 89, 91–92, 93
Middleton, Simon, 71
Mihm, Stephen, 176
Miller, Jonah, 138
Minty, Christopher, 181
Mintz, Sidney, 50, 80
Mitchell, John, 88
modernity, and slavery, 47, 74, 80–81, 82
Mohout, Jean-François, 56
Morgan, Edmund S.: American Revolution, 110–11, 178; colonial local institutions, 150–51; historiography, 5, 150, 152, 226n4; imperialism, 106–7, 172
Morgan, Philip D., 29, 205
Morison, Samuel Eliot, 10
Morrissey, Robert Michael, 13, 57–58
Mt. Pleasant, Alyssa, 85–86, 87
Murphy, Anne L., 158
Murphy, Tommy E., 43

Namier, Lewis, 139, 150, 151, 152
Nash, Gary, 175
Natchez War (1729), 89, 145
national identity. See identity

nation-state, and United States, 36, 37, 38, 176, 178–79, 188
Native American and Indigenous Studies (NAIS), 12, 90
Neem, Johann N.: British imperialism, 100; empires, 36–37, 100; interdisciplinary approach, 13; race and American Revolution, 37, 100; traditional themes critique, 32, 39, 198; #VastEarlyAmerica critique, 35–36, 38, 196, 240n74, 240n76; White settlers' identity, 184
neoliberalism, 14, 35, 37, 38, 39, 105, 240n76
New England: free Blacks, 65, 66; imperialism, 113, 117, 123; slavery, 65–66, 80; traditional themes, 23–24, 27; wealth data, 45. See also British North America
New France. See French America (New France)
Newman, Brooke, 102
Newman, Simon P., 13, 70, 207
Newton, Melanie J., 83
Nooe, Evan, 88

Oatsvall, Neil, 46, 56
O'Brien, Jean M., 85
O'Brien, Patrick K., 105, 157–59
O'Malley, Gregory, 77
Onuf, Peter S., 116, 207–8
Ostler, Jeffrey, 15–16, 73–74, 99
Otis, James, 40

Palmer, R. R., 111
Panza, Laura, 44
Parkinson, Robert G., 7
parochialism, 34, 119, 162, 172, 198, 207
Parsons, Christopher M., 75
Parthasarti, Prasannan, 162
Pateman, Carole, 147
Paton, Diana, 9, 49, 50, 143–44, 147
patriarchy: Great Britain, 121, 137, 138; household governance, 140–41, 173, 178; plantations, 48, 69–70; White women and, 27, 137, 138
Pelham, Henry, 153–54, 167

Perkins, John, 9, 67–68
Perkins, Simeon, 146
Perl-Rosenthal, Nathan, 13, 109–10
Peterson, Mark, 81–82, 174
Petiver, James, 9
Phillips, Nathaniel, 8, 50
Piker, Joshua, 34
Pincus, Steven, 52, 226n4
Pitt, William, 115–16, 161
plantations: abolitionism and, 45–46, 50; American Revolution's effects, 45–46, 50, 51; childcare practices, 143–44, 147; enslaved women, 49–50, 143–44, 147; industrialization and, 46, 51; living standards, 136; merchants and, 50–51, 66; modernity and, 80–81; patriarchy, 48, 69–70; productivity/profitability data, 46, 49, 76, 156; sugar plantations, 46–47, 49, 50–51, 81, 136, 144, 201; urban life and, 76–77, 252n39. *See also* enslaved people; Jamaica, and plantations; violence, and plantations
Pocock, J. G. A., 10, 111–12, 162
Polasky, Janet, 108
Pole, J. R., 23
politeness, 137–38, 146–48, 151
politics: American Revolution and, 37, 99, 174, 181, 186, 189; archives, 12, 68; gender, 137, 139, 140. *See also* British history, and politics; democracy
Pomeranz, Kenneth, 55–56, 155, 198, 199
population data. *See* demography
Porter, Roy, 151
postcolonialism, 14, 33, 41–42, 115
power, and space/spaces of power, 87, 90–91, 92, 94, 95, 96–97. *See also* Indigenous peoples, and power
Price, Jacob, 76
proslavery movement, 47, 72, 73, 74, 192. *See also* abolitionism; enslaved people; enslaved women
Protestants: British history, 154, 159, 161, 167, 170, 171, 266n99; British North America, 72, 75, 100, 119–20

race: American Revolution, 8, 37, 101, 161–62, 180, 184; current themes, 7, 16, 28–29, 37; household governance, 140, 141; slavery, 7, 28, 63, 68, 75; traditional themes, 3, 28, 31; US and, 37, 101, 190; whiteness, 37, 98, 99, 101–2, 180, 185; White settlers, 8, 37, 98–99, 101, 161–62, 184
Radburn, Nicholas, 49, 53, 76–77, 207
Rakove, Jack, 7–8
Rao, Gautham, 116
Raphael, Ray, 175–76
Ravano, Lorenzo, 101–2
Raynal, Abbé, 41, 42, 59
Rediker, Marcus, 10
Reese, Ty M., 79
Reichardt, A. Zuercher, 226n4
Reid, Ahmed, 46, 51
Reinart, Sophus, 9, 52–53
religion, 72–73, 74–75, 82, 138, 142. *See also* Catholics; Protestants
republicanism, 10, 24, 104, 107, 120, 152, 188, 190
research methodologies, 2–6, 13–16, 195, 226n4
Reynolds, Joseph, 153
Rice, James, 56, 57
Richardson, David, 46
Richter, Daniel K., 26–27, 84–85
Ridge, Martin, 10
Riello, Giorgio, 78
Roberts, Justin, 49
Robertson, William, 41, 42, 59
Rodgers, Thomas G., 181–82
Rogers, Dominique, 68
Roney, Jessica Chopin, 8–9, 95, 96–97, 118
Rönnbäck, Klas, 51, 135–36, 156, 242n26
Rosenbloom, Joshua L., 44, 46
Royal Proclamation (1763), 100, 182
Ruderman, Anne, 79
runaway enslaved people, 13, 66, 70–71
Rusert, Britt, 47–48
Ryden, David B., 46

sailors/seamen, 29, 40, 87–88, 170
Saint Domingue (Haiti), 45, 80–81, 108, 109, 174, 204, 206
Sarson, Steven, 39
Sassen, Saskia, 35–36

304　INDEX

Saunders, Robert, 114
Saunt, Claudio, 32, 33–34, 92, 183–84
Schneider, Eric B., 43
Schwarz, Bill, 112
Schweger, Tristan, 48
Scotland: Jacobitism, 124, 152, 160, 162, 166–67; regions and, 164–65, 166–69; the Union and, 100, 166–67; White settlers and, 21–22, 162–63, 164
Scribner, Vaughn, 46, 56
Sensbach, Jon, 27, 28, 29
Serieux, John, 50, 51
settler colonialism: overview, 95; American West, 87, 96–97; authority and, 115–18; borderlands, 93, 94–95, 99, 164; British history, 1, 161–63; current themes, 13–16; empires, 13–14, 15, 41, 95–97, 100, 101; identity, 100, 161, 183, 184; Indigenous peoples and, 13–14, 87, 91–92, 95–97, 161; space/spaces of power, 87, 90–91, 92, 94, 95, 96–97; US, 13–14, 15, 41, 95–97, 101; violence, 14, 16, 99. *See also* White settlers
Seven Years' War (1756–63), 21, 88, 90–91, 97–98, 107
sexuality: overview, 131; Great Britain, 138–39; Indigenous women, 144–45; Jamaica, 141, 142; White men, 138–39, 148–49; White women, 138–40, 142
Seymour, Susanne, 50
Shammas, Carole, 137, 148, 178
Shankman, Andrew, 115, 116
Shannon, Timothy, 9
Shoemaker, Nancy, 15
Sidbury, James, 91, 92
Siddique, Asheesh Kapur, 125
1619 Project, 16, 29, 63, 191–92
slavery: age of revolutions, 108–9; American Revolution and, 66–67, 77, 101, 176, 177, 178–79; British America, 30, 44, 46, 54, 63; British North America, 30, 44, 64–65, 76, 77–78, 101, 122; capitalism and, 80–81, 155–57, 160, 230n37; commerce, 6, 28, 58–59, 76, 78; current themes, 16, 22, 42, 63, 80–81, 254n54; enslaved children, 50, 63, 66, 68–69, 143–44, 147; French America, 68, 80, 186; imperialism and, 63, 82, 117, 122; manumission, 66–67; modernity and, 47, 74, 80–81, 82; Protestants and, 72, 75; race, 7, 28, 63, 68, 75; racial capitalism, 81, 183, 254n54; religion, 72, 73, 74–75; runaway enslaved people, 13, 66, 70–71; 1619 Project, 16, 29, 63, 191–92; socio-economic development, 53, 54; *Somerset* case (1772), 101, 122; traditional themes, 26, 27, 28, 29, 31; US, 122, 173. *See also* abolitionism; enslaved men; enslaved people; enslaved women; Jamaica, and slavery; plantations; wealth/plantation wealth
slave trade: abolitionism and, 46, 63; Africa/Africans, 75–76, 78, 79, 80, 81, 127, 136; capitalism, 53, 74–75, 79, 160; data, 63, 76; Indigenous peoples, 59, 89–90; merchants, 76–77, 78; settler colonialism critiques, 41, 42; urban life, 77–78. *See also* slavery
Smallwood, Stephanie, 67
Smith, Barbara Clark, 7
Smith, David Chan, 125–26, 165
Smithers, Gregory D., 89
Snyder, Terri L., 131, 132, 136–37
social science, 11, 12–13, 22–26, 234n9, 234n12
Soll, Jacob, 123, 124, 126
Solow, Barbara L., 28, 64
Somerset case (1772), 101, 122
South Africa, 41–42, 100–101, 254n54
Spain: age of revolutions, 180; early American history and, 205; imperialism, 102, 104, 113, 126; Indigenous peoples and, 87, 88, 90; US and, 176
Sparks, Randy J., 80
Spear, Jennifer M., 15
Spero, Patrick, 188
Staloff, Darren Marcus, 26
Stamp Act (1765), 98, 107, 182, 259n63
standards of living. *See* living standards
Stanley, Amy Dru, 132–33
Stapleton, William, 69–70
Stobart, Jon, 157
Stock, Paul, 171–72
Sweeney, Shauna J., 207

Sweet, James H., 92
Swift, Jonathan, 170–71

Tacky's Revolt (1760–61), 67, 166
Tailyour, John, 76–77
Tawney, R. H., 10
Taylor, Alan: American Revolution, 37, 175, 177, 179–80, 186–87, 205–6; empires, 37, 239n72
Taylor, Jordan, 71
Thompson, E. Pl, 9
Toft, Mary, 139–40
Tomlins, Christopher, 175–76
trade. *See* commerce; slave trade
traditional themes: overview, 11, 21, 22, 39; academic journals, 3; critiques, 32–34, 39, 198, 238n53; literature critiques, 195, 197–98, 207; scholarship, 22–26, 31, 238n46; social science, 11, 12–13, 22–26, 234n9, 234n12. *See also* current themes
Trahey, Erin, 133, 143
Trevor-Roper, Hugh, 10
Truett, Samuel, 86, 91, 93, 94
Truxes, Thomas M., 63
Turner, Frederick Jackson, 93, 94, 95
Turner, Sasha, 68–69

United States: overview, 22, 26, 37; authority, 115, 116, 117, 118; Constitution, 25, 34, 188, 192, 206; exceptionalism, 24, 29, 33, 34, 178–79, 191; imperialism and, 113, 115, 116, 117, 122; internationalism, 114, 176, 189, 190, 191; nation-state, 36, 37, 38, 176, 178–79, 188; postcolonialism, 33, 115; race and, 37, 101, 190; republicanism, 107, 152, 188, 190; settler colonialism, 13–14, 15, 41, 95–97, 101; slavery, 122, 173. *See also* American Revolution (1776–83)
urban life, 8–9, 53, 54, 76–78, 252n39

#VastEarlyAmerica: overview, 22, 34–35, 38, 39, 97, 209–10; critiques, 35–36, 38, 93, 196, 240n74, 240n76; globalization, 195, 207–8; neoliberalism and, 35, 38, 39, 240n76
Vickers, Daniel, 29, 237n39

Vickery, Amanda, 139
Vidal, Cécile, 68, 86, 200
violence: American Revolution and, 178–79, 180–81; Indigenous peoples, 16, 58, 89, 97, 98–99; settler colonialism, 14, 16, 99
violence, and plantations: Caribbean islands, 48, 49–50, 64, 71, 143, 186; enslaved men, 49, 67, 68, 70; enslaved women, 49–50, 68–69, 143; rape, 49, 64; runaway enslaved peoples, 70–71. *See also* plantations; violence

Wahrman, Dror, 139
Waldstreicher, David: age of revolutions, 151; American Revolution, 7–8, 119, 175, 178, 180, 187, 188; historiography, 6, 7; imperialism, 172; Wheatley biography, 82, 122
Wales, 50, 51, 153, 157
Walker, Christine, 54, 64, 133, 138, 142
Wallis, Aaron, 120, 121
Walpole, Robert, 153–54, 167, 168, 169
Ward, Richard, 164
Warde, Paul, 55–56
Warren, Wendy, 65, 66
wars: Carib-European War (1769–73), 102; Seven Years' War, 21, 88, 90–91, 97–98, 107; War for/of American Independence (1775–83), 42, 77, 174–75, 179, 181, 182. *See also* American Revolution (1776–83); Indigenous peoples, and American Revolution; Indigenous peoples, and wars
Warsh, Molly A., 205
Washington, George, 9, 183
Watson, Amy, 168
Watt, Timothy D., 165
Way, Peter, 125
wealth, 17, 42, 44, 45, 51, 58–59
wealth/plantation wealth: Blacks and, 42, 43, 44, 52, 242n20; British America, 45, 46–47, 63; British North America, 43, 44, 54, 158, 242n26; Caribbean islands, 42–43, 45–47, 48, 50, 242n26; enslaved people, 42–44, 45–47, 48, 50, 242n20, 242n26;

wealth/plantation wealth (*continued*)
  French America, 42–43, 45, 242n20; White settlers, 43, 44, 52, 54, 158, 242n20, 246n28. *See also* living standards; wealth
Weisdorf, Jacob, 134–35
Weiss, Thomas, 44, 46
Wells, Andrew, 102
West, the (American West). *See* American West (the West)
West Africa: British imperialism, 79, 126–27; commerce, 79, 81, 157; domestic slavery, 80, 136; living standards, 135–36; merchants, 50, 78, 79, 80, 136; slave trade, 78, 80, 81, 127, 136; women's role, 80, 136. *See also* Africa/Africans
West Indies, 45–46, 68, 102, 148, 159
West Indies, and slavery: abolitionism, 45–46; American Revolution and, 177; demography, 44; violence, 48, 50; wealth/plantation wealth, 42–43, 45–47, 48, 50–51, 76, 242n26. *See also* West Indies
Whatley, Christopher, 166
Wheatley, Phyllis, 9, 65, 81–82, 122
Whigs, 151, 153, 154, 166–67, 168, 169, 170
White, Richard, 89
White, Sophie, 68, 145–46
White children, 134–35, 144, 147, 148
Whitefield, George, 9, 72, 73
White men: farmers, 8, 29–30, 50, 66, 237n39; household governance, 140–41, 173; imperialism, 132, 147; inheritance practices, 142; living standards, 134–35; marriage, 137, 147–48; masculinity, 28, 132, 146–49; politeness, 137–38; rape, 49, 64, 138, 143; sexuality, 138–39, 148–49. *See also* Blacks; White people; White settlers; White women
whiteness, 37, 98, 99, 101–2, 180, 185. *See also* American Revolution (1776–83), and White people; White men; White settlers; White supremacy; White women
White people: Caribbean islands, 50, 159, 279n45; children, 134–35, 144, 147, 148; Creole people, 49, 55, 63, 92, 109, 124, 142, 143; poverty, 43, 49, 65, 124–25; whiteness, 37, 98, 99, 101–2, 180, 185. *See also* American Revolution (1776–83), and White people; White men; White settlers; White women
White settlers: American Revolution, 8, 37, 101, 115, 118, 161–62, 184; British North America, 8, 40, 42, 43, 137; critiques, 40, 41–42, 52, 54, 59, 98; current themes, 13–16, 21–22; environmental impact, 55; farmers, 8, 29–30, 50, 66, 237n39; identity, 26, 37, 100, 152, 161–62, 184; imperialism, 100, 132, 137, 147, 183; Indigenous peoples and, 42, 52, 54, 63, 96, 100, 163, 180, 185; race and, 8, 37, 98–99, 101, 161–62, 184; Scots-Irish people, 21–22, 164; traditional themes, 1, 21–22, 33; wealth/plantation wealth, 43, 44, 52, 54, 158, 242n20, 246n28; White supremacy, 14, 99, 101, 102, 143. *See also* White men; White people; White women
White supremacy, 14, 99, 101, 102, 143, 190. *See also* whiteness
White women: American Revolution, 17, 137, 183; archives, 134; capitalism, 54, 132–33, 135; childcare practices, 144; current themes, 8, 21–22, 27–28; embodiment and, 139–40; femininity, 28, 131, 139; household governance, 137; imperialism, 132, 137, 147; living standards, 134–35; marriage, 137, 147–48; patriarchy and, 27, 137, 138; religion and, 75, 138; sexuality, 133, 138–40, 142; as slaveholders, 133, 137, 142. *See also* White men; White people; women
Whiting, Gloria McCahon, 65–67
Wigginton, Caroline, 85–86
Williams, Eric, 45–46, 50, 74, 155–56, 230n37
Williamson, Jeffrey, 43–44, 45
Wilson, Kathleen, 114, 131, 140–41, 142, 147, 151
Wisecup, Kelly, 67, 85–86
Witgen, Michael, 15, 84, 91
Wolfe, Patrick, 14–15, 95

women: Black women, 65–66, 80, 133, 136, 141, 142–43; Indigenous women, 144–45. *See also* enslaved women; White women

Wood, Gordon S.: American Revolution, 175, 178, 187; Indigenous people's lands, 85; traditional themes survey, 24–26, 33, 34, 85, 234n12; #VastEarlyAmerica critique, 35

Wood, Peter, 203

Worsley, Lucy, 169

Wrigley, E. A., 55

Wulf, Karin, 32, 33, 35, 39

Yeh, Sarah, 48

Ylivuori, Soile, 138

Yong Hwi Yoon, 72

Young, Arthur, 124

Zabin, Serena, 177, 179, 180, 207

Zagarri, Rosemarie, 178, 179, 180, 189, 190, 193, 209

Zahedieh, Nuala, 51, 156–57

Zappia, Natale, 56–57

Zelnik, Eran, 96, 101

Zuckerman, Michael, 175, 189

The Revolutionary Age

Spain and the American Revolution: New Approaches and Perspectives
Gabriel Paquette and Gonzalo M. Quintero Saravia, editors

The Habsburg Monarchy and the American Revolution
Jonathan Singerton

Navigating Neutrality: Early American Governance in the Turbulent Atlantic
Sandra Moats

Ireland and America: Empire, Revolution, and Sovereignty
Patrick Griffin and Francis D. Cogliano, editors

www.ingramcontent.com/pod-product-compliance
Lightning Source LLC
Chambersburg PA
CBHW031803130825

31059CB00014B/69